# Ethics, Education and Administrative Decisions

# American University Studies

Series XIV
Education

Vol. 8

PETER LANG
New York · Berne · Frankfurt am Main

# Ethics, Education and Administrative Decisions

## A Book of Readings

Edited
by
Peter Andre Sola

Footnote and Bibliographic Format
by
Paula Pedersen

PETER LANG
New York · Berne · Frankfurt am Main

Library of Congress Cataloging in Publication Data
Main entry under title:

**Ethics, Education and Administrative Decisions:**
(American University Studies. Series XIV, Education;
v. 8)
Bibliography: p.
1. Universities and colleges – Administration –
Addresses, essays, lectures. 2. School management and
organization – Decision making – Addresses, essays, lectures.
3. Decision making (Ethics) – Addresses, essays, lectures.
4. Professional ethics – Addresses, essays, lectures.
I. Sola, Peter Andre, 1940–        .    II. Series.
LB2341.E77   1984      371.2      84-47867
ISBN 0-8204-0148-X


CIP-Kurztitelaufnahme der Deutschen Bibliothek

**Ethics, Education and Administrative Decisions:**
A Book of Readings / ed. by Peter Andre Sola. Foot-
note and bibliogr. format by Paula Pedersen. –
New York; Berne; Frankfort on the Main;
Lang, 1984.
(American University Studies: Ser. 14, Education;
Vol. 8)
ISBN 0-8204-0148-X

NE: Sola, Peter Andre [Hrsg.]; American University
Studies / 14

© Peter Lang Publishing, Inc., New York 1984

Printed by Lang Druck, Inc., Liebefeld/Berne (Switzerland)

## DEDICATION

This Book is dedicated to my family; Mary Beth my wife and friend, and my children Christopher Andre and Rachel Levine.

# LIST OF PERMISSIONS

1. The Philosophical Base of Ethical Theory. Excerpted from _Principles of Biomedical Ethics_ by Tom L. Beauchamp and James F. Childress. Copyright C 1979 by Oxford University Press, Inc. Reprinted by permission of the publisher and the authors.

2. "A Social Humanities View of Educational Policy and Administration" by Thomas Sergiovanni, in _Educational Administrative Quarterly_, Vol. 16, No. 1, 1980, pp. 1-20. Reprinted by permission.

3. "The Changing Administrator: Developing Managerial Praxis" by William Foster, in _Educational Theory_, Vol. 30, No. 1, pp. 11- 21. Reprinted by permission.

4. "Values and Educational Decisions" by George Newsome, Jr., and Harold Gentry, in _National Elementary Principal_, Vol. xii, No. 2, November 1962, pp. 24-29. Reprinted by permission.

5. "Morality and the Ideal of Rationality in Formal Organizations." by John Ladd, in _Monist_, Vol. 54, 1970, pp. 488-516. Reprinted by permission.

6. "Administration and the Crisis of Legitimacy: A Review of Habermasian Thought" by William Foster, in _Harvard Educational Review_, Vol. 50, 1980, pp. 496-505. Copyright C 1980 by President and Fellows of Harvard College. Reprinted by permission.

7. "Moral Dilemmas of Schooling by H. Millard Clements and James B. Macdonald, in _Educational Leadership_, Vol. 23, No. 1, 1965, pp. 29-32. Reprinted with permission of the Association for Supervision and Curriculum Development and H. Millard Clements and James B. Macdonald. Copyright C 1965 by the Association for Supervision and Curriculum Development. All rights reserved.

8. "Values Clarification and Civil Liberties" by Howard Kirschenbaum, in _Turning Points: New Developments, New Directions in Values Clarification_, ed. by Joel Goodman, Saratoga Springs, New York: Creative Resources Press, 1978. Reprinted by permission.

9. "Can Schools Teach Kids Moral Values?" by Amitai Etzioni, in _New York University Education Quarterly_, Vol. 9, No. 1, Fall 1977, pp. 2-7. Copyright C New York University. Reprinted by permission.

10. "Who Says Its Unethical?" by Estelle Faulconer, in _Today's Education_, Vol. 58, No. 1, January 1970, pp. 62-63. Reprinted by permission.

11. The _AASA Code of Ethics_ by The American Association of School Administrators Ethics Committee, American Association of School Administrators, pp. 17-34. Reprinted by permission.

## ACKNOWLEDGEMENTS

My interest in this topic extends over the past 12 years. However, the encouragement to begin the book came from Dr. Earle H. West, Associate Dean, School of Education, Howard University. The opportunity to explore the topic of ethics and educational decision making in a seminar was given to me by Dr. Alexander Kloster, Director of the Educational Administrator Specialist Program at Northern Michigan University, Marquette, Michigan. Funds were provided for the 1978-1979 academic year by the Howard University Sponsored Grants Awards (OA-SRP-913).

This book could not have been completed without the help of my efficient and hard working graduate assistants. Mrs. Annette Davis helped with the initial survey of the literature. Her abilities were the bench-mark for the graduate assistants that followed. Mr. Herbert Nembhard continued the literature search.

I wish to give special thanks and recognition to my graduate assistant for the past two years, Mrs. Paula Pedersen. Mrs. Pedersen has converted every footnote and bibliographic reference into a uniform reference style. Finally, I wish to thank Ms. Joyce Bonaparte, who typed every page of the manuscript from the title page to the bibliography.

Peter Sola
Washington, D.C.   1983

# TABLE OF CONTENTS

PRACTICAL APPLICATIONS OF ETHICS AND EDUCATIONAL DECISION MAKING

# INTRODUCTION

For quite a few years, I've been concerned with a particular aspect of the decision making process. This aspect has to do with ethics. Could or should the decision making process incorporate an ethical component?

In raising this issue I realize that I am creating a great many problems. I am trying to operate between an objective, rationally designed mechanism, decision making, and a concept that is usually perceived as subjective and personal - ethics. Yet the truth is that decision makers do make their decisions from a personal, subjective base, as well as a rational, objective base. I am trying to discuss two concepts; Can decision making encompass an ethical dimension? Can (or does) the individual incorporate ethics into a decision? Perhaps it might be useful to rephrase the questions in a slightly different manner. How do individuals, say school administrators, decide an issue that has an ethical aspect? Here are some possible mechanisms that may be utilized: (1) the administrators can inject their own set of values, either overtly or covertly, into the decision making process, (2) they can use commonly held ethical concepts that might cut across the various ethical systems, (3) they can ignore the ethical aspect by hiding behind the law or even logic.

It would be appropriate to begin discussing these possible solutions by first assuming that the decision maker will be brought to an awareness of the ethical aspect of the problem. When this is done she cannot say she did not see this aspect of the problem. She can, of course, still ignore it. However, I believe that once the ethical aspect is recognized ethics will play a part in the administrators' decision making process.

This ethical awareness must come from either a clear understanding of the decision maker "seeing" the ethical aspect of the issue, or that the decision maker brings to the particular situation a set of personal ethical beliefs that act covertly on the issue to shape the decision. In the first instance the decision makers should bring to bear on the issue at hand their ethical position. Their position should be open, publicly explainable and dealt with in the arena of public debate. In the second instance this would result in a subjective analysis based on a private ethical system. Thus the decision maker sees the decision based on their own value system.

This issue raises the question of the public, open and explicit aspect of decision making vs. the private, implicit aspect of decision making. This is to say the administrator arrives at a policy either overtly or covertly. Everyone brings to the decision making process his own subjective values, attitudes, beliefs, political views, etc. Most administrators are quite aware that in the process of decision making all of these personal perspectives shape the decision. Indeed, if the issue being decided has an ethical aspect they consciously and deliberately use their beliefs to shape the decision, subject to public scrutiny.

A second possible solution, the use of commonly held ethical concepts that might cut across various ethical systems, could be viewed in the following light. Every philosophy has an ethical system which contains ethical elements that could be teased out and utilized in the decision making process. The school administrator deals with a diverse constituency. The administrator must accommodate in his decision making process, the wide range of ethical commitments held by that constituency. These conflicting ethical systems may lead the administrator to exclude the ethical dimension from the decision making process. Another option is for the administrator to seek to forge an eclectic ethical system using elements common to all the views held by her constituency. There are, of course, many problems involved in creating a set of common values. They could become so diluted that they become vague and general. The decision maker might then be tempted to create a formula to apply to the appropriate situation that would tend to almost exclude her from taking a position.

A possible solution to the problem of shared ethical values and its application to a decision might be to look at the consequences of the decision. Does the decision result in the enhancing of a person, or group, or might it reflect a societal, i.e., an anti-person orientation? In other words, are we viewing the decision in terms of people being manipulated as objects for a societal end or are people viewed as ends in themselves?

Finally, the third possible solution, ignoring the ethical aspect of the issue by hiding behind the law or even logic, might be viewed from this perspective. We need to show the decision maker that the concepts of law and ethics are usually intertwined and that we use or sometimes abuse the law as a justification for a decision that ignores the ethical aspects of the issue. This could show us that ethics is either linked or not linked to the legality of the issue. Thus, an unethical situation could result if a decision is based on the law. Or does the law have a built-in or hidden perspective regarding ethics? Or does the law have an immoral or unethical or even an amoral perspective?

By clearly showing the above concept we might demonstrate that ethics is part of a decision making situation in either a positive, i.e., ethics and law agree, or negative manner, i.e., ethics and law do not agree. To push this solution a bit more, we need to demonstrate that by using the law, individuals might be forced into an either/or situation: that is, if the decision with the force of the law behind it is unjust, unethical or immoral, can we break the law? However, the issue regarding the decision makers and their position, might be that they can use the law as a scapegoat to let them disavow responsibility regarding the consequences of the decision. Obviously, the decision maker can then not be held accountable. In conclusion, the decision makers may also hide behind the so-called objective methodology of decision making, bootlegging their own personal view into the decision without having to justify the decision in terms of personal preference.

So far in this essay you have read my personal ruminations about ethics and decision making as it pertains to education. I would like to believe that this view of the decision making process is accurate and that it might point a way to improve on the process of decision making. However, we need to examine the above concept in a much broader context.

This text is focused on the use of ethics in decision making. It is addressed to educational administrators at every level in the bureaucracy, graduate students in education, parents and teachers.

The thrust of the book is to develop sensitivity to the ethical issues that are always part of the daily decisions with which educational administrators deal. In addition, I hope to begin to develop a framework to help educational administrators become aware of, and include as part of their decisions, the ethics of the situation.

This book consists of two parts. The first part illustrates the philosophical-theoretical aspects of developing and using ethics in decision making. The second part gives us a picture of how ethics may be utilized in specific practical situations by the use of essays and case studies. It is not my intention to write a "how to" book of decision making. My intent is to illustrate the fact that we need to incorporate ethics into the decision making process.

This introductory essay is a general summary of the theme and articles of each of the first four chapters. Chapters Five and Six are simply, and briefly, noted.

Chapter One begins the book with a general analysis of the concept of ethics without relying on any particular philosophy for justification. The concepts of law and ethics as well as decision making and ethics are closely linked. In Chapter One Professor Crittenden separates these concepts and analyzes them one at a time. Only after thoroughly explaining these concepts does the author show how law and ethics are linked, and the implications of such a linkage. The author describes the characteristics of the moral framework within which we make our decisions. How can we be moral in our daily lives? The means-end argument, the author notes, does not, at this point in the chapter, get us to a more central issue. Therefore Professor Crittenden removes us from this line of reasoning and directs us along another path in search of the meaning of morality: ". . . by describing the kinds of practices that are undoubtedly central to what engaging in morality involves."[1] One of the characteristics of human kind is that we act in a moral manner. We also (sometimes) act rationally and hopefully, morally; emphasis, notes the author, on morality: The moral criteria should, he states; ". . . exercise the decisive arbitrating role."[2] In other words the "right" decision might be morally "wrong" if one does not have the proper perspective of ethics.

Professor Crittenden draws a clear distinction between public and private morality. The emphasis is, of course, placed on the role of public morality. A strong case is made to support morality on rational grounds. Not be appealing to authority or by a mathematical formula but by ". . . having reasons whose relevance and adequacy can be submitted to public assessment . . . ."[3] There should be open scrutiny of how one arrives at a decision.

The concluding pages of this chapter bring us back to illustrate the linkage between law and morality. The issue is quite clear, and had been hinted at above, do we obey decisions that are morally wrong? How should we react in applying the decision if the affected parties are opposed to the policy?

An excellent essay, like a good classroom lecture, raises more questions than it answers. Professor Crittenden has given us many issues to mull over. Some of these issues we will deal with in later chapters, other issues are food for thought to be discussed with your colleagues.

Now that we have an idea of what it is to be moral we need to have a better picture of the basis of morality and ethical theory. Chapter Two, adopted by Professor West, combines two chapters of a work by Professors Beauchamp and Childress that illustrates morality, ethics and ethical theories. The focus of this chapter is on the distinction between utilitarian and deontological ethical theories. The ethical theories are presented in a concise, objective manner.

The concept of utilitarianism is defined as the greatest good for the greatest number, or "human actions are to be morally assessed in terms of their production of maximal non moral value."[4] The article illustrates the pros and cons of extrinsic and intrinsic value, act and rule utilitarianism.

The definition of deontological theories, as noted by the authors, in the essay is based on the assumption that "at least some acts are wrong and others are right independent of their consequences."[5] The analysis of these theories are separated into three topics for discussion: the rightness or wrongness of acts; the difference between monestic and pluralistic theories, and rule deontology.

Finally, the essay, in the last two sections, shows us the place of rules in the moral life and the concept of rights.

Having explored these ethical theories that one may operate through, we now must ask whether or not administrative decisions can have, as an integral part of the process, an ethical component. There are many theoretical frameworks one can adopt to help one arrive at a decision. Administrators need process in order to formulate policy and make decisions. Chapter Three demonstrates that ethical concerns should be incorporated into the decision making model.

One of the key issues in decision making is the dilemma of objective vs. subjective concepts. We understand that we cannot be subjective in making decisions. Since ethics are personal, hence subjective, they cannot be incorporated into the decision making process. The above statement may be logical but is it correct? Sometimes we can avoid an issue by ignoring it, sometimes we rationalize it away. However, as noted earlier in the introduction, the person making the decision does operate with a set of ethical beliefs. These beliefs, whether consciously used or not, do affect the decision. A possible way out of the dilemma might be to formulate a code of ethics. Perhaps this would resolve any ethical conflict by giving us a set of principles that would enable use to answer the problem. One simply has to look at the numerous codes of ethics to see that they tend to be, in many instances, quite useless.

I believe it is time that administrators began to deal with issues as they exist in the real world. The decisions they make affect real people and have real consequences. Most issues have ethical aspects and should be decided by examining the social, and moral consequences of the decision. I am sure we would be moving in the right direction if we incorporated ethical awareness into our decision making process, as opposed to a hidden agenda of personal beliefs as part of the decision making process, or worse yet, an amoral perspective.

The articles in Chapter Three point out to us various ways one might begin to include ethics into her decision making process. Professor Sergiovanni begins the chapter with a possible method of bridging policy making, ethics, and administration. The author notes that in search for a science of administration, the seeking for laws of management is never ending. However, recently a shift has occured in the thinking of many social scientists. Now inductive "modes of inquiry" as well as deductive theories are gaining recognition.

Professor Sergiovanni discusses the concept of administration as science and art. Both play a role in administrative and policy areas. The author assumes that administration is an art that utilizes both scientific and normative concepts, which he defines as "a good normative theory . . . include(s) assumptions, beliefs, realities and prescriptions about some issues or problem which, when taken as a whole, represents a new standard, a higher order or existence, or ideal to which person, organization, and society strive."[6] The decision making process must include both scientific and normative aspects: He states, ". . . how might insights from the humanities - particularly values issues - and those from social science be meaningfully integrated?"[7] Professor Sergiovanni begins to explore how the linkage of science and normative theory can ". . . improve educational decision making."[8] Utilizing the writings of R.D. Gastil and the phrase he coined, social humanities, the author sketches out a potential framework that would incorporate both scientific and normative theories in the decision making process.

Four concepts are outlined in this article to help the administrator adjust his decision making method: They are utility, transcendence, justice, and ethical limits. These four elements are fully explained and examples are used to illustrate the practicality of the theory.

The author recognizes that educational decisions must be made in a multi-dimensional rather than a one dimensional frame of reference, hence the use of normative and scientific theory.

The next article in this chapter, written by Professor Worsfold, moves deeper into the marrying of science and ethics by suggesting that university administrators need to develop their own code of ethics. The author believes that a university must develop a set of operational guidelines in order to be properly governed. Professor Worsfold suggests that if a code is not developed within the university, then such a code would be imposed by either the state or federal governments. Such a code, he believes, should be developed by the administrators. The code would be of great use, he states, because it would be based on the firsthand perceptions of what is necessary and proper regarding university decisions. The author asserts that the purpose of this article; ". . . (is) a code of ethics for educational administrators (that) would establish the interests of the university as these are conceived by those who must live with them in their administration of them. The principles which might form the content within which to frame such a code are the business of this essay."[9]

Professor Worsfold then develops these four principles; what is of educational worth, a morally acceptable administration, the moral accountability of the university, and finally professional integrity. From these concepts the author generates three general principles that form the bases for a code of ethics.

The final article in this chapter demonstrates a possible method of going beyond the simple development of the technology of making decisions. The decision maker must begin to recognize that many of the decisions he makes have social consequences that ought not be ignored. Professor Foster discusses the process of administration. He notes that the "science" of administrative decision making is not, in fact, a science. While we have numerous theories regarding the administrative process, we have very little explanation on how these theories relate to the social implications of decisions. The author believes that school administration must ". . . be restructured and reformulated . . . with the focus on our study of management on . . . organizational morality and ethics . . . ."[10] The theme of this essay is that we have ignored ". . . the basic problems of running an organization . . . in favor of attempts to find a technology of management."[11] Process then becomes the end and not a means to an end. One problem noted by the author is that we do not bother with the social consequences of the decisions that we make. The author suggests that when we have an administrator that separates facts (science)from values, we have a decision making process by which the administrator neither knows nor cares how the decision affects the individual or group in terms of justice and equality. One approach to help overcome the above situation would be, according to the author, to incorporate into the fact finding process the culture within which the organizational forms occur. For example, the relationship between the educational system and the larger social-economic system in this society.[12] Professor Foster develops a very strong argument for his position against administrative processes as currently utilized. He implies a very disturbing question in his article; namely for whom does the administrative structure operate, the ends of the institution or the people it serves?

Chapter Four brings together the impact of philosophy, in general and ethics in particular, on the process of decision making. Administrators have tried to separate the objective from the subjective, that is, facts from values. On the surface this would appear quite logical since the outcome, the goal of decisions, would then be objectively arrived at hence, a value neutral decision. I think we all can see under this superficial logic.

School administrators are subjected to issues that are important because of the consequences of the decision on specific
communities of people. Sometimes it is quite difficult to see the
common ground that we think exists between the diverse communities
that make up our society. Therefore, decisions that are made will
cause conflict. If we in reality have very little in the way of
options, then the use of philosophy, indeed the use of ethics in
the decision making process may be possible.

This chapter raises a variety of questions: can philosophy
help us to justify our decisions and policies? Should a person
remove her philosophical hat when she becomes an administrator?
Is situational ethics a valid approach to moral decisions? Is
there a paradox between the ideas of morality for the individual
and the rationality of organizations? Should we begin to rethink
the relationship between means-ends?

The question of means-ends might be one of the keys we can
use in attempting to solve the problem of the separation of
science from normative theory in the decision making process.
Perhaps instead of simply finding a suitable technology to solving
problems, we can begin to examine the consequences of the solution
to the problems. Perhaps by beginning to look beyond the tip of
our collective nose and finally seeing what are the results of a
particular decision, we will know the impact of the decision and,
perhaps, alter our verdict. A classic example was the
development of the atom bomb.

Maybe it's time that the decision makers begin to address the
issue of the consequences of their actions in light of the impact
on people. Does, for example, the decision enhance the person or
group affected, or does the decision enhance the aim of the
organization disregarding the people involved? In other words, as
I stated earlier in the introduction, do we view the decision in
terms of people being manipulated as objects for organizational
ends or do we view people as ends in and of themselves?

There is an interesting and revealing footnote to the above
concepts. The first managing editor of the journal
Educational Administration and Supervision, was Charles Hughes
Johnston. In a 1916 editorial Professor Johnston asked the school
administrator if; ". . . the school man (can) find something to
his purpose in relating his policy of school administration
definitely to some modern system of philosophical thought?"[13]
Professor Johnston may have been fearful of the direction the then
just emerging science of administration was taking; that is all
scientific facts, and no philosophical reflection. He believed
that a decision needed to be grounded on a firm foundation. This
was quite clear to him when he stated:

> . . . to force oneself to work back to
> fundamental considerations when initiating
> school reform or justifying school procedure,
> (philosophy) ought to be an essential part of
> the professional equipment of the school
> administrator. Otherwise, curriculum
> construction, to select a typical administra-
> tive function, must degenerate into mere

checkboard manipulation of programs and
schedules, or at most into adjustments to the
merely more obvious and pressing demands of an
economic, political or traditional sort.[14]

It is interesting to note that over 65 years ago Professor
Johnston asked administrators to justify their decisions on a firm
philosophical basis and not simply get caught up in the action –
the process of the decision making; of doing something without
really reflecting upon the consequences of their action.  I wonder
if educational administration would have been altered if Professor
Johnston had not died in an auto accident in 1917 at the age of
43.

Forty years later Professor McDonald asked us, in his essay,
if philosophy can give substance to a decision on policy
formulated by an administrator.  According to the author, the
foundation of an educational policy would be a systematic
philosophy that would give to the administrator "consistent and
comprehensive guidance in selecting reasons for his practices in
education."[15]  The author's essay, while not  focusing on the
theme of ethics, gives the reader the broader picture.  That is to
say, we see the role of philosophy as applied to educational
policy and practices. We can draw an analogy between this concept
and the use of ethics in decision making.

However, everyone does not agree that the philosopher can be
an administrator.  Philosophers, according to Professor Morris,
cannot sit in an administrative chair because philosophical
concepts grow out of assumptions that are quite contradictory to
the role of the administrator.  Therefore, philosophy cannot give
much guidance to the administrator.

Professor Morris in his essay illustrates three areas in
which conflict between philosophy and educational administration
occurs; People as ends and means; open communication of academia
vs. administration's closed, restricted communications; and
finally the philosophic temperament vs. the administrative
temperament.

The issues raised by the author are quite serious from a
general philosophical perspective as well as an ethical
perspective.  The following article brings us back to the specific
issues of values and the educational administrator.  Both
ProfessorsNewsome and Gentry stated that values are very critical
to the decision maker.  The authors discuss the concepts of cause-
effect, means-ends, and the problem of defining the terms value
and decision.

As the authors noted, ". . . decisions are made by various
means . . ."[16], and values should be a part of that process
depending upon the type of decision one makes.  The authors
analyze five types of decisions and the values inherent in them.
Professors Newsome and Gentry noted that in a pluralistic society
the problem of values is quite critical.  By facing the issue of
ethics and morals, and openly addressing it, we might be able to
become rational and ethical in our decisions.

Professor Ladd  takes up this  issue of  values and decisions
from the perspective of means-ends especially between individuals

and the ". . . formal organizations (or bureaucracies) in our society."[17] Professor Ladd addresses the twin issues of the "rationality of formal organizations, and its regard to individuals inside and outside the organizations to individuals and to the public at large."[18] The author, like Professor Morris, makes a similar point about morality and administration. Professor Ladd stated, ". . . certain facts of the organizational ideal are incompatable with the ordinary principles of morality . . .."[19] Another problem that grows out of bureaucracies is the feeling of "alienation," which ". . . is a logical consequence of the particular language-game one is playing in organizational decision making."[20] This is one of the problems that trap us because of the structures we have created and the consequences of these structures.

This essay utilizes the following perspectives to illustrate the authors' theme. First is the ". . . 'ideology', . . . presupposed by organizational decision making."[21] The second is the language-game as the mode of analysis because as Professor Ladd stated, ". . . it provides us with a method of analyzing a rational activity without committing ourselves to whether or not it is also moral."[22] Four topics are covered by the author: the moral relationship of individuals to organizations; the moral relationship of organizations to individuals; utilitarianism and alienation; and closing remarks on the paradox that individuals who make corporate decisions do so, not on the basis of values or beliefs in a personal sense, but on the aims and goals of the organization. Finally, these individuals are not responsible for the consequences of their actions because they are acting for the corporation.

It is just this issue, the consequences of decisions that the author of the final article in this chapter addresses. Professor Foster engages us in the issue of how facts and values are part of the decision making process. The author objects to the current methodology of decision making, especially in the separating of the solution of a problem from the consequences of that solution.

The basis of the author's discussion of the concepts of facts and values are the writings of Jurgen Habermas. Habermas, according to Professor Foster; ". . . provides a compelling framework for analyzing the nature of an administrative science, the fact value distinction and the role of the administrative apparatus in maintaining its legitimacy."[23]

This legitimacy can be brought about if we can work through linking a theory of the science of administration and a normative theory, as long as we do not orient the science of administration ". . . towards increasing technical control but toward a systematic search for social justice and freedom."[24]

Finally, the author, in echoing comments made by Professor Ladd, stated that we must break the cycle of means-ends. Perhaps then we can begin the process of re-establishing administrations ". . . lost legitimacy."[25]

The first four chapters of this book constitute the theoretical aspect of ethics and educational decision making. Chapters Five and Six will examine the practical applications of the use of ethics in decision making. Chapter Five consists of

articles in which an ethical perspective is clearly present.
Chapter Six is a series of case studies in educational decision
making.

Chapter Five's lead article is about ethics and the
politician. While the article does not specifically discuss
education and educational decision making, the theme of the essay
is universal in its application. In the article the concepts of
what is just and what is necessary collide. Professor Bailey
raises many issues regarding ethical problems that confront
public officials. The author shows us that the application of
ethics to "real" situations may not be as clear cut as many of us
would like to believe. We need to remember that administration,
whether politically or educationally derived, is the art of doing
what is possible.

We now move from the area of the general implications of
ethics and decision making towards specific issues of ethical
importance. Professor Clements and Macdonald present to us a
brief summary of seven papers that were presented at a conference
that dealt with morality and schooling. Almost twenty years after
the conference was held, the issues raised are still fresh and
critical to educators. The following essay, by Professor
Kirschenbaum, argues that values clarification is a method that
allows students to come to grips with issues that are, in
themselves, controversial. The author also notes that value
clarification is, ". . . most consistent with democratic
thought."[26] The theme of this article, as stated by the author,
is the political implications of values clarification. The author
discusses how we might decide what specific topics are useful for
values clarification. That, in and of itself, is a difficult
concept because of the many divergent perceptions parents and
teachers have regarding exposing students to controversial topics.
If we are to discuss controversial issues we need to respect the
various viewpoints of the individuals. Professor Kirschenbaum
also notes that, contrary to popular opinion, values clarification
does not impose upon the students ". . . to conform to the group
opinion."[27] The author takes a very interesting position on the
uses of values clarification.

Professor Etzioni believes that we can do ethics in the
school if we separate ethics based on religious doctrine from what
he calls "civil ethics": ". . . The acceptance by members of
society, as an ethical imperative (as opposed to a mere pragmatic
expedient), that pursuing private and public goals ought to be
done by legitimate means - i.e., according to rules demarcating
right from wrong."[28] This would be in line with the ideas of
Professor Kirschenbaum. The final article by Professor Faulconer
presents to us an additional set of problems regarding ethics and
the schools. What are the standards of ethics we ought to operate
by? Who applies the standards, and what are the consequences of
unethical acts?

Chapter Six consists of case studies. The chapter opens with
an introduction by Professor Burnett who gives us a possible
method of how we might be ethical in our decision making. The
author states four concepts that he believes will help us act in
an ethical manner. If we rephrase these four concepts into four

questions, and keep them in mind as we read the case studies in this chapter, I believe we can begin to deal with the issues raised in these cases. The four concepts rephrased are:

1. Does your decision deliberately draw from a set of genuine options?
2. Are you, the decision maker, capable of acting sanely and maturely?
3. Do you have a firm grasp of the facts and the consequences of the various choices you have in making the decision?
4. How does the choice affect the welfare of individuals?

The case studies in the chapter have been picked to represent many areas where ethics would be logically involved. The cases are drawn from the following areas: Professional development (Professor Sayer); Analyzing your value system (Professor Carlson); Issues based on a code of ethics (Professor Dexheimer); Sexism (Ms. Carol Sarvello); Race relations (Professor Katz); Educational politics (Professor Fisher); Fiscal concerns (Professor Krinsky); and an article on several issues including free speech and the teachers' role in shaping policy (Professor Tyner). In some of the case studies I have added questions in order to help you better focus upon the issues.

In conclusion, it is my hope that ethics can become an integral part of one's decision making process. I believe that the linkage of facts and values, means-ends, and the welfare of people over organizations, will begin to re-establish a more humanistic decision making process by the educational decision makers.

## FOOTNOTES

[1]Crittenden, Brian, Chapter I, p. 16.

[2]Ibid., p. 17.

[3]Ibid., p. 22.

[4]West, Earle, ed., Chapter II, p. 45.

[5]Ibid., p. 51.

[6]Sergiovanni, Thomas, Chapter III, p. 70.

[7]Ibid.

[8]Ibid.

[9]Worsfold, Victor, Chapter III, p. 89.

[10]Foster, William, Chapter III, p. 104.

[11]Ibid.

[12]Ibid., p. 108.

[13]Johnson, Charles H., _Educational Administration and Supervision_ 2 (November 1916): p. 591.

[14]Ibid.

[15]McDonald, Gerald, Chapter IV, p. 124.

[16]Newsome, George and Gentry, Harold, Chapter IV, p. 137.

[17]Ladd, John, Chapter IV, p. 145.

[18]Ibid.

[19]Ibid.

[20]Ibid., p. 146.

[21]Ibid.

[22]Ibid., p. 147.

[23]Foster, William, Chapter IV, p. 172.

[24]Ibid., p. 184.

[25]Ibid., p. 186.

[26]Kirschenbaum, Howard, Chapter V, p. 209.

[27]Ibid., p. 211.

[28]Etzioni, Amitai, Chapter V, p. 216.

# CHAPTER I

## THE MORAL CONTEXT OF DECISION MAKING IN EDUCATION

### Brian Crittenden

### Characteristics of the Moral Domain

The Appeal Court in England recently decided, contrary to the wishes of the parents, that it was in the best interests of an infant born with Down's syndrome that it should live. In California a 'wrongful life' suit has been brought against a hospital on behalf of a 26 month-old boy born with the same condition. While there may be significant differences in the particular cases, the contrast dramatically illustrates how diversely a moral issue can be interpreted. But people differ not only on the relative weight they give to moral values, or what they take to be the morally significant facts of the case, or even on the moral status of various principles or standards. They also radically dispute the nature of morality itself. Thus, we cannot embark on the effort of characterizing the moral domain without making claims that, to some extent at least, are contentious.

The attempt to distinguish morality in purely formal terms -- for example, judgments in which 'ought' or its equivalent is used in a prescriptive and universalizable way[1] -- may avoid the more obvious differences over the content of moral beliefs and principles. However, there is serious argument on what formal criteria are appropriate, and more importantly, on whether any purely formal account can be sufficient. In the present century, the extent of the differences in moral belief and theory (or ethics) has induced many people to take a pessimistic view about the possibility of being objective and of reaching rational agreement in morality. Relativists have supposed that moral claims can only apply and be upheld within the way of life shared by the members of a group; emotivists have interpreted moral claims as nothing more than the expression of one's feelings or tastes; existentialists have based the moral life on a commitment of the will to certain ultimate standards and values for one's life, a choice beyond the scope of rational reflection.[2]

But these and other similar responses exaggerate the problem of diversity. The ideals and standards of how human beings ought to live can be rationally examined in the light of their characteristic needs and the general conditions in which they live. Given the kind of experience that pain is, for example, we do not have to make an arbitrary choice on whether cruelty is morally bad or not; and its moral badness does not depend on whether one is disgusted by cruelty or takes pleasure in it. It is precisely because cruelty is morally bad that it deserves to be found disgusting. (Of course, morality would not be possible unless most human beings were inclined to be repulsed by cruelty and other actions that disregard human welfare.) Because human beings everywhere share a common evolutionary background, possess the same neuro-anatomical structure, and contend with similar conditions of life in the one physical world, it is hardly surprising that there would be at least some common ideals and standards for how they should live their lives.[3] Relativists tend to exaggerate the differences by ignoring the common underlying moral values that are often interpreted diversely in the details of moral practice.[4] The conflicting views on whether infants born with Down's syndrome should be kept alive or not may be based on a common principle of respect for human life.

It should be stressed that, in any case, diversity does not entail relativism. Societies can be mistaken in their moral estimation of particular practices (e.g. slavery, human sacrifice, child labor), and one group may have a better general understanding of morality than another. At least in regard to fundamental beliefs about how human beings should treat one another, relativism is an untenable position. We cannot seriously hold such beliefs (e.g. that genocide, enforced apartheid, imprisonment without trial, dishonesty are morally wrong) and at the same time insist that they may not apply outside our own cultural or social group.[5] The most we can accept is that our fundamental moral beliefs (which in the nature of the case must apply in some fashion to everyone) may be wholly or partly mistaken and that we would be prepared to revise them in the light of more adequate understanding and experience.

In examining the nature of morality we need to keep in mind the serious differences in the moral beliefs that people hold and the way they interpret morality. However, we have some ground for proceeding confidently with a discussion of the nature of morality from the fact that there are at least some moral values that are generally recognized and that can be upheld objectively by appealing to characteristics of the things and actions involved together with facts about human nature and experience. If nothing more, there is the possibility of a genuine argument.

It is clear that morality is concerned, in some fashion, what the question of how people should live their lives. In attempting to identify its nature more specifically, we are likely to beg disputed questions if we appeal to formal conditions that any judgment claiming to be moral must satisfy or if we identify morality as a means for the efficient achievement of a particular non-moral end (such as happiness, welfare, rational self-interest). I think it is more satisfactory to approach the meaning of 'morality' by describing the kinds of practices that are undoubtedly central to what engaging in morality involve.[6] Each of these practices contains various normative concepts, ideals, attitudes, prescriptions and prohibitions. At the very least, morality has to do with respect for human life, with such notions as love, loyalty, justice, honesty, courage, and generosity, with truth telling and promise keeping, with the institutions of political authority, property, and family (along with the more general, but associated, regulation of sexual relations). Whether a specific belief or practice is intelligible as a moral one depends on the extent to which it is consistent with the central and distinctive issues of morality. In general, we tell when individuals are raising a moral question, stating a moral problem, making a moral judgment, from the kind of substantive concepts in which they describe or argue about the situation. In other words, it is content more than form that distinguishes a moral argument.

Upon this basis, I would wish to go further and support the following interpretation of morality. It consists of the standards and ideals of action that are thought to be fitting for human beings when they are viewed in the broad range of their distinctive characteristics and within the pattern of relationships they inevitably have as members of the physical and socio-cultural world. The existence and specific content of morality depend on certain facts about human beings: for example, that they are capable of rational choice and can be held responsible within certain limits for what they do; that they are sentient beings prone to pain and mortal injury; that they live in a world of limited resources; that the decisions of one generation can have serious consequences for those that follow.

In this interpretation of morality it is obvious that, whatever values may enter into decisions on what one should do, moral criteria exercise the decisive arbitrating role. This is not to say, however, that one can always appeal to a moral criterion to settle competing claims of different values (e.g. aesthetic and economic) or that moral criteria may not themselves conflict in a way that has no clear resolution. On many occasions, the morally right or good action issues in the attainment of one or another of the non-moral values that make up human life. The values that people enjoy through being treated justly, for example, are the values of the things they receive, or are not prevented from acquiring, as their due (such as income, property, health care, education). Does this mean that there are really no distinctively moral values to be realized, that what is morally good consists in the attainment of non-moral values in various combinations and degrees? If we concentrate simply on the consequences of moral action, I believe this is the case. However, if actions are seen from the perspective of the intentions, motives, reasons, and dispositions of the agent, we can distinguish in them distinctively moral value (or disvalue). When, for example, a person treats others fairly out of a sense of respect for them as human beings, moral value is realized in the quality of such actions even though a recipient may fail to gain some non-moral good as a result and may not even be aware of the treatment. While various non-moral benefits usually flow from genuine love or friendship between human beings, moral value exists directly in the quality of such a relationship. Speaking the truth may be useful for achieving many non-moral ends. Whether there is specifically moral value in it depends on the speaker's motives and reasons (such as concern for others or the belief that the truth matters). In general, it seems that moral value (or disvalue) is found directly in the kinds of regard we have for others and ourselves (and the non-human world) and in the extent of our commitment to realize the non-moral goods that are constituents in a worthwhile human life or are at least conditions on which the possibility of such a life depends.

Because of the special interests of philosophy, ethical theorists have tended to concentrate on a few general concepts

(such as 'ought' and 'good'), on the logical status of moral
claims, and on the logic of moral argument. Through the powerful
influence of Kantian and utilitarian ethics, the domain of
morality (and moral education) has often been interpreted in
contemporary thought as predominantly a matter of making rational
decisions about particular questions of what ought to be done; and
the model of argument has been that of theoretical reasoning --
the subsuming of particular situations under general moral
principles.[7] In reality, the moral domain is much broader and
more complex in its scope. In moral decision making, the mode of
reasoning is practical, not theoretical. So many indeterminate
factors come into play (such as past experience, the
interpretation of principles and circumstances, the estimation of
consequences) that relatively simple models drawn from theoretical
reasoning are inappropriate. In particular, moral principles and
dispositions do not lend themselves to being organized into a
completely harmonious system. Conflicts between moral values
inevitably occur. In particular situations one must face the
contrary attraction of such values as truthfulness and loyalty,
candor and kindness, freedom and equality, justice and compassion.
Thus, as Stuart Hampshire has pointed out, rational decision
making in morality must accommodate the fact "that no sufficient
reason of any kind is on occasion available to explain a decision
made after careful reflection in a situation of moral conflict."[8]
But reasoning and decision making are only a part of what morality
encompasses. It is concerned with the way in which we typically
regard ourselves and others (and the social and physical world in
which we live) as well as how we act; with the range of stable
dispositions, attitudes and emotions that incline us to see and
act as we do.[9] If these are developed adequately through
education and experience, we should be able to perceive more or
less directly (i.e. without any formal process of reasoning) the
morally significant features of everyday situations and to act
accordingly. Morality also extends beyond the range of strict
obligations and duties to include public and personal ideals of
what is good or desirable in moral character and action.

Public Morality
    Because this book focuses on the relationship of ethical
theory and moral values to the decision making of educational
administrators, it is not necessary to examine the nature of
morality in its full complexity. I shall draw attention to two
distinctions which help to identify the moral context within which
administrative decisions in a communal practice such as education
need to be placed. These distinctions also provide a basis for
treating the problem of diversity which, as I have noted, exists
both in fact and in the nature of morality.
    In the first place, we need to distinguish between the basic
social morality -- the values and practices without which society
could hardly survive and would certainly not be tolerable -- and
the comprehensive bodies of moral belief about what is good or
desirable for social and individual human life.[10] As a minimum,
the basic social morality includes the practices of justice, truth
telling and honesty, concern for others at least to the extent of

avoiding the infliction of injury, mutual help in satisfying essential physical and cultural needs, and the willingness to recognize the claims that others make on us on the basis of these practices. In the context of any particular society, the strict obligations and duties that everyone must recognize as affecting interpersonal relationships and the general life of the society are those which reflect the broad principles of the basic social morality. In addition to this level of morality, individuals and groups within a society may hold other values that they believe are essential or at least desirable for the conduct of social and individual life. At any time, some of these values will probably be accepted in the society generally -- although the actual content of this category is likely to vary.

The full range of moral beliefs and practices that individuals or groups recognize varies in its comprehensiveness (it may extend from common desirable standards to personal ideals in one's way of life) and in the degree to which its content forms a system. Some inclusive moral outlooks are largely eclectic, others form a carefully ordered pattern based on a theory or ideology, in which, for example, there may be an overriding single aim of moral practices or a dominant moral value or definite procedural principles for resolving conflict among values. It is probably correct to say that, in contemporary western culture, the moral obligations and personal moral ideals that many people accept are not characterized by any systematic unity but reflect the influence of diverse, and perhaps incompatible, traditions. But there are also, of course, important comprehensive moral outlooks that, in varying degrees, are systematic. Moralities based on religion tend to be of this kind; among systematic secular moralities there are the various versions of utilitarianism and those that give primacy to a single moral value (such as equality in socialist morality and individual freedom in liberal morality).

The second distinction to be noted is between personal and public morality.[11] This distinction can be applied to the content of both the basic social morality and comprehensive moral systems (although in a pluralist democratic society public morality will be associated mainly with the former). It also cuts across the division of principles into strict obligations or duties and moral ideals. Although the boundaries between personal and public morality cannot be sharply drawn, the key distinguishing condition is whether one is acting as a private citizen in the direction of one's own life and in relationship to other particular individuals or whether, by virtue of power or authority, one makes decisions that often affect large numbers of people. The distinction applies most obviously to those who hold positions of authority in the state. But it extends to anyone whose actions in a public office seriously affect the interests of others. As Thomas Nagel has pointed out, there is a dangerous sense of insulation for those who make decisions in a public role.[12] They are often seen by themselves and others as part of a complex public system in which they have a certain range of decisions to make; they are subject to orders themselves and are curtailed by actions taken elsewhere in the system. The aspect of personal responsibility can easily be obscured. Blame is shifted from the individual by appealing to the moral defects of the system. While to some extent this defense may be justifiable, individuals nevertheless do make decisions in public morality and cannot escape responsibility for assessing their own actions and their consequences in the light of the fundamental social moral values.

There are various ways in which the relationship between personal and public morality can be interpreted. Although the issues cannot be argued here, I believe the most satisfactory position is one in which the differences between them, while important, are matters of degree and emphasis; that the same general moral values and principles apply in both contexts. In general terms, there are at least three main respects in which public and private morality differ.

1. Public morality is subject to stricter conditions of impartiality. Those who make decisions in a public role are usually exercising power over a large number of people. They are justified on the assumption that they are acting for the welfare of the whole society or an institution or group within it and for individuals insofar as they are members of the relevant group. In making judgments their normal standpoint should be the welfare of the whole group they serve; there is no place for personal interest. In personal morality, on the other hand, the normal perspective is one that admits the particular circumstances of the individual. (I act in a certain way because the person involved is my husband or wife, my child, my friend and so on.) In taking the welfare of other human beings generally into account, individuals are not in most cases morally required to choose actions that confer benefit, but only to avoid those that inflict harm. I have used 'normal' in referring to both domains because there are occasions when a general perspective needs to take precedence in personal morality and when the general perspective in public morality needs to be broadened. A policy that serves the welfare of an institution or even a whole society may be morally undesirable in the light of the needs of more inclusive groups and its effects upon them.

2. In considering the intrinsic moral quality of an action and the value of the consequences, more weight tends to be given to the consequences in public than in private morality. On the question of justifying the means in terms of the end, I do not see that there is any difference in principle between public and personal morality. However, because of the scale of the decisions commonly made in public morality and their direct bearing on the welfare of groups rather than individuals, there are important differences of degree. (Compare, for example, the question of one individual coercing another for some desirable end and the state using coercion for the public good.)

It should be emphasized, however, that apart from the general moral values that apply to an action (and to the full range of its consequences), the choice of means in public morality is constrained in particular by the moral and legal rights of individuals. In this respect, Nagel draws attention to the special role of the law. As an institution it is expected to make impartial but non-consequentialist decisions, to protect individual rights and thus to limit the means that other institutions may employ.

3.  Decisions in public morality are generally subject to more demanding conditions of explicit rational justification than in private morality. In the latter, because the scale of decisions is usually small and the context familiar to the agent, there is less need -- and often less opportunity -- for explicit reasoning in coming to a decision on what one should do. In fact there are many occasions on which we recognize what ought to be done without any explicit process of reasoning. Even when reflection is appropriate, we might not be able to express adequately in words our reasons for assessing a situation as we do. In public morality experience also plays a significant part in judgment. However, because of the power exercised by agents in the domain of public morality, the adverse consequences that often follow for some individuals, and the strict condition of impartiality, it is reasonable to expect that the decisions of public morality should normally be backed by explicit justifying reasons.

In a society that upholds respect for diverse comprehensive moral ideals and systems, it is obvious that decisions in the domain of public morality should be based on the principles of the essential core of social morality together with those values on which the policy of moral pluralism itself directly depends (personal freedom, the equal worth of all individuals as moral agents, tolerance of diverse ways of thinking and acting, the use of non-violent persuasion). In the political and legal system of the society these values are translated into more specific principles and procedures (for example, consent of the governed, majority rule, due process of law, various specific rights of freedom). Certain moral ideals of a particular system may, in fact, be accepted by everyone although in a pluralist society one must be wary about assuming that this is the case. With an exception to be noted shortly, decisions in public morality should not reflect the distinctive outlook of any particular inclusive moral system or theory. Whether an official is committed to asceticism or hedonism as a personal moral ideal, it should make no difference to the way in which he or she administers a program of unemployment benefits.

Moral principles, as we saw, are intimately related to the attainment of non-moral goods in human life. In regard to distributive justice, for example, it is necessary to identify what count as benefits and burdens, for it is the equitable sharing of these among the members of the society that is required by distributive justice. There are certain goods that all human beings need and may reasonably be presumed to desire (e.g. protection of life, food, shelter, health care, induction into a culture, friendship). The precise form of human needs and the related values placed on them vary, of course, from one culture and society to another. Decisions in public morality must give priority to the claims people make for commonly desired human goods. It must be recognized, however, that in addition to variations among individuals and groups on what are perceived as good-making features of life, there are serious differences over the relative weight given to the commonly accepted goods.

In the practice of democracy, the conditions I have sketched for public morality have to be qualified in one important respect. The holders of public office often seek to implement policies based on the order of priority and interpretation of values in a particular moral system. They claim that success at an election has given them at least an implicit mandate to act in this way. In an election one party may stand for the primacy of individual freedom, initiative and competition while another emphasizes egalitarian values in the form of, say, welfare services and a narrower range in the distribution of incomes. Each party may believe that its policies are best for everyone. In fact it is known that each is upholding value preferences of a section of the whole society. The party elected to government may win by a narrow majority. This practice has to be accepted as a qualification of the pluralist principle on the grounds that though periodic election everyone has the opportunity to express an opinion on certain values that should be given priority in shaping public policy. Through the legal system, the constitution, charters of human and civil rights and so on, there are also checks on what a government and its agencies may do in implementing its objectives.

It must also be recognized that no actual pluralist society will exactly meet the conditions I have been describing. The contemporary nation states that uphold substantial diversity of moral and other cultural values among their citizens inevitably reflect in their practices and traditions the influence of particular value systems dominant in the past. In countries such as the United States, Canada and Australia public attitudes to the family and sexual morality are still fairly strongly influenced by Christian ideals; the values of individualism still tend to shape the practices of their economic life.

## On Being Rational In Morality

In a general way I have already defended the view that moral principles can be rationally supported and criticized by appealing to the common needs and capacities of human beings, to the characteristic condition on which the flourishing of life depends, and to human experience viewed as broadly as possible. I have also indicated that moral reasoning is practical not theoretical; that because of such features as the competing claims of different moral values we should not expect the justification of a moral decision to be like a mathematical proof. Keeping in mind particularly the kinds of decision that come within the ambit of public morality, I wish now to comment further on the characteristics of rationality and reasoning in the moral domain.

I shall not attempt a detailed defense of the claim that human beings should have rational grounds for their moral beliefs and should proceed rationally in making moral decisions. Being rational is understood here in contrast to appealing simply to authority, to an intuition or feeling, to a blind decision or to chance. It consists in having reasons whose relevance and adequacy can be submitted to public assessment, being receptive to criticism, and taking account of the evidence of human experience on the broadest possible scale. Rationality as an ideal in the moral sphere does not reduce the acceptance of moral beliefs and the making of moral decisions to a purely intellectual activity in which reasons are always to be fully explicit and organized in a rigorously logical way. To attempt to impose an abstract model of reasoning that disregards the actual nature of morality is itself to act irrationally. Being rational in morality recognizes the conditions of practical reasoning, the crucial role of experience and of judgment based on experience, the need to have clear guidelines for certain occasions on which it is not possible or appropriate to reflect, the fundamental place of emotions and attitudes (which themselves may or may not be rationally defensible).

To claim that we can (and should) be rational about morality is not, of course, to suggest that simply by being rational we will necessarily hold sound moral values or apply them in a way that issues in morally defensible judgments -- much less that we will translate our rational moral judgments into action. The claim is also to be distinguished from the issue of whether a person may rationally reject the priority of moral reasons in making decisions. On this issue it seems clear that people can, in particular cases and even in substantial areas of their life, make rational decisions (e.g. for the sake of self-interest) that ignore or violate moral values. However, to attempt to give primacy to non-moral values in the whole of one's life would be such a distortion of what it is to be human that such a position could hardly be described as rational.[13]

Whatever the gap between thought and action, moral beliefs and values are among the fundamental guides for how life should be lived and are commonly accepted as such. Given that human beings have some capacity for self-determination and for making choices rationally (i.e. on the basis of reasons, experience, and logically consistent arguments) rather than capriciously, it seems obvious that moral beliefs should be among the first objects of rational reflection and application. If morality is to be practiced in a rational way, people must at least to some extent communicate and discuss their reasons for believing and acting as they do. Certainly, in public morality, it is an essential safeguard for rational (and morally sound) decision making that those affected by the decision should be informed as fully as possible of the reasons on which it is based. To justify a moral decision in this way is also, of course, to acknowledge the respect that is due to others as rational moral agents.

There are at least five main elements that enter into the rational justification of moral decisions: (a) the matters of fact in the situation that are thought to be related to a moral judgment; (b) the consequences that are estimated as being likely if various decisions are followed; (c) the moral concepts and principles that are believed to apply or the concepts and principles that are believed to have moral status in the case; (d) the way in which the key evaluative terms are interpreted; (e) the relative weight given to moral principles when their application leads to conflicting decisions. There is a different level of justification to which I have referred earlier and will not comment on further; why human beings should be moral (i.e. just, honest, compassionate, etc.) at all.

While the identification of matters of fact and possible consequences is often crucially important in a moral argument, what distinguishes such an argument is the way in which the facts are described or assessed in morally evaluative language. It is this process which is at the heart of the moral argument. The form of the argument is neither strictly deductive nor inductive. It is a matter of arguing, in regard to what we know of this case and others like it, that a particular description in moral terms is appropriate. On some occasions, the task may be simple: to act in such a way is to deceive, or to break a promise or to be unfair, and there are no complicating circumstances. But on other occasions it is by no means obvious how an action or situation is to be interpreted in moral terms. Is the withholding of the truth in these particular circumstances to be called a lie? Does this way of using another person's work constitute cheating? Is taking the life of this (or any) fetus to be described as murder? Is this act of violence to be regarded as terrorism?

The application of moral concepts in this way has something in common with a much wider range of terms, namely, those in which human intentions and purposes determine what count as an object or activity of a particular kind (e.g. is this piece of furniture a table or a bench?).[14] However, unlike many of these terms, morally evaluative descriptions engage certain attitudes and feelings. We cannot possess 'cruelty', 'injustice', 'dishonesty' and so on as moral concepts unless we also disapprove of what we recognize as cruel, unjust, dishonest. In this respect, the attempt to describe a situation accurately in moral terms is analogous to aesthetic description (e.g. are the metaphors banal? Isthe design of this painting coherent?). In both, the form of argument -- whether we are reflecting to ourselves or addressing someone else -- is persuasive; feelings and attitudes play an integral part in it.

Obviously, the attempt to win agreement is a particularly important aspect of argument in support of a moral judgment. But insofar as the argument is rational, it is also an attempt to test the adequacy of the judgment on which a policy (or a particular decision) is based. We saw earlier that although facts about human nature do not entail values, we cannot intelligibly propose moral standards and ideals that are not closely related to characteristic human desires and wants. In the process of the descriptive evaluation involved in moral argument the appropriate description is not simply entailed by the 'bare' facts or inferred from them; but it is an exercise of judgment that is answerable to the facts. For this reason, although disagreement may not necessarily be resolved, there can be objective arguments.

Beyond the question of what are seen as the 'bare' facts and what evaluative descriptions are thought to be appropriate, moral argument often must include a defense of the precise interpretation of the moral concepts and of the basis on which a decision is reached when conflicting evaluative moral descriptions of a situation are given from the viewpoint of different moral values. It may be agreed, for example, that a policy of providing special funds for the education of the poor is to be seen and justified in terms of the moral value of equality. However, one person may interpret this value as requiring that everyone be given an equal chance, as far as this is humanly possible, to compete for very unequal goods on the basis of personal ability and effort. Another person may see the value in relation to the distribution of commonly desired human goods so that the total of such goods possessed by each person is, in balance, approximately the same or, at least, that no one should gain an advantage that leaves anyone else worse off. It may not always be possible to resolve such conflicts of interpretation. But a rational moral argument requires the meaning in which the key moral concepts are being employed and the context of justifying theory to be made explicit.

In the determination of public policies -- and even in particular applications of a policy -- there are often different value perspectives that yield conflicting moral evaluative descriptions. The enforced busing of children to secure racially integrated schools provides a clear illustration. It may be seen as an effective means of promoting the ideal of racial harmony or integration in the society, or as a way of ensuring that minority groups have equal economic opportunity through schooling, or as a serious abridgement of the freedom of parents and students, or as a denial of the value of community in the relationship between a school and its neighborhood. And these are by no means all the moral values that affect the question of enforced busing. Such value conflicts could in principle be resolved -- and moral argument would be relatively simplified -- if a clear hierarchy of values could be objectively established or if there were a single good to be achieved through all moral action. There are some common principles of priority, such as the protection of life before the protection of property. However, as we saw earlier, it is only within particular inclusive moral systems that the values characteristic of the moral domain (e.g. freedom, benevolence, justice, equality, honesty) are given a relative weight. In the public morality of a pluralist society the moral vision of a particular system cannot be justifiably imposed on the whole society. There is, of course, the qualification to which I have already referred: the endorsement of certain moral value priorities held by a political party when it is democratically elected. Among the distinguishing characteristics of political parties in Western democracies is the relative weight they give to individual freedom and social equality. The difference will be clearly reflected in such issues as compulsory busing, the provision of public funds for private schools, the setting of enrollment quotas for minority groups. But, apart from the general constraints mentioned earlier, political parties usually do not have a complete hierarchy of values that provides a clear guideline for assessing all the competing values in complex cases, such as that of busing.

The most notable attempt to overcome the problem of conflicting values has been made by the utilitarians. They assume that there is a single end (happiness) to be achieved by a moral action, and that all experiences of happiness are comparable and measurable on a single scale. Hence, in any situation, the morally correct decision is the one that promotes the greatest happiness of the greatest number. Moral judgment is a matter of careful calculation. Although this may prove difficult in particular cases, it means that, in principle, value conflicts are eliminated. In its promise of precision and efficiency in moral decision making, utilitarianism has a strong appeal for administrators. With the development of sophisticated computers it might seem that even the practical difficulties of calculation are within sight of resolution.

In the first part of this chapter I defended an interpretation of morality that is obviously imcompatible with utilitarianism. It drew attention, in particular, to the collection of ideals and principles that mark out for human beings the ways of acting that are worthy or disgraceful in themselves. Utilitarianism has been the object of much systematic criticism.[15] In summary, the main objections are that the forms and expression of human happiness or well-being cannot be quantified and measured on a single scale, and that the utilitarian principle leads to the sanctioning of means and consequences that violate basic moral values (e.g. infliction of torture, condemnation of an innocent person, the repression of dissidents, the disfigurement of the physical environment--when the net result is that the happiness of the majority is increased). Some utilitarians have themselves recognised the latter problem by insisting on the following of rules that in general are found to meet the utilitarian criterion. But this modification does not avoid the sanctioning of immoral conclusions unless it is pushed to the point of undermining utilitarianism itself. In any case, a utilitarian has no good reason for objecting to the breaking of a rule when, in a particular case, it is known that to do so promotes greater utility.

Apart from the problems that may arise from cultural pluralism, the attempt to resolve competing moral claims by giving priority to a single value misunderstands the general nature of morality and moral reasoning. In complex cases, rational moral argument is not served by giving priority as a matter of course to one kind of value. What is required is sympathetic, careful attention to the full range of values that are at stake and an attempt to reach a judgment on the policy or action which, in the particular circumstances, respects these values as fully as possible. As we have already seen, to act rationally in making such a judgment it is necessary, insofar as conditions allow, to submit one's interpretation of the situation to critical scrutiny.

The attempt to take due account of the diverse values that may affect a moral decision often requires a considerable effort of imagination. In given conditions, there may seen to be no choice but to sacrifice one moral value for another. However, it may be possible to alter the conditions so that the dilemma is avoided or that both values can be realized in a way that is preferable to achieving one at the expense of the other. The approach to the question of busing suggested by James Coleman illustrates this use of imagination.[16] He discusses the tendency to determine such an issue as compulsory busing by giving priority either to equality (as in Rawls' theory) or to individual freedom (as in Nozick's theory). Coleman wishes to avoid the undesirable increase in social and economic inequality that follows when there are no constraints on the individual right of choice in schooling. At the same time he wishes to avoid "coercive reassignment". What he proposes is that people should have the opportunity to choose an integrated school and that there should be incentives (such as tax deductions) to encourage the choice of these schools.

It will be obvious from the foregoing comments on moral reasoning that the process cannot be reduced to a few simple formal rules. There are, of course, various logical conditions relating to consistency and non-contradiction that need to be observed. But these are far from sufficient. As we have seen, critical judgment in the application of substantial moral concepts is the central element of the process. The full test of rationality in moral argument must include the way in which motives, actions, consequences, situations are interpreted in moral terms.[17] When moral concepts have been properly acquired their application involves attitudes of approval or disapproval and, in some cases, related feelings. To imagine oneself acting in a certain way may provoke an anticipated sense of guilt or disgust. This affective aspect of moral thought provides a bridge between judgment and action. However, it must also be recognized that because moral decisions prescribe action and can significantly affect the interests of individuals and groups, they can also arouse strong emotions that seriously inhibit rational reflection. In the public sphere, issues of power often overwhelm those of morality.

Being rational in the making of moral judgments does not, of course, guarantee correct decisions; on complex issues there may not be a best or single correct decision. However, some judgments are morally more satisfactory than others. The best chance of reaching such a judgment and of overcoming the distorting influence of self-interest and the struggle for power is to test the rationality of a moral argument in each of its main aspects. While there are few clear-cut rules, it is possible to identify inconsistency, contradiction, and the overlooking of important facts or moral criteria, and to show that some evaluative descriptions or the relative ordering of values in a particular case are more defensible than others.

Given the characteristics of moral argument discussed in this section, it is obvious that in the domain of public morality all the key elements in the justification of a proposed policy or decision should be submitted to wide public criticism. When decisions affecting particular individuals are made, they or their representatives should be fully informed of the grounds for the decision and given the opportunity to challenge the argument.

## Morality and Other Values in Educational Decisions

Moral values and criteria are obviously not the only ones that need to be taken into account in the exercise of practical judgment. There is often a broad range of other values -- aesthetic, economic, political and so on -- that may affect the quality of a decision. In these cases, respect for moral values is necessary but not sufficient for a sound judgment. Two proposals for the building of an expressway, for example, may satisfy the relevant moral conditions, but one may be clearly preferable on economic grounds while the other achieves a better aesthetic effect. The decision thought best in the circumstances would thus depend on the relevant weight given to non-moral values. In the present context I shall not attempt to discuss the full variety of value perspectives that may have bearing on questions of educational policy and the decisions of educational administrators. Questions of economy and technical efficiency clearly play a large part; important aesthetic values are often at stake, although I believe that in practice they are commonly neglected. Leaving aside these and other values, I shall comment on only two of the value perspectives that are closely associated with moral standards in policies and decisions: the legal and the educational.

## Law and Morality

In many of the decisions, general as well as particular, made by educational administrators the application or interpretation of legally binding directives is the main issue. These directives may come from legislatures, courts of law, or higher levels in the educational bureaucracy. In moral terms, educational administrators have a duty to ensure that the decisions they make accord with the relevant laws and regulations. The scope of their authority, even at the highest levels, is itself at least broadly determined by law. Given the significant role that laws and regulations play in the decisions of educational administrators, it is necessary to comment directly on the place of moral values and inquiry in this context. I shall first refer briefly to the nature of the general relationship between law and morality.

Although this topic is a complex and controversial one, there are several key claims that I think can reasonably be made.[18] In the first place, whatever the precise logical connection between law and morality, it does not seem possible that a legal system could be developed without reflecting moral beliefs about what is good or bad in the conduct of human life. The legal prohibition on many activities -- assault, murder, theft, false advertising, publication of pornography, cruelty to animals and so on -- is obviously influenced by the belief that they are morally undesirable ways of acting. There are many laws requiring or prohibiting practices (such as the wearing of safety belts in automobiles, school attendance, being prevented from drinking alcohol or gambling) that are defended on paternalistic grounds; for what is thought to be in their best interests or for their good, the law constrains the freedom of certain people -- and, in the process, sometimes that of others.[19]

How far the law should go in attempting to enforce morality has been a strongly disputed question. At least in the conditions of a pluralist society, the distinction that was discussed earlier between the basic social morality and inclusive moral systems is crucial to this question. In such a society the law should not extend to matters that lie strictly within the domain of personal moral ideals or are distinctive of a particular moral system. But even apart from the conditions of a contemporary liberal pluralist society, it can be argued that the laws of any society should be restricted to the aspects of life that human beings share as citizens. That is, the moral values that the law may justifiably uphold are those affecting the common welfare. It is not within the purpose of the law to forbid everything that is morally evil or to prescribe everything that is morally good.

For the sake of the common good, many laws and regulations prescribe or prohibit matters that are in themselves morally neutral (e.g. traffic rules). But laws have also forbidden or even criminalized activities that in themselves are morally permissible and, what is more important, have prescribed or at least defended activities that are morally undesirable. This leads us to another basic and disputed question about the relationship between law and morality; whether there are any moral criteria that the directives of a public authority must satisfy if they are to be legally valid. Some have taken the view (defended by Augustine) that unless an enactment of a civil authority satisfies the moral conditions of justice it cannot have the status of a law. In varying ways legal positivists have rejected such a condition. Following the positivist tradition, H.L.A. Hart has argued for a clear distinction between the validity of a law and its morality.[20] But, as he has emphasized, to know that a rule is legally valid does not settle conclusively the question of whether it ought to (morally) be obeyed. As long as this difference is recognized, we reach the same practical conclusion on the question of obeying a law that violates moral criteria. In one case, the immoral law is not even valid; in the other, it is valid but not morally binding. Whether, for example, the notorious racist laws that have applied in a number of countries during the present century have had legal validity or not, there can be no doubt that they have violated fundamental moral values and could make no moral claim to be obeyed. On the contrary, there is a moral presumption against complying with such laws. Just what an individual member of the society could morally be expected to do in regard to an unjust law would depend on an assessment of his or her particular circumstances. In many cases, people may be permitted or even morally obliged to obey in order to avoid greater evil. However, when the evil of an act prescribed by law is such that it could not be offset by any desirable consequences (for example, an order to massacre innocent civilians in wartime), there would be a moral obligation to resist unconditionally.

The general issues of law and morality affect educational administrators somewhat differently depending on the level at which they make decisions. Many are involved, for the most part, in applying laws, regulations, directives and so on to particular cases; some have the responsibility for formulating general directives within a system of schools, although they must work within the framework set by more general laws and regulations; a few have a direct part in making major policy decisions that affect the practice of education. It is obvious that many policies of this kind, particularly in their legal formulation, are shaped by individuals and groups beyond the educational administrators and even the whole professional body of educators.

What has been said in this chapter about moral argument and justification applies clearly enough to the making of policies and general directives. Such issues as compulsory schooling, enforced busing, special funds for disadvantaged groups certainly involve legal questions; but whether the policy is finally determined by a legislature or a court or some other body, it is evident that there are many values at stake including basic, and often conflicting, moral values. A law in such cases cannot be adequately justified simply by reference to other laws. The question of what the law should be is inescapably linked with questions about what is desirable or undesirable in human life. Thus the justification for the decision must be a moral as well as legal one.

Educational administrators, particularly at the lower levels of the system, may agree that such moral justification is required in the making of policies and general regulations. But they may argue that their job is to apply these policies and regulations and that the justification for their decisions must be predominantly in terms of the rules they administer.

It can readily be granted that a substantial proportion of decisions by administrators in an educational system are of this kind. The appropriate scale of an educational system and the pattern of authority that should characterize it are themselves questions in which important moral and other values are involved. But I would claim that even at the school level, moral values have a significant part in administrative decisions.

In the first part, it is necessary to ensure that as far as possible such moral values as fairness, honesty, respect for persons, sympathy and concern are reflected in the organization of the school as a social institution and place of education. There are also many situations not covered by laws and regulations in which a decision on how a teacher or student is to be treated must be made and for which standards of fairness and other moral values are immediately relevant. In any judgment about improving the quality of education in a school (e.g. whether there should be more or fewer electives in the curriculum or what the limited equipment funds should be spent on) certain assumptions are inevitably made about what is humanly worthwhile and the kind of role schools ought to play in the society.

In the case of decisions that are directly related to regulations, administrators often need to make a judgment on how a regulation should be applied in particular circumstances. Given the underlying purpose of law to promote human good, a sound interpretation will depend, at least in part, on applying moral criteria of what is desirable.

Finally administrators at the school level are in an excellent position to observe any undesirable consequences in practice from the application of general policies and regulations. It might be found, for example, that a bilingual program was being imposed on parents rather than being chosen or that the emphasis in the program on the maintenance of an ethnic language and culture was putting the children affected at a serious educational and social disadvantage and promoting cultural separatism. In a particular case, the withholding of federal funds from a school that refused to integrate might seem to be unjustified because of the harm done to the children in that school. In general, where the practical consequences of a policy are morally (or educationally) undesirable, local administrators have the responsibility of criticizing the policy and resisting its application.

At the levels of educational administration at which regulations and policy are determined, it follows from what has been said about the general relationship between law and morality that moral values should play a crucial part in shaping the substance of the decisions and in their justification.

Educational administrators at any level may be subject to morally undesirable directives. The most dramatic cases would be those determined by a legislature or court. A state might make a particular kind of sex education program compulsory in all schools or insist that every school teaching evolutionary theory in science courses should present religious beliefs about creation as an alternative. Both these directives would raise serious moral questions about the scope of the states' authority in education. The first relates particularly to the freedom of parents and students in an area that so directly reflects the diversity of personal moral ideals and inclusive moral systems respected in a pluralist society; the second affects the intellectual integrity and academic freedom of teachers. Whatever the present status of evolutionary theory as a scientific explanation, a religious belief in creation cannot be presented as an <u>alternative</u> -- although it might be considered as a quite different way of thinking about the origins of the world. As we have seen, the moral issues in the policy of enforced busing to achieve racial integration are complex; there are grounds on which its moral justification can at least be questioned. The same may be said for the policy of setting enrollment quotas on the basis of sex, ethnic group, social class and so on for entry to various professional programs. It is not possible to say in advance precisely what educational administrators ought to do when confronted with a directive they believe is morally objectionable. What I wish to emphasize is that an appeal to a legally enacted regulation may not be a sufficient justification for acting in a certain way, and that when it seems that moral values are being violated, administrators have the responsibility to decide on moral grounds what action they should take.

Because a legal approach to decision making is common in the work of educational administrators, they may be inclined to assume that even when moral values need to be applied the process of argument and justification is essentially the same. In particular, they may assume that moral values are expressed in a set of clear-cut rules. In the earlier sections of this chapter I tried to stress the extent to which judgment and interpretation enter into moral deliberation and argument, particularly when there are several, perhaps competing, moral values at stake. Moral rules, as distinct from ideals and principles, do have a place in morality.[21] Their importance has been exaggerated because of the strong influence in our cultural tradition of theistic morality with its emphasis on Divine commands and laws.

Moral rules are useful guides to action when deliberation is not possible. But in situations of any complexity they can be crude instruments. It is precisely when there is no single overriding law that clearly applies in the given case that the procedures of legal reasoning themselves tend to be like those of moral reasoning.

## Educational Values

Policies for education or particular administrative decisions may satisfy moral and legal conditions but fail from an educational point of view. In fact, it is not uncommon for public policies to be devised mainly for the sake of non-educational ends. In the past few decades, the ideal of social equality -- whether it is interpreted as equal opportunity to compete for the prizes of the society or as a more equitable distribution of goods -- has been the dominant objective of many policies in education.

Apart from the link between educational achievement and other themes in human life, the school as a social institution can and does serve a variety of non-educational objectives. It is hardly surprising, then, that the school would be seen as a useful instrument for promoting all kinds of interests. In some cases, decisions may have little, if any, connection with the school's educational role (e.g. they might be about a dental care program or the building up of a champion football team). In others, they may use the educational work of the school for the sake of some other good without necessarily distorting the values of education (e.g. a special program in language skills for a socially disadvantaged ethnic group). But in other cases, the values that distinguish the practice of education may be undermined in order to achieve certain social, political, economic or other objectives -- such as laissez-faire freedom for the learner, equality of learning outcomes, political conformity, military superiority, technical efficiency.

It is too late in the course of this chapter to explore the difficult question of what constitutes distinctively educational values.[22] It must be recognized that there is much legitimately contested ground and that, to a substantial degree, the differences reflect controversy about moral values. Any form of education is necessarily shaped by assumptions about what is of worth in human life, about how human beings ought to live. However, I think it can at least be fairly claimed that teaching and learning fail to be educational when they neglect the conditions for a critical understanding of the beliefs, skills, attitudes and values that are being acquired. These conditions are, for the most part, tested and refined in the institutions of systematic inquiry that comprise the disciplines. When the conditions are neglected, learning is, at best, shallow and mechanical; when the beliefs interpret human life and have consequences for how people ought to act, the practice amounts to indoctrination.

Over any substantial part of the curriculum (at least in the schooling of children and adolescents) there are other broad criteria of its educational value: the cultural and social significance of what is being learned; the scope of the program in relation to the major symbolic modes of culture and the degree of coherence among the different elements of the program; the depth and coherence that is achieved within each element over time.

The point I wish to stress is that such conditions of educational value should be given a central place in the deliberations that lead to the making of policies for schools and to the particular decisions of administrators. To a certain extent educational values are protected by a regard for moral values (e.g. in rejecting indoctrination). However, there are distinct criteria of what is educationally desirable. It must be acknowledged, of course, that in some circumstances the claims of educational values should be overridden on moral grounds. Consider, for example, the decision to give limited resources to the building of more hospitals rather than to the improvement of schooling, or to concentrate the resources available for education on bringing everyone to a minimally acceptable standard of literacy rather than on the development of a broad educational program.

Everyone who has a part in making decisions that affect education ought to be concerned for the moral values that are at stake. But even when this condition is satisfied, it is inevitable that politicians, economists, judges and so on will tend to interpret the issues in terms of the criteria of judgment with which they are most closely associated by virtue of their role. What may be expected, I think, is that <u>educational</u> administrators would be among the chief defenders of the specifically educational values.

On many occasions, administrators apply these values (as well as moral and legal criteria) to questions about the appropriate educational means for achieving a predetermined end. However, it would be a serious mistake to interpret their role (or that of educational theorists) as a purely technical one. In the practice of education, as in other fundamental human activities, means and ends cannot be neatly separated in this way. They interact and modify one another. While there may need to be compromises in shaping general policies for education, it is essential that educational values should at least be represented in the process of deliberation. In regard to the decisions that come within the control of educational administrators, these values should be given priority next to the basic moral criteria.

In discussing the nature of moral decision making, particularly in the public domain, I stressed the need to make as explicit as possible the ingredients that go to form the final judgment. As we saw, the nature of the argument is persuasive; but at the same time it is an attempt to test the adequacy of an interpretation. There are, of course, occasions on which it is not possible for public officials to test and justify the decisions they propose to take. Despite some recently popular metaphors of schooling, educational administrators are not, however, commonly faced with the urgency of a casualty ward or a battlefield. In any case, as defenders of educational values, they should be particularly concerned to uphold the conditions of reasoned judgment in their own decisions.

## Moral Authority for Educational Decisions

In this chapter I have focused on general characteristics of morality and the nature of moral argument as a background for a further examination of moral values and administrative decision making in education. I have related morality in a general way to other values that play a particularly important role in such decisions. I shall conclude by drawing attention briefly to the fundamental moral issues in the question of who may exercise authority over education (particularly the education of children) and what the scope of their authority should be.

It is commonly argued that parents have the primary moral right to choose the kind of education their own children shall receive.[23] At the same time, this right must be exercised for the good of their children and must respect the moral claim that children have to a sound and adequate education. As students acquire sufficient maturity (not later than about 15 or 16 years) they should take over from their parents the exercise of choice in their education. I am doubtful whether even mature students have a moral claim to authority in determining what is done in the name of education. However, there are many decisions in the life of an educational institution in which students as they mature are morally entitled to participate.

The state has a morally defensible authority over education both to protect the interests and good of children and to act for the welfare of the society.[24] It is obvious that education is not simply a personal matter. It is one of the major processes by which the members of a society maintain and develop their common cultural and social life from one generation to another. Within the framework of liberal pluralist societies, the state has played a remarkably large role in education. It has not restricted itself to providing resources and to insisting on certain conditions in the practice of education that would protect the interests of students and the common welfare. It has also been directly engaged in the management of a whole system of educational institutions. There are obvious dangers in this situation for the values of pluralism. In a liberal pluralist society the state should not attempt to impose or even favor any particular ideal of a desirable human life. Yet, it is very difficult for a school to avoid reflecting at least some of the moral values that belong to a particular way of life in a society rather than to the basic social morality; certainly a school will embody a particular interpretation of educational theory and practice. The decisions of legislatures and government departments affecting education need to be closely assessed in relation to the moral constraints that are at least implicit in pluralism.

The moral authority of teachers and administrators is also a complex matter. In part, they act as delegates of the parents and the state. But this delegation is based on the assumption that they possess appropriate competence. As R.S. Peters argued some years ago, to be in authority as a teacher is dependent on being an authority in what one teaches.[25] The exercise of authority on the basis of competence (and not simply power) is an additional ground for expecting that decisions would be firmly grounded in arguments and evidence.

In common with others who make morally significant decisions in the public domain, educational administrators have a general responsibility to rationally justify their decisions as thoroughly as possible. But, as we have also seen, it is part of their special responsibility to educational values and, in relation to students, of their role as educators.

**FOOTNOTES**

[1]See R.M. Hare, <u>The Language of Morals</u> (Oxford: Oxford University Press, 1964).

[2]For an interesting critique of these views particularly the last, see Mary Midgley, <u>Beast and Man: The Roots of Human Nature</u> (Ithaca: Cornell University Press, 1978), especially Ch. 9.

[3]These common features are discussed by Stephen Toulmin, <u>Human Understanding</u>, Vol. 1, (Oxford: Clarendon Press, 1972) pp. 97, 485.

[4]See M. Ginsberg, <u>On the Diversity of Morals</u> (London: Mercury Books, 1956).

[5]Mary Midgley makes this point well in "Trying Out One's New Sword," <u>The Listener</u> (December 15, 1977), pp. 787-88. She is criticizing what she calls "moral isolationism."

[6]I have discussed this interpretation in <u>Form and Content in Moral Education</u> (Toronto: Ontario Institute for Studies in Education, 1972) esp. pp. 32-48. Several paragraphs in the present chapter have been taken from an unpublished paper, "Moral Education: Some Aspects of its Relationship to General Values Education and the Study of Religion."
Among writings to which I referred in the immediate preparation for this chapter, I should mention, in particular, A.L. Lockwood, "Moral Reasoning and Public Policy Debate," in <u>Moral Development and Behavior</u> ed. Thomas Lickona (New York: Holt, Rinehart and Winston, 1976) Ch. 18. Fred Newman, <u>Clarifying Controversial Issues: An Approach to Teaching Social Studies</u> (Boston: Little, Brown & Co., 1970).

[7]For a discussion of this point see Stuart Hampshire, "Public and Private Morality," in <u>Public and Private Morality</u> ed. Stuart Hampshire (Cambridge University Press, 1978) esp. pp. 36-38. This essay and his other contribution to the book <u>Morality and Pessimism</u> are critiques of what he calls "abstract and computational" moral theory.

[8]Hampshire, <u>Public and Private Morality</u>, p. 44.

[9]This aspect of morality is brought out well by Iris Murdoch, <u>The Sovereignty of Good</u> (London: Routledge and Kegan Paul, 1970).

[10]For a discussion of almost the same distinction see P.F. Strawson, "Social Morality and Individual Ideal," in <u>Christian Ethics and Contemporary Philosophy</u>, ed. I.T. Ramsey, (London: SCM Press, 1966); A similar distinction is made by J.L. Mackie in <u>Ethics: Inventing Right and Wrong</u> (Harmondsworth

Penguin Books, 1977) pp. 106-7.

[11]The distinction and the characteristics of public morality that I discuss in this chapter are based on the chapters by Stuart Hampshire and Thomas Nagel in Public and Private Morality. There are some differences in the details of my interpretation.

[12]Thomas Nagel, "Ruthlessness in Public Life," Public and Private Morality, ed. Stuart Hampshire, p. 75.

[13]cf. Midgley, Man and Beast, p. 212.

[14]Concepts of this kind are discussed by Julius Kovesi, Moral Nations (New York: The Humanities Press, 1967) Ch. 1.

[15]For general critiques of utilitarianism see, for example, David Lyons, The Forms and Limits of Utilitarianism (Oxford: Clarendon Press, 1969); Bernard Williams, "A Critique of Utilitarianism," in J.J.C. Smart and Bernard Williams, Utilitarianism: For and Against (Cambridge: Cambridge University Press, 1973); A brief critique by Williams is contained in his book Morality: An Introduction to Ethics (Cambridge: Cambridge University Press, 1972) pp. 96-112.

[16]James S. Coleman, "Rawls, Nozick, and Educational Equality," The Public Interest 43 (Spring 1976): 121-28.

[17]Earlier, I referred to the question of whether a person can rationally refuse to be guided by moral standards. Certainly, on the basis of general conditions of rationality, particular judgments about what ought to be done can be rational but immoral (just as a person may make a moral decision that is objectively sound on the basis of an irrational process). One may doubt, however, whether a person who generally disregarded or misapplied moral criteria really satisfied the conditions of rational judgment.

[18]For general discussion of law and morality see, for example, Lon L. Fuller, The Morality of Law, rev. ed. (New Haven: Yale University Press, 1969); H.L.A. Hart, The Concept of Law (Oxford: Clarendon Press, 1961); Richard A. Wasserstrom, ed., Morality and the Law (Belmont, California: Wadsworth, 1971).

[19]On the points in this paragraph see, in particular, A.R. Louch, "Sins and Crimes" and Gerald Dworkin, "Paternalism," in Morality and the Law, ed. Richard A. Wasserstrom.

[20]H.L.A. Hart, The Concept of Law, Ch. 9.

[21]For a discussion of moral rules, see G.J. Warnock, The Object of Morality (London: Methuen, 1971) Chs. 4 and 5. Although I would disagree with T.D. Perry's account of moral argument, he offers useful comments on the nature of judicial reasoning in Moral Reasoning and Truth (Oxford: Clarendon Press,

1976) Ch. 4.

[22]I have discussed the question in <u>Education and Social Ideals</u> (Toronto:  Academic Press Canada, 1973) Ch. 1,  and  in  <u>Education for Rational Understanding</u> (Melbourne:    Australia  Council  for Educational Research, 1981) Ch. 3.

[23]See,  for example,  H.J. McCloskey, "The Rights of Parents," in <u>Rights and Inequality in Australian Education</u>, ed. P.J. Fensham (Melbourne:    Cheshire,  1970);  Francis  Shrag,  "The  Right  to Educate," <u>School Review</u> 79 (May 1971):  359-78.

[24]cf.   M.J.  Charlesworth, "The Liberal State and the Control of Education" in <u>Melbourne Studies in Education 1967</u>,  ed.  R.J.W. Selleck (Melbourne University Press, 1968).

[25]R.S.  Peters,  <u>Ethics and Education</u> (London:  Allen & Unwin, 1966) p. 252.

# CHAPTER II

## MORALITY, ETHICS, AND ETHICAL THEORIES

### Tom L. Beauchamp
### James F. Childress
### Adopted by Earle West

People in a variety of roles frequently must make difficult decisions. The difficulties inherent in the decision making process may involve legal issues, financial and budgetary problems, personal conflicts, political considerations, and moral issues. What makes any situation a moral dilemma or quandary? The purpose of this chapter is to clarify moral dilemmas, to distinguish them from other kinds of dilemmas, and to outline types of ethical theories which are often used to resolve moral issues.

The Realm of Morality
In dilemmatic situations the reasons on each side of a problem are weighty ones, and none is in any obvious way the right set of reasons. If one acts on either set of reasons, one's actions will be desirable in some respects but undesirable in other respects. Yet one thinks that ideally one ought to act on all the reasons, for each is, considered by itself, a good reason. If there is a conflict between moral obligation, on the one hand, and self-interest or personal inclination, on the other, we do not usually conceive the situation as presenting a moral dilemma, for moral dilemmas arise when one can appeal to moral consideration for taking each of two opposing courses of action. If moral reasons compete with nonmoral reasons, difficult questions can be posed (for example, why be moral?), without creating a moral dilemma. Some situations, however, clearly involve moral dilemmas. They take the following forms:[1] (1) Some evidence indicates that act X is morally right, and some evidence indicates that act X is morally wrong, but the evidence on both sides is inconclusive. Abortion, for example, is sometimes said to be "a terrible dilemma" for women who see the evidence in this way. (2) It is clear to the agent that on moral grounds he or she both ought and ought not to perform act X. For example, some have viewed the intentional cessation of lifesaving therapies in the case of comatose patients as dilemmatic in this way. Our approach to moral reasoning in deliberation and justification can be diagrammed in the form of hierarchical levels or tiers, which we will call levels of moral justification:

4  Ethical Theories
↑
3  Principles
↑
2  Rules
↑
1  Judgments and Actions

According to this diagram, judgments about what ought to be done in particular situations are justified by moral rules, which in turn are grounded in principles and ultimately in ethical theories. Finally, the particular judgment, the rule, and the principle may be grounded in an ethical theory (a theory that for many people may be only implicit and inchoate).

Although our diagram may be oversimplified, it is designed to indicate that in the process of moral reasoning we appeal to different reasons of varying degrees of abstraction and systematization. Let us start with the lowest level and move upwards. A judgment is a decision, verdict, or conclusion about a particular action. Although the precise nature of the distinction between rules and principles is somewhat controversial, rules state that actions of a certain kind ought (or ought not) to be done because they are right (or wrong). A simple example is, "It is wrong to lie to a student." Principles are more general and fundamental than moral rules and serve as their foundation. The principle of respect for persons, for example, may ground several moral rules of the "it is wrong to lie" sort. Finally, theories are bodies of principles and rules, more or less systematically related. They include second-order principles and rules about what to do when there are conflicts. Utilitarian theories, as we shall see, are one important example of ethical theories. Following William Frankena, we will refer to all these levels or tiers, but especially to principles and rules, as "action-guides." Which action-guides are worthy of moral acceptance and why? General normative ethics is a field of inquiry which attempts to answer this question. It is constituted by what in our levels of justification are called ethical theories. Such theories seek to formulate and defend a system of moral principles and rules that determine which actions are right and which are wrong. These action-guides are presumably valid for everyone. Ideally, any such ethical theory will include a complete set of ethical action-guides and will defend the claim that they are universally valid. While general normative ethics is an attempt to construct an ethical theory, numerous ethical questions would remain even if a fully satisfactory theory were to be developed. For example, what do the various principles and rules imply for concrete decisions that people must make in everyday life? An attempt to apply these action-guides to different problem areas can be labelled applied normative ethics. The term "applied" is used because general ethical principles and rules are applied to illuminate and resolve moral problems.

In addition to normative ethics, either general or applied, there are at least two non-normative approaches to morality. First, there is descriptive ethics, the factual investigation of moral behavior and beliefs. Anthropologists, sociologists, and historians determine, for example, whether and in what ways moral attitudes and codes differ from society to society. They study different beliefs about sexual relations, the treatment of the dying, etc. Second, there is the field of metaethics. This approach to morality, which has been warmly embraced by numerous philosophers in this century, involves analysis of the meanings of crucial ethical terms such as "right," "obligation," and "responsibility." Students of metaethics also analyze the logic of moral reasoning, including the nature of moral justification.

Descriptive ethics and metaethics can be grouped together because both are nonnormative; that is, they do not attempt to provide prescriptive action-guides. Instead, they attempt to establish what factually or conceptually is the case, not what ethically ought to be the case.[2]

A general moral code consists of fundamental moral principles and rules. There should not be so many rules, or rules so heavily qualified, that some members of society cannot remember or grasp them. These rules are usually general statements such as "Whenever you have promised to do something then you ought to do it." By contrast, a special moral code is composed of derivative and very specific moral rules that are justified by reference to more general and fundamental rules and principles (although the justification may only be implicit in the codes themselves). Again, there should not be so many rules that members of the group cannot master them; but some of these rules will be more professional, and technical in detail, than those in the general moral code.

A professional code represents an articulated statement of role morality as seen by members of the profession. It is distinguished from sets of standards imposed from the outside by other bodies such as governments.

Professional codes are justified if they serve as effective ways to express moral principles and rules in special relationships. Their function is to facilitate relationships of trust and confidence that permit and encourage certain activities to be performed for socially valued ends, such as the promotion of health. No doubt some professional codes oversimplify moral requirements and lead professionals to think that they have met all the relevant moral requirements if they have followed the rules of the code; but such failures may be outweighed by their value in controlling moral conduct.

But what is meant by "public policy," and how is it connected to ethics? According to one recent author, "Public policy is whatever governments choose to do or not to do."[3] More adequately, public policy is purposive action or inaction by government officials in such a way as to display a course or pattern. As such, public policies typically involve one or more of the following actions: regulation (e.g., prohibition of an activity) and allocation and distribution of both social benefits (e.g., services and goods) and social burdens (e.g., taxation). However, it is rarely possible to move assuredly from a judgment that act X is morally right (or wrong) to a judgment that policy X is morally right (or wrong), because of numerous factors such as the symbolic value of law and the cost of enforcement. Thus, the judgment that an act is morally wrong does not necessarily lead to the judgment that the government should prohibit it or even refuse to allocate funds for it. Nor does the judgment that an act is morally acceptable in some circumstances imply that the law should permit it.

## Tests of Ethical Theories

Several general tests can be used to determine the adequacy of ethical theories. Although it is possible that no ethical theory will satisfactorily meet all the tests, we do and should appeal to them in trying to determine which elements in a theory are acceptable.

First, an ethical theory should be internally consistent and coherent. Ralph Waldo Emerson dismissed a foolish consistency as "the hobgoblin of little minds," but a theory that is not internally consistent and coherent is to that extent unacceptable. Indeed, it is questionable that such a "theory" could really count as a theory, because it would not yield similar results when used by different people or even by the same persons in different but relevantly similar circumstances. Second, a theory should be complete and comprehensive. There should be no major gaps or holes in the theory. A theory that is more complete and comprehensive is, ceteris paribus, preferable to less complete and comprehensive theories. Third, simplicity is a virtue of theories. For example, a theory should have no more rules, principles, and concepts than are necessary, and certainly no more than people are able to remember and able to apply without confusion.

Fourth, a theory must be complex enough to account for the whole range of moral experience, including our ordinary judgments. We daily participate in morality as we make decisions, reach judgments, and offer reasons in the name of morality. Ethical theories must account for what we already do. Indeed, they build on, systematize, and criticize our ordinary notions. Our moral experience and our moral theories are also dialectically related. We develop theories to illuminate experience and to determine what we ought to do, but we also use experience to test, corroborate, and criticize theories. If a theory yields conclusions that are totally incompatible with our ordinary judgments - for example, if it allows human subjects to be used purely as means to the ends of scientific research - we have reason to be suspicious of that theory and to look for another. But in many matters of morality, we may be uncertain whether the theory is in error and needs to be modified, whether the theory should be rejected, or whether our ordinary judgments are mistaken. As Joel Feinberg suggests, our procedure is similar to the dialectical reasoning which occurs in courts of law:

> If a principle commits one to an antecedently unacceptable judgment, then one has to modify or supplement the principle in a way that does the least damage to the harmony of one's particular and general opinions taken as a group. On the other hand, when a solid well-entrenched principle entails a change in a particular judgment, the overriding claims of consistency may require that the judgment be adjusted.[4]

## Moral and Nonmoral Action-Guides

What makes some dilemmas and judgments - and not others - moral? That is, by what criteria can we say that any given normative standard is properly moral rather than religious, political, legal, or whatever?[5]

Although many believe they can recognize moral action-guides when they see them, there is pronounced disagreement about the criteria that make them moral. We shall indicate some of the main criteria for distinguishing moral and nonmoral action-guides. However, it should be noted from the outset that some action-guides, involve both moral and nonmoral elements, and that several diverse action-guides thus may be employed in judgments about a single act.

Contemporary philosophers have delineated three main conditions of moral action-guides (in contrast to nonmoral ones). The first two conditions are formal. They refer to the form, not the content, of moral judgments, rules, and principles. Because they do not pertain to content, they would (if used alone) allow more action-guides to be counted as moral than the third condition would allow. According to the first condition, moral action-guides are whatever a person or, alternatively, a society accepts as supreme, final, or overriding in judgments about actions. Unless this condition of overridingness is combined with other conditions, it permits almost anything to count as moral if a person, or a society, is committed to its overriding pursuit. For example, a person's primary commitment to scientific knowledge could be taken as that person's morality. True, we often do say that a person or a society has a morality even when we think that it is an unacceptable morality. It is difficult, however, to hold that supremacy is either necessary or sufficient for morality. Because other conditions such as the second one to be mentioned (universalizability) appear to be indispensable, we cannot say that every overriding action-guide counts as moral. Furthermore, to hold that supremacy is a necessary condition of morality is to prejudge the weight that moral action-guides should have in our deliberations when they conflict with political, legal, and religious action-guides. We cannot with certainty say that moral considerations, by definition, must outweigh or override all other considerations in competition with them.

A second and widely accepted condition for moral action-guides is universalizability, which requires that all relevantly similar cases be treated in a similar way. This formal condition may be a necessary condition of moral thinking, but it is insufficient to distinguish moral judgments from other judgments which also meet this requirement. A judgment that an act is right (or wrong) commits one to judging relevantly similar acts right (or wrong); and if a person holds that act X is right and act Y is wrong but cannot point to any significant differences between them, the person is not making a moral judgment. But clearly many universalizable action-guiding propositions are not moral - e.g., "Always train your dogs before they are one month old."

Some philosophers have also proposed a third criterion of morality, one which has moral content. They argue that it is necessary for a moral action-guide to have some direct reference to the welfare of others.

However, the contention that moral action-guides must have some reference to the welfare of others does not indicate that the welfare of all parties must receive the same weight.

In order to determine the grounds on which any policy could be held to be immoral, we shall now turn to an examination of major ethical theories and their moral principles, rules, and judgments.

## Ethical Theories

In this section, we shall concentrate on two types of ethical theories that have received the most attention in recent years: utilitarian and deontological theories.

The classical origins of utilitarianism are found in the writings of David Hume (1711-76), Jeremy Bentham (1748-1832), and John Stuart Mill (1806-73). Utilitarianism is only one of several ethical theories that gauge the worth of actions by their ends and consequences. These theories are sometimes said to be consequentialist or teleological (derived from the Greek term telos, meaning "end"). They hold that morally right actions are determined by the nonmoral value (e.g., pleasure, friendship, knowledge, or health) produced by their performance. The value is said to be nonmoral because it is the general goal of human strivings (e.g., in art, athletics, and academics), and thus is not a distinctly moral value as is, for example, fulfilling a moral obligation. A common feature of these theories is that duty and right conduct are subordinated to what is good, for right and duty are defined in terms of goods or that which produces goods.

By contrast, deontological theories (derived from the Greek term deon, meaning "duty") deny precisely what teleological theories affirm. Their classical origins are more diverse and include, for example, some religious ethics that concentrate on divine commands; but the ethical theory of Immanuel Kant (1734-1804) is generally regarded as the first unambiguous formulation. Deontologists maintain that the concept of duty is independent of the concept of good and that right actions are not determined exclusively by the production of nonmoral goods. The basic difference between these two general approaches may be briefly expressed as follows: the teleologist (and thus the utilitarian) holds that actions are determined to be right or wrong by only one of their features, viz., their consequences, while the deontologist contends that even if this feature sometimes determines the rightness and wrongness of acts, it does not always do so. Other features are also relevant, e.g., the fact that an act involves telling a lie or breaking a promise.

## Utilitarianism

While the term "utilitarianism" is familiar to most of us, its popular usage can be confusing and misleading. It is said, for example, to be the theory that "the end justifies the means." It is also said to be the view that "we ought to promote the greatest good of the greatest number." Since "utility" is commonly translated as "usefulness," this theory is also said to be the view that what is right is that which is most useful. In some respects each of these popular characterizations is accurate, but utilitarianism is considerably more sophisticated and refined than such characterizations indicate. Here, the term "utilitarianism" refers to the moral theory that there is one and only one basic principle in ethics, the principle of utility. This principle asserts that we ought in all circumstances to produce the greatest possible balance of value over disvalue for all persons affected (or the least possible balance of disvalue if only evil results can be brought about).

## The Concept of Utility

We have seen that all utilitarians share the conviction that human actions are to be morally assessed in terms of their production of maximal nonmoral value. But how are we to determine, it may be asked, what value could and should be produced in any given circumstance? Utilitarians agree that ultimately we ought to look to the production of what is intrinsically valuable rather than extrinsically valuable. That is, what is good in itself and not merely what is good as a means to something else ought to be produced. For example, neither undergoing nor performing an abortion is considered by anyone to be an intrinsically good event. However, many people would sometimes consider it extrinsically good as a means to another end, such as the restoration of an ill woman to a state of health. Utilitarians believe that we really ought to seek certain experiences and conditions in life that are good in themselves without reference to their further consequences, and that all values are ultimately to be gauged in terms of these intrinsic goods. Health and freedom from pain would be included among such values by most utilitarians.

An intrinsic value, then, is a value in life that we wish to possess and enjoy just for its own sake and not for something else which it produces. Without such values, the things we pursue as means to other things would probably lose their value.

Still, the main task for utilitarians is to provide an acceptable theory that explains why things are intrinsically good and that develops lists and categories of such goods.

A major distinction within utilitarian theories of intrinsic value is drawn between hedonistic utilitarians and pluralistic utilitarians. Bentham and Mill are referred to as hedonistic utilitarians because they conceived utility entirely in terms of happiness or pleasure – two terms that may here be taken as synonymous and as very broad in scope. Bentham, for example, viewed utility as that aspect of any object or event whereby it tends to produce different pleasures in the form of benefit, advantage, good, the prevention of pain, etc.[6] Mill went to considerable lengths not to be misunderstood on the matter of what "happiness" means. He insisted that happiness does not refer to "a continuity of highly pleasurable excitement," but rather encompasses a realistic appraisal of the pleasurable moments afforded in life, whether they take the form of tranquility or passionate excitement.[7]

The principle of utility for Bentham and Mill thus demands courses of action which produce the maximum possible happiness in the broad sense of the term employed by these philosophers. That is, an action ought to be performed if the sum of the happiness interests of all affected individuals would be maximized by the performance of that action. If Mill and Bentham had believed other things in life besides happiness were desirable as ends in themselves, they no doubt would have held a different view. But both believed that pleasure and freedom from pain are the only things desirable as ends, and therefore that all desirable things (which are numerous) are desirable because they either produce pleasure or prevent pain.

Mill and Bentham knew, of course, that many human actions do not appear to be performed merely for the sake of happiness. For example, they were aware that highly motivated professionals - such as research scientists - can work themselves to the point of exhaustion for the sake of knowledge they hope to gain, even though they might have chosen different and more pleasurable pursuits. Mill's explanation of this phenomenon is that such persons are initially motivated by pleasure. They are at that time interested either in prestige or in the prospect of money, both of which promise pleasure. Along the way, however, either the pursuit of knowledge becomes itself productive of happiness or else such persons never stop associating the money or prestige they hope to gain with an ultimate goal of pleasure (despite their not actually deriving much, if any, pleasure). Mill also believed that there are qualitatively different kinds of pleasure, some worth cultivating more than others because intrinsically more valuable. This claim proved difficult to sustain, but Mill's problems with it cannot be considered here. The main point is that for some utilitarians, including two of its leading proponents, happiness or pleasure is the single form of intrinsic value, even though it may be analyzed into many different subtypes.

Later utilitarian philosophers have not looked kindly on this monistic conception of intrinsic value. They have argued that other values besides happiness possess intrinsic worth - e.g., values such as friendship, knowledge, courage, health, beauty, and perhaps even certain moral qualities. According to one defender of this view, G.E. Moore, even some states of consciousness can be valuable apart from their pleasantness.[8] The idea that there are many kinds of intrinsic value eventually received widespread acceptance among utilitarians. Its proponents held that the rightness or wrongness of an action is to be assessed in terms of the total range of intrinsic value ultimately produced by the action.

In recent philosophy, economics, and psychology, neither the approach of the hedonists nor that of the pluralists has pre-vailed. Both approaches have seemed relatively useless for purposes of objectively aggregating widely different interests in order to determine where maximal value and, therefore, right action, lies. The major alternative approach is to appeal to the language of individual preferences. For this approach, the concept of utility refers not to experiences or states of affairs, but rather to one's actual preferences, as determined by one's behavior. To maximize a single person's utility is to provide

what one has chosen or would choose from among the available
alternatives that might be produced. To maximize the utility of
all persons affected by an action or policy is to maximize the
utility of the aggregate group. This approach is indifferent as
regards hedonistic or pluralistic views of intrinsic value. What
is intrinsically valuable is what individuals prefer to obtain,
and utility is thus translated into the satisfaction of those
needs and desires that individuals choose to satisfy.

This modern approach to value is preferable to its
predecessors for two main reasons. First, recent disputes about
hedonism and pluralism have proved interminable, sometimes
ideological, and in the view of many, irresolvable. One's choice
of a range of these values seems deeply affected by personal
experiences - a problem the concept of preference seems to provide
a way of avoiding. Second, to make utilitarian calculations it is
necessary in some way to measure values. In the monistic theory
espoused by Bentham and Mill, for example, we must be able to
measure pleasurable and painful states and then compare one
person's pleasures with another's in order to decide which are
quantitatively greater. Yet, it is uncertain what it means to
measure and then compare the values of pleasure, health, and
knowledge - or any value at all, for that matter. It does make
sense, however, to measure preferences by devising a utility scale
that measures strengths of individual and group preferences
numerically. This approach has proved fruitful in recent
discussions of health economics, to take just one of many
examples. It might also hold promise for helping to clarify and
resolve educational issues, since the schools are frequently the
focal point of conflicting values and ideologies.

The preference approach nonetheless is not trouble-free. A
major theoretical problem for utilitarianism arises when
individuals have what are, according to ordinary views about
morality, immoral or at least morally unacceptable preferences.
For example, if a skillful researcher derived supreme satisfaction
from inflicting pain on animals or human subjects in experiments,
we would condemn and discount this person's preference and would
seek to prevent it from being actualized. Utilitarianism based on
subjective preferences is satisfactory only if a range of
acceptable values can be formulated. This task has proved
difficult, however, and may even be inconsistent with the
preference approach. This problem cannot be ignored, but since
most people are not deviant in the manner envisioned and do have
acceptable (even if we may think odd) values, we shall proceed
here under the assumption that the utilitarian approach makes
sense and is not wildly implausible if a theory of appropriate
(nonmoral) values could be provided to buttress its moral
perspective.

If utilitarianism could be fully worked out along the lines
we have envisioned, it would give us a definite procedure for
making ethical choices. We would first calculate to the best of
our knowledge the consequences that would result from our
performance of the various options open to us. In making this
calculation we would ask how much value and how much disvalue - as
gauged by the preferences of those affected by our actions - would

result in the lives of all affected, including ourselves. Once we have completed all these calculations for all relevant courses of action, we are morally obliged to choose that action which maximizes intrinsic value (or minimizes intrinsic disvalue). Knowingly to perform any other action is to take a morally wrong course.

It would be easy to overestimate the demands of this moral theory. While we must always attempt to make accurate measurements of the preferences of others, this seldom can be done because of our limited knowledge and time. Often in everyday affairs we must act on severely limited knowledge of the consequences of our action. The utilitarian does not condemn any sincere attempt to maximize value merely because the consequences of the attempt turn out to be less than ideal. What is important, morally speaking, is that one conscientiously attempts to determine the most favorable action, and then with equal seriousness attempts to perform this action. Since common sense and fair-minded deliberation will ordinarily suffice for these calculations, utilitarians cannot be accused of presenting overly demanding moral requirements, as some critics have alleged.

## Act and Rule Utilitarianism

The next and most important distinction to be considered is that between act and rule utilitarians. For all utilitarians the principle of utility is the ultimate source of appeal for the determination of morally right and wrong actions. Controversy has arisen, however, over whether this principle is to be applied to particular acts in particular circumstances in order to determine which act is right or whether it is to be applied instead to rules of conduct which themselves determine the acts that are right and wrong. Using the scheme of ascending levels of justification introduced earlier, we may outline how utilitarians attempt to justify moral actions and, at the same time, illustrate how act and rule utilitarians differ:

Rule Utilitarianism | Act Utilitarianism
---|---
Principle of Utility | Principle of Utility
↑ | ↑
Moral Rules | Individual Actions
↑ |
Individual Actions |

According to the schema on the left, actions are justified by appeal to rules, which in turn are justified by appeal to utility. An act utilitarian simply skips the level of rules and justifies actions directly by appeal to the principle of utility.

The act utilitarian considers the consequences of each particular act, while the rule utilitarian considers the consequences of generally observing a rule. Accordingly, the act utilitarian asks, "What good and evil consequences will result from this action in this circumstance?" and not "What good and evil consequences will result from this sort of action in general in these sorts of circumstances?" The act utilitarian sees rules such as "You ought to tell the truth" as useful rules of thumb in guiding human actions, but not as unbreakable prescriptions. According to this species of utilitarian the question is always, "What should I do now?" and not "What has proved generally valuable in the past?" Act utilitarians take this position because they think observance of a general rule (of truth-telling in this case) would not on some occasions be for the general good.

For roughly this latter reason, act utilitarians regard rule utilitarians as unfaithful to the demands of the principle of utility. This principle requires that we maximize happiness, or at least that we maximize intrinsic value. But there are individual cases in which abiding by a generally beneficial rule will not prove most beneficial to the persons involved, even in the long run. So, why then ought the rule to be obeyed in individual cases when obedience does not maximize value? The contemporary utilitarian, J.J.C. Smart, has argued that the rule utilitarian cannot reply to this criticism that it would be better that everybody should obey the rule than that nobody should. This objection fails, according to Smart, because there is a third possibility between never obeying a rule and always obeying it-- viz., that it should sometimes be obeyed.[9] For example, physicians do not always tell the truth to patients. They withhold information and even lie. Perhaps they invoke the legal doctrine of therapeutic privilege as a justification for their action, but they nonetheless violate general moral rules of truth-telling. They do so because they think it is better for the patient and for all concerned, and they do not think their act really undermines morality. Smart's objection seems in the end reducible to the empirical prediction that we will be better off in the moral life if we sometimes obey and sometimes disobey rules, because this selective obedience will not erode either moral rules or our general respect for morality. The rule utilitarian would, of course, challenge Smart's apparent empirical prediction that less rather than more damage will be done to the institution of morality by adopting an act-utilitarian position.

According to rule utilitarians, rules themselves have a central position in morality and cannot be disregarded because of the exigencies of particular situations. Because rules maximize utility, the act of a physician who withheld information from a patient would be immoral unless he were able to justify it by appeal to a moral rule strong enough to override the rule requiring that the truth be told. Because of the substantial contributions made to society by the general observance of rules of truth-telling, the rule utilitarian would not compromise them for a particular situation. Such compromise would threaten the integrity and existence of the rule itself, and a rule is selected in the first instance because its general observance would maximize social utility better than would any alternative rule, or no rule. For the rule utilitarian, then, the conformity of an act to a valuable rule makes the act right, whereas for the act utilitarian the beneficial consequences of the act alone make it right.

Although many rule utilitarians justify various rules by their consequences, some rule utilitarians propose that we consider the utility of whole codes or systems of rules rather than independent rules. Among the defenders of different versions of this position are David Hume, the eighteenth-century Scottish philosopher, and R.B. Brandt, a contemporary American philosopher.[10] According to this approach, the rightness or wrongness of individual acts is determined by reference to moral rules that have a place in a code or system of rules. The system is assessed as a whole in terms of its overall consequences. It is necessary to consider the consequences of moral rules not as independent rules, then, but as parts of a whole code of rules. By again using the scheme of ascending levels of justification, we may illustrate this version of rule utilitarianism:

Principle of Utility    (Supreme Principle)

      ↑

Moral Code    (Whole Scheme of Rules)

      ↑

Moral Rules    (Single Rules)

      ↑

Individual Actions    (Judgments and Actions)

While this whole code approach bears a resemblance to simple rule utilitarianism, it allegedly has additional advantages. Most importantly, proponents claim that we are more likely to be able to maximize utility across a society by the advocacy of a whole system of rules than merely by testing and attempting to gain adherence to single rules, each isolated from the consequences of other rules in the system. It would be difficult to motivate individuals in society to conform to rules if they were individually tested for their consequences, and we rarely think of morality in this way. Most of us are motivated to the acceptance of a whole way of life that is moral, and we generally think of morality as a system of integrated principles and rules, none of which stands in isolation.[11]

It is important to note, in concluding this section, that from the rule utilitarian's perspective no rule (and hence no moral action) is ever absolutely wrong in itself, and no rule in the system of rules is absolute and unrevisable. A rule's acceptability in the system of rules depends strictly on its consequences. If a given series of consequences, which now provides the utilitarian basis for some well established rule, were no longer to occur, then the utilitarian would see no reason in principle why the rule (e.g., a rule against killing or lying) should not be abandoned. Thus it is clear that utilitarianism is strictly a consequentialist theory.

## Deontological Theories

We have seen that a teleological or consequentialist theory holds that the right is a function of the good, specifically of intrinsically valuable ends or consequences. Within such a theory one would determine what is right or wrong by asking whether an act or class of acts would probably produce the greatest possible balance of good over evil in the world. By contrast, deontological theories (sometimes called formalist theories) hold that features of some acts other than their consequences make them right or wrong. For many deontologists deception is a wrong-making characteristic regardless of its consequences. As we shall see, a deontologist need not hold that deception is absolutely wrong and never justifiable. However, to be a deontologist, one must hold that at least some acts are wrong and others are right independent of their consequences. Examples of right-making characteristics in deontological systems include fidelity to promises and contracts, gratitude for benefits received, truthfulness, and justice.

## Versions of Deontology

Different deontological theories compete with each other, as well as against teleological theories. It is possible to analyze these theories from several perspectives. First, we could explore the different ways deontologists try to vindicate their judgments that certain acts are right or wrong. Some moralists in religious traditions appeal to divine revelation (e.g., to God's promulgation of the Ten Commandments), while others appeal to natural law, which they contend can be known by human reason. Some philosophers, including W.D. Ross, find intuition and common sense sufficient, while others, such as John Rawls, derive their principles from the notion of a hypothetical social contract.[12] To analyze and assess these and other warrants for judgments about moral acts would lead us into the thickets of metaethics (theories of the meaning and justification of ethical terms), and this pursuit would consume too much space. Most of the principles and rules that we will consider are accepted by most deontological theories and can also be discovered in the "common morality."[13] Thus, for our purposes it is not necessary to examine different metaethical theories.

Second, like utilitarian theories, deontological theories may be monistic or pluralistic. A monistic deontological theory holds that there is one single rule or principle from which one can derive all other rules or judgments about right and wrong. Thus, one could affirm basic principles such as love and respect for persons and derive other rules such as truth-telling and fidelity from them. In his classic attempt, Immanuel Kant proposed a single "categorical imperative" through which he tested all maxims of action. As an example, consider a person who desperately needs money and knows that she/he will not be able to borrow it unless she/he promises to repay it in a definite time, although she/he also knows that she/he will not be able to repay it within this time period. She/he decides to make a promise that she/he knows she/he will break. According to Kant, when we examine the maxim of his action - "When I think myself in want of money, I will borrow money and promise to pay it, although I know that I never can do so" - we discover that it cannot pass the basic test of what Kant calls the categorical imperative, according to which maxims must be universalizable. To be universalizable, the maxim must be capable of being conceived and willed without contradiction as a universal law. The above maxim about misleading promises cannot be conceived as a universal law, for it would contradict itself. As Kant writes,

> How would things stand if my maxim became a universal law? I then see straight away that this maxim can never rank as a universal law of nature and be self-consistent, but must necessarily contradict itself. For the universality of a law that everyone believing himself to be in need can make any promise he pleases with the intention not to keep it would make promising, and the very purpose of promising, itself impossible, since no one would believe he was being promised anything, but would laugh at utterances of this kind as empty shams.[14]

Some maxims which can be conceived as universal nonetheless cannot be willed without contradiction. Consider the maxim of a person who is well-off but refuses to help those who are struggling. According to Kant, an agent cannot, without contradiction, will that one's maxim of refusing help become universal law, for one might be in need of others at some point in time, and one would certainly want their help.

Although few philosophers would hold, as Kant appears to, that the universalizability of a maxim is both necessary and sufficient for determining its acceptability, most concur that it is a necessary condition of the validity of ethical judgments, rules, and principles. Kant may actually have had more than one basic principle, since the several formulations he offers of the categorical imperative are not clearly equivalent. In any case, neither Kant not others who have proposed monistic theories have carried the day.

Pluralistic deontologists, by contrast, affirm more than one basic rule or principle. For example, W.D. Ross, a prominent twentieth-century deontologist, held that there are several basic and irreducible moral principles, such as fidelity, beneficence, and justice. While this pluralistic approach may at first glance appear more plausible than monistic approaches because it is closer to our ordinary judgments, it quickly encounters the difficulty - as Ross recognized - of what to do when these principles or rules come into conflict. The pluralistic deontologist may give us little guidance about which rules or principles take priority in such cases of conflict. For example, Ross held that the principle of nonmaleficence (noninfliction of harm) takes precedence over the principle of beneficence (production of benefit) when they come into conflict, but he gave no answer about the priorities among the other principles except to say that several duties (such as keeping promises) have "a great deal of stringency." Finally, he quoted Aristotle: "The decision rests with perception."[15] While we intuit the principles, according to Ross, we do not intuit what is right in the situation; rather we have to find "the greatest balance" of right over wrong. If a pluralistic deontological theory does not provide some ordering or ranking of its principles and rules, it offers little guidance in the moment of decision making.

One major recent attempt to overcome the difficulties of

pluralistic theories is John Rawls' <u>A Theory of Justice</u>, which provides a serial or lexical ordering of quite general principles of justice (but not the whole of morality). Rawls' lexical order avoids the need to balance principles, since we have to satisfy the first principle before we consider the second; the prior principle has absolute weight relative to the later ones. Using this approach he argues that the principle of equal liberty is prior to the principle of distributing social and economic benefits. Rawls does not, however, propose this sort of ordering for all moral principles.[16]

Finally, just as there can be act and rule utilitarians, deontologists may focus on acts or rules that cover classes of acts. Few philosophers or theologians have tried to defend act deontology, though traces of it can be seen here and there. It has been held, for example, that an individual by intuition, or conscience, or faith in God's revelation and grace, can immediately and directly perceive what he or she ought to do. But act deontology is problematic for several reasons. We do not have firm grounds for confidence in our own or others' intuition, conscience, or faith to perceive right and wrong in the situation - particularly in the light of immediate pressures, lack of time for deliberation, and the power self-interest has to distort perception. Rules appear to be an important stabilizing influence in the moral life. Furthermore, to judge that a particular act is wrong in the situation is implicitly to appeal to a rule. If we are making a moral judgment when we say that act X is wrong, we are saying that all relevantly similar acts in similar circumstances are wrong. To say it is wrong to tell a lie to a patient who asks a direct question about his prognosis is to say that it is wrong to tell such a lie in similar circumstances. Such a statement is at least an incipient rule.

For rule deontologists, the heart of morality is a set of principles and rules that identify classes of acts that are right or wrong and obligatory or prohibited. Kant, for example, held that several rules could be derived from the basic categorical imperative. According to Ross, there are several independent duties that can be stated as rules or principles. Some of these duties rest on one's own previous acts. For example, promises and implicit promises give rise to duties of fidelity. And one's previous wrongful acts engender duties of reparation. Some other duties rest on the previous acts of other persons. When they render services to us, we have duties of gratitude. Ross goes on to develop duties of self-improvement, nonmaleficence, benefi- cence, and justice.

## Deontology As An Ethical Theory

What are some of the major characteristics, as well as the strengths and weaknesses, of deontological theories as compared to utilitarian theories? First, utilitarians hold that ultimately there is only one significant moral relationship between persons: the relationship of benefactor and beneficiary. Deontologists, however, take seriously various relationships between people. For them it is not sufficient to say, as utilitarians do, that we should maximize the good and that each person counts as one and only one. They claim that we do not encounter other people merely as depositories of good, as beneficiaries, each one counting as one and only one; rather, we are related to them in various ways by their and our own previous acts. The texture of the moral life thus seems richer and more complicated than any simple utilitarian model suggests, for numerous relationships with others have special moral significance: parent and child, friend and friend, promisor and promisee, teacher and student. Parents assume certain obligations to their children, and the children incur certain obligations to their parents.

A second and closely connected point concerns the role of past actions in our moral assessments. Utilitarianism seems to have little room for the past in moral judgments, because of its orientation toward the present and future. If utilitarianism considers the past from a moral standpoint, it is only because paying attention to the past appears to be important for future consequences. For example, to reward people for what they have done may encourage them to act in similar ways in the present and the future. But for a rule deontologist like Ross, the fact that one has performed certain acts in the past by itself creates certain obligations. If I have made a promise, I am bound in certain ways to the promisee, independent of the consequences of keeping or not keeping the promise.

Third, utilitarianism conceives the moral life in terms of means to ends reasoning. It asks: "What is our objective?" and "How can we most effectively realize our objective (e.g., the production of the greatest possible good)?" This conception of the moral life in terms of means to ends makes it congenial to empirical science. Deontologists, by contrast, hold not only that there are standards independent of the ends for judging the means, but that it is a mistake to conceive the moral life in terms of means and ends. Why? In part, because it seems to presuppose a greater capacity to predict and control than we actually have. We lack the level of capacity to predict and control the future that act utilitarians and some rule utilitarians seem to presuppose. Deontologists also insist that the utilitarian model of choosing effective and efficient means to good ends distorts the moral life in fundamental ways. As Antony Flew argues,

> To do one's duty, or to discover what it is, is rarely if ever to achieve, or to find a way to achieve, an objective. Rather and typically, it is to meet, or to find a way to meet, claims; and also, of course, to eschew misdemeanors. Promises must be kept, debts must be paid, dependents must be looked after; and stealing, lying, and cruelty must be avoided.[18]

From this view we are not merely agents who initiate acts for good ends; we are also responders who encounter the claims of others. Our responsibilities to others are more varied and more specific than the responsibility to promote good.

Fourth, the deontologist's standard and perhaps most

attractive objection is that utilitarianism can lead to morally unacceptable conclusions. One test of moral theories, as we saw earlier, is their congruence with our ordinary moral convictions. Deontologists pose this situation against act utilitarians: suppose that we have two acts, A and B, which appear to yield the same score when we balance their respective good and evil results. The scales appear to be perfectly balanced. But suppose that A involves lying to a patient, while B does not. In the end, the result is the same: the patient can be expected to get well. The consistent act utilitarian must say that the acts are equally right. Now suppose that act A, which involves lying to a patient about his or her condition, is preferable on utilitarian grounds because it offers a greater chance of success in restoring the patient's health, while act B, which does not involve lying, has a slightly lesser chance of success. According to act utilitarianism, A is right and obligatory and the physician should therefore lie to the patient. The deontologist claims that in both cases act utilitarianism leads to judgments that are morally unacceptable.[19]

The rule utilitarian perhaps can avoid these difficulties by holding that a fuller analysis of the consequences, including the remote or long-term consequences, leads us to assign greater weight to the rule of truth-telling. But while rule utilitarianism thus appears to be more congruent with our ordinary judgments, it does not, according to many critics, adequately account for rules of justice, which we find valid apart from the consequences of those rules or principles. For example, consider fairness in bearing the burdens of some common enterprise such as conserving water in a crisis. According to one utilitarian, "if a person happened to know that nearly everybody else was in fact going to make a sacrifice that no one wants to make, and if one knew that, as a result, a similar sacrifice by one was not really essential for the public welfare, then one need not make it."[20] If one has good grounds for thinking that one's act will not be known (and emulated) by others and that the enterprise will in no way suffer from one's using water, he/she appears to have no obligation to conserve water on either act- or rule-utilitarian grounds. Nevertheless, according to some interpretations of our ordinary judgments about fairness, we would insist that the person acts unfairly and wrongly, regardless of the consequences. Such a case indicates that our sense of fairness or justice may not be reducible to utility.[21]

On balance, which ethical theory is to be preferred? For one author of this chapter, rule utilitarianism is preferable to any deontological theory presently available, while for the other, rule deontology is more acceptable than utilitarianism. We come to these different conclusions after testing the various theories for their consistency and coherence, their simplicity, their completeness and comprehensiveness, and their capacity to take account of and to account for our moral experience, including our ordinary judgments. Still, for each of us, the theory that we find more satisfactory is only slightly preferable, and no theory is fully satisfactory on all the tests. Whether one takes the utilitarian or deontological standpoint no doubt makes a great deal of difference at many points in the moral life and in moral reflection and justification. Nevertheless, the differences can easily be overemphasized. In fact, we find that many forms of rule utilitarianism and rule deontology lead to identical rules and actions. It is possible from both utilitarian and deontological standpoints to defend the same rules (such as truth-telling and confidentiality) and to assign them roughly the same weight. These standpoints draw even closer if utilitarians take a broad view of the values that support the rules and consider a wide range of direct and indirect, immediate and remote consequences of classes of acts, while deontologists admit that moral principles or rules such as beneficence and nonmaleficence require us to maximize good and minimize evil outcomes.

An indication that rule utilitarianism and rule deontology lead to similar or identical rules, and therefore to a similar conception of the moral life as rule-governed, is found in the writings of the utilitarian philosopher R.B. Brandt. As we have seen, he argues that morality should be conceived as an ideal code consisting of a set of rules that guides the members of a society to maximize intrinsic value. While Brandt appeals to utilitarian reasoning to justify the rules in the code, the following statement is a revealing one:

> (The best set of rules) would contain rules giving directions for recurrent situations which involve conflicts of human interests. Presumably, then, it would contain rules rather similar to W.D. Ross's list of prima facie obligations: rules about the keeping of promises and contracts, rules about debts of gratitude such as we may owe to our parents, and, of course, rules about not injuring other persons and about promoting the welfare of others where this does not work a comparable hardship on us.[22]

That Brandt appeals to utility and that Ross appeals to intuition to ground an identical set of rules is a significant difference on the level of ethical theory, but it is a trivial difference when it comes to what we ought to do as a matter of moral rightness and how we should judge the actions of others.

Moreover, within what we would consider the most adequate rule-utilitarian theory and the most adequate rule deontology, moral agents have to face some of the same issues. What should we do when rules come into conflict? What should we do when we cannot realize all the claims upon us or all the goods that we seek? How can we resolve these competing demands? The fact that no presently available rule utilitarianism or rule deontology adequately resolves all moral conflicts perhaps points to their incompleteness. But this incompleteness may reflect more the complexity and tragedy of the moral life than any failures of the theories.

## The Place of Rules

Many utilitarians and deontologists, as we have seen, find that the moral life requires various rules. They reject "situation ethics," which may take either act-deontological or act-utilitarian forms. Although there are several versions of situation ethics, many of its proponents hold that there is a single fundamental principle such as utility, love, or obedience to the divine command, and that all the moral agent has to do is discern the meaning of that principle in the situation. Thus, the agent asks what would serve the greatest good for the greatest number, what would be the most loving deed, or what God commands at the moment, without relying on intermediate rules, i.e., rules connecting the basic principle and the situation. In defending both rule deontology and rule utilitarianism, we have rejected situation ethics. Such a rejection does not, of course, deny the importance of factual considerations, empirical data, and the like, in moral decision making and justification; it only contends that some rules and derivative principles are also required in the situation.

Along the way, we have given several reasons for favoring either rule utilitarianism or rule deontology over their act competitors. Some of those reasons are general; e.g., rules are essential in decision making, since agents frequently do not have the time to recapitulate all the steps from basic principles to conclusions. Other reasons may hold against act utilitarianism, but not against act deontology, and vice versa. Any form of situation ethics, however, appears to run into serious problems of coordination, cooperation, and trust. The following encounter between act utilitarians in a medical setting, as envisioned by G.J. Warnock, is instructive:

> Suppose that I, a simple Utilitarian, entrust the care of my health to a simple Utilitarian doctor. Now I know, of course, that his intentions are generally beneficent, but equally that they are not uniquely beneficent towards me. Thus, while he will not malevolently kill me off, I cannot be sure that he will always try to cure me of my afflictions; I can be sure only that he will do so, unless his assessment of the 'general happiness' leads him to do otherwise. I cannot of course condemn this attitude, since it is the same as my own; but it is more than possible that I might not much like it, and might find myself put to much anxiety and fuss in trying to detect, at successive consultations, what his intentions actually were. But conspicuously, there are two things that I could not do to diminish my anxieties: I could not get him to promise, in the style of the Hippocratic Oath, always and only to deploy his skills to my advantage; nor could I usefully ask him to disclose his intentions.

The reason is essentially the same in each case. Though he might, if I asked him to, promise not to kill me off, he would of course keep this promise only if he judged it best on the whole to do so; knowing that, I could not unquestioningly rely on his keeping it; and knowing that, he would realize that, since I would not do so, it would matter that much less if he did not keep it. And so on, until his 'promise' becomes perfectly idle. Similarly, if I ask him what his intentions are, he will answer truthfully only if he judges it best on the whole to do so; knowing that, I will not unqualifiedly believe him; and knowing that, he will realize that, since I will not do so, it will matter that much less if he professes intentions that he does not actually have. And so on, until my asking and his answering become a pure waste of breath. And this is quite general; if general felicific beneficence were the only criterion, then promising and talking alike would become wholly idle pursuits. At best, as perhaps in diplomacy, what people said would become merely a part of the evidence on the basis of which one might try to decide what they really believed, or intended, or were likely to do; and it is not always obvious that there is much point in diplomacy.[23]

Situation ethics, of course, can recognize rules, but it treats them as summary rules or rules of thumb that are expendable in decision making, since they only summarize the wisdom of the past. Such rules illuminate but do not prescribe what we ought to do. A rule of thumb in baseball is "Don't bunt on third strike," but in some situations it would be advisable for the batter to bunt despite having two strikes. For act deontology or act utilitarianism, all moral rules are like this rule of thumb in baseball. We have argued against this view of moral rules. Although some moral rules may resemble rules of thumb, others are more binding, e.g., the rules that prohibit murder, rape, and cruelty. It is, therefore, important to consider whether some rules are absolute.

If moral rules are conceived as absolute, they cannot be overridden under any circumstances. Obviously, there are good reasons for being suspicious of such a view of moral rules. It undermines the freedom and discretion of moral agents, and it sometimes results in moral victims who suffer the consequences of overly rigid adherence to rules. Even if it is not true that everything depends on the consequences, it may be true that in some cases, such as emergencies, the consequences of following some rules would be so terrible that those rules should be overridden.

Nevertheless, we have to face the possibility that some moral rules are virtually exceptionless or absolute: (a) Some rules that refer to traits of character whose development and expression are always good may be absolute. To exhort a physician colleague to "Be caring" or "Be a loving physician" or "Be conscientious" is to call for the development and expression of traits of character that are good. Of course, one may be too loving or too conscientious and thereby obscure important aspects of one's responsibilities; (b) We might also state some rules of action so as to include all exceptions. These rules, with all exceptions built into them, would be absolute. An example might be, "Always obtain the informed consent of your competent patients except in emergency or low-risk situations." There might still be considerable debate about what constitutes an "emergency" or a "low risk," but the rule would be absolute; (c) Finally, some rules that do not specify exceptions may also be virtually absolute. If "murder" is taken to mean "unjustified killing," then its prohibition would be absolute; and the prohibition of cruelty can be considered absolute if the term means "do not inflict suffering for the sake of suffering."

These examples indicate that the debate about whether some rules can be defended as absolute hinges in part on the definition of moral terms such as "murder," "cruelty," and "lying." Suppose Nazi soldiers had come to a hospital in Germany in the late 1930s and asked the administrator whether there were any Jewish patients in the hospital. If the administrator insisted that the hospital had no Jewish patients, although he knew there were in fact several, how should we describe this exchange and, in particular, the administrator's statement? Consider two possibilities: (1) the administrator's statement is a lie, but the lie is justified because it is intended to save the lives of several innocent patients. (2) The administrator's statement is not a lie because his questioners have no right to the truth. In (1), "lying" may be defined as intentionally telling a person what one believes to be untrue in order to deceive the person. In (2), "lying" may be defined as not giving the truth to a person to whom it is due. The first involves a "neutral and relatively definite description" of lying, while the second involves a "nonneutral and relatively indefinite description."[24] The first definition indicates what counts as lying or truth-telling, but not how much moral weight lying or truth-telling has. The second definition, however, indicates how much lying or truth-telling counts, but not what is to count as lying or truth-telling. Although the second approach holds that lying is always wrong, it leaves open the question when the truth is due someone. If one takes the first approach, one could stress the reality that the moral life often involves doing the "lesser of two evils." For one taking the second approach, harmony between moral principles and rules is more evident than conflict, once their range of applicability is understood. Often this view of harmony is joined with the conviction that one should never do evil that good might result.

In addition to conceiving of moral rules as rules of thumb and absolute rules, a third possibility is to conceive them as prima facie binding. W.D. Ross has usefully distinguished prima facie duties from actual duties. He uses the phrase "prima facie duty" to indicate that duties of certain kinds are on all occasions binding unless they are in conflict with stronger duties. One's actual duty in the situation is determined by an examination of the weight of all the competing prima facie duties. Prima facie duties such as beneficence and promise-keeping are not absolute, since they can be overridden under some conditions. Yet they are more than rules of thumb. Because they are always morally relevant, they constitute strong moral reasons for performing the acts in question, although they may not always prevail over all other prima facie duties. One might say that they count even when they do not win.

For example, Ross considers nonmaleficence-noninfliction of harm as a prima facie duty. While it may make sense, as we have seen, to say that murder is absolutely prohibited because of what "murder" means, it does not make sense for most moral theories to say that killing is absolutely prohibited. Even the prohibition against killing in the Ten Commandments is more accurately translated as the prohibition of "murder" or "unjustified killing," since the Hebrew people recognized justified killing in self-defense, in war, and as a form of punishment. But "killing" nonetheless is prima facie wrong, because it is an act of maleficence. To call "killing" prima facie wrong, then, is to say that insofar as an act involves killing, it is wrong. But since acts have many features, these features may lead to moral conflicts. For example, the duty not to kill someone may come into conflict with the duty of justice, which includes protecting innocent persons from aggression. But it may also come into conflict with the duty of beneficence, the duty to benefit others. Mercy killing provides an example. Imagine a patient suffering from what appears to be uncontrollable and unmanageable pain. Ross holds that the duty of nonmaleficence takes precedence over the duty of beneficence, but he apparently thought about these duties in relation to different individuals; thus, it would not be right to injure A in order to benefit B (although it might be right to injure A in order to prevent A from injuring B). But suppose the duties of nonmaleficence and beneficence come into conflict in the case of the same suffering patient. It is not clear that killing a person in order to alleviate that person's pain would always be wrong. A person trapped in a burning wreck provides such a case. The point of the notion of prima facie duties, however, is that insofar as the act involves killing, it is wrong. Yet killing may be the only way to satisfy some other prima facie duties. If so, then killing can become an actual duty.

Furthermore, when a prima facie duty, such as veracity, is outweighed or overridden, it does not simply disappear or evaporate. It leaves what Nozick calls "moral traces."[25] The agent should not only approach the decision conscientiously, but should also experience regret and, perhaps, even remorse at having to neglect or violate this duty. The duty's "moral traces" should also lead the agent to minimize the effects of the violation, and possibly later to provide an explanation and an apology to the person or persons affected.

## Rights

Throughout our discussion we have used terms like "right," "wrong," "obligatory," "obligation," and "duty." We have stressed rightness and duty with some attention to goodness. And we have examined how principles and rules in both deontological and utilitarian theories establish our duties and obligations, as well as the rightness and wrongness of our acts. It may seem odd that we have not employed the language of rights. We have witnessed an explosion of rights language in numerous contexts, from biomedicine to foreign policy - e.g., the debates about "human rights" on the international level. Indeed, our moral, political, and legal debates often appear to presuppose that no arguments or reasons can be persuasive unless they can be couched in the language of rights.

Rights language is especially congenial to the liberal individualism that is pervasive in our society. From Thomas Hobbes and John Locke to the present, liberal individualists have employed the language of rights to make their moral, social, and political arguments. Our Anglo-American legal tradition has broadly incorporated this language. In the tradition of liberal individualism, the language of rights has often served such functions as opposing the status quo and forcing social reforms. Historically it was instrumental in securing certain freedoms from established orders of religion, society, and state, e.g., freedom of conscience and freedom of the press. Although statements of important rights are shared across many societies, such statements are not universal. As has often been pointed out, many languages, such as ancient Hebrew and Greek, do not have equivalent expressions for our terms "a right" or "rights." Nevertheless, rights language is very important, not only because of its symbolic significance in our society but also because it plays a legitimate role in ethical theory. It is difficult, however, to determine the status and content of those rights that deserve recognition.

Most recent writers in ethics recognize that "rights" should be defined in terms of claims. In our framework, rights are best seen as justified claims that individuals and groups can make upon others or upon society. Just as legal rights are claims that are justified by existing legal principles and rules, so moral rights are claims that are justified by moral principles and rules. A moral right, then, is a morally justified claim - i.e., a claim validated in terms of moral principles and rules.[26] Just as obligations and duties may take many different forms (religious, legal, moral, etc.), rights may be justified by different forms of principles and rules. In dealing with the abortion issue, the Supreme Court had to determine whether the Constitution and the law embodies rights relevant to this issue. It did not confront the question of moral rights (except by implication), but moral rights and legal rights often are similar and sometimes even identical.

We have concentrated on moral principles and rules, some of which establish duties and obligations, as well as on the rightness and wrongness of acts. In this context we use "duty" and "obligation" interchangeably, though it is important in some other contexts to distinguish them. From our standpoint, there exists what David Braybrooke calls "a firm but untidy correlativity" between obligations and rights, and both obligations and rights can be analyzed in terms of principles and rules.[27] According to the doctrine of the "logical correlativity" of obligations and rights, a right implies that someone else has an obligation to act in certain ways.[28] Rights thus imply obligations. The doctrine of the logical correlativity of rights and obligations holds that it is possible to start from a right and infer a correlative obligation, and vice versa. It indicates that we can secure the same moral content from either standpoint, that of the right or of the obligation. However, the doctrine does not tell us whether obligations are grounded in rights or vice versa, and we take no stand on this issue here.

While the doctrine of the logical correlativity of rights and duties is for the most part sound, there is a generalized use of "requirement," "obligation," and "duty" which sometimes appears not to imply correlative rights. For example, we sometimes refer to "duties" or "requirements" of love, charity, and self-sacrifice that do not seem to be restatable in terms of rights. It seems awkward in most instances to hold that one person can claim another person's love or charity as a matter of right. The problem is that some so-called duties and obligations express what we ought to do in the light of ideals and supererogatory actions, such as those of heroes and saints, that may not be appropriately labelled moral requirements. Often they express self-imposed requirements, as when we believe that we ought to contribute substantially to charity, even though morality does not require it.

John Stuart Mill usefully approached this problem by employing the distinction between duties of perfect obligation and duties of imperfect obligation: "duties of perfect obligation are those duties in virtue of which a correlative right resides in some person or persons; duties of imperfect obligation are those moral obligations which do not give birth to any right."[29] Mill goes on to indicate that duties of perfect obligation are duties of justice, while duties of imperfect obligation belong to other spheres of morality: "Justice implies something which is not only right to do, and wrong not to do, but which some individual person can claim from us as his moral right. No one has a moral right to our generosity or beneficence, because we are not morally bound to practice those virtues towards any given individual."[30]

Either rule utilitarianism or rule deontology, as obligation-oriented theories, can incorporate the language and substance of rights. This claim may appear to be somewhat surprising, since some utilitarians have vigorously opposed certain conceptions of rights, and many of the strongest supporters and theoreticians of rights have operated within deontological frameworks, emphasizing particularly respect for persons. Indeed, in our ordinary moral discourse, we frequently set the rights of individuals and groups in opposition to social utility. Nevertheless, it follows from the doctrine of the logical correlativity of rights and obligations that the rule utilitarianism as well as rule deontology can provide a foundation for both rights and obligations.[31]

Ronald Dworkin's argument about the possibility of rights within a rule-utilitarian political theory also holds for moral theory:

> a political theory might provide for a right to free speech, for example, on the hypothesis that the general acceptance of that right by courts and other political institutions would promote the highest average utility of the community in the long run. . . If the theory provides that an official of a particular institution is justified in making a political decision, and not justified in refusing to make it, whenever that decision is necessary to protect the freedom to speak of any individual, without regard to the impact of the decision on collective goals, the theory provides free speech as a right.[32]

Rights, according to this view, may serve as constraints or "political trumps" within either rule utilitarianism or rule deontology. In rule utilitarianism, they are justified by their likely contributions to utility, and Mill defended rights of autonomy and liberty in these terms. In a deontological framework, on the other hand, rights are likely to be based on respect for persons, autonomy, and similar nonutilitarian principles; rights express and embody those principles and are not merely instrumental to the maximization of good consequences. Of course, there will be disputes about whether certain claims are "rights," about their relative weight, etc., but these disputes will probably be no more frequent or intractable between rule utilitarians and rule deontologists than within these two approaches to ethical theory.

An important distinction is that between positive rights and negative rights. As Joel Feinberg writes, "A positive right is a right to other persons' positive actions; a negative right is a right to other persons' omissions or forebearances. For every positive right I have, someone else has a duty to do something; for every negative right I have, someone else has a duty to refrain from doing something."[33]

The liberal tradition has generally found it easier to justify negative rights, especially those that call for noninterference with liberty, than positive rights; but the recognition of welfare rights has extended the range and power of positive rights.

How much weight do we assign to these different rights? When they come into conflict, which right takes precedence? Answers to these questions, which may finally be unanswerable to everyone's satisfaction, can only come through the framework of systematic reflection on moral principles and rules, including duties, obligations, and rights.

**FOOTNOTES**

[1]See John Lemmon, "Moral Dilemmas," Philosophical Review 71 (1962): 139-58.

[2]For various reasons it is controversial whether such a sharp distinction can be drawn between mathematics and normative ethics. See for example Philippa Foot, "Goodness and Choice" and J.R. Searle, "How to Derive 'Ought' from 'Is'," in W.D. Hudson, ed., The Is/Ought Question (London: Macmillan, 1969).

[3]Thomas R. Dye, Understanding Public Policy, 2nd ed. (Englewood Cliffs, New Jersey: Prentice-Hall, 1975), p. 1.

[4]Joel Feinberg, Social Philosophy (Englewood Cliffs, New Jersey: Prentice-Hall, 1973), p. 34.

[5]For a discussion of some of the issues and major positions, see James F. Childress, "The Identification of Ethical Principles," Journal of Religious Ethics 5 (Spring 1977): 39-68. We will often use the terms "moral" and "ethical" interchangeably, although some distinctions can be drawn between them. Cicero apparently formed the Latin word moralis (from mores) to translate the Greek term ethikos. Etymologically their meanings are similar and stress manners, character, and customs. Contemporary usage suggests some rough but not very precise distinctions between them. "Ethics" often refers to reflective and theoretical perspectives, while "morality" often refers more clearly to actual conduct and practice. Our use of the terms "ethics" and "morality" in this chapter respects this rough distinction, although we use the adjectives "moral" and "ethical" less precisely.

[6]Jeremy Bentham, An Introduction to the Principles of Morals and Legislation (New York: Hafner Publishing Co., 1948). Cf. Chapter I.3.

[7]John Stuart Mill, Utilitarianism, On Liberty, and Essay on Bentham, ed. with an Introduction by Mary Warnock (Cleveland: World Publishing Co., 1962), pp. 256-78.

[8]G.E. Moore, Principia Ethica (Cambridge: Cambridge University Press, 1962), pp. 90 f.

[9]J.J.C. Smart, An Outline of a System of Utilitarian Ethics (Melbourne: University Press, 1961), and "Extreme and Restricted Utilitarianism," The Philosophical Quarterly 6 (1956), as reprinted in M. Bayles, ed., Contemporary Utilitarianism (Garden City: Doubleday Anchor Books, 1968), especially pp. 104 ff in the latter source.

[10]David Hume, _A Treatise of Human Nature_, ed. L.A. Selby-Bigge (Oxford: Oxford University Press, 1888). Book III, Parts I and II, especially pp. 494-500. Richard B. Brandt, "Toward a Credible Form of Utilitarianism," in Bayles, ed., _Contemporary Utilitarianism_, pp. 143-86.

[11]Moral Code Utilitarianism also may provide a way of circumventing a prominent objection against the act/rule distinction that has been advanced by David Lyons in _Forms and Limits of Utilitarianism_ (Oxford: Clarendon Press, 1965). He urges that whatever would count for an act utilitarian as a good reason for _breaking_ a rule would count equally for a rule utilitarian as a good reason for emending a rule - and hence the two come in practice to the same theory. It would be very difficult and perhaps impossible to emend an entire code with the frequency with which a rule could be validly broken by act utilitarians.

[12]See W.D. Ross, _The Right and the Good_ (Oxford: Clarendon Press, 1939); and John Rawls, _A Theory of Justice_ (Cambridge, Massachusetts: Harvard University Press, 1971).

[13]See Alan Donagen, _The Theory of Morality_ (Chicago: University of Chicago Press, 1977).

[14]Immanuel Kant, _Groundwork of the Metaphysics of Morals_ trans. H.J. Paton (New York: Harper and Row, Harper Torchbooks, 1964), pp. 90-91.

[15]Ross, _The Right and the Good_, pp. 22, 41-42.

[16]Rawls, _A Theory of Justice_, Chaps. 8, 11, 51, especially pp. 339-40.

[17]See Ross, _The Right and the Good_ and _The Foundations of Ethics_.

[18]Anthony Flew, "Ends and Means," _The Encyclopedia of Philosophy_, ed. Paul Edwards (New York: Macmillan and the Free Press, 1967), p. 510.

[19]See William Frankena, _Ethics_, 2d. ed. (Englewood Cliffs, N.J.: Prentice-Hall, 1973).

[20]Richard B. Brandt, _Ethical Theory_ (Englewood Cliffs, N.J.: Prentice-Hall, 1959), p. 404.

[21]See Lyons, _The Forms and Limits of Utilitarianism_.

[22]"Toward a Credible Form of Utilitarianism," in Bayles, ed., _Contemporary Utilitarianism_, p. 166.

[23]G.J. Warnock, _The Object of Morality_ (London: Methuen and Co., 1971), p. 33.

[24]Donald Evans, "Paul Ramsey on Exceptionless Moral Rules," American Journal of Jurisprudence 16 (1971): 184-214. See also Sissela Bok, Lying: Moral Choice in Public and Private Life (New York: Pantheon Books, 1978), pp. 13-16.

[25]See Robert Nozick, "Moral Complications and Moral Structures," Natural Law Forum 13 (1968): 1-50.

[26]See Joel Feinberg, Social Philosophy (Englewood Cliffs, N.J.: Prentice-Hall, 1973), p. 67. Feinberg prefers the narrower term "validity" to the broader term "justification," since validity "is justification of a peculiar and narrow kind, namely justification within a system of rules."

[27]David Braybrooke, "The Firm but Untidy Correlativity of Rights and Obligations," Canadian Journal of Philosophy 1 (March 1972): 351-63.

[28]Feinberg, Social Philosophy, p. 61.

[29]Mill, Utilitarianism, p. 305.

[30]Ibid. It is still largely undecided whether we should ascribe rights to nonpersons, such as trees and animals. We have a duty not to be cruel to animals, for example, but is it appropriate to ascribe rights to them? The answer to this question will obviously depend upon one's theory of rights and their foundation. According to one recent theory, only entities capable of having interests can have rights, and therefore trees and vegetables cannot have rights. However, since both animals and future generations can be said to have interests they can be said meaningfully to have rights. See Joel Feinberg, "The Rights of Animals and Unborn Generations," in Philosophy and Environmental Crisis, ed. W.T. Blackstone (Athens, Ga.: University of Georgia Press, 1974).

[31]Act utilitarians, by contrast, seem committed to the translation of rights into interests and needs in order to facilitate utilitarian calculation; but rule utilitarians need not resort to this maneuver. The utilitarian critique of natural rights offered by Bentham is well-known: "Natural rights is simple nonsense: natural and imprescriptible rights, rhetorical nonsense - nonsense upon stilts." That critique, however, was aimed at the epistemology of natural rights, not at any use of the language of rights or at any development of a theory of moral rights. Bentham's invectives were directed against "naturalistic" theories rather than "rights." Bentham, Anarchical Fallacies, in The Collected Papers of Jeremy Bentham, vol. 2, ed. John Bowring (Edinburgh, 1843), as reprinted in Human Rights, ed. A.I. Melden (Belmont, Cal.: Wadsworth Press, 1970), p. 32.

[32]Ronald Dworkin, Taking Rights Seriously (Cambridge, Mass.: Harvard University Press, 1977), pp. 96-97. See also Richard Flathman's justification of the practice of rights in

<u>The Practice of Rights</u>   (Cambridge:   Cambridge University  Press, 1976).

[33]Feinberg, <u>Social Philosophy</u>, p. 59.

# CHAPTER III

## PERSPECTIVE:  A SOCIAL HUMANITIES VIEW OF EDUCATIONAL POLICY
## AND ADMINISTRATION

### Thomas J. Sergiovanni

The quest for a science of administration continues.  To many, the social sciences represent the disciplines from which accurate, reliable, and relevant ideas, concepts, and postulates can be generated.  These in turn can provide a general theory of administration or, more modestly, an array of middle-range theories.  The scenario peaks with the belief that through the process of logical deduction and hypothesis testing, theories can be translated into a series of practices to form the core of a science of educational administration.  Following this line of reasoning, as engineering is to physics and chemistry, so administration and policy are to the social sciences.  In recent years more inductive modes of inquiry which rely on observation, description, and classification have regained popularity.[1]  Here, knowledge is formulated by inference and intuition.

The ends sought by both inductively and deductively oriented science are the same:  to develop accurate and reliable descriptions of the real world and how it works and to refine the task necessary for making accurate and reliable predictions about this reality.  In this sense, knowledge so produced might be referred to as descriptive.  Deductive methods provide us with descriptive postulates and theories of the real world and inductive methods with descriptive arrays, representations, classifications, and inferences about what the real world is like.

## The Nature of Applied Science

If one views educational policy and administration as sciences, then major concern is given to describing, explaining, analyzing, and predicting societal and organizational phenomena and human behavior as they relate to the resolution of relevant issues and to the accomplishment of goals.  The scientific approach is one of accuracy, reliability, objectivity, and neutrality.  Emphasis is given to the identification and articulation of principles which have wide applicability, and variables are examined in cause and effect relationships so that action propositions can be developed to guide policy and administrative decisions.

But neither policy science nor administrative science are sciences in the strictest sense.  Both go beyond mere description of what is and mere projecting of interrelations among aspects of a problem to the development of the most effective ways to achieve desired ends.  Thus, being concerned with what is desirable as well as what is fact, with standards as well as bench marks, and with change for the better as well as mapping present circumstances makes these fields applied sciences.

Administration is perhaps better viewed as an art which uses science in seeking its ends. Quantitative methods, theoretical analyses, characteristics of objectivity, and other artifacts of science should be viewed as perspectives for understanding the art of administration and not as surrogates for this art.[2] The role of science in decision making is not to replace but rather to inform intuition. Normative aspects of educational policy and administration are and should be omnipresent. A good normative theory is much like an educational or management platform. Both include assumptions, beliefs, realities, and prescriptions about some issue or problem which, when taken as a whole, represents a new standard, a higher order of existence, or ideal to which person, organization, and society strive. Issues of confirmation are not wholly determined by what is fact as in the case of descriptive theories, but by internal consistency of assumptions, postulates, and prescriptions (deductive logic); moral and ethical reasoning (adequacy of assumptions of the nature of humankind, for example); consistency with other normative theories which comprise and define the broader culture (normative political and religious theories, for example, as in the case of democracy and Judeo-Christian ideals); and adequacy of the ends defined for future reference.

## Toward a Social Humanities View of Educational Decision-Making

One test of leadership in an applied field is the ability of the leader to sort through both the perspectives of science (the descriptive) and value (the normative) in a fashion which provides some balance and which permits reasonable action. Descriptive views of educational policy and administration typically are derived from the social sciences and other related fields such as management science and systems analysis. Normative views, by contrast, seem more imbedded in the humanities. Statements of philosophy and underlying models of humanism and assumptions about how humans behave and of what they are capable, though often portrayed in a "scientific" manner, are typically more hopes and ideals or statements of value than accurate descriptions of reality. Indeed, it should be expected that since normative theories are designed to change, rather than reflect, the social order, they frequently are at odds with reality.

The question remains, how might insights from the humanities -- particularly value issues -- and those from social science be meaningfully integrated? The need for integration is generally undisputed but has not been systematically attacked.[3] Gastil has suggested that a new discipline be established to work out this problem and to offer decision-makers a set of guidelines for action.[4] He coins the phrase, "social humanities", to describe this discipline. Following his work, I examine how a social humanities view of educational administration might take shape and provide an example of how such a view might be used to improve educational decision-making. The purpose of this discussion is to present a set of ideas for examination, discourse, and elaboration. No pretense is made that the ideas are fully developed. If the social humanities concept is usable, widespread further study will be needed, and many more proposals will need to be considered before a workable methodology can be developed.

Applying the Social Humanities View
     Applying the social humanities view to educational policy and
administration requires the acceptance of two assumptions about
the nature of humankind. The first, a bio-social view, assumes
that humans are basically self-interested and self-serving. As
such, they assume a calculative posture responding to the costs
and benefits of various situations. Their biological capabilities
and cultural conditioning determine what is of value and the
nature of desirable interchange between cost and benefit. The
goal of such interchange is to maximize one's advantage. This
view provides much of the impetus for the scientific-descriptive
study of our field and, indeed, is the target of such inquiry.
The second, a humanistic view, assumes that humans are capable of
reflection, responsible action, and valuing. Further, it assumes
that agreements are possible, goals can be determined, and persons
as individuals and as human systems of an organization are capable
of intrinsic, goal-seeking behavior. This in turn implies the
ability of people to commit themselves to action. Normative
theories in our culture rely heavily on this humanistic view. The
above assumptions underlying these two views of humankind should
be considered as alternate and somewhat competing dispositions of
human nature rather than as mutually exclusive entities.
     Educational decision-making requires that one give some
attention to problem analysis and to selecting from among
alternatives. If each of the assumptions of humankind is to be
reflected in an evaluation of decision alternatives or in an
analysis of a problem, then we need a set of pluralistic criteria
to help guide this analysis and evaluation. The guidelines would
be pluralistic in the sense that both descriptive and normative
views of human nature and administrative action would be taken
into account. Following Gastil,[5] four elements will be considered
in developing a pluralistic framework for analysis and evaluation:
1.  Utility:  This element is concerned with the practical, with
    social maximization, with costs and benefits, and with other
    standards of production and achievement. Utility contributes
    to the goals of a good society by expanding its wealth and
    other aspects of material production. Being decision-
    oriented, the applied sciences of policy and administration
    are naturally concerned with utility. The traditional
    distinctions between policy and administration involve
    considerations of scope and breadth. The former refers to a
    more general course of action intended to guide and determine
    present and future decisions, and the latter refers to a more
    specific course of action.[6] But each is concerned,
    nevertheless, with action toward some end, and each is
    ultimately practical and instrumental. As educational
    administrators and policy makers evaluate decision
    alternatives, they give attention to the practical utility of
    each to the school community and to society in general.
2.  Transcendence:  Though practical matters suggested by utility
    are important, they bespeak of routine and project an
    instrumental view of achievement without necessarily
    considering growth in new understanding or in establishing
    higher standards of achievement. Transcendence is going

beyond the ordinary to creativity and excellence. From a psychological point of view, transcendence refers to the capacity of an alternative to build esteem, autonomy, and self-actualization. From a societal point of view, transcendence refers to the capacity of an alternative to increase the potential of society for achieving humanness in the pursuit of happiness. This is a qualitative dimension concerned with the aesthetic, creative, spiritual, and intellectual enrichment of the individual and society. As educational administrators and policy makers evaluate decision alternatives, they give attention to the potential of each to help individuals, organizations, the community, and society to move beyond the ordinary, to grow to new levels of understanding, to higher standards of operation.

3. Justice: This element is concerned with equity in the distribution of benefits accrued by each decision alternative. Utility and transcendence both require benefits to the school and society, but they do not speak to the matter of equitable distribution. Although the concept of justice used in this framework is from Rawls, his position is too extreme for direct use. (The good society as envisioned by Rawls in his Theory of Justice evolves from the principles of full political and social equality and from full equality in the distribution of primary goods.[7] Justice, in his normative theory, would be the primary criterion for decision-making.) In the framework for decision-making offered here, justice is but one of four elements each of which would be balanced against the other. As educational administrators and policy makers evaluate decision alternatives, they give attention to the extent each provides for a just distribution of benefits.

4. Ethical Limits: In this framework justice is considered as a universal ethical concern and, therefore, is present in all decision settings. Ethical limits, on the other hand, refer to other moral questions raised by, or germane to, the problems at hand. Lying and deception, for example, are often ethical considerations which surface in problem situations. Consider a superintendent who wants to do everything he or she can to help pass a school tax increase. Is it appropriate to deceive the public a bit by exaggerating the school's fiscal plight?[8] Obviously, passing the tax increase means much more for students. No easy answer exists to this or any other ethical dilemma, but they must, nevertheless, be addressed. As administrators and policy makers evaluate decision alternatives on the basis of utility, transcendence, and justice, they should consider as well the ethical questions which surface.

The four elements of this pluralistic framework for analyzing and evaluating educational decision are illustrated in Figure 1. Note that the elements are grouped by the extent to which they represent competing action forces as opposed to competing control forces. Action forces tend to be instrumental and achievement-oriented, suggesting progress or moving ahead. Control forces tend to be substantive and value-oriented, suggesting guides and restraints on action rather than action itself. One system of checks and balances within the framework is the tension which results from trying to maximize both action and control forces. Often optimal plans of action, be they utilitarian or transcendental in nature, are modified because of ethical limits or constraints of justice. Within the action and control categories, another system of checks and balances results from the tension of trying to maximize both utility and transcendence on the one hand and justice and other ethical limits on the other.

## The Limits of Choice Among Alternatives

A basic assumption underlying this policy and decision framework is the fact that problems can be analyzed and

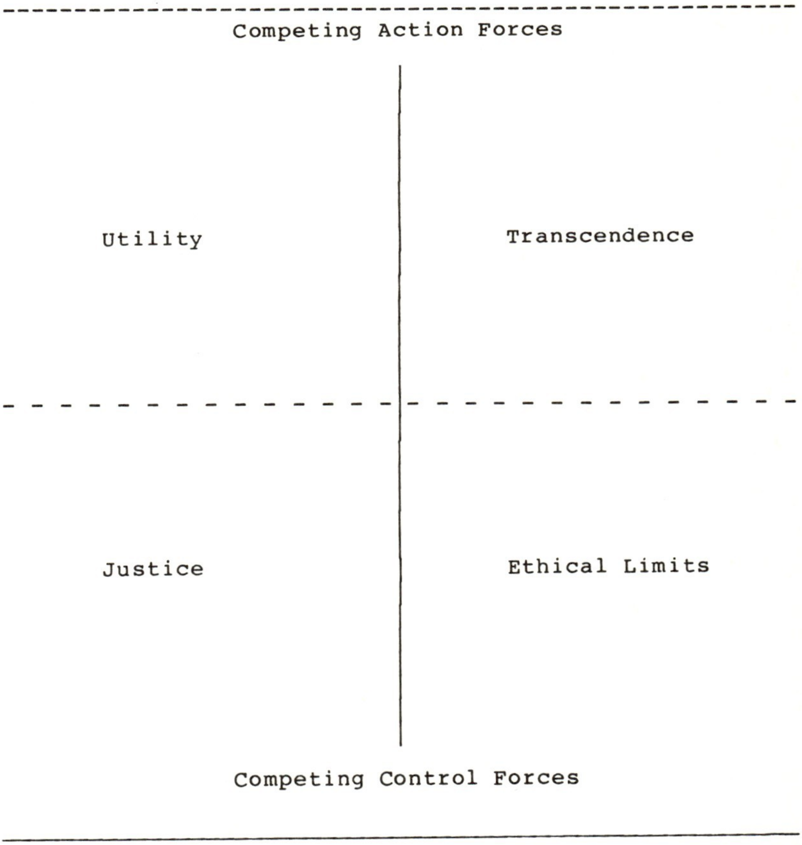

- - - - - - - - - - - - - - - - - - - - - - - - - - - - - - - - - - - - - -

Competing Action Forces

Utility                          Transcendence

- - - - - - - - - - - - - - - - - -|- - - - - - - - - - - - - - -

Justice                          Ethical Limits

Competing Control Forces

Figure 1

A Pluralistic Framework for Evaluating Education Decisions

alternatives can be considered in terms of each of the four criteria -- utility, transcendence, justice, and ethical limits. Ideally, a proposal would maximize each of the four. Realistically, however, each of the four should be viewed as having an acceptable range. A curriculum proposal, for example, might have only marginal utility with regard to increasing the basic skills but offer a great deal of transcendence potential and be considered both just and ethical. If this proposal had very little utility, it would likely be found unacceptable regardless of its ability to meet the other criteria. It follows that a second proposal offering a great deal utility and found as well to be just, but only marginally strong in the areas of ethical limits and transcendence, might be found acceptable. Another proposal with less than marginal strength in one or both of these latter areas would not be acceptable. Although a perfect balance among the criteria is the ideal in evaluating decision alternatives, it is likely that decisions will be made on the basis of acceptable limits.

A serious excess in any one element of the framework is likely to upset an acceptable level of balance among the four. An over-emphasis on justice (equal treatment of individuals and equal distribution of resources and benefits), for example, could negatively influence the transcendence potential of a proposal. "Sameness" often discourages creativity and takes the edge off individual initiative. Further, it is likely that commitment to organizational purposes would be bland and the organizational incentive system dulled. This dullness of transcendence, persisting over time, would eventually lower the more routine performance capability (utility) of the organization and would raise as well a series of ethical questions. Is it fair to treat everyone equally when their contributions are different? Should we persist in distributing resources equally even though the need may be greater in one area than another? As utility, transcendence, and ethics are limited, the organization's health and productive capability are endangered. This, then, could lead to a decline in organizational productivity and esteem -- the raw materials of a just distribution system. Having less to distribute, justice itself suffers from its initial excess.

A proposition of limits is proposed, therefore, as a necessary assumption and guide in the framework for maintaining an acceptable level of balance among the four dimensions. Over time, a serious deficit or excess in any one dimension of the pluralistic framework for evaluating educational decision alternatives negatively influences each of the other dimensions.

## Toward a Strategy for Decision Analysis

The analysis of problems and the evaluation of alternatives can take a variety of forms. This process is typically implicit and informal, but if made explicit it is likely to include some concern for the statement of a problem; a descriptive account of relevant information; a search for theoretical or intuitive frameworks to help understand and clarify the problem; a values analysis whereby the evaluator's preferences, biases, and assumptions would come into play; and, finally, some decision intended to improve things would be formulated. These steps are not necessarily executed in order but typically all are employed by the educational decision maker.[9]

Consider, for example, the problem of evaluating and deciding among several educational program proposals.[10] Assume that the setting is an elementary school and the problem is deciding which model or model combination of educational programs should be selected as the standard from which guiding principles are drawn for making curricular, classroom organizational, instructional, and evaluative decisions.[11] An analysis conducted on behalf of a school actually facing this problem would need to be more elaborate than can be attempted here. The author proposes only to provide a broad outline of an analysis and will assume that the model programs described are generally familiar to readers and, thus, require only parsimonious definition and description. These model programs will be referred to as curriculum, child, teacher, and problem centered.

One form of the curriculum centered program places reliance on carefully defined objectives for each subject matter area, with areas arranged according to level and grouped into teaching-learning modules. Objectives are accompanied by carefully developed curriculum formats and learning activities. Curriculum formats, in turn, come complete with tests of various kinds which are designed to determine when students have mastered a set of learning materials and are ready to progress to the next module. Objectives and materials are typically purchased commercially or assembled from various commercial and other sources by school committees. In sum, the controlling force in this type of program is the highly structured and sequenced curriculum. Another form of this approach is far less precise but curriculum-centered nevertheless. In this form, grade level syllabi are developed and textbooks or workbooks are selected to guide instruction. Indeed, syllabi and textbook content are highly correlated. Teachers proceed page by page through an array of books selected to cover the material designated as important for a particular grade level. Students progress from grade to grade as they pass tests on this material. In sum, the controlling force is the content of the books used.

Child-centered programs can be described as those which make the self-determined needs of children the basic decision criteria. Objectives emerge, curriculum materials are selected, and instructional decisions are made to suit the needs and interests of students. The setting is informal and unstructured with a great deal of reliance placed on students accepting responsibility and taking the initiative in deciding what will be scheduled, when, and how. Teachers guide and facilitate this effort. Texts, curriculum materials, and other instructional materials are viewed as resources to be drawn upon as, and if, needed. The driving force is, in sum, the self-determined needs of the students.

Teacher-centered programs place the teacher at the center of the decision-making apparatus. Although a set curriculum exists and certain objectives are expected to be pursued, teachers are afforded broad authority and wide discretion in deciding what, when, how, and where to teach. Since the curriculum is broadly conceived, learning materials, schedules, equipment, and other instructional elements are viewed as resources to be used as the teacher sees fit. The teacher is the controlling force in this type of program, and student needs are determined by the teacher.

Problem-centered programs require that teachers and students together assume major responsibility for planning, organizing, and controlling the learning environment. Although a general curriculum exists and certain objectives are presumed, it is expected that they serve as a context from which teachers and students jointly select for study and develop mutual goals and plans to guide activity as well as the evaluation of their efforts. What goals should be pursued and what activities need to be completed to accomplish these goals are the questions which set the tone for student-teacher collaboration. Teachers and students are both assertive in answering these questions, but the focus is less on who decides and more on the decisions that are required to achieve goals. Problems, goals, and shared decisions are the driving forces which govern activity in this program mode.

A variety of approaches and a number of criteria could be applied in evaluating each of these program designs. For purposes of illustration, an analysis using some of the factors suggested by the curriculum theorist Starratt in his conceptualization of the context for learning will be employed to assess these alternatives for program decision guidelines or standards.[12] His framework will comprise the basis for a "scientific" or descriptive analysis of each program alternative. He suggests that the amount and mix of intrinsic and extrinsic motivation that characterizes a particular program model, the extent to which personal and culturally defined meanings are emphasized, and the interpersonal settings emphasized in the learning context are important considerations in describing, understanding, and evaluating. (Of further interest to this analysis is the issue of power and authority. Who decides, in the view of the author of this article, is intimately related to the matters of motivation, meaning, and interpersonal setting in classrooms.)

Starratt proposes first that programs be examined for the extent to which both intrinsic and extrinsic content are manifested. He is concerned with intrinsic and extrinsic cognition, activity, motivation, inquiry, and creativity.[13] Intrinsic content is concerned with appreciation and enjoyment and extrinsic content with more practical and instrumental activity. Most agree that healthy adults are able to function in both intrinsic and extrinsic ways. It seems reasonable, then, to suggest that educational programs should contribute to healthy adult functioning by including opportunities for students to function for both intrinsic and extrinsic reasons.

Second, the extent to which personal and cultural meanings are emphasized in programs should be considered. Personal meanings are those which students bring to learning encounters. They act as filters through which learnings are processed. Activities which emphasize personal meanings result in outcomes which differ for each learner. Personal meanings both enrich learning experiences and are themselves enriched by these experiences. Culturally defined meanings, on the other hand, are heavily laden with expectations that reflect the values which others (the teacher, textbook writers, or the state) hold for learners. Macdonald, in concurring with Starratt, also feels that the two contribute to healthy adult functioning as follows:

> It would be apparent to all that the growing self must have personal meanings and cultural meanings for adequate realization. Further, it follows from this that the two meaning systems are not separate compartments within the individual. They are (in a healthy state) functionally integrated into the purposive striving of the person.[14]

Starratt believes that the interpersonal context for learning is a third and key factor in any program design. The typical classroom is characterized by a pattern of interpersonal relationships which can be described as "one to one." The teacher, for example, typically interacts with students one at a time. Even in a large group session of teacher lecturing and questioning the teacher relates to one student at a time and students relate individually in response to the teacher's queries. In adult life interpersonal competence requires that one function reasonably well in three settings: alone, paired, and as a group member. As Starratt suggests:

> We may then speak of a general dimension of human growth which moves from individual thought and action to conversation with another, to action and discussion in a group. All three experiences are formative of the person and make up that person's environment of learning. Group activities and discussion contribute to the person's ability to relate to others, to share in group goals, and to surrender selfish attitudes and values for the benefit of the group.[15]

Given the importance of interpersonal competence in adult functioning, it seems reasonable for the school to provide students with learning experiences in each of the three settings.

Using the extent to which teacher and students are able to influence classroom decisions as its abscissa and ordinate, the four quadrants of Figure 2 each represents one of the program alternatives under consideration. The extent to which the curriculum context factors of Starratt are likely to be manifested by a particular alternative is summarized in each program quadrant.

In child-centered programs intrinsic motivation dominates and personal meanings are emphasized to the virtual exclusion of culturally-defined meanings. Since students assume the controlling position with respect to decisions, the interpersonal setting depends upon student choice. In teacher-centered programs where teachers enjoy wide discretion, they can emphasize both intrinsic and extrinsic motivation and both culturally-defined and personal meanings, although extrinsic motivation and culturally-defined meanings are likely to enjoy greater prominence. Interpersonal setting opportunities depend on teacher choice. In curriculum-centered programs where the controlling force is the structured and highly sequenced curriculum, teacher and student influence is very low. Thus, motivation must be built into the curriculum and is likely to be extrinsic. Culturally-defined meanings are emphasized to the virtual exclusion of personal meanings, and individual activity predominates the interpersonal setting. Problem-centered programs, characterized by high teacher and student influence, enable both intrinsic and extrinsic motivation, and both personal and culturally-defined meanings, to be emphasized. The problems under consideration determine the appropriate interpersonal setting. (See Figure 2)

Applying the Pluralistic Framework

Having now conducted a brief scientific or descriptive analysis of each program possibility with respect to the important curriculum context aspect of program decisions, we can now proceed with a social humanistic evaluation using the pluralistic framework of utility, transcendence, justice, and ethical limits. The issue remains, which program combination or alternative should be selected as representative of the overall model from which day by day decisions can be made about curriculum and instruction in an elementary school? Of necessity, the analysis must continue to proceed abstractly since we have no scenario of concrete facts about an actual school and its environment in mind. Further, although other decision aspects or issues are important (such as curriculum objectives, instructional materials, or pupil evaluation), the analysis here is concerned primarily with the context for learning.

With respect to utility, it is reasonable for society to require that certain expectations for learning be met, that certain knowledge imperatives be taught, and that certain basic competencies be emphasized. Although some would debate the school's role in influencing society, few indeed would debate the right of society to influence the schools. Further, our educational system is such that certain performance expectations must be met for students to qualify for certain jobs and to gain access to higher education.

Issues of school political and financial support often revolve around questions of utility with regard to school performance. As utility is evidenced, political and financial support tend to increase. Culturally-defined meanings typically encompass demands for utility. A similar line of reasoning applies as well to extrinsic motivation. Utilitarian demands are related to aspects of social responsibility and this, in turn, requires that one go beyond narcissism which would result from an exclusive or dominant emphasis on intrinsic satisfaction and personally-defined meanings.[16]

Transcendence, however, requires that students and teacher move beyond the mere dispensing and assimilation of information to a fuller involvement, one characterized by intellectual activity

| Child Centered | Problem Centered |
|---|---|
| Goals are de-emphasized but when in evidence are informal and ad hoc. | Formal and informal goals present. |
| Students assume a controlling position with teachers acting as facilitators. | Students and teacher have wide discretion in planning, organizing, and controlling the learning environment. |
| Intrinsic motivation clearly dominates. | Intrinsic and extrinsic motivation are both present with intrinsic slightly more than extrinsic. |
| Personal meanings are emphasized to the virtual exclusion of culturally-defined meanings. | Personal and culturally-defined meanings are emphasized. |
| Interpersonal setting depends upon student choice. | Interpersonal setting opportunities depend upon the problem to be solved. |
| Formal goals are emphasized but they are impersonal. | Formal goals are emphasized with informal permitted at teacher discretion. |
| The curriculum is in control with minimum discretion exercised by students and teacher. | Teacher assumes control amd enjoys wide discretion. |
| To the extent that motivation is emphasized, it is extrinsic. Motivation is built into the curriculum. | Intrinsic and extrinsic both present with extrinsic emphasized. |
| Culturally-defined meanings are emphasized to the virtual exclusion of personal meanings. | Personal and culturally-defined meanings are present with cultural emphasized. |
| Interpersonal setting is typically individual. | Interpersonal setting opportunities depend on the teacher's choice. |

Curriculum-centered       Teacher-centered

Low    (Teacher Influence)    High

*(left vertical axis: high ... (Student Influence) ... low)*

Figure 2
Program Alternatives Under Consideration

and personal enrichment. Intellectual activity is dynamic, creative, and expansive - conditions not possible in the absence of the interplay of personal meanings and knowledge. Personal enrichment requires that one attain the fuller meanings implicit in learning activity and derive a sense of appreciation and satisfaction from them.

Justice requires that those involved in a program have some influence on decisions which affect them. Certainly influence need not be equal among groups, but students should be afforded some choice, teachers should be able to exercise professional judgment, and parents, too, should have some influence on matters of curriculum and instruction. The literature on the availability and use of power and authority by individuals in organizations provides additional insights. Individuals who feel more like "origins" than "pawns"[17] are likely to be more committed and better motivated. Commitment and motivation, in turn, affect the values of utility and transcendence.

Although a number of ethical issues can be raised, the issues of democracy and job or work satisfaction seem most obvious. The school, for example, is charged with inculcating values of democracy in students. This is done by direct teaching and by implicit and explicit modeling. It seems reasonable, therefore, to expect educational program designs not only to teach the values of democracy but also to model them. On the issue of job satisfaction, humanistic capitalism has gained acceptance in North America as has industrialized democracy in Western Europe and paternalistic management in Japan. These patterns differ both conceptually and culturally but share a common theme. Individual job satisfaction and high group morale are goals of the workplace and are to be pursued in their own right. Heretofore, job satisfaction was considered as a legitimate goal among North American managers as long as performance and production increases either preceded or followed increases in job satisfaction. For our purposes, regardless of an educational program's performance potential, we need as well to be concerned with issues of job or work satisfaction for both teachers and students.

Framing the Decision

This line of analysis suggests that when judged against the pluralistic framework, child-centered and curriculum-centered models are not sufficiently balanced and should, therefore, not be considered as possibilities in selecting standards or guidelines for program decisions. Although utility would be high in curriculum-centered programs in the sense that they promise the most reliable coverage of subject matter, personal meanings and intrinsic satisfaction (transcendence) are neglected. The pattern of low student and teacher influence on decision-making raises serious questions of justice. Further, without some reasonable influence patterns, values of democracy would be difficult to articulate in classroom functioning and job or work satisfaction would likely be low. Child-centered programs could afford students a great deal of initial satisfaction, and intrinsic motivation would be high. But the teacher is not sufficiently active in this approach to ensure the culturally-defined meanings are emphasized or to participate fully in the democratic process. Overall, initial transcendence would be high, but utility and justice would be low and ethical limits moderate.

The problem-centered program model would earn very high ratings on transcendence, justice, and ethical limits and fairly high ratings on utility. Built on the principles of democracy and on a just distribution of influence, intrinsic and extrinsic motivation as well as personal and culturally-defined meanings would be high. Some would argue that the teacher's authority would be limited somewhat and, therefore, the matter of utility would likely be compromised. A program such as this would require a great deal of skill from the teacher, commitment from the student, and understanding from parents. Despite its merits, and understanding from parents. Despite its merits, this program is not recommended as an exclusive model.

The teacher-centered model, by placing the teacher at the center of the decision-making apparatus, is a bit easier to understand and implement than the problem-centered model. Limits of justice, to this analyst, are acceptable given the general belief in our society that teachers should be in control. Students become influential as teachers decide to share some of their authority. Satisfaction probably would be high for teachers and moderate for students. The potential for utility is high and for transcendence moderate.

On the basis of this analysis, it is recommended that a combination model reflecting problem-centered and teacher-centered approaches be adopted as the source of standards or guidelines for school program decisions. The teacher-centered model would, for example, represent the core set of values and ideas for organizing and deciding issues of curriculum and instruction. The problem-centered model would represent a desirable area of functioning and mode of operation to be selected for periods of time or certain activities at the discretion of the teacher. The transcendence potential of the problem-centered model, as compared with the teacher-centered model, would require that teachers select this option often.

Naturally, in a real-world analysis, other issues (such as local politics, talents and dispositions of teachers, and community expectations) would need to be taken into consideration. But, by and large, the analysis would proceed in a fashion similar to that outlined here.

Issues of Validating
The social humanities view of educational decision-making has a number of key features. It offers a pluralistic evaluation framework that is comprehensive in its concern for a number of competing forces. Ethical matters are not considered as a separate issue but remain integral to the analysis. The approach recognizes the cognitive and affective limits on the rationality of humankind and relies on a process of "muddling through" to reach a decision rather than adopting a more tidy but less realistic linear approach. An evaluation strategy is offered that provides for the use of alternating patterns of normative and descriptive analysis. Basically, a balance is sought between the

standards implied in normative analysis and the facts of the real world as suggested by descriptive analysis. Social humanities has as its goal the development, accumulation, and analysis of normative and descriptive information to be offered in a mode which permits educational decision-makers to achieve as much of the ideal as is possible. The role of science in this process is not to replace but to inform intuition and humanistic judgment. The humanities similarly serve as a source of direction and conscience in informing the educational decision-maker's intuition.

But how does one confirm the validity of a particular type of analysis or decide that one kind of analysis is better than another. And, since the social humanities view relies on reaching a sense of balance or harmony among several competing forces, how likely are we to choose well? After all, compromise and mediocrity are considered by some to be first cousins. The issues raise more questions than answers. One could look to principles of the marketplace and to rules governing the political process for possible answers. Here several different analyses could be developed and offered for general discourse and debate. A particular analysis would be validated on the basis of its preference in the eyes of decision-makers on the one hand, and its estimates of likely acceptance by clients and the public on the other. Some might prefer a more social-psychological path in searching for a resolution of this issue. Perhaps Chris Arygris' work on intervention strategies and the role of the consultant-analyst might provide leads. He suggests that generating valid information, helping people make free and informal choices based on this information, and striving for internal commitment once choices are made are proper roles for consultant-analysts who intervene in organizations with the intent to change them in some way.[18]

On the issue of balance, since the nature of the applied sciences of educational policy and administration require that practical issues be addressed, decisions be made, and action taken, immediacy becomes a necessity and bounded rationality becomes a reality. An educational decision-maker cannot take the best solutions which address the problems of social equality, for example, and hold on to them until the world is ready to accept them. Rather, decisions must be made in the face of reality. Changes are evolutionary and progress gained today, when added to that of tomorrow, moves one closer to goals or ideals. The pluralistic framework offered as a guide to evaluation seeks to test the tension between the opposing forces of action and control with the intent that the ideal is approached a little more with each decision that is made. Nonetheless, this balance among competing forces is delicate. Any one factor which over a period of time is over or under-emphasized results in an eventual decline in each of the other factors. Perhaps the Chinese philosophy of tien-jen-heh-yi (the embodiment of heaven and man into one) and of Chung Yung (The Golden Mean) can help us to understand better the nature of harmony and balance in educational decision-making. This is the doctrine of "half and half" proposed by Tsesse, a grandson of Confucius. Lin Yutang's comments on realism and idealism illustrate aspects of this doctrine.

> Mankind seems to be divided into idealists and
> realists, and idealism and realism are the two
> great forces molding human progress. The clay
> of humanity is made soft and pliable by the
> water of idealism, but the stuff that holds it
> together is after all the clay itself, or we
> might all evaporate into Ariels. The forces
> of idealism and realism tug at each other in
> all human activities, personal, social and
> national, and real progress is made posssible
> by the proper mixture of these two ingredients
> so that the clay is kept in the ideal pliable
> plastic condition, half moist and half dry,
> not hardened and unmanageable, nor dissolving
> into mud.[19]

Educational administration is an applied field concerned with
the professional problems of education. As Hill suggests, "While
no less concerned about the maintenance, transmission, and
extension of knowledge than are the academic professions, the
applied professions also assume responsibility for managing ongoing practical processes and for seeking and implementing
solutions for concrete, practical problems."[20] Applied fields
face the problem of integrating issues of fact and value in
decision-making activities. Significant further developments in
our field await greater acceptance of the importance of this
problem. Perhaps adopting a social humanities view as suggested
in this article can help us progress more rapidly in this
direction.

## FOOTNOTES

[1]It is generally recognized that the "natural history" phase of more inductive inquiry should precede as a full blown effort at developing a more deductive science. Thus, the "return" to inductive methods such as the case study are viewed by many as encouraging. See, for example, International Encyclopedia of United Science, 1939 ed., s.v. "The Technique of Theory Construction," by J. H. Woodger.

[2]See, for example, R.E. Strauch, "A Critical Look at Quantitative Methodology," Policy Analysis 2 (1976): 121-144, and E.R. House, The Logic of Evaluative Argument (Center for the Study of Evalution, University of California at Los Angeles, 1977).

[3]See, for example, F.S.C. Northrup, The Logic of the Sciences and the Humanities (New York: The Macmillan Company, 1948).

[4]R.D. Gastil, Social Humanities (San Francisco: Jossey-Bass Publishers, 1977). Gastil's pioneering proposal for establishing a discipline of social humanities is seminal to this discussion. The context of his analysis is that of broad policy, particularly as it affects national and international developments. Though true to his basic ideas, many liberties are taken in articulating the social humanities view within the context of education. Any defects in my analysis, therefore, should not be attributed to Gastil.

[5]Ibid., pp. 109-121.

[6]Despite this pedagogical distinction, eminent scholars have long since suggested that policy and administration are confounded both conceptually and in practice - a conclusion generally accepted by practicing "policy-makers" and administrators. Freidrich, for example notes: "Public policy, to put it flatly, is a continuous process, the formation of which is inseparable from its execution. Public policy is being formed as it is being executed, and it is being executed as it is being formed. Politics and administration play a continuous role, in both formation and execution, though there is probably more politics in the formation of policy, more administration in the execution of it." C.J. Friedrich, "Public Policy and the Nature of Administrative Responsibility," in Public Policy, C.J. Friedrich and E.S. Mason, eds. (Cambridge: Harvard University Press, 1940), pp. 6-7. Simon notes: "Recognition of this distinction in the meanings of 'correctness' would lend clarity to the distinction that is commonly made in the literature of political science between 'policy questions' and 'administrative questions'. These latter terms were given currency by Goodrow's classic treatise, Politics and Administration, published in 1900. Yet neither in Goodrow's study nor in any of the innumerable discussions that

follow it have any clear-cut criteria or marks of identification been suggested that would enable one to recognize a 'policy question' on sight, or to distinguish it from an 'administrative question'." H.A. Simon, Administrative Behavior: A Study of Decision-Making Processes in Administrative Organization (New York: The Macmillan Company, 1950), pp. 53-54. The Goodrow reference as cited in Simon is: F.J. Goodrow, Politics and Administration (New York: Macmillan, 1900).

[7]J. Rawls, A Theory of Justice (Cambridge: Harvard University Press, 1971).

[8]See, for example, S. Bok, Lying: Moral Choice in Public and Private Life (New York: Patheon Books, 1978).

[9]The author agrees with Lindblom, Cohen and March, Allison, and others that decision-making is not nearly as rational a process as is typically portrayed in the literature. C.E. Lindblom, "The Science of Muddling Through," Public Administrative Review 19 (Spring 1959): 79-88; M.D. Cohen and J.G. March, Leadership and Ambiguity: The American College Presidency (New York: McGraw Hill, 1972); G.T. Allison, "Conceptual Models and the Cuban Missile Crisis," The American Political Science Review 63 (1969): 684-718. Indeed rational models are normative views of the world. In any event, the steps outlined here tend to come into play in one form or another in decision-making.

[10]An organizational example dealing with the example of centralization and decentralization in a secondary school, can be found in T. J. Sergiovanni and F. D. Carver, The New School Executive: A Theory of Administration, 2d ed. (New York: Harper and Row, 1980), pp. 321-25.

[11]A similar analysis could be conducted to help a state department develop accreditation of educational program policies or policies to guide the consulting services they extend to local school districts, or to assist funding agencies develop policies for determining programs worthy of support or in analyzing other broad policy issues related to educational programs.

[12]See Chapter 13 in, T.J. Sergiovanni and R.J. Starratt, Supervision: Human Perspectives, 2d ed. (New York: McGraw Hill, 1979), pp. 250-66.

[13]See, for example, A.H. Maslow, "Some Basic Propositions of a Growth and Self-Actualization Psychology," in Perceiving, Behaving, Becoming, A.W. Combs, ed. (Washington, D.C.: Association for Supervision and Curriculum Development, 1962).

[14]J. Macdonald, "An Image of Man: The Learner Himself," in Individualizing Instruction, R.C. Doll, ed. (Washington, D.C.: Association for Supervision and Curriculum Development, 1964), p. 39.

[15]Sergiovanni and Starratt, _Supervision_, pp. 257-58.

[16]See, for example, C. Lasch, _The Culture of Narcissism: American Life in an Age of Diminishing Expectation_ (New York: Norton, 1978).

[17]R. de Charms, et al., "The Origin-Pawn Variable in Person Perception," _Sociometry_ 28 (1965): 241-58.

[18]C. Arygris, _Intervention Theory and Method: A Behavioral Science View_ (Reading, Mass.: Addison-Wesley, 1970).

[19]L. Yutang, _The Importance of Living_ (New York: The John Day Co., 1937), p. 4.

[20]J. Hills, "Problems in the Production and Utilization of Knowledge in Educational Administration," _Educational Administration Quarterly_ 14 (Winter 1978): 2.

# TOWARD A CODE OF ETHICS FOR UNIVERSITY ADMINISTRATORS

## Victor L. Worsfold

## Introduction:  The Need for a Code of Ethics

As university administrators lead their universities into the
'eighties, perhaps more than ever the strictures of the times
demand an ethical stance on the part of these leaders.  For, if
the Carnegie Foundation is to be believed, "All of the major
controversies on American college campuses are centered on moral
issues."[1]  Reciting the charges of the misuses of authority, of
prejudice and discrimination in student admission and faculty
appointments, and of the misappropriation of funds, society has
begun to view universities, and consequently the institutions'
principals, with jaundiced eyes.  Moreover, as the supply of
students steadily decreases in the rest of the decade the
temptation to abuse the moral standards inherent in the laws
governing the conduct of universities may well increase.  For
while the monies required for the business of the state
universities remain tied to student body count, in an age of
diminishing enrollment, as the money decreases so the temptation
to dissemble increases.  But for educational administrators to
give in to the pressure caused by less monies is to invite not
simply further societal scorn but also societal interference in
the form of governmental supervision.  In a word, not to be
morally responsible within the university is to ensure
governmental control from without the university.  On the eve of
the creation of a federal Department of Education, one of whose
functions will already be the regulation of universities by its
control of the flow of federal funds, the need for a code of
ethics for university administrators has never been more pressing.

The context within which such a code of ethics might be
worked out would seem to be supplied by the administrative
regulations and court decisions which provide impersonal formulae
for correct procedure.  But impersonality has been confused with
impartiality so that in an effort to bring standardized solutions
to the problems of all universities the society has removed the
possibility of individual discretion on the part of university
administrators almost to the point at which institutions can no
longer develop individual characters and their leaders a sense of
personal style in their administering of these institutions.  As
the Commissioner of Higher Education in Texas has written "the
presumption seems to be that since a person who has latitude to
act has the latitude to do wrong, the danger of independent
decision (on the part of college presidents) must be removed."[2]

If independence of judgment is to be restored to university
administrators, however, their ability to be morally responsible
in dealing with the complexities of the conduct of their
institutions must be patent.  To demonstrate their moral
responsibility, university administrators must see beyond the
never-ending stream of administrative and legal guidance to the

very purposes which their institutions serve. For without this
sense of purpose administrators cannot have the vision required to
lead their institutions through the hamstringing effect of
governmental interference in the pursuit of the values their
universities must perpetuate. Thus if universities are to be
accountable to the society which they serve, nothing short of a
consideration of what is educationally worthwhile and of a morally
acceptable way of promoting this conception will do as the context
within which to frame a code of ethics for the conduct of a
university. Only by addressing these issues within its particular
circumstances can a university develop a sense of individual
identity and begin to be morally responsible to the society of
which it is a part. Administrators being at the interface between
the university and the society must take the lead in this attempt
at accountability.

Clearly these issues of educational worth and acceptable
procedures permit of both theoretical and practical approaches.
Indeed the comprehensive issues of the university's moral
accountability to the society might be addressed from both a
theoretical point of view--in what ways might a university be
morally responsible--and a practical viewpoint--in what ways does
a university become morally responsible? By comparing both
approaches to the issues of educational worth and morally
acceptable procedures within the broader issue of the university's
accountability, it is hoped that principles for a code of ethics
for university administrators which would be both theoretically
sound and practical to implement might begin to develop. But
first, the very desirability of such a code must be discussed, for
recently some have questioned this on the grounds of the
unfeasibility of such a code.

Commenting on the need for an academic code of ethics in
general, Daniel Callahan points out what might be said on behalf
of developing such a code.[3] It might remind academics of the
values to which the pursuits of academic life commit them. It
might specify the rights and duties of those who make up the
academic communities. It might provide standards against which to
begin to resolve the procedural issues involved in retention,
promotion and tenure of the faculty, help delineate the
substantive issues of the ongoing debate about the moral necessity
for excellence in teaching and research--a debate engaged in by
those within and without the university--and might even "provide
faculty members with visible standards of integrity that could
serve as a protection against the encroachments of
administrators."[4] Yet Callahan is against a code of ethics as a
means of grappling with the moral problems of academic life in
general, and so, we presume, against a code as a basis for dealing
with the ethical problems of academic administration in
particular. Arguing that he is hardly against confronting these
kinds of problems, Callahan insists that codes rarely help in
dealing with the ethical problems of professions--medicine, law
and journalism, for example--since "at best they only serve to
help formulate and make public some ideals of the professions,"[5]
and, because of the particular complexities of the pursuits of
academic life, an acceptable formulation of such a code would be

"extraordinarily hard to imagine."[6] Moreover, even if it is decided to formulate such a code, ought only academics be consulted in its devising or should not the public have a role also?

But Callahan's major objection to attempting to devise a code of ethics is its need for enforcement. What he and others like him fear most is the establishment of quasi-governmental regulatory agency to oversee the code's acceptable implementation--and with the founding of a Department of Education Callahan's agency is not so quasi![7] Yet it is precisely because such an agency has come into existence that the need for a code of ethics at least for those involved in the administration of a university seems so crucial. For because they are at the interface between the university community and the society at large, all academic administrators must cope most with the society's demands for accountability, however this notion is construed, by whatever agency demands it.

Surely it is in university administrators' best interests, therefore, to set about the task of devising a code to guide their ethical practice based on their perceptions of how best to proceed with the conduct of academic life, before the external demands become urgent commands based upon external perceptions of academic life. While there may be no internal constraint on administrators to abide by it, a code of ethics for educational administrators would establish the interests of the university as these are conceived by those who must live with them in their administration of them. The principles which might form the content within which to frame such a code are the business of this essay.

## What is of Educational Worth?

In beginning the task of devising a code of ethics for their administration, the central issue confronting educational administrators is their conception of education. Drawing on the most recent work of R.S. Peters, these administrators might argue that the traditional dichotomy between knowledge for its own sake and knowledge pursued for the sake of some practical end seems false when applied to the notion of liberal education.[8] For what ultimately matters is the student's "concern to assess the significance of the context in which he has to live his life"[9] and such an ability is likely to evolve not simply by the in depth pursuit of knowledge for the joy of mastery and intellectual discovery, nor by the apparent usefulness of particularly relevant sets of information--physics, ethics, or economics, for example-- but rather by having both kinds of knowledge presented in an interactive way so that the student learns the intellectual virtues of clarity of expression, humility before accomplishment and impartiality of mind which would inform any educated assessment of a student's human predicament. In a word, what is of educational worth at any level is the development of autonomy-- autonomy conceived to be the ability to think critically and creatively, examining justifications for beliefs and demanding reasons for proposed actions.

If such an attitude is not simply to remain a pious hope, however, university administrators must ensure that students have access to the different conceptual schemes by which knowledge is organized, that they can come to understand the criteria for truth on which these truths rest and that they can be encouraged to apply such an understanding to problems both theoretical and practical in an imaginative way. Such a construction of educational worth will cut across the diversities of purpose and organization which characterize academic life but which, traditionally, are based on a single assumption, namely, that knowledge is to be acquired for the sake of more specialized knowledge. On the view of educational worth set out here, the incremental view of knowledge as the university's purpose is replaced by a developmental view of knowledge--a view which conceives knowledge as means for the development not of some radical authenticity with its falsely egalitarian views of never acquiescing to any authority but one's own, but rather for the development of "self-origination,"[10] based on the ability to assess the authoritative quality of the instruction offered by mastery of the reasoning involved and the appropriateness of the specific belief's applicability where appropriate. Yet it is the incremental view of knowledge with which university administrators must deal as they examine the typical practice of their institutions.

Arguing their case on the basis of their responsibility to their subject-matters as their prime, if not their sole, responsibility in academic life, many faculty members and administrators would insist that any notion of educational worth which university administrators might use as an assumption underlying their modus operandi must be couched in terms of this responsibility. Indeed such faculty members and administrators will argue that the diversity of conceptions of knowledge and of standards imminent in these conceptions, together with the diversity in the kinds of organizational structure required to support such conceptions, are entailed by their responsibility to their subjects. Thus, the familiar departmental structure, with research centers attached, is justified in terms of its functioning as the guardian of these subjects' standards and, as a result, as the educative context for students. In essence, the argument amounts to the claim that to meet the departmental requirements is to meet the subject's requirements, since the latter dictate the creation of the former. What is of educational worth, in this view, is for the student to have met these requirements, thereby allowing the faculty member and administrators who hold this view to have discharged their duty to their subjects.

Now, the temptation to judge this view of educational worth as self-serving on the part of those who hold it must be resisted. For despite the abuses to which it may be subject--perhaps the worst to which departmentalization has led is the notion of their being "two cultures" amongst scientists and humanists, as if physicians and historians had nothing in common--the notion that educational worth must be tied to mastery of standards imminent in the various subject-matters is necessary to a sense of being educated in the subjects. For how else could students be said to be creatively critical in them? The difficulty is that in the inculcating of these standards, the traditional departmental organization of the university has not served the student body well. The main reasons for this turn of events is that those within the departments have taken such inculcation to be the sole end of their educational duties. As a result, students attempting to meet these standards have not been encouraged to develop autonomy, but rather what Peters calls "a slavish reproduction of the views of some authority"[11] as the achievement for their education. Thus many students have come to learn only for the sake, at best, of imitating the practices of their mentors and, at worst, of pleasing them in their every whim. Thus the popular press has come to claim that "America's colleges and universities have grievously failed to maintain minimum academic standards."[12] If this is true, then surely it cannot but be the case that it is such in part, at least, because instead of permitting students to develop critico-creative thinking at all levels of their education, universities have insisted on conformity to the dictates of their departments as the sina qua non of a university education. What is required, therefore, is an abandonment of the departmental structure and in its place a welcoming of programmatic guidelines arranged such that students may learn what they require in order to stimulate their imaginations within the boundaries created by genuine intellectual problems. Certainly such a conception will require disciplinary competence. But it also allows for interdisciplinary formulations when the solution to the particular problem at hand necessitated these. Indeed a consideration of the courses offered in the Harvard Core Curriculum reform will reveal that it is precisely this kind of thinking which informs the new courses.[13] The titles of the course listing alone seem reflective of the view outlined here.

Under Literature and the Arts, we find (a) Literature, (b) Fine Arts and Music, (c) Contexts of Culture; while Social Analysis with such course titles as Conceptions of Human Nature which examines "certain important ideas about human nature in terms of their origins in philosophy, their status as assertions in behavioral science and the social and political consequences of accepting or rejecting them,"[14] speaks for itself. Even Science with its division between courses dealing with deductive and quantitative aspects of natural science and those dealing with "the description of complex natural systems and courses that have a substantial or evolutionary component,"[15] seems to conform to the idea of disciplinary competence within an interdisciplinary context.

Thus, with respect to what is of educational worth, university administrators, if they are to be morally responsible, must see to it that their curricula are reflective of a principle of balance--a principle which realizes the natural interaction between knowledge which is pursued for its own sake and knowledge pursued for the sake of some instrumental end such as the interdisciplinary solution to some practical issue about living well. By insisting on such a principle as the basis of educational worth, university administrators can do justice to the dictates of the subjects their faculties teach. More importantly, however, in effecting such a principle, administrators can address

the need for students' autonomy in decision-making which the
quality of life to which students must aspire, demands.

## A Morally Acceptable Administration?

Following from the need to arrive at such a principle,
university administrators, in the conduct of their administration
would seem to need to consider a multiplicity of opinions--in
theory, at least. At its best, a university, as Lord Ashby has
reminded us is "a society of scholars who agree to cooperate to
effectively advance and transmit knowledge,"[16] and we might now
add, so that autonomy might be gained by those who are students of
the knowledge. But, Ashby insists, despite this cooperation, or
perhaps because of it, "administrators must administer."[17] Thus,
administrators must not succumb to indecision because such a lack
of decision constitutes an amelioration of the strain that comes
from always being "in the driver's seat." For such indecision on
the part of administrative leaders makes for a drift toward
indecision by all who must make decisions in the academic
community. Thus, educational administrators must find principles
which are faithful to the dictates of their posts of leadership
but which account for the cooperative nature of the institutions
which they head. In theory, what is required, therefore, is an
ethics of coordination.

The task of university administration can best be
characterized as an attempt to balance the component parts of the
institution so that the institution's cohesion is preserved and
its purpose furthered. Only in this way can the administration
realize integrity of conduct. But Lord Ashby declares the
vitality of a university "depends on conflicts"[18]--conflicts which
generate disequilibrium whose continual resolution is the
administrator's task, thereby returning the university to a state
of stability. It is in pursuit of such stability that university
administrators must be willing to make decisions in such a way
that they are seen to care for those affected by the decision so
that the vitality which characterized their initial willingness to
be critical does not die. Thus administrators can continue to
maximize the contribution of their faculties, while maintaining
their own integrity as supportive individuals themselves. In
moral terms this means that administrative conduct must be
informed by such notions as a concern for others, fair treatment
and a sense of impersonality in such treatment.

Writing about the art of administration, Kenneth Eble has
said that "nothing is so necessary to administrators as an
understanding of and caring for human beings."[19] In the academy
such a concern for others surely amounts to the ability to
understand students' and faculty members' needs, an understanding
of and willingness to accept the ways in which these individuals
develop the satisfaction of their needs, and a respect for the
dissatisfaction which eventuates when these needs are not
satisfied. Central to this kind of concern for others, however,
is a concern for self. For how effective administrators are
depends upon what they have made of themselves, upon what choices
they have made, and perhaps most importantly upon how they go
about their administration--their personal styles. It is only

from a sense of confidence in themselves and their ability to execute the tasks of leadership that university administrators can exert the kind of authority which is informed by a concern for others.

Yet the concern for others which university administrators must evince, must be evidenced fairly. Thus, in acknowledging the conflict endemic to the life of a university, administrators must be willing to permit the members of their institution the maximum amount of freedom of self-expression compatible with a like amount for all. This means that each member of the university community can exercise the rights which constitute the role each plays in the educative process. Thus the university administrator has a duty to guarantee, for example, that the faculty's rights in deciding about appropriate curricular demands are not abridged by students' demands for oversight of these, or that students' rights to due process are not abridged by a desire to protect particular faculty members from embarrassment. Most importantly, administrators have duties to each other to monitor the use of the discretionary authority that pertains to their office in order to ensure that its exercise is justifiable in terms of furthering the stated purpose of the institution. In essence, then, addressing a concern for others, _fairly_, seems to amount to a willingness on the part of university administrators to conduct their institutions with the impartiality necessary for its perpetuation to the mutual advantage of all its members. Fairness demands this kind of distributive justice from those holding office in the university.

In addition to demanding this kind of impartiality of treatment, a morally acceptable academic administration calls for a certain kind of impersonality of outlook. Intuitively, talk of impersonality may appear totally contradictory to our earlier insistence on the need for administrators to exercise a concern for others in their leadership. Yet, this concern for others is not to be compared with therapy or even friendship. Rather, it is the realization that each individual in the university is worthy of consideration, not because the individuals work for their educational leaders and so require pampering, but because the institution has a set of goals which the leader represents and therefore must be at pains to identify and describe clearly and persuasively to all so as to avoid dissension and promote a commonality of purpose. Thus, the members of an academic community are not so interested in each other as persons as they are in the joint pursuit of a commonly held set of goals. To borrow from R.S. Downie, the framework within which education is conducted might be somewhat Platonically characterized as "the eyes of each look toward a third thing--(the purpose of the university)--and it is only by reflection from it that they see each other at all: the discipline of (the purpose) requires them (the members of the academic community) to look at _it_, and only out of the corner of the eye, as it were to look at each other."[20] To the extent that this construction of the administrative framework is accurate, the administrator's attitude must be impersonal in character.

In theory, then, the university administrators' ethics of

coordination must be exercised in an impersonal framework, in which the administrators must demonstrate a blend of impartiality and a concern for the self-expression of others. It is this apparent contradictoriness of attitude which is required of university administrators that may provide something of an explanation for why educational administration is so difficult to execute and is so shunned by many faculty members. Furthermore, the kind of moral balancing of priorities which the coordination of the members of a university demands--indeed, on occasion, the kind of self-effacement on the part of educational administrators which the development of administrative skills in others may call for--can lead to much administrative abuse in practice. By devaluing the sense of impersonality which their administration morally requires of them administrators may come to treat members of the academic community as objects of manipulation rather than as individuals with opinions and aspirations. Moreover, a diminution in their concern for others can lead administrators to overbalance in their enthusiasm for taking the initiative, or attempting to be persuasive, so that their insistence that the purposes of the institution are right can so easily move from an ethically justifiable stance to one of rank authoritarian insistence, unless kept in check by the thinking of their academic community. Finally, should they pervert the demand for impartiality with respect to their decisions, university administrators risk the possibility of turning the ethics of coordination into the practice of injustice. In dealing with the reward system of their institution, for example, university administrators must take the lead to ensure that the systems of reward fairly reflect the stated goals of the institution. It is Eble who has warned administrators who must work with institutional reward systems which are ill-fitting of their institution's goals, which pose constant threat to job security for the untenured, and which arouse competition, fear and even jealousy, that such an adjudicatory task is as complex as any an administrator is likely to face. For it is the reward system which "affects notions of self-worth central to the well being and performance of faculty."[21] If administrators fail to coordinate the reward system ethically, that is, act in a partial way with respect to faculty, then they may justifiably be charged with injustice. And it is precisely such allegations which constitute perhaps the typical response of faculty to university administration and which are most frequently couched in terms of Machiavellianism.

In the course of the exercise of their leadership, administrators must often make decisions and set priorities which are perceived to pervert the nature and purpose of academic life, and serve particular institutional interests, usually alleged to be the administrator's own. To continue, and make specific, the example of the reward system--it is not unusual for particular faculty members to be awarded tenure on grounds which, while they may rely on an adequate interpretation of tenure criteria, give one desideratum of a tenured faculty member--excellence in teaching, say, more weight than another--brilliance of research productivity, for example. Instead of accepting the

administrator's claim that in her or his view, excellence in
teaching requires balancing against brilliance of research if the
university is to continue to attract students, those who feel
agrieved by the decision (normally because their man did not get
tenure) accuse the administrator of plying academic politics. As
a result, trust in the administrator's judgment, which alone
allows the administrator credence with the faculty, is vitiated.
Charges of Machiavellianism are then brought against the
administrator, by which is meant a lack of magnanimity, a
secretive superintending of decisions, and sometimes utter
callousness. But, what those who bring such charges rarely
consider is whether the so-called Machiavellianism is, in fact,
compatible with an ethics of coordination in the practice of
university administration. Could a Machiavellian administrator
exercise his or her authority in a morally acceptable way thereby
preserving her or his integrity?

For Machiavelli, what is central to his notion of value is
that men continually change their desires and so continually value
different things.[22] What men most desire, however, is their
ability to bestow value on whatever they please. Thus matters of
value, and so moral value, are subjective in nature, though the
desire to retain the ability to designate value is absolute.
Given the subjective nature of value then, it is hardly surprising
that we find Machiavelli insisting that it is in the interplay of
each man's ambition that the tension which is typical of any
political order is to be found. For each man is ambitious to have
his or her particular desires satisfied. So blinding is the
effect of this ambition, however, that the limits to it must be
imposed on individuals from without the individual. Thus men
develop what Machiavelli calls "inganno," "ingegno," and
"prudenza" as character traits helpful in dealing with ubiquitous
ambition, and in creating a social order.

Now, what this excursion into Machiavelli's psychology
provides is a possible understanding of why individuals act as
they do in the social order that is the university. For example,
because Machiavelli thought that appearances constitute the
reality of political life, the continuing ability to exercise
political authority was "a function of what people believed,
whether true or not."[23] Thus men must develop "inganno"--the
ability to scheme, plot and even, for Machiavelli, to deceive,
precisely the kind of attributes disgruntled faculty members
allege pertain to administrators. Additionally, men must have the
ability to contrive the situations in which they find themselves
such that what they desire is what is attained--ingenuity or
"ingegno," perhaps what might be said to constitute a rough
characterization of administrative functioning. Most importantly,
men must develop "prudenza"--practical reason in the conduct of
one's political life. Martin Fleisher characterizes Machiavellian
"prudenza" as "the cool calculation of what must be done in a
given situation to accomplish one's purposes,"[24] exactly what is
required of a university administrator who understands that he or
she must administer. Thus "prudenza," in conjunction with
"inganno" and "ingegno," serves ambition. It demands what most
men find so difficult in the practice of their political lives

(and many administrators in academic life), namely, a willingness to change their ways, especially those which may have been successful in the past. When "prudenza" does function correctly, however, and men do come to understand what must be done for the proper ordering of social life, then such men are said by Machiavelli to possess "virtue," for they possess the authority of knowing what to do and how to do it. Such men are Machiavellian leaders. Our query of such leaders in university administration is whether their administrative practice can be counted morally acceptable. To put the question bluntly; is prudent administration, moral administration?

To begin to address the moral propriety of the prudent administrator the relation between prudence and the accomplishing of purpose must be emphasized. In exercising their authority as administrators, university leaders, by coordinating the desires of the members of the university based upon the purpose of the university, are, in essence, serving the university. Thus the ethics of coordination is an ethics of service--service to the purpose of the university. Acting prudently, however, may also be construed as acting in the service of the university's purpose, provided that is the goal on behalf of which administrators exercise their prudence. Prudent administration, then, can be moral administration provided its ambition is the service of the university.

Indeed, it may well be prudence, construed as Machiavelli construed it, which provides the answer to those, like Christopher Lasch, who would damn the participatory view of the exercise of authority which leadership by coordination connotes. [25] For administrators, knowing what to do, namely pursuing the university's purpose, and how to do it, does not permit of a therapeutic view of authority in which each individual affected by the decision is made to feel good about the fact that he or she has contributed their own authority in the making of the decision. Rather, by pursuing the university's purpose prudently, the administrator realizes the need to balance competing ambitions amongst the university's members on the basis of overall purpose. Thus the administrator retains the leadership role to which his authority entitles him, while evincing concern for others' ambitions. Holding to the purpose of the university will keep the administrator impartial and impersonal with respect to those over whom he or she exercises authority.

To administer in a moral manner, then, requires a principle of coordination which demonstrates respect for others, impartially and impersonally, thereby permitting the prudent balancing of interests which the pursuit of the university's purpose dictates.

## The Moral Accountability of the University

By insisting that university administrators are answerable for a conception of educational worth and a morally acceptable construction of the execution of that conception, the matter of the accountability of these leaders has already begun to be addressed. For in addressing these ideas, university administrators are, in effect, providing society with a basis on which to judge the quality of their institutional practice. As a result, these leaders can lay claim to a willingness to combat the skepticism with which so much of what they attempt is viewed. Ivan Illich, for example, has recently written that "instruction has deadened self-confident curiosity"[26] so that what is required is a society in which professionals no longer tell one what she or he needs, but individuals come to understand and fulfill their needs for themselves. In the pursuit of such autonomy, society would require deschooling--and deschooling "is nothing less than a cultural mutation by which a people recovers the effective use of its constitutional freedoms," (which, for Illich, means) "learning and teaching by men who know they are born free rather than treated to freedom."[27] In the teeth of such a polemic, university administrators can, if our conception of educational worth with its emphasis on autonomous decision-making is accepted, begin to offer a reasoned response. If the moral constraints on the effecting of this purpose are realized in addition, then university leaders can also begin to offer a response to the kind of criticism of society's practices which Lasch and Sissela Bok have recently rendered.[28]

Essentially Lasch sees cultural narcissism, construed to mean an inability to self-validate on the part of each individual, and Bok, societal lying, understood in terms of institutional willingness to engage in purveying unjustifiable untruth, as the paramount failing in today's society.[29] Both critics, however, appear to perceive the current state of society as a moral affront to personhood. Now, without wishing to diminish the university's responsibility for this regretable state of affairs, university leaders can, in comporting themselves with the moral constraints involved, begin to create of their universities the kind of moral communities which Lasch and Bok by implication appear to think desirable. For by exercising the authority of their office in a way which is morally acceptable, particularly with respect to the faculty of the university, university administrators will establish the kind of moral atmosphere which alone is conducive to the educative purpose of the university. The point of arguing for a _morally_ acceptable administration together with a conception of educational worth as the hallmarks of a responsible university leadership is that such attributes are by their very natures susceptible to justification and, therefore, to the general debate which the idea of accountability demands. Yet it may be thought that in defending educational worth and morally acceptable administrative procedures, university leaders are not in fact acting in an accountable way, since neither of these notions is neutral in nature. For by grounding their administration in what is of educational worth and what is morally acceptable, university administrators would lead their institutions in a certain direction which they believe is necessitated by the nature of their task. But it might be asked whether the university could better fulfill the dictates of accountability by remaining neutral with respect to the nature of education and the exercise of administrative authority. Such a query naturally raises another, however; namely, what would it mean for a university to remain neutral?[30]

To argue the case for the university's accountability to society in terms of the institution remaining neutral is

intuitively to argue that the university discharges its
responsibility to society by not adopting a particular position on
specific issues but, in contrast, opting for a state of affairs in
which free and open discussion pertain. Such a stance, it might
be averred, is designed to combat particular interest groups, the
military establishment or the local lettuce growers association,
say, demanding that the university support their particular
ideology; indeed this kind of stance may be adduced in defense of
those who deny the right of those who pay for higher education--
the taxpayers--to an assurance that their tax dollars will be
consumed in the education of patriots rather than radicals. Free
and open discussion, then, is considered a neutralizing antidote
to these concerns. But to proclaim free and open discussion as
the pursuit of the university is not 'not taking a stand.'
Rather, it is the replacement of one desideratum by another. And
it is this realization which leads to the conclusion that
neutrality so far from being desirable, may be impossible. In
fact, in his comments on the institutional behavior of an ideal
university, Robert Paul Wolff declares that "(A) large university
in contemporary America simply cannot adopt a value-rental
stance . . . no matter how hard it tries."[31] Thus, in this view
it becomes impossible for the university not to take a stand.

In his debate on Wolff's remarks, Kenneth Strike has,
however, pointed out that Wolff's argument is based on the
presupposition that if it does adopt neutrality then the
university is forced into the position of adopting either A or not
A as a course of action. Similarly in the case of the university
asserting an opinion, Strike argues that Wolff's position can be
schematized into either the university believes 0 or not 0. But
Strike rightly points points out that there is a third option in
both situations for the university. For "it is . . . the case
that it cannot be inferred from the fact that one does not believe
0 that he believes not-0."[33] Logic allows, in other words, that
it is perfectly possible for a person--and by extension a
university--to have no opinion, and thereby to remain neutral. In
the case where action is demanded, Strike again seems correct to
insist that it is quite possible for the university to act in
such a way that neither party to a dispute is helped or hindered
by the university's actions, so that once more the university
remains neutral. But in both these cases it must be noted that
the university is not without a stance. In point of fact, what
the university appears to be doing is playing the role of ideal
observer, that is, listening to each side and deciding for
neither, on the basis of the arguments presented.

In essence, then, while the university may decide to remain
neutral with respect to the outcome of debate on such contemporary
social problems as the Middle East crisis or abortion on demand,
it can function as a forum for the debates themselves. In doing
so, the university might indeed become an arbiter of the debate,
attempting to adjudicate the form of the debates by insisting that
they comply with acceptable procedural standards for debates
generally. The university's principle is one of impartiality with
respect to the content of the decision made, but partiality to the
procedures under which it comes to be made. Such a stance seems

theoretically sound, if Strike is correct, and practically
possible as the arguments shows. Moreover, it seems to flow
naturally from our conception of educational worth construed in
terms of the development of autonomous decision-making on the part
of students, and our demand that the execution of this conception
be morally justifiable. Such a stance permits the university a
consistency of practice between what it does internally and
externally. For what do concerns for educational worth and moral
administration amount to but concerns for impartiality with
respect to the content of the decisions necessitated by our formal
conception of educational worth and partiality with respect to
standards by which this sense of worth is pursued. By adopting
such notions as the basis of its accountability to the society the
university's leaders can avoid charges of unconcern for the
society which pays its bills and restore the principle of respect
for persons as the basis for the institution's moral stance both
within and without its domain.

Principles for a Code of Ethics

The principles which might constitute the context within
which a code of ethics for administrators could be worked out are
as follows, then,

    (i)    a principle of balance with respect to the kinds of
           knowledge which recognizes the natural interaction
           between knowledge pursued for its own sake and knowledge
           pursued for the sake of some instrumental end;

    (ii)   a principle of concern for others, allowing for
           impartiality of treatment and impersonality of outlook,
           and leading to the prudent co-ordination of interests;

    (iii)  a principle of impartiality with respect to societal
           issues, but partiality with respect to the standards of
           intellectual life.

On reflection, these principles may seem very (perhaps too)
general in nature, much as Callahan had feared. In essence, they
are ideals which, because of our insistence that they be such, are
implementable. The principles function, therefore, as the basis
on which the university's administrators can make decisions--
decisions which, when they conform to the principles, proclaim the
values the principles contain. To make such decisions does not
demand of administrators that they be philosophers. Rather, such
decision-making demands that administrators administer not on the
basis of prejudice but on the basis of well-defined principles
grounded on philosophical considerations, developed with regard
for the pursuit of the process of education. What could be more
institutionally efficient?

Embedded in this notion of administration, however, is one
last principle, namely, a principle of professional integrity
which, because it informs all the decisions the administrator must
make, provides a moral coherence and cogency to these decisions.
It is by the resolution to hold to such principles that university
administrators will create a code of ethics for themselves--and
thereby attempt to create the kind of moral community to which the
university must aspire if it is to be truly educative in the
'eighties.

100

**FOOTNOTES**

[1]_Missions of the College Curriculum: A Commentary of the Carnegie Foundation for the Advancement of Teaching_ (San Francisco, Jossey-Bass, 1977), p. 241.

[2]Kenneth H. Ashworth, _American Higher Education in Decline_ (College Station, Texas, A&M University Press, 1979), p. 89.

[3]Daniel Callahan, "Should There Be an Academic Code of Ethics?" paper presented at the National Conference on Higher Education, American Association of Higher Education, Washington, D.C., April 1979.

[4]Ibid., p. 5.

[5]Ibid.

[6]Ibid.

[7]C.F. George M. Schurr, "Toward a Code of Ethics for Academics," Unpublished paper.

[8]R.S. Peters, "Ambiguities in Liberal Education and the Problem of Its Content," in _Ethics and Educational Policy_, ed. Kenneth A. Strike and Kieran Egan (Boston: Routledge and Kegan Paul, 1978) pp. 3-21.

[9]Ibid., p. 11.

[10]Ibid., p. 17.

[11]Ibid., p. 19.

[12]Alstan Chase, "Skipping Through College," _The Atlantic_ 24 (Sept. 1978): 35.

[13]Office of the Dean, Faculty of Arts and Sciences, _Report to the Faculty and Students on the Core Curriculum_ (Harvard University, May 1979).

[14]Ibid., p. 19.

[15]Ibid., p. 27.

[16]Eric Ashby, _Adapting Universities to a Technological Society_ (San Francisco, Jossey-Bass, 1974), p. 93.

[17]Ibid., p. 98.

[18]Ibid., p. 97.

[19]Kenneth E. Eble, <u>The Art of Administration</u> (San Francisco, Jossey-Bass, 1978), p. 80.

[20]R. S. Downie, "Personal and Impersonal Relationships," <u>Proceedings of the Philosophy of Education Society of Great Britain</u> 1 (July 1971): 129-130.

[21]Eble, <u>The Art of Administration</u>, p. 143.

[22]This section owes much (to) Martin Fleischer, ed., "A Passion for Politics: The Vital Core of the World of Machiavelli." In <u>Machiavelli and the Nature of Political Thought</u> (New York: Atheneum, 1972), pp. 114-147.

[23]Ibid., p. 134.

[24]Ibid., p. 140.

[25]Christopher Lasch, <u>The Culture of Narcissism: American Life in an Age of Diminishing Expectations</u> (New York, W.W. Norton & Co., Inc., 1978), pp. 182-86.

[26]Ivan Illich, <u>Toward a History of Needs</u> (New York, Pantheon Books, 1977) p. 13.

[27]Ibid., p. 85.

[28]Lasch, <u>The Culture of Narcissism</u>, passim.

[29]Sissela Bok, <u>Lying: Moral Choice in Public and Private Life</u>, passim.

[30]This section owes something to Kenneth Strike, "Liberality, Neutrality and the Modern University," in Strike and Egan, eds., <u>Ethics and Educational Policy</u>, pp. 22-35.

[31]Quoted by Strike, "Liberality, Neutrality and the Modern University." p. 23.

[32]Ibid., p. 26.

[33]Ibid., pp. 26-27.

# THE CHANGING ADMINISTRATOR:

## DEVELOPING MANAGERIAL PRAXIS

### William P. Foster

It is common now to speak of a science of administration, or of a management science, as if the running of organizations has finally been put on a secure and safe footing. We know from our experience with schools, whose organizational problems are certainly not minor, that this is hardly the case. The school administrator, in particular, runs time and again into the theory-praxis problem: the theory of administration has little or no relevance to the development and maintenance of effective and responsive institutions, institutions that at one and the same time provide for the body and soul of their constituents.

It does not seem unreasonable to ask that American organizations - in particular, the schools - be administered and managed according to some social theory. Yet managers and school administrators perennially face the question of what the organizational response should be to such issues as equality of opportunity, effective teaching, and racial desegregation. These issues reflect the dynamics of a pluralistic society, where groups conflict with each other for positions of power, yet a science of management avoids confronting such questions with the excuse that they lie outside of legitimate science: ". . . an administrative science, like any science, is concerned purely with factual statements. There is no place for ethical assertions in the body of a science."[1]

This, however, is distinctly unhelpful when it comes to the actual management of organizations. Two writers of a popular text in educational administration, for example, note that:

> Scientific approaches to administration-while able to provide invaluable inputs to educational decision-making in the form of hard knowledge, concepts, and fundamental understanding-offer little direct help in formulating operational strategies for school administrators.[2]

In similar vein, Erickson, reviewing the "state-of-the-art" of educational administration, has concluded that "It is time, I believe, for a major reconsideration of what research on educational organization is, or should be, all about."[3] This malaise is not only confined to educational organizations: it also appears in the field of general administration.[4] Writing on the field of public administration, Denhardt and Denhardt have observed that:

> As an academic discipline, public administra-
> tion has failed to produce a coherent and

reflectively informed body of knowledge capable of connecting theory and practice . . . . [5]

A critical evaluation of management sciences and
administrative studies, including those pertinent to education,
reveals a peculiar weakness, where, in the pursuit of scientific
status, the cultural ramifications of functioning organizations
are ignored.

This paper asserts that management science in general and
school administration in particular need, as disciplines, to be
restructured and reformulated. Our society is a society of
organizations and institutions, yet we are unable to vigorously
confront the nature of the organization and its role in providing
social justice. We talk about roles and about leadership, but pay
scant attention to organizational morality and ethics. We are
unable to decode the relationship between types of administration
and school success. These should be at the heart of the study of
management.

In its present position, the science of administration cannot
adequately account for the interaction between the administration
of organizations and organizational influence over culture. A
critical theory of organizations would enhance the dialectical
growth of the individual in society. Such issues as class,
structure, organizational cultures and the formalization of reason
do, however, need to be considered. These aspects of culture and
society can be studied from the point of view of the
rerationalization of organizational forms - that is, by examining
social processes in light of their relevance to organizations in
order to provide the knowledge needed to manage such organizations
rationally without domination.

Our argument in this respect is threefold: one, that the
thrust of modern managerial studies has been to accept a positive
science view of management and administration, a view that results
in an inability to come to grips with the cultural performance of
organizations; two, that more significant types of questions about
the administration of organizations can be asked if organizations
are considered reflectively in cultural terms; and, three, that
administrators can begin to reconcile the theory-praxis problem by
examining the role of the organization as a social entity. We
will try to develop an argument that proposes that administration
- as a cultural science - can base its analysis of, and program
for, institutional development in a critical sociology of
management, using arguments from a variety of intellectual
endeavors, such as sociology and social linguistics, aimed at
restructuring the modern institution so that it can respond to the
needs of all groups in society.

Essentially, the argument claims that the basic problems of
running an organization - educational or otherwise - have been
ignored in favor of attempts to find a technology of management.
Administration in its most radical form involves the design of
organizational structures which meet certain redoubtable human
needs - equality, liberty, justice - and it lies with the study of
organizations and their administration to discover how modern
institutions can cope with the practical dimensions of such

issues.

## The Present Nature of Administrative Studies

The trend in this century in the field of administration has been to attempt to develop an essential technology of management, an uncritical technique. There has been a somewhat embarrassed but conscious effort to make administration a positive science. The lure of scientific status is one reason behind the concerted efforts of researchers to scientize management, but it should be remembered that a positive science of management would fulfill a strong social need for absolute control by a technical elite.

This scientization, however, must be complemented by the depolitization of administrative studies. Putting administrative management on a scientific pedestal is to remove it from the realm of ethics and the consequent debate over the politics of issues. This position has been best stated by recent Nobel laureate Herbert Simon, in his now-classic <u>Administrative Behavior</u> a volume that asserted that administration can and should avoid the practitioner's tricks and folkways in order to develop a rational and scientific footing.[6] This volume, building on, yet departing from, previous administrative theories, is perhaps the best example of contemporary trends in administrative studies. It is the beginning of the behavioral science emphasis.

Simon's volume asserted the boundaries of the rationality of man: confronted with boundless choices, man can only make limited selections; this later was termed "satisficing" in honor of our penchant for taking not the best but the most-satisfactory-at-the-time alternative.[7]

<u>Administrative Behavior</u> found its inspiration in one major source -- logical positivism.[8] The interpretation of the positivists' tenents led to the conclusion expressed in Simon's work that administrators could only be concerned with the factual verification of decisions, not with their ethical or moral content. Of importance to administration was the maximization of efficiency, not the essential rightness nor wrongness of the decisions. The perfect administrator would be one who could perfectly separate fact from value, who could easily live in the bifurcated universe Whitehead so dreaded.

Simon suggested that "rationality" was solely a cognitive function, wherein fact was divorced from value. Rationality, for him, reflects the dichotimization of fact from value, ignoring the real interrelationships between the valued-facts and factual-values, and dismissing Susanne Langer's observation that "the very idea of non-rational source of any knowledge vitiates the concept of mind as an organ of understanding."[9]

Through treating rationality only formally, administrative theorists foreclosed other ways of rational knowing. They ascribed to rationality certain limits. If rationality is composed of only the selection of "best" means to achieve prescribed ends, then it followed that man, unable to actually consider all alternative means because of incomplete information, was necessarily of limited rationality. This conception made a certain degree of sense if one accepted that particular definition proffered by these students of administration - a type of linear selection process which belied the complex passageways of our thinking-valuing organ.

Not only did some students of administration often make the rash assumption that rationality and rationalism are the same, they assumed that organizational studies can, and should, be neutral, the purpose of management lying in the determination of "how the problem is to be solved, not the solution to be adopted."[10] Neutrality, for many organizational students, was the machine that powered the unemotional process of choice-making, ignoring Horkeimer's admonition that any:

> . . . neutralization of reason that deprives it of any relation of objective content and of its powers of judging the latter, and that degrades it to an executive agency concerned with the how rather than with the what, transforms it to an ever-increasing extent into a mere dull apparatus for registering facts.[11]

Administrative study, accepting the degeneration of the rational, became concerned with asserting its status as a science. Administrative studies, it was claimed, could objectively measure and discover the inner workings of the processes of decision-making within organizations. Such a social physics had not yet come about, but was perhaps on its way:

> The field of management is now going through a metamorphosis that is paralled to that occurring in the development of all sciences. Gradually a field of knowledge breaks away from its origins in philosophy, adopts the value system of science, and finally stands as a full-fledged science in its own right. Management appears to be somewhere in the transitional process between philosophy and science.[12]

The natural sciences provided the paradigm case for managerial and organizational students. These students concurred with Simon's finding that "there are no logical differences which distinguish the sentences of one science from another. Whatever differences exist must arise from the subject matter of the several sciences, rather than from the intrinsic nature of their sentences."[13] Here was a theory of unity for all science. There is, Simon seemed to say, no logical difference between our investigations in management or sociology or psychology and those in chemistry and physics. And further, such social disciplines could profitably adopt the patterns and pretensions of their more methodologically rigorous natural sisters.

There is, Simon claimed, a difference between natural and social phennmena (for example, in degree of complexity) but these differences, he asserted, "must be dismissed as superficial."[14] The science of management could be a positive one, and Simon was its Newton. His own faith in this new science was to guide a generation of managerial students, and to set the tone for the development of the various administrative disciplines.

Simon, and his later colleague, James March, developed a number of ingenious insights into the functioning of organizations and provided, as Perrow has noted, further contributions to the structure that Weber built.[15] Yet the essential framework for the integration and development of their observations is a shaky one, and tends to prejudice the type of administrative studies that followed: "endless, witless administrations of the LBDQ, OCDQ, POS, ABC, and XYZ scales to haphazard collections of teachers and administrators,"[16] as one critic of work in the field of educational administration put it. This framework-the assumption of scientific status for this social discipline-is open to dispute. Peter Winch, for example, created something of a minor stir when he asserted in his The Idea of a Social Science and Its Relation to Philosophy, that the differences between natural and social phenomena involved transformations not simply of degree but of kind and that our social concepts are more than measurement.[17]

Winch approached the traditional goal of the German Geisteswissenschaften, the development of a "science of understanding" (as opposed to the natural world's science of explanation) but, as Richard Bernstein and Karl Otto Apel have both observed, developed more of a caricature than a picture of science. Winch, says Apel,

> . . . due to his Wittgensteinian presupposi-
> tion that the language games determine the
> limits of understanding and that any question
> can be asked meaningfully only within a speci-
> fic language game, arrives at a kind of
> monadology of different cultural systems.[18]

Bernstein emphasizes the fact that Winch's arguments do not appear to restrict a social science per se, but rather establish the preconditions for its conduct. ". . . Winch is right," says Bernstein, "when he emphasizes that, in the systematic study of some social phenomena, we must pay careful attention to the rules governing the activity of the participants and to their criteria for what counts as 'doing the same kind of thing.'"[19] Yet we do find in the science of management a disposition to apply scientific technique and methodology uncritically to obscure problems without considering the presuppositions that undergird the field. Mintzberg, a management scientist, underscores this argument when he talks about the future of managerial science:

> In his search for elegance the management
> scientist has hindered his ability to
> participate in solving policy problems.
> Without corrupting his science, the management
> scientist must be prepared to forego elegance,
> to adjust his technique to the problem rather
> than searching for problems that fit the
> technique. (Emphasis added.)[20]

The radical transformation of administrative studies would involve first, I believe, the recognition of the possibility of differing organizational forms, each reflecting to some degree that particular culture in which they develop. This recognition requires understanding rather than explanation. With this understanding, the possibility of reforming the administration of American organizations becomes a reality, for the regularity and predictability of administrative decision-making, of organizational life itself, is a human regularity, one bound to the nature of culture and of thought. It is, in essence, a hermeneutically derived regularity.

In assuming that organizations must behave in regular and predictable fashion according to rules that we presume to know, management scientists face the possibility of two choices: either people are of a limited rationality (because they will, on occasion, ignore or circumvent rules to be followed) or else our system of observation is incomplete - there are rules which people follow which we have not "discovered." If administrative scientists and organizational theorists could, however, study the nature of administration and of organization from a cultural perspective, looking for the ethnographic details that give the organization life, what a difference in our understanding of organized man that they may make.

For one thing, it may allow us to reconsider the relationship between our educational system and greater social-economic system of which it is a part. If we look at much of the current science of organizations, we find that certain social assumptions are present. There is, for example, the assumption that management study not only simply provides information to policy makers but provides wise information. "Wisdom" now becomes a function of organizational analysis; it is derived through the rational study of alternatives suitable to organizational growth, rather than through any individual valuational processes.

At the heart of much administrative science there is a confusion of what Northrop termed the theory of natural science, the theory of social science, and the theory of norms.[21] Social theory, designed to describe the "as is" in society is confused for normative theory - the "should." This leads to such a conception of management science as Simon's later assertion that it is a "meta-technology" designed for the objective application of technological systems.[22] Such aspects of administrative studies reflect the dominant thought in the field, reflecting Northrop's "primitive concepts and postulates" which define our vision of man.

In educational administration, particularly, we have become concerned with the science of administration as it impacts solely on administrators. What, for example, is the "scientifically" appropriate style of leadership for a given school? How should our school "climate" be measured? What does the literature advise about "motivation"? These concepts point to a concern with the development of administrative techniques rather than with an examination of the basic process or organizing relationships between people. The question becomes what are the primitive postulates which underlie our notions of organization and administration? The study of organization and administration needs to be placed in context: schooling occurs in a historically developed social system with its own peculiar economy, polity, and sociology. Can we understand the wise administration of schools, for example, without understanding the social context? And if the social context can be looked at in relationship to organizations, then administrators will have taken the first step in finding valid operational strategies, in finding praxis.

## The School as an Administered Organization

Managers generally are notably ambivalent to the findings of management scientist and for, I think, the notable reason that administrative studies have provided little help in dealing with the basic problems of organizations.[23] Looking at administration as a cultural science may assist in this regard - not in providing firm rules of behavior but in providing illustrations of the theory and praxis that may underlie our conceptions of organization.

The reformulation of administrative studies would require the new administrator to become conscious about the interrelationships that may occur between the social arena and the organization in question, and to recognize through a reflective bracketing how the primitive concepts of his science may covertly serve these social needs.

The school may be an organization ripe for such an administrative analysis. This would involve viewing the school as an organization in a cultural and historical milieu in an attempt to relate the objective need for schooling with social and economic realities. This, it must be asserted, is necessary to a fully administrative understanding of the organization-in-time. The educational administrator must ask, "Manage for what end?" Why do schools, for example, tend to dominate certain (underclass) children, perhaps without even realizing it? It is clear that for many children, including minority children, schools are places of success where the future glows bright. But for many others, it is the uncertain and unhappy place that so much of the literature describes. What is it about schools organizationally - and a simple concept such as "mindlessness" doesn't explain it - that allows the success of certain groups and the failure of others despite the attempted equalization of resources? Who wins in the educational game, and why? It is these questions, I think, that are the significant ones for educational administrators. It is true, of course, that administrators are faced with such seemingly "clear" issues as building maintenance and school construction but there are few administrators, I think, who have considered even these aspects of administration apart from their social and political implications - does not school construction impact with the sensitive areas of residential segregation? Considering the more basic issues is of prime importance to the practicing administrator.

Many of the issues are political and sociological in character, but without the possibility of administrative intervention they remain only interesting observations. Administrative science, especially in schools, can be a science of praxis - that is, encouraging practical action, grounded in theory, by practical persons. This is social action, designed for social betterment rather than organizational maintenace.

There appear a number of issues which the science of administration has not yet dealt with, but which remain very much present in the actual administration of schools. While we can only hint at some, the examination of these may perhaps provide a glimpse of the way in which administration as a cultural science might be structured.

There are four major assumptions that lie behind the discussion that follows and which indicate the directions in which a reformulated administrative science might go:

1. The prime managerial issue in our time has been the problem of equalizing opportunities for individuals through organizations. This has been true racially, economically and educationally. Even in the private sector this issue remains, as evidenced by unionization activity and such slogans as "equal pay for equal work."

2. Organizations are transition points between the individual and the social collective. That is, they shape individual performance so that it conforms to social norms.

3. Administrators and managers are capable of changing organizational structures in significant ways: thus they are capable of modifying the requirements organizations put on individuals.

4. The field of administration, particularly educational administration, has much to profit from looking at related social disciplines, e.g., sociology, history and sociolinguistics. The information these disciplines convey provides a basis for the rational assessment of needed organizational change in terms of providing a liberating praxis.

Given these assumptions, the changing administrator can address some of the very basic issues which confront a rational administration of organizations. For the school administrator, these issues will have to do with the very nature of schooling itself: only by confronting a critical assessment of schools can there be any kind of dialectical growth wherein steps to greater provision of equality by organizations can be taken. The first question asks, what is the role, purpose or function of schooling in our society? The second asks, why do schools impact differently on certain groups? If an administrator can confront these issues to his or her own satisfaction, then individual steps can be developed to improve the organizational functioning. None of this, it should be stressed, means the abandonment of the traditional areas of administrative expertise - planning, coordinating and so on; it does mean placing these in a meaningful context so that they become value-full and purpose-full. It is the solution to be adopted that matters. Administrators in such important institutions as schools cannot afford to ignore the realities of class and race as they are affected by the organization. The analysis that follows is offered as a preliminary statement of possible directions that administrative studies might take in an effort to rerationalize our institutions.

There is, Aries has pointed out, a definite and unavoidable

connection between the rise of formal schools and beginnings of the class system.[24] As it developed, the conjugal family was shaped and molded to fit the needs of evolving industrial society.[25] This, in turn, was to be a factor of some importance for the structuration of schools. the very concept of a conjugal family diminished in importance the traditional authority structures (the "line"), weakening the ties that provided normative stability and allowing for the frequent acceptance of social innovation.

The combination of this shift in authority with the rise of nationalism and then industrialism provided the school with a role as an arm of social control. Knowledge became linked to class structure: ". . . what had been virtually unrestricted education (before the eighteenth century) became a class monopoly the symbol of a social stratum and the means of its selection."[26] The school became the link between individual and society, and as the American society became more complex, so did its need to control the educational process. Everhart reports that:

> The growth and transformation of organized American education is the story of change from an informal, loosely structured, discontinuous educational process to a school system that was both formal and explicit, increasingly centralized, and based upon greater continuity and flow from one unit to the next.[27]

The difference, as Kaestle has observed, was that later schools, unlike their colonial forbears, became critical for literacy, career training and cultural transmission.[28]

The school became the primary means for the organization of a class system supporting the new nation-states:

> The old society concentrated the maximum number of ways of life into the minimum of space and accepted, if it did not impose, the bizarre juxtaposition of the most widely different classes. The new society, on the contrary, provided each way of life with a confined space in which it was understood that the dominant features should be respected and that each person had to resemble a conventional model, an ideal type. . . .[29]

The school began to exhibit a dominant structural feature: it mediated tensions between social spheres which appeared contradictory, and by linking the person to the body collective, the school could act as a means for the formation of attitudes as well as a dissipator of emerging tensions. Two spheres of human involvement structured capitalist systems - the political and the economic, and the school's role as a social link became apparent.[30] Like a feudal kingdom, the modern state has a need for legitimacy in the eyes of its subjects. Contemporary states premise this right on principles of exchange, most notably the "exchange" of political rights and protection for legitimate support by the people. The modern state does not have any right to govern based on particular extra-rational characteristics (such as divine right) and must base its legitimacy on its protection in principle of individual political rights. It is apparent that modern societies accept in principle, and have embodied in the notion of representative government, the basic conception of man's equality. This can be observed in the United States, although its applicability extends beyond our system, despite the presence of practical impediments to its full implementation both here and elsewhere. But this version of equality is apparent only in the political sphere; under a capitalistic system the economic sphere is generally free from political intervention, except at the point where the economic sphere begins to threaten or otherwise jeopardize the political sphere. This produces, however, a dilemma particular to modern capitalism: equal rights are interpretable only in political, and not in economic terms. But true political equality (in terms of the equal distribution of power) demands, as a precondition, economic equality. A certain tension between these spheres becomes apparent when we examine capitalistic societies; there is, for example, no overtly political solution for the disparity in the distribution of wealth but only ameliorative solutions designed in large part to dissipate the tension that the disparity creates. Federal school legislation seems to be an example of this process.

Schools are now socially necessary not only for the particular skills they may teach but also for their role as mediative agents. They are, to pursue the above example, secondary distributors of wealth, offering direct services (such as poverty-bridging school lunch programs) as well as exchange-value services (such as compensatory programs designed to improve the "marketability" of minority or underclass youngsters). Any tension caused by the realization that political equality does not yield economic equality is dissipated by these school-oriented services. In this way, the school becomes an arm of the state, allowing for the social normalization and routinization of modern capitalism.

Had societies evolved in a different fashion, undoubtedly some other institution could have performed these functions. Organizationally, however, schools became admirably suited for performing socially required mediative functions because they were mandated by the state, had state-certified employees, and required the participation of, at one time or another, almost the entire population. Compulsory attendance and compulsory certification are organizational indicators that schools do in fact perform certain covert or at least not easily recognizable functions in the service of the state. This should be distinguished from those functions they perform in the service of society - the more easily recognized functions of knowledge and value transmission.

The political sphere represents the interaction of actual power configurations with ideal power conceptions: it is, in a sense, the distribution of control among the powerful tempered by awareness of ideals by the masses. Freedom and equality are, of course, two such ideals. The political sphere reflects an emphasis on the equality of all citizens, despite their class position (to the degree that they may be aware of this) and their native ability (the right-to-vote cases illustrate this). The political sphere has been governed by the recognition of a substantive rationality, i.e., a "higher order" to which human rules must be attuned. "Liberty" and "justice" and similar end points of reason suggest an orientation of this sphere, in pre-industrial times at least, to a concern with the determination of social ends. The political sphere recognizes the (potential) equality of all despite class and ability.

But the economic sphere is governed by another rationality, a technical rationality designed to uncover means without a concern for ends. The economic sphere recognizes the (actual) variability of all according to class and ability. Efficiency is the guiding word here, coupled to growth, innovation and the consolidation of profit-seeking abilities:

> The central trait of modern capitalism is to be found in its character as a system of rationally calculated, routinized production - exemplified in the formally rational principles of organization in the capitalist enterprise.[31]

The rationality here is economic rationality; the violation of rational rules in this context is considered incompetence, whereas the violation of rational rules in a political/normative context is deviance.[32] Administrative rationality is largely technical rationality.

The schools, then, to a certain extent mediate between these spheres and these competing definitions of the rational. Initially, they would tend to develop in the student an appreciation of what Horkheimer termed "objective" rationality, the substantive, person-oriented definition of the rational in which ends were objective features of desire.[33] Economic rationality - the means-to-an-end scheme - would be embedded, as Habermas has put it, within, and subservient to, political rationality.[34] That is to say that means of action - technical activity - would be dependent on ends of action - symbolic activity. The use of technical rationality could only be legitimated by reference to the substantially rational. But:

> . . . Marx showed that capitalism is the point in history where there is a reversal of the order of legitimation. This is the beginning of what in our own time has become known as the technological society. In this phase the extension of the systems of purposive rational behavior begins to legitimate itself.
> . . . The principle that lies behind today's advanced societies is not free competition but systems maintenance. Growth of industrial society has seen the extention of economic rationality into every sphere of society -

until the entire institutional configuration
can be conceived as organized for a self-
regulating production and consumption
system.[35]

Organizationally, schools mediate between the political and
the economic spheres by legitimating the separateness of the two.
However, insofar as schooling presents the political sphere, and
the ideals it incorporates, as a question amenable to technical
manipulation - as a "problem" whose solution awaits only the
development of proper technical means - then it allows the
economic rationality to escape from its former context and to
begin to guide political decisions. "Equal opportunity," for
example, becomes presented as an issue awaiting the proper
development of technical delivery systems rather than a more
fundamental question of social structure. Thus, the
organizational design of schools is such that they serve to
legitimate the state, whose existence in turn is justified by the
promise of human rights. The school functions to mediate the
tensions caused by the absence of rights in one sphere and their
presence in another, but in the act of mediation, the school
subverts the rationality of social development to the rationality
of systems maintenance. The institutionalization of the school
serves as a force designed for systemic regulation. The
institution legitimates the activity of the economic sphere by
maintaining the rationality of its separation.

This then is, I believe, the established social context of
education, about which - as an objective force - little can be
done, other than changing our economic system. But with the
knowledge of the context of schools as tension-mediating
organizations, the administrator can more readily appreciate the
political shifts and swings which occur when one sector in society
is faced with a legitimation problem requiring scholastic
intervention. In other words, the changing administrator needs to
ask, what is the relationship between curricular movements and
economic or political shifts? Is, for example, "back-to-basics"
related to a national leadership crisis where the legitimacy of
those in power seems to depend on the re-emergence of "old
values?" Such analysis can be used in the support of a reasoned
position which assesses social developments in terms of their
effect on human liberation and equality.

## The School Organization and the Individual

The new administrator will look not only at the metastructure
of the organization in society, but also at the infrastructure:
how the school as an organization mediates between the social
sphere and the individual biography and how social differentiation
is reinforced.

The concept that the organizing principle of modern society
is system maintenance explains partly the organization's
reluctance to change modes and styles of operation. Systems
maintenance, however, is, unlike previous epochs, consciously
planned through administrative decision-making. It is "direct
administrative processing of cultural tradition."[36] Habermas

says:

> Whereas school administrations formerly had to codify a canon that had taken shape in an unplanned, nature-like manner, present curriculum planning is based on the premise that traditional patterns could as well be otherwise. Administrative planning produces a universal pressure for legitimation in a sphere that was once distinguished precisely for its power of self-legitimation.[37]

The direct administrative planning of the curriculum can be analyzed in terms of its contribution to the structuring of the class system and, in particular, in terms of the relationship between organizational and systemic requirements and individual abilities. Thus, in part because of its role as a mediating agent, the school system may be forced to reproduce curricularly the logic and rationality of the economic system (in order that competent workers may be produced); if, however, the logic and rationality of the individual (influenced traditionally by class position) is counter to the organizational logic, that individual may be forced out of the system. Educational administrators need to be conscious of the requirements that organizational rationality may put on individuals whose rationalism arises from a more relational and less analytic or heuristic perspective.[38] Schools, for example, require the display of heuristic ability: "Heuristics come before all else in school for they are the intellectual building blocks of education."[39] But a heuristic style of thought is not the only universal style even though such a pattern is apparently necessary in industrial society. A child who fails in school does so often because he is a victim of a biography formed through reactions to organizational requirements. When cultural patterns developed in the individual family are inadequate in dealing with social demands, such as changing from relational to innovative or heuristic thought, withdrawal may occur. The individual's particular biography is always pre-class; it does not depend on forms of class consciousness for its own self-definition yet must, as it develops, encounter class society and the style of cognition required by that society.

The middle class child, for example, early on learns the use and value of a context-free language; this is one in which the context of speech cannot be assumed to be known by all speakers and listeners. The relevant context must be established in the process of speaking; it must be "created" as the speaker moves from point to point. Let us say then that the middle class speaker establishes universal meanings in his speech. The underclass child, on the other hand, depends on particular meanings - those that are context-specific. The middle class child can be said to be able to move between universal and particular meanings with some ease while the underclass child is often solely dependent on context and consequently at loss in a school situation where the context of speech is universal.

Bernstein's work is seminal in this regard. He suggests

that:

> . . . it is reasonable to argue that the genes
> of social class may well be carried less
> through a genetic code but far more a
> communication code that social class itself
> promotes . . . between the school and
> community of the working-class child there may
> exist a cultural discontinuity based upon two
> radically different systems of communica-
> tion.[40]

Yet the important point for administrators is that such
communicative strategies - despite their apparent inadequacy in
the middle class context of the school - are not inherently
irrational or illogical. Labov, for example, finds that:

> . . . in fact, Black children in the urban
> ghettos receive a great deal of verbal
> stimulation, hear more well-formed sentences
> than middle-class children, and participate
> fully in a highly verbal culture. They have
> the same basic vocabulary, possess the same
> capacity for conceptual learning, and use the
> same logic as anyone else who learns to speak
> and understand English.[41]

A child whose style of thought is practical and traditional may
not develop the standard English facility needed by a heuristic-
oriented teacher; that teacher, in turn, may find certain
linguistic difficulties in the child's community.
Both the teacher and the child live in logical universes:
the teacher, however, is required organizationally to have the
child cross from his universe into the teacher's. The school
adopts an organizational structure that is industrial, urban and
centralized in form (and anonymously individualized). A pre-class
youngster enters this structure possibly from an organizational
form which is communal, traditional and decentralized (true even
in the city). The pre-class youngster may well have an objective
rationality but this will be mediated by the school to emphasize
the absence of essential truths and to stress the formality of
reason. These factors act to introduce the child to class
society, to select the child whose circumstances pre-dispose him
to "middle classism." Access to knowledge, governed by class
position, is distributed organizationally, (and the knowledge
itself becomes distorted as it begins to reflect class interests).
For many, the situation is exacerbated by the objective
conditions in which they have been raised. Triandis and his
colleagues find, for example, that ghetto Blacks have a high
degree of "eco-system distrust," and that "in short, the economic
and social conditions of the ghetto create psychological
conditions which make adjustment to industrial or to middle-class
environments extremely difficult, if not impossible."[42] The
subjective cultures that have developed cannot accommodate the

realities of the organizational situation as this reflects its own
dominant rationality and cognitive style.

This type of information would seem to be important for
educational administrators insofar as they may wish to restructure
and reformulate within the possible limits the school
organization's requirements for children. The question is whether
differential organizational structures can be developed in
response to the knowledge developed in a number of disciplines.
The changing administrator will of necessity be concerned less
with the maintenance of formal structures than with their radical
reformulation. This requires the educational administrator to be
concerned with the development of the individual biography as this
has been influenced by organizational and social requirements. A
knowledgeable administrator, for example, will probably dismiss
the deficit or deprived theory of class and race and attempt to
programmatically regulate the educational environment so that it
can account for different cognitive/logical styles.

## Conclusion

At issue is the nature of administrative studies and their
relation to the organizational structuring of an individual
biography. If in fact such concepts as human justice, equality
and freedom are to be meaningful to us, we need to integrate them
onto the totality of our academic reflections. Administrative and
managerial theory does not do this adequately. I believe that
school administrations in particular must devise a study of
administration that asks how our fundamental organizational
structures influence social relations. How, in other words, does
the organization of schooling in this country perpetuate class and
racial divisions and allow one group to succeed where another
fails? It is not a simple matter. We need to address questions
of rationality, of sociology, of language, but not from the sole
perspective of a philosopher, a sociologist, or a linguist. We
need, Habermas has said and as Giddens seems to say, to
rationalize our institutions so that they serve human ends.[43]
This requires abandoning a "natural" science of administration and
formulating a new cultural science.

It seems no longer profitable to think in terms of a single
rationality in organizations. It is more productive, I believe,
to think in terms of different styles of thought and different
forms of rationality, each influenced by one's surrounding culture
and social conditions. It seems no longer profitable to
concentrate on managerial neutrality in implementing decisions.
Administrators must take a value position and defend it to their
constituency. In short, a positive science of administration will
be empty indeed without some type of dialectical movement towards
adjusting and improving our institutions. If administrators can
be taught the need for praxis, and for the relevance of social
analysis, at least a significant debate can begin.

Disparate themes, reluctant to join together, have been
broached here; the pertinence of the analysis to the area of
administration may appear stretched, yet I think it is a necessary
stretching, given our present orientations in the field of
educational administration. Our question must be: Is it possible

to develop in this century a praxis of administration, one that, in combining theory and practice, attempts to overcome in organizations and institutions, the structural weaknesses that result in inequality?

## FOOTNOTES

[1]Herbert A. Simon, _Administrative Behavior_, 2d ed. (New York: The Free Press, 1965), p. 253.

[2]Thomas J. Sergiovanni and Fred D. Carver, _The New School Executive: A Theory of Administration_ (New York: Harper and Row, 1973), p. 4.

[3]Donald A. Erickson, "Research on Educational Administration: The State-of-the-Art," _Educational Researcher_ 8 (March 1979): 12.

[4]See Stephen Wood and John Kelly, "Toward a Critical Management Science," _Journal of Management Studies_ 15 (February 1978): 1-24; M. Hales, "Management Science and the 'Second Industrial Revolution'," _Radical Science Journal_ 1 (January 1974): 5-28.

[5]Robert B. Denhardt and Kathryn G. Denhardt, "Public Administration and the Critique of Domination," _Administration and Society_ 11 (May 1979): 107.

[6]Simon, _Administrative Behavior_.

[7]James March and Herbert A. Simon, _Organizations_ (New York: John Wiley and Sons, 1958), Ch. 6. For a far-reaching critique of Simon's thought, see Herbert Storing, "The Science of Administration: Herbert A. Simon," in _Essays on the Scientific Study of Politics_, ed. Herbert J. Storing (New York: Holt, Rinehart & Winston, 1962).

[8]As Simon says, "the conclusions reached by . . . logical positivism - will be accepted as a starting point . . . ." _Administrative Behavior_, p. 45. His citations include works by Rudolf Carnap and A.J. Ayer. Note that Simon's work "opened a whole new vista of administration theory" Amitai Etzioni, _Modern Operations_ (Englewood Cliffs, N.J.: Prentice-Hall, Inc., 1964) p. 30.

[9]Susanne Langer, _Philosophy in a New Key_, 3d ed. (Cambridge, Mass.: Harvard University Press, 1972), p. 98.

[10]Victor Vroom, "A New Look at Managerial Decision-Making," in _Emerging Concepts in Management_, 2d ed., Edited by Max S. Wortman and Fred Luthans (New York: Macmillan Co., 1975), p. 121.

[11]Max Horkheimer, _Eclipse of Reason_ (New York: The Seabury Press, 1974), p. 55.

[12]John B. Miner, _Management Theory_ (New York: Macmillan Co., 1971), p. 143. Note that Henry Mintzberg agrees that "There is as

120

yet no science in managerial work" but holds out hope for developing such a science. Henry Mintzberg, <u>The Nature of Managerial Work</u> (New York: Harper and Row, 1973), p. 161.

[13]Simon, <u>Administrative Behavior</u>, p. 250.

[14]Ibid., p. 250.

[15]Charles Perrow, <u>Complex Organizations: A Critical Essay</u>, 2d ed. (Glenview, Ill.: Scott, Foresman and Co., 1979), p. 172.

[16]W.W. Charters, Jr., "A Critical Review of Erickson's Readings in Educational Organization and Administration," paper prepared for presentation at Annual Meeting of the American Educational Research Association, Toronto, Canada, March 30, 1978, p. 11 and quoted in Erickson, "Research on Educational Administration," p. 10.

[17]Peter Winch, <u>The Idea of a Social Science and Its Relation to Philosophy</u> (London: Routledge and Kegan Paul, 1965).

[18]Karl Otto Apel, <u>Analytic Philosophy of Language and the Geisteswissenschaften</u>, trans. H. Holstelilie (Dordrecht, Holland: D. Reidel and Co., 1967), p. 56.

[19]Richard J. Bernstein, <u>The Restructuring of Social and Political Theory</u> (New York: Harcourt, Brace and Jovanovich, 1976), p. 71.

[20]Henry Mintzberg, <u>The Nature of Managerial Work</u> (New York: Harper and Row, 1973), p. 196.

[21]F.S.C. Northrop, <u>The Logic of the Sciences and the Humanities</u> (New York: Meridian Books, 1959).

[22]Herbert A. Simon, "Technology and Environment," in <u>Emerging Concepts in Management</u>, 2d ed., edited by Max S. Wortman and Fred Luthans (New York: Macmillan Co., 1975).

[23]See Mintzberg, <u>The Nature of Managerial Work</u>, p. 161.

[24]Philippe Aries, <u>Centuries of Childhood</u>, trans. R. Baldick (New York: Vintage Books, 1962), p. 335.

[25]See, William Goode, <u>The Family</u> (Englewood Cliffs, N.J.: Prentice Hall, 1964), p. 109.

[26]Aries, <u>Centuries of Childhood</u>, p. 313.

[27]Robert B. Everhart, "From Universalism to Usurpation: An Essay on the Antecedents to Compulsory School Attendance Legislation," <u>Review of Educational Research</u> 47 (Summer 1977): 502.

[28]Carl F. Kaestle, The Evolution of an Urban School System, New York City, 1750-1850 (Cambridge, Mass.: Harvard University Press, 1970), p. 186.

[29]Aries, Centuries of Childhood, p. 415.

[30]Anthony Giddens distinguishes political and economic "spheres" and continues the distinction between "state" and "society." The interpretation of his work is my own. See, Anthony Giddens, The Class Structure of the Advanced Societies (New York: Harper and Row, 1975).

[31]Ibid., p. 139.

[32]Jurgen Habermas makes this distinction in, Toward a Rational Society, trans. Jeremy J. Shapiro (Boston: Beacon Press, 1971), p. 92.

[33]Horkheimer, Eclipse of Reason.

[34]Habermas, Toward a Rational Society, p. 94.

[35]Trent Schroyer, "Toward a Critical Theory for Advanced Industrial Society," in Recent Sociology No. 2, ed. Han Peter Dreitzel (New York: Macmillan Co., 1970), p. 218-19.

[36]Jurgen Habermas, Legitimation Crisis, trans. Thomas McCarthy (Boston: Beacon Press, 1975) p. 71.

[37]Ibid., p. 71.

[38]For an overview of cognitive styles and their relation to schooling, see M.C. Wittrock, "The Cognitive Movement in Instruction," Educational Researcher 8 (February 1979): 5-11.

[39]Thomas Gladwin, East Is a Big Bird (Cambridge, Mass.: Harvard University Press, 1970), p. 231. See Gladwin's work, particularly Ch. 6, for a cross-cultural analysis of cognitive "styles."

[40]Basil Bernstein, Class, Codes and Control 1 (London: Routledge and Kegan Paul, 1971): 143-44.

[41]William Labov, Language in the Inner City (Philadelphia: University of Pennsylvania Press, 1972), p. 201.

[42]Harry C. Triandis, ed., Variations in Black and White Perceptions of the Social Environment (Urbana, Ill.: University of Illinois Press, 1976), p. 175.

[43]Habermas, Toward a Rational Society; Giddens, The Class Structure of the Advanced Societies, n.p.

# CHAPTER IV

## IS THE SCHOOL ADMINISTRATOR CAPABLE

## OF RECEIVING EFFECTIVE GUIDANCE FROM PHILOSOPHY?

### Gerald Edmund McDonald

If an administrator were asked to give a reason which justifies his advocating the use of the lecture method in his educational program, he most likely could provide a ready answer. Perhaps, he might reply that the lecture method is an accepted way of communicating a logically organized body of subject matter. If, however, he were asked to give a reason which justifies his advocating the communication of a logically organized body of subject matter, his answer might be slower in forthcoming. He might reply after some deliberation that knowledge is an end in itself worth knowing for its own sake.

Why should one question cause more deliberation than the other? The answer, it seems, is that the first reason is a common-sense reason. It is a reason, or better still, a conviction which the administrator shares in common with many of his colleagues and which a large segment of the people familiar with education endorse. Also, it is a conviction which has existed in the minds of many educators and laymen over a long period of time. The second reason is a philosophical reason. It refines the common-sense reason by giving an explanation which is the result of rigorous and logical thinking. Certainly, it is not the type of reason that an administrator easily or readily calls to mind, and it is not likely to be endorsed by people unless they uphold a particular philosophical system.

Both types of reasons can guide an administrator in directing an educational program. The common-sense reason is useful in resolving an immediate and specific problem. Since its reference to a specific practice has been determined by wide agreement, an administrator is aided by an easy and ready explanation as a basis for the practice. However, a common-sense explanation can very soon make "uncommon" sense. To the people of yesterday learning by the rod may have made good common sense; to a modern community it does not make sense at all. Furthermore, a common-sense explanation presupposes no systematic theory; it may very well be an isolated and specific solution to a specific problem. The second type of reason is useful in formulating long-range policies or in guiding an administrator in the solution of a class of problems. Since its reference to practice has been determined by rigorous and logical thinking, an administrator is aided by a considered and stable explanation as a basis for the practice. It is not an isolated explanation. Rather, it is consistent with other explanations and other practices because it is consistent with a systematic philosophy of education. Ultimately, the philosophical reason provides more consistent and comprehensive guidance for an administrator because it grows out of a systematic philosophy.

But why must its reference to a systematic philosophy be

emphasized? Why cannot a philosophical reason be consistent merely with an educational practice? The answer to this question is that an administrator needs a unifying system which will give consistent and comprehensive guidance in selecting reasons for practices in education. There may be several reasons which are consistent with a particular educational practice. They may also be philosophically inconsistent with one another, and, unless administrators can identify one of these reasons as being consistent with their philosophy of education, they may give contradictory reasons for their practices. Admittedly, a systematic theory which is remote from educational practice is no more significant to administrators than a motley group of practices for which they have no intelligent explanation. Both theory and practice are needed by them; yet only that systematic theory which actually guides administrators will be of practical value. Ultimately, the effective guidance with a systematic philosophy provides requires a philosophical reason to be referred to an entire philosophical system.

However, an objection may be raised to the above conclusions. It may be granted that unrefined common sense has a limited value for an administrator; yet it may be asserted that philosophy is too general or too speculative to be of much practical value in helping to direct an educational program. Science also may be said to refine common sense while being a more concrete, practical guide.

The answer to this objection is that philosophy and science have different functions to perform in education. Both may guide an administrator, but where science discovers facts, philosophy formulates values and criticizes assumptions. For example, science may aid an administrator in discovering the effectiveness of an educational program in achieving its aims. It may even aid the administrator in discovering the aims of other programs of interest, but it cannot formulate the aims which the administrator "ought" to have or designate those aims which are the valuable ones.

Similarly, science can aid an administrator in selecting practices which are effective in achieving the aims of an educational program, but it cannot tell which practices one "should" select. These practices, because they are chosen or should be chosen in view of the aims which had been decided upon, are now seen as values and have philosophical implications. Faced with the problem of selecting the valuable educational practices from among perplexing and oftentimes conflicting practices, an administrator is required to go beyond science to a systematic philosophy of education.

Are administrators in education receiving effective philosophical guidance? There is increasing evidence to suggest that they are not. Where they lack such guidance, their educational program lacks fundamental justification and thoroughly considered direction. Yet this lack of planning does not mean necessarily that administrators are insensitive to philosophy or that they are incapable of receiving guidance from this source. Perhaps they are not using it because of sociological, psychological or historical reasons. If administrators are capable of receiving effective guidance from philosophy, they already possess a powerful means which they could use in directing their educational program. Yet, if administrators are to be so guided, what must be determined first is the extent to which they possess a consistent body of philosophical concepts which they understand to underlie their educational practices. The extent to which administrators manifest a philosophical consistency (where that consistency is orientated toward practice) should be a proper index of the extent to which they are capable of receiving effective philosophical guidance.[1] But how can this degree of consistency be determined? Here is a problem of measurement which requires an empirical solution.

In what follows, an analysis of the logical and systematic character of philosophy is offered from which a method of solution could be devised.

Underlying the statement of the problem are two assumptions: First, successive philosophical reasons chosen by administrators for upholding certain practices in education can be judged as "consistent" or "inconsistent" with a system of philosophy. Secondly, a particular system can be ascribed to administrators. Their very eclecticism, if such be their plight, depends upon their holding this and some opposing philosophical system. If these two assumptions were groundless, the problem could not admit of a solution. Fortunately, however, philosophy provides ground for these assumptions and consequently a rational basis for a solution.

First, a philosophical system does provide grounds for determining the consistency or inconsistency of successive philosophical choices made by administrators. Among the several areas of a philosophical system is the epistemological area, and it is logically prior to the others. The other areas are logically consistent with it not in the sense that their conclusions follow immediately from principles in epistemology, but in the sense that their principles imply logically prior principles in epistemology.[2]

For example, an administrator may uphold the educational practice that occasions are to be provided in which the student develops a personal set of moral values. The administrator may give the following philosophical reason for upholding this practice: the goodness or badness of an act depends upon its consequences in the personal and social life of an individual. This is an ethical principle, and it implies the logically prior epistemological principle that the meaning of any mental response is determined by its consequences in experience. The epistemological principle comes first logically in the sense that it is more fundamental, a more basic conception. The ethical principle in turn looks to it for its logical justification.

Since epistemology is logically prior to the other areas within a philosophical system, it designates or identifies the system. An epistemological view identifies the system by implying characteristic views in other philosophical areas of that system. For example, given the epistemology of pragmatism, the ethics of pragmatism, the philosophy of man of pragmatism, and the pragmatic view in other philosophical areas in the system are identified.

Consequently, the philosophical choices of administrators can be judged to be consistent or inconsistent according to whether they accept or do not accept the appropriate views within other areas of a system. The choices of administrators can be judged in terms of a system, and if a particular system can be ascribed to administrators, then the consistency or inconsistency of their choices can be ascribed to them.

However, how can a philosophical choice be shown to belong to a systematic view within a philosophical area? The answer is that the choice must be shown to be logically consistent with a philosophical viewpoint in that area. Fortunately, each viewpoint in an area possesses an internal consistency in the sense that its conclusions are correctly drawn from its principles. A philosophical choice, an ethical choice for example, can be shown to be logically consistent with a distinctive system of ethics. To identify such a choice as belonging to a system of ethics is to place it in the logical context of that system.

Secondly, a particular philosophical system can be ascribed to administrators because an epistemological viewpoint, the viewpoint which implies a system of philosophy, is internally consistent and allows an epistemological choice made by an administrator or a group of administrators to be identified with a particular system of epistemology. Moreover, there are notions in opposing epistemologies which are at issue with one another regarding the same epistemological topic. The nature of truth is such a topic and opposing epistemologies have their respective notions about the nature of truth. These notions are representative in the sense that they are logically consistent with only one system of epistemology. They can be phrased as possible reasons for upholding an educational practice. The reason which an administrator chooses as acceptable, can logically constitute one's choice of epistemology and system of philosophy.

This analysis which borrows heavily from the logical and systematic character of philosophy is designed to provide a rationale for an instrument of research. While the specific character of the instrument will depend upon the appropriate practices of a particular area and level of education together with the group to be tested, its generic character will be determined by philosophical assertions taken from leading philosophies of education in the United States. These assertions will be formulated as possible reasons or assumptions for upholding a specified number of educational practices. Certain of the assumptions will be distincly representative of their respective system of epistemology. Others will refer to one or more areas within opposing philosophical systems.

## FOOTNOTES

[1]The word effective in this context denotes "having an effect" upon educational practice. The quality or value of that effect is discussed in the latter portions of this article.

[2]It should be noted that for realists an intelligible reality which is antecedent to the knower is the starting point in philosophy. Their epistemology follows as a critical defense of their position and constitutes a logical starting point.

# PLATO'S "PHILOSOPHER-KING":  POSITION IMPOSSIBLE

## Van Cleve Morris

In his master work, <u>The Republic</u>, Plato held out a special place for those individuals who had risen to the top of the political heap and who, through a life-time of service to their countrymen, were finally rewarded with a position of ultimate leadership in the perfect state. He called them "philosopher-kings," and had in mind for them a mode of leadershop which combined the characteristics of thoughtful reflection on the one hand and executive decision-making on the other. In this union, thought Plato, was the perfect blend of reason and action so necessary to the functioning of a truly democratic state, the perfect republic.

Alfred North Whitehead once remarked that "all of Western philosophy is but a footnote to Plato." If so, it must be reported that very little thought has been given in either our philosophical or political literature to just how the philosopher-king role would get worked out in practice. Instead, most of our philosophical footnotes to Plato have been directed to his transcendent ideas, to the definition of ideal forms like love, justice and friendship, and sometimes to his bizarre educational ideas. Little has been said about his politics and specifically how the top person, the philosopher-king, would function in the political apparatus.

I have given some thought to this problem over the last several years, largely as an outgrowth of my experience as a middle-level executive in a large university, a dean of a college of education. Since a university is an attempt at a perfect republic--what one might call the academic's paradigm answer to the politics of the wider society--it may be worthwhile to investigate somewhat more closely how philosophy and executive leadership combine in the real world.

Now obviously a dean is not a king, but there is nonetheless a sense in which a dean wields power, however modest it may be. I am using Plato's word 'king' in a metaphoric, generic sense, referring to all administrators from low to high, up to and including the king, who make decisions and carry responsibility for the functioning of the whole. It is this element of decision-making responsibility which sets this group off from the remainder of the citizenry. Is Plato correct in recommending that philosophers occupy the administrative chair?

I have no idea whether philosophers are suited to this kind of work nor am I sanguine about Plato's assumption that philosopher-kings are good for the republic. What I have encountered, however, is more disquieting and disturbing, namely, that contradictions between the two roles are unavoidable. In their most extreme form, these contradictions represent a collision of values which Plato may never have thought of. For the present purpose, I would like to focus on three spheres

of conflict which seem to me endemic to the marriage of philosophy
with educational administration.  I will state them briefly,  and
then comment on each:
    First,  we  need to restudy the anomaly of treating people as
both ends and means.
    Second,  it  is  important  to  reexamine  the  contradiction
between  open communication in the academic community and  closed,
restricted information management in the administrative suite.
    Finally,  we  need  to  look  into the possibility  that  the
philosophic  temperament  itself  may  be  inimical  to  effective
management,  and that philosophers can be successful administrators
only if they shut down their philosophical tendencies.

People As Ends and Means
    We  have come to learn,  not only from Immanuel Kant but from
our  liberal heritage,  that an ultimate human value is  to  treat
persons  as ends and never as means.  This notion is driven  deep
into  Western values,  and it comes naturally to us and  coincides
with  our  sense of fitness in this society.  There is  hardly  a
mischief so mean and abhorrent as the attempt to use people.
    However,  when one becomes an administrator, it turns out that
virtually the central feature of the job is precisely that--to use
people,  their motivations,  their drives, their ambitions, not to
mention  their  abilities,  skills and services on behalf  of  the
entire enterprise.  The function of an administrator is to run an
organization.  His  or her decisions must be measured not by  how
humane they are,  but by a more severe criterion:  How  effective
they  are  in  advancing the interests of the  organization  as  a
whole.
    A  dean,  like a baseball manager or a football  coach,  must
treat people as things,  as interchangeable parts in a machine.  A
professor may be given an asssignment he doesn't like, may be sent
on errands he does not consider part of his job,  or may be forced
to  collaborate  with colleagues for whom he has  little  respect.
The  dean must enforce these directives for the good of the entire
organization.  Sometimes,  in  extremity,  the dean may  know  in
advance  that a certain decision--for example,  a termination  for
incompetence--will  destroy  the  morale  of  an  individual
subordinate,  but in spite of this knowledge must proceed with the
decision  on  behalf  of the organization over  which  he  or  she
presides.
    It  is certainly true that an employee consents to a  certain
measure  of  manipulation merely by accepting a contract to  work.
The  signature  thereon  signifies  an  acquiesance  to  a  larger
purpose,  to which one's own personal goals must be  subordinated.
But that is just the point.  By the very fact of this consent, the
employees  are  turned  into instruments of the  corporate  group.
They  present themselves to the executive not as persons,  but  as
operating centers of skills and abilities,  assignable to  various
tasks  in  the organization.  Accordingly,  the  administrator
obliges,  and deals with them as functioning pieces of a large and
intricate mechanism.
    What  any given individual may want--especially those  things
which  contribute to a sense of self such as salary,  status,  and

intellectual respect--must yield to what everybody else, i.e., the organization, wants. By definition the administrator is the paymaster of these social goods and is put in the position of controlling the psychic income of the employee. I do not mean by this that the dean must be prepared merely to deliver bad news. Rather, the dean must be ready to sacrifice an otherwise whole and healthy human personality to the needs of the larger entity.

## Open vs. Closed Communications

Another Western value, perhaps even more troublesome to the practicing administrator, is the commitment to an open communication network. In educational work, especially in academe, we are committed to the free flow of ideas, to freedom of information, and to unrestricted exchange of findings. Choosing an academic career means to devote oneself to the pursuit of truth and to the sharing of whatever one discovers or leans in this pursuit. Among academics, there is something almost holy about the obligation among scholars not to keep secrets from one another.

This mentality, cultivated over years of training, makes it difficult for academics to work with other people. It probably explains why universities and government agencies (especially secret-prone intelligence bureaus and military establishments) have so much difficulty collaborating with one another. In the academic community itself, there is hardly a more heinous sin than withholding relevant information.

Enter the educational administrator. This person is a political functionary. His or her job is to see to it that the interests of the entire organization come first. On behalf of this loyalty, it is sometimes necessary to withhold certain kinds of information and to deal it out, piece by piece, to the people who must have it, deliberately keeping it from others, especially those who may use the information in a disruptive and destructive way. The messages that flow across an administrator's desk are of a special sort. Although not literally personal, they are nevertheless privileged, an adjective which could never be applied to any sort of information in the academic marketplace.

Is the dean's in-box a public place. Absolutely not. Administration is politics, and politics, whatever else it may be, is the exercise of power. And, as we all know, knowledge is power. Hence, the management and control of information is essential to the successful administrator. Contrast this with the ethic out of which the dean has come--an environment in which all information is open, where the term "privileged information" would have no meaning, and where everyone is entitled to know everything that everybody else knows.

The two worlds, one open and accessible, the other closed and restricted, must coexist side by side. In the passage from faculty status to administrative responsibility, this shift in commitments is abrupt and troubling. It means giving up the exhilarating fresh air of intellectual sharing in favor of the cramped quarters of protecting secrets and managing the news. Philosophers don't keep secrets. Deans sometimes must.

132

## The Philosophic vs. The Administrative Temperament

With the foregoing commentary as a backdrop, we can now begin
to see that the philosophic temperament as such may not be the
ideal qualification for administrative service. The philosopher
is the quintessential interrogator, the seeker after alternatives
and options, the explorer of the terrain of other possibilities.
In cultivating this approach to life's contingencies, the
philosopher's stock in trade is the question. Indeed, in Plato's
time, the very definition of philosophy as expressed in his
teacher, Socrates, was the art of questioning. For the most part,
we cling to this notion today. Philosophy is inquiry into
meaning, it is the exploration of understanding, of comprehending
the world. The philosopher, by training and disposition, is not
interested in making things happen. Too much has happened
already. The central task is to comprehend what past and present
events mean, not to generate new events which will require their
own analysis.

Thus, the Holy Grail of the philosopher is insight and
understanding, what we used to call wisdom. It is an awareness of
the texture and depth of events, not their consequences. It is a
comprehension of how they all fit together into a larger whole,
not how they bump into one another or lead on one to the next.
The philosopher's attention is fixed on a distant clarity. Even
when a philosopher acts, as he or she must in the course of a
life, it is tentative and provisional, forever on the lookout for
some alternative that might have been chosen instead.

An administrator's life does not lend itself to these
requirements. The administrator may have a desire to understand,
but there isn't time. Understanding can wait. By definition, the
administrator is situational, oriented to a circumstance which
calls out for resolution or redefinition. The situation may, in
the long future, be understood as part of a larger whole, but
right now it is a situation requiring movement to a new condition,
a new situation. The administrator's life is focused on this
priority of immediacy.

I think this truth was not lost on Plato. Indeed, I think
precisely because of this political focus on the immediate, he
recommended that his high politicians be capable of the longer
view. But in the hurly burly of contemporary administration--
educational or otherwise--it appears that the "longer view" may
not be all that valuable to us. The world nowadays changes so
radically so rapidly that the philosopher's curiosity as to what
it all means may turn out to be a kind of metaphysical joke. By
the time the "longer view" is in hand, the human condition has
changed enough to make that view neither true nor false, but
merely irrelevant, and the search for another "longer view" must
begin anew. And, says the administrator, if longer views are this
perishable, why then must they occupy us so much of the time?

Philosophy, or at least the philosophic temperament, can
therefore be seen as an impediment to decisive administration.
The administrator is oriented to the situtation and its immediate
features. And, of course, there must be a gathering of
information on which to act. But once having acted, the
administrator does not dwell on--indeed is agressively <u>not</u>

interested in--what would have happened if something else had been done. The second-guessing syndrome, so popular among political pundits and social commentators, is not a good trait in an administrator.

It can possibly be argued that administration itself, as a field of endeavor and as a career specialty, has come into prominence in the twentieth century precisely because our mode of social action requires a different focus. Institutional life in a technological society puts a premium on facility with the foreground of action. Individuals who function well in the foreground are therefore highly valued,. and philosophers, more comfortable somewhere out on the horizon of understanding, do not fully qualify.

In conclusion, as we look back on the anomaly of ends and means, on the collision between open and closed information networks, and on the contradictions between the philosophic and managerial temperaments, it is easy to see why Plato never anticipated any of these difficulties. He rather assumed, I suppose, that everybody in The Republic would be competent and ambitious, hard-working and obedient. No one would have to be treated as a thing because one's personal goals would always coincide with those of the state. No one would be disciplined or fired because no one would have to be disciplined or fired. Everyone would do his or her job well and gladly. There would be no secrets, because no one would use information improperly or merely for one's own private gain. Finally, administration, the work of the king, could be made to coincide with philosophy because, in a slowly evolving city-state, where all would know their place, there would be a closer fit between thinking and doing.

In my next life, I want to live there. I think it would be even better than Eden. Meanwhile, I think we must all settle for a world that is not only imperfect, but more explicitly, a world chopped up into ethical spheres. In such a world, traditional values will be expected to operate, but only up to a point. Beyond this point, another code takes over, another set of rules, another catalog of expectations. We need to know when we cross this frontier into the adjoining ethical province. Given this knowledge, educational administration can become more comprehensible and manageable, and we will abandon the attempt to be a philosopher and a king at the same time.

# VALUES AND EDUCATIONAL DECISIONS

### George L. Newsome, Jr.
### Harold W. Gentry

It has been said that common men react to life and its problems more often in terms of values than in terms of facts.[1] It has also been said that "directly or indirectly, questions of value are involved in nearly every decision which the educator makes."[2] Some administrators contend that values are so practical and so essential that "adequate conceptions of administration cannot be developed without a clearly formulated value framework . . ."[3]

Although these claims are probably more or less true, they tend to be confusing and logically inadequate. It is often difficult, if not impossible, to determine what kind of behavior represents a value reaction, or to determine whether it is to personal or social values that one is reacting. It seems equally difficult to specify the particular values incorporated into a decision, or to state precisely how values enter into the decision-making process. A considerable portion of the difficulty stems from the prevailing pattern of decision making and from educational language.

The typical pattern for decision making treats values, including needs projected as values, as aims or objectives, and decision making as means.[4] This pattern is inadequate because educators must deal with complex problems in which multiple ends (values) and multiple means are in question.[5] In most cases, one cannot clearly state or accurately anticipate the relevant ends or values. Moreover, in practical situations, it is often impossible to separate means from ends. Decisions are made in a time sequence and often against time and deadlines. They cannot be postponed indefinitely in the hope of getting enough evidence. For this reason, the means-end model and the terminology used with it tend to obscure the time element in decision making.[6] Finally, it seems doubtful that the language of education is precise enough or educational phenomena so well isolated and controlled that a one-to-one ends-means relationship can be definitely established.

## What Do Value and Decision Mean?

Much discussion about the role of values in decision making seems to consist of disputes about the meanings of vague and ambiguous words. Words like "value" and "decision" are vague because they refer to unspecified matters of degree. How valuable is a value? How decisive is a decision? These terms are also ambiguous because one frequently cannot tell from the context to what they refer. "Value" may refer to process or product, the ideal or the actual, or to some unit or degree of worth. "Decision" is equally ambiguous because it, too, may refer to process or product, intention or action, or established policy.

The word "value" is sometimes used to refer to "the good,"

for no one considers a value to be bad (disvalue). In common usage, "good" is the most general term of approval in the English language. Therefore, terms like "value" and "good" have a halo effect. It is not surprising that some philosophers have claimed that the word "good" is verbally indefinable.[7] Others have held that statements of value ". . . insofar as they are not scientific, . . . are not in the literal sense significant, but are simply expressions of emotion which can be neither true nor false."[8] Statements that describe personal or cultural values would be factual and scientific, but statements of value would serve only to express feeling or evoke feeling in others. Of course, statements of the latter kind serve a purpose in persuasive discourse.

The word "decision" is also nebulous and honorific. "Decision" means that one's mind is made up, that a course of action has been selected, that a legal judgment has been rendered, that a logical conclusion has been drawn from premises, or that a consensus of group thought or feeling has been reached. "Decision" also suggests wisdom, courage, and integrity on the part of the decision-maker. For this reason, the power and ability to make decisions is often associated with individuals in executive positions. The ability to make reasoned and effective decisions is, of course a very important aspect of leadership.

Decisions that can be called "reasoned and effective" are not easily described. They seem to be decisions that logically relate factual evidence to values. The logical problem is quite complex. Although the decision, and the reasoning that supports it, may be rather persuasive, it is not always logically valid. One can derive neither a value conclusion from a factual argument nor a factual conclusion from value premises. Moreover, when value premises are related to factual premises, one can often affirm the premises in principle and deny the conclusion in fact. Consider the conclusion in the following argument:

Every employee should be paid according to merit.
Teachers are employees of the school board.
Therefore, teachers' salaries should be based upon merit.

The first statement (major premise) is a value statement and the second (minor premise), a factual statement. One can, and many do, affirm both premises in principle and deny the conclusion on the grounds that merit cannot be fairly and adequately determined.

In still other cases, the conclusion may be feasible, and yet rejected, even though the premises are accepted. For example:

A principal should always tell the truth (value).
Miss X is an ineffective teacher (fact).
Therefore, if asked by a parent, the principal should
say Miss X is an ineffective teacher (conclusion).

The premises may be affirmed in principle and the conclusion denied on the grounds of "professionalism" or "general good of the school."

The rather disturbing fact is that decisions based upon

established facts logically related to generally accepted values
do not always gain acceptance. Wisdom is seldom a substitute for
prudence and it is frequently prudent to appear to be morally good
rather than wise. If one perceives socially accepted values
accurately, and reasons well, then one may be excused for some
socially unacceptable and ineffective decisions or for some "error
of judgment."

The foregoing discussion points up some of the confusion and
problems that beset a discussion of values and educational
decisions. Some theoretical considerations are now in order.
What operationally defensible meanings can be given to words like
"value" and "decision"? In precisely what ways do value
considerations enter into educational decisions?

## Value Determinants

The values people live by appear to be biologically
determined and culturally engendered predispositions to thought
and action, which are expressed in preferential behavior.⁵
Behavior preferences tend to show that those things which sustain
and support life are generally valued over things which merely
enhance and embellish it. For example, the hungry man is likely
to prefer food to money or entertainment. In other cases, value
preferences may be more cultural than biological. Some
individuals and groups, as a result of cultural conditioning,
prefer tea to coffee, classical to popular music, religious
devotion to agnosticism, liberal to vocational education.
Cultural values, including psycho-cultural values, are not innate.
They are learned from one's environment, including formal
schooling as part of that environment.

To say that values are biologically or culturally determined
does not mean that they are instinctive or soaked up sponge-like
from the environment. Man is a creature of preferences - a
creature that can, and does to some degree, regulate biological
urges and social conditioning in expressing preferences. In some
measure, man demonstrates characteristics of independent and
intellectual choice by critically examining his own biological
urges and cultural experiences. Herein are found the seeds of
science and the hope of education.

## Types of Educational Decisions

Despite science and education, people continue to make
decisions by various and sundry means. Some read tea leaves,
others pray for divine guidance, some trust to luck, others accept
fashion and custom, and some follow dogmatic authority. Although
principals are not entirely emancipated from such procedures,
their educational decisions are usually of five specific types:

. Routine decisions based upon personal habit and custom
. Legalistic decisions based upon appeal to and interpretation of, laws, policies, or well-established social customs
(precedents)
. Rational decisions based upon conclusions that logically
follow from premises or evidence in either inductive or deductive
argument

. Decisions that result from consensus or common agreements
. Persuasive decisions that must be sold to a majority to be accepted and implemented.

Values enter into decisions of each type. In routine decisions, values are implicit in one's own personal habits and customs. In legalistic decisions, the values are contained in, or implied by, the laws, policies, or social customs to which appeal is made. Rational decisions imply the values of factual evidence and logical reasoning. Consensus suggests the values of group thought and deliberation. Persuasive decisions make use of many personal and social values in an effort to influence others for or against some idea, person, or action. By confusing personal feeling with matters of fact concerning social and cultural values, all decisions are made emotive, persuasive, and non-cognitive in meaning. All but the first and last types of decisions can be made on the basis of facts concerning the social and cultural values implied by, or contained in, the principles to which appeal is made.

Because values reflect personal preferences and cultural peculiarities, it is unlikely that value conflicts can be completely resolved in a pluralistic society that allows freedom of thought and expression. Disagreement about values and about decisions involving appeal to values seems inevitable. Value conflict can, however, be minimized by clearly stating values and decisions by avoiding as much as possible personal and emotional expressions of value, and by providing logical arguments in support of the decisions. Prudence suggests that it may be more advantageous to clarify and interpret values than to expound new or partisan ones. There is no poverty of values in American culture. On this score we are embarrassingly rich.

An elementary school principal is confronted with situations which call for decisions about such diverse things as buildings, buses, budgets, school organization, curriculum, pupils' behavior, community relations, and the like. The kinds of decisions identified in the previous section could be applied to any of these situations. For purposes of illustration, only one example will be given for each kind of decision.

Routine Decision

Routine decisions based upon personal habits and customs are almost too common to require illustration. A routine decision, when called in question, is usually reformulated as a decision of another type. For example, the principal who habitually interrupts school activities with announcements over the intercom will likely claim, if challenged, that his decision to make frequent use of the intercom is a reasonable one. His argument may take the following form:

Directives and information, to be effective, must be communicated immediately and directly.

The intercom is the most direct and immediate means of communication.

Therefore, I will use the intercom.

The values in the original decision were contained in the

principal's own uncritically examined habits and customs. When her/his decision, as represented by his/her actions, was challenged, he/she was probably reluctant to admit that it was based on personal preferences and habits. A more reasonable argument was then formulated, the premises of which serve as evidence for the conclusion. Since the conclusion is the decision, the decision is supported and explained by the evidence contained in the premises. Those who accept the premises will tend to accept the conclusion. An appeal to values of impersonal evidence and logical reasoning is implied in choosing a rational explanation.

## Legalistic Decisions

Legalistic decisions are also common and easily identified by their appeal to laws, policies, and the precedents of established social customs (common law). Those who question legalistic decisions are questioning either the interpretations of the laws, policies, or social customs or questioning their legality and justice. In either case, the recourse of the questioner is that of appeal to higher authority. In other cases, individuals do not challenge a decision, but plead instead for special consideration on the basis of extenuating circumstances. Unless the principal has authority to deviate from law and policy in judging these cases, appeal must still be made to higher authority. Many decisions concerning personnel administration are of this type.

For example, a teacher who had taught fifth grade in the Flatrock School for ten years, was transferred to the Rockeypoint School in the same system. The principal assigned the teacher to teach the third grade. The teacher challenged the decision on the basis of special qualifications and experience as a teacher of the fifth grade. The principal justified the decision on the following grounds:

1. Rockeypoint School needed a teacher for the third grade.
2. It is customary to give teachers, in so far as possible, choice of teaching assignments on the basis of seniority in the school. The teacher has no seniority in Rockeypoint School.
3. According to the legal provisions and general policies of teacher certification in the state, elementary school teachers are not certified by grade level or subjects.
4. Specific board policy, clearly and emphatically stated in teaching contracts, says that teachers may be assigned to teach any grade level or subject for which they are properly certified.

The principal's decision to assign the transferred teacher rather than some other teacher to the third grade was made on the basis of laws, policies, and established school customs. The values at issue are those found in, or implied by, the laws, policies, and customs. The transferred teacher's only recourse is appeal to higher authority.

If individuals are unaware of the values contained in laws, policies, and school customs, the principal may find it helpful to explain them. For example, the principal could have pointed out that the laws, policies, and customs imply that the general

welfare of the school and pupils must take precedence over
personal preferences (appeal to the greater good). The principal
could also have pointed out that the laws and policies governing
certification were based upon the ideal (value) of having
elementary teachers prepared to teach all elementary grades, thus
giving them a better understanding of the total program and
providing flexibility in employment and assignment. These
advantages (values) are reflected in teacher preparation and
policies governing contractual agreements.

## Rational Decisions

Rational decisions may be based upon either inductive or
deductive arguments, or some combination of the two. Induction
can be used to establish facts, and statements of facts can be
made the premises of deductive arguments which demonstrate the
conclusion that follows logically from them. Because it is a
logical process of sampling and generalizing from observed cases,
induction seldom, if ever, provides certainty. The universal
(all) statements so often found in deductive arguments cannot be
established inductively by getting enough particulars to make a
universal – that is, all relevant evidence or possible cases
cannot be had. It is, therefore, virtually impossible to
formulate a rational argument that is at the same time both
factually true of all possible cases and demonstratively certain.

Recognizing these difficulties, some philosophers have
stressed what is called "informal logic" for dealing with
practical issues.[10] This logic utilizes both induction and
deduction and provides for rational decisions based upon "good
reasons" and "logical force," though not necessarily valid
arguments.[11] In this respect, it is more like the logic of legal
decisions that the logic of scientific proof.

The Lakeville School is noted for its excellent scientific
materials and equipment. Since the "Sputnik scare," the lion's
share of the materials and equipment budget has gone to the
science program. The creative arts and social studies have had to
make do with rather limited and somewhat obsolete materials and
equipment.

The principal, after an inventory of equipment and careful
examination of budgetary expenditures, suspected that instruction
in the creative arts and social studies might be impaired for lack
of enough up-to-date materials and equipment. The principal
conferred with teachers on this problem, obtained advice from
qualified people in the state department of education, and judged
materials and equipment against several recommended standards for
instruction in creative arts and social studies. Opinions of both
teachers and state department officials, and recommended standards
for curriculum and instruction, indicated that Lakeville School's
creative arts and social studies programs were dangerously weak
for lack of adequate material and equipment. As a result, the
principal decided to allot a substantially larger portion of the
material and equipment budget to these areas of the curriculum and
less to science.

This decision was reasonable and rational, if not logically
valid. The underlying values were those found in the appeal to

informed opinion, fact, and observable evidence. One may contest
the decision, but would be hard pressed to arrive at another on
the basis of relevant factual evidence.

## Group Decisions

Decision by group action and consensus seems to be rather
prevalent in educational institutions. The advantages of
unanimous or majority decisions based upon either assent or
consent are well known. The value of a united front and agreement
among reasonable and rational persons is obvious. On the other
hand, good people, wise people, and people with access to factual
information do, for a fact, often disagree about important
matters. The "one mind idea" of group decisions is a popular
myth, for group decisions do not imply commonly accepted values
and goals. Some agree because of values and goals, others because
of means, and some for much more mundane and selfish reasons.

Committees charged with making decisions do not always make
relevant, correct, or good decisions. For example, a curriculum
committee asked to make a decision about curriculum content, after
much discussion, decided instead to change the daily schedule of
classes. Situations like this indicate why principals must judge
the decisions made by groups to which they have delegated
authority. Indeed, principals are morally and often legally
responsible for decisions made under their authority. They may
reasonably exercise their veto power over decisions that are
illegal, foolish, irrelevant, or obviously selfish.

## Persuasive Decisions

Persuasive decisions are made on the basis of "selling" other
people on some idea. Through emotive language, praise,
suggestion, slogans, threats, and other techniques that make
people receptive to ideas, a favorable attitude is created as the
basis for the decisions. Persuasive decision making, seeking to
"win friends and influence people," often emphasizes "positive
thinking" about the ideas being pushed and utilizes the standard
propaganda appeals. Persuasive decision making is sometimes
thought unbecoming on the part of the educator who should eschew
propagandistic appeals and huckstering. In other cases, this
behavior is approved in the interest of good causes under
respectable titles such as "leadership" or "statesmanship."

For example, a principal had strong feelings about
departmentalization and ability grouping in the upper elementary
grades, but had not raised the issue because "the time was not
ripe for it." Recent trends in elementary education, however,
demonstrated that the time had come to begin preparing the ground.
Three faculty members were selected and several influential
members of the community power structure, whom the principal
believed would be receptive if the idea were put to them in a
positive way. Moreover, ways were considered in which
departmentalization and ability grouping might be allied with
known interests of each person.

The principal first approached each person informally to test
their opinions, and finding no strong antagonism, waited several
weeks and again approached each person on a more formal basis.

The principal, however, left the impression that the ideas received came from the individuals approached. Each person was assured that they had been approached because they were known for wisdom and good judgment, and were persons who could be relied upon for good advice.

The principal cultivated this new group of "advisors" and arranged for them to "carry the ball" in the PTA and in community clubs. As the issue built up in both school and community, the principal played the role of an interested but uncommitted educator. When the tide began to turn more in favor of the idea, the principal started speaking in favor of it, but urging a "go slow and reasonable approach." When strong opposition began melting away, the principal announced the decision to departmentalize the upper grades and introduce ability grouping on a trial basis the following year.

In this case, a principal successfully made a persuasive decision. There is, however, considerable danger in this method of operation. It suggests that the end (value) justifies the means. It is propagandistic and, if exposed, appears as knavery and use of people for selfish ends.

In Conclusion

Discussions about the role of values in decision making are often confused and logically inadequate because of lack of clarity in language and the inadequacy of the means-end model. Attempts to relate facts to values in order to formulate logically adequate arguments or decisions do not measure up to expectations. They fail because decisions must often be made against time and in absence of facts, and because one can often affirm the premises and deny the conclusion. This problem has not yet been resolved, although it can be clarified by more carefully defining key terms, identifying the types of decisions a principal is likely to make, and formulating the logical arguments that produce or support decisions.

In the interest of clarity "values" can be defined as biologically determined and culturally engendered predispositions to thought and action. "Decision" may be defined as choice, and "decision making" as choosing ideas, policies, or plans of action. Choice may be based upon personal preferences and habits, laws and established social customs, reason, group actions, or persuasions of other people to accept some idea. Except for the first and last types, decisions can be made on a nonpersonal, unemotional, and factual basis by an appeal to the values which are in fact rather generally held by people. Decisions of the first and last kind are both psychological and emotional in character.

Value conflicts are inevitable in a pluralistic and open society. They may be minimized, however, by more precise terminology, by clearly stating decisions and supporting arguments, and by avoiding personal and emotional expressions of value. Descriptive statements of the more immediate values contained in, or implied by, laws, policies, established social customs, and reason (facts and logic) will serve as adequate value appeals for most educational decisions. People are more likely to accept and work for these kinds of short-range and practical values than for more ultimate and esoteric values.

In many cases, for many principals, the major problem is neither values nor the psychological aspects of making decisions, but rather the much more difficult problem of formulating logical arguments to support and justify the decisions made on a more informal and less rational basis.

144

**FOOTNOTES**

[1]Harold A. Larrabee, Reliable Knowledge (Boston:  Houghton Mifflin Co., 1945), p. 601.

[2]John S. Brubacher, Modern Philosophies of Education  (New York:  McGraw-Hill Book Co., 1962), p. 97.

[3]Orin B. Graff and Calvin M. Street, "Developing a Value Framework for Educational Administration," Administrative Behavior in Education, ed. Rose F. Campbell and Russell T. Gregg (New York:  Harper and Bros., 1957), p. 129.

[4]For an analysis of the word "need" and the comparison it has produced in education, see Paul Komisar, "Need and the Needs-Curriculum," Language and Concepts in Education, ed. B. Othanel Smith and Robert H. Ennis (Chicago:  Rand McNally and Company, 1961), pp. 24-42.

[5]Jack A. Culbertson, Paul B. Jacobson, and Theodore L. Reller, Administrative Relationships (Englewood Cliffs:  Prentice-Hall, 1960), pp. 464-465.

[6]Herbert A. Simon, Administrative Behavior (New York:  Macmillan Co., 1957), pp. 64-65.

[7]G.E. Moore, "The Indefinability of Good," A Modern Introduction to Philosophy, ed. Paul Edwards and Arthur Pap (New York:  Free Press of Glencoe, 1957), pp. 411-417.

[8]Alfred Jules Ayer, Language, Truth and Logic (New York:  Dover Publications, n.d.), p. 103.

[9]Some philosophers have considered value theory as primarily scientific study of preferences.  For example, see Charles S. Morris, "Axiology as the Science of Preferential Behavior," Value: A Cooperative Inquiry, ed. Ray Lepley (New York:  Columbia University Press, 1949), pp. 211-222.

[10]Gilbert Ryle, Dilemmas (Cambridge:  Cambridge University Press, 1954), pp. 111-120.

[11]See Stephen Toulmin, The Uses of Argument (Cambridge:  Cambridge University Press, 1958).

# MORALITY AND THE IDEAL OF RATIONALITY

## IN FORMAL ORGANIZATIONS

### John Ladd

Introductory
        The purpose of this paper is to explore some of the moral
problems that arise out of the interrelationships between
individuals and formal organizations (or bureaucracies) in our
society.  In particular, I shall be concerned with the moral
implications of the so-called ideal of rationality of formal
organizations with regard to, on the one hand, the obligations of
individuals both inside and outside an organization to that
organization and, on the other hand, the moral responsibilities of
organizations to individuals and to the public at large.  I shall
argue that certain facets of the organizational ideal are
incompatible with the ordinary principles of morality and that the
dilemma created by this incompatibility is one source of
alienation in our contemporary, industrial society.  The very
conception of a formal organization of bureaucracy presents us
with an ideological challenge that desperately needs to be met in
some way or other.
        The term "formal organization" will be used in a more or less
technical sense to cover all sorts of bureaucracies, private and
public.  A distinctive mark of such organizations is that they
make a clear-cut distinction between the acts and relationships of
individuals in their official capacity within the organization and
in their private capacity. Decisions of individual decision-
makers in an organization are attributed to the organization and
not to the individual.  In that sense, they are impersonal.
Individual office-holders are in principle replaceable by other
individuals without affecting the continuity or identity of the
organization.  In this sense, it has sometimes been said that an
organization is "immortal."
        This kind of impersonality, in particular, the
substitutability of individuals, is one way in which formal
organizations differ from other kinds of social systems, e.g. the
family, the community or the nation, which are collectivities that
are dependent for their existence on specific individuals or
groups of specific individuals and that change when they change.
        Under formal organizations I shall include not only all sorts
of industrial, military and governmental bureaucracies but also
formal organizations like large universities (multiversities),
hospitals, labor unions, and political machines.  For our
purposes, we may even include illegal and undercover organizations
like the Mafia, the Communist party, the FBI, and the CIA.  The
general characteristics of all these organizations are that they
are "planned units, deliberately structured for the purpose of
attaining specific goals,"[1] and such that each formal organization
is a "continuous organization of official functions bound by

rules."[2] One of the distinctive features of formal organizations of the type we are interested in is that they are ordinarily hierarchical in structure; they not only have a "horizontal" division of labor but a "vertical" one as well - a "pyramid of authority."[3]

There is good reason for choosing the ethics of formal organizations as a subject for philosophical inquiry, for many of the older and traditional issues of political philosophy, e.g. those relating to authority, obedience, welfare, and justice, have now turned into issues involving the relationship of individuals to formal organizations and of formal organizations to society. Formal organizations of all types have in fact come to dominate our individual and social life in a way that was earlier thought to characterize only the state. The extraordinary growth in power, scope, and complexity of large formal organizations requires us to revamp, e.g. the traditional question of the freedom of the individual. Traditional political theory conceived of authority and responsibility as more or less concentrated in one sovereign power, but now we have a new problem that comes from the fact that through formal organizations, authority and responsibility have become quite diffused. As a result the "point of contact" between the individual and the powers that be can hardly be ascertained, for indeed there is no such point; our contact with formal organizations, their power and authority over us is continuous and blurred.

Social critics, e.g. W.H. Whyte, use phrases like the "smothering of the individual" to describe the contemporary situation created by organizations. It is not my purpose here to decry once more the unhappy condition of man occasioned by his submergence as an individual in the vast social, economic and political processes created by formal organizations. Instead, I shall try to show that the kind of alienation that we all feel and complain about is, at least in part, a logical necessity flowing from the concept of formal organizations itself, that is, it is a logical consequence of the particular language-game one is playing in organizational decision-making. My analysis is intended to be a logical analysis, but one that also has important ethical implications.

Accordingly, I shall not be concerned with empirical studies of organizations, with their typology, with their functions and dysfunctions, with studies of informal groupings within organizations, etc.[4] Rather, I shall approach the subject in terms of the "ideology" presupposed by organizational decision-making. This may be one way of interpreting Weber's ideal-type, from which his classical analysis of bureaucracy takes its point of departure. There have been many different interpretations of Weber's concept of an ideal-type; it has variously been taken to be a heuristic device, a method of describing data, or a logical construction. Instead of any of these, I shall try to formulate Weber's ideal-type of bureaucracy as a way of representing a certain pattern of thinking about actions and social relationships, that is, as a kind of rational or moral order.

For our purpose, we may construe Weber's analysis of bureaucracies as describing a certain language-game, since it is almost exclusively concerned with the "formally instituted aspects of bureaucracy."[5] The ideal-type is literally an ideal, that is, a limit which actual organizations approach more or less closely. In philosophical terminology, it is a normative concept, albeit perhaps not an ethical one.[6] This point comes out clearly when Herbert Simon says of his account that it is "not a description of how administrators decide so much as a description of how <u>good</u> administrators decide."[7]

Here we may find the concept of a language-game, as advanced by Wittgenstein and others, a useful tool of analysis. The point about a language-game is that it emphasizes the way language and action are interwoven: "I shall call the whole, consisting of language and the actions into which it is woven, the language-game."[8] A language-game is thus more than simply an abstract set of propositions constituting, say, a formal system. The game not only determines what should and what should not be done, but also sets forth the goals and the moves by which they are to be attained. More important even than these, a particular language-game determines how the activities within it are to be conceptualized, prescribed, justified and evaluated. Take as an example what is meant by a "good" move in chess: we have to refer to the rules of chess to determine what a "move" is, how to make one, what its consequences will be, what its objective is and whether or not it is a good move in the light of this objective.[9] Finally this system of rules performs the logical function of defining the game itself.

One advantage of the language-game model is, therefore, that it enables us to describe a kind of activity by reference to a set of rules that determine not only what should or should not be done, but also how what is done is to be rationally evaluated and defended. And it allows us to describe the activity without reference to moral rules (or norms). In other words, it provides us with a method of analyzing a rational activity without committing ourselves to whether or not it is also moral.

If we pursue the game-analogy one step further, we find that there may be even more striking similarities between the language-game of formal organizations and the language-game of other types of games. For instance, the rules and rationale obtaining in most typical games like chess and baseball tend to make the activity logically autonomous, i.e. the moves, defenses and evaluations are made independently of external considerations. In this sense they are self-contained. Furthermore, while playing a game it is thought to be "unfair" to challenge the rules. Sometimes it is even maintained that any questioning of the rules is unintelligible. In any case, there is a kind of sanctity attached to the rules of a game that renders them immune to criticism on the part of those engaged in playing the game. The resemblance of the autonomy of the activity and the immunity of the rules governing the game to the operations of bureaucracies can hardly be coincidental![10]

## The Concept of Social Decision and Social Action

Let us take as our point of departure Herbert Simon's definition of a formal organization as a "decision-making structure."[11]  The central concept with which we must deal is that of a decision (or action) that is attributable to the organization rather than to the individuals who are actually involved in the decisional process.  The decision is regarded as the organization's decision even though it is made by certain individuals acting as its representatives.  The latter make the decision only for and on behalf of the organization.  Their role is, i.e. is supposed to be, impersonal.  Such nonindividual decisions will be called <u>social decisions</u>, choices or actions.  (I borrow the term "social choice" from Arrow, who uses it to refer to a choice made on behalf of a group as distinct from the aggregate of individual choices.)[12]

The officials of an organization are "envisaged as more or less ethically neutral . . . (and) the values to be taken as data are not those which would guide the individual if he were a private citizen. . . ."[13]  When the official decides for the organization, his aim is (or should be) to implement the objectives of the organization <u>impersonally</u>, as it were.  The decisions are made for the organization, with a view to its objectives and not on the basis of the personal interests or convictions of the individual official who makes the decision. This is the theory of organizational decision-making.

One might be tempted to call such organizational decisions "collective decisions," but that would be a misnomer if we take a collective decision to be a decision made by a collection of individuals.  Social decisions are precisely decisions (or actions) that are to be <u>attributed</u> to the organizations themselves and not to collections of individuals.  In practice, of course, the organizational decisions made by officials may actually be collective decisions.  But in theory the two must be kept separate; for the "logic" of decisions attributed to organizations is critically different from the "logic" of collective decisions, i.e. those attributed to a collection of individuals.

Underlying the concept of social decisions (choices, actions) as outlined here is the notion that a person (or group of persons) can make decisions that are not theirs, i.e. are not attributable to them.  They make the decisions on behalf of someoneelse and with a view to the latter's interest, not their own.  In such cases, we ordinarily consider the person (or group) that acts to be a representative or agent of the person or thing  acted for.

The classic description of this conception of acting for another is given by Hobbes in the following passage:

> . . . Some (persons) have their words and actions owned by those whom they represent. And then the person is the <u>actor</u>, and he that owns his words and actions is the AUTHOR; in which case the actor acts by authority. . . . So that by <u>authority</u> is always understood the right of doing any act; and <u>done by authority</u>, done by commission or license from whose right it is.

From hence it follows that when the actor makes a covenant by authority, he binds thereby the author no less than if he had made it himself, and no less subjects him to all the consequences of the same.[14]

Accordingly, a social decision, as intended here, would be an action performed by an official as actor but owned by the organization as author. For all the consequences of the decision so made are imputed to the organization and not to the individual decision-maker. The individual decision-making official is not personally bound by the agreements he makes for the organization, nor is he personally responsible for the results of these decisions.

The theory of social decision-making that we are considering becomes even clearer if we examine the theory of organizational authority with which it is conjoined. Formal organizations are hierarchical in structure, that is, they are organized along the principle that superiors issue commands to those below them. The superior exercises authority over the subordinates. What does this mean?

Simon defines this authority as follows:

> A subordinate is said to accept the authority whenever he permits his behavior to be guided by the decision of a superior, without independently examining the merits of the decision. Hence, the subordinate holds in abeyance his own critical faculties for choosing between alternatives and uses the formal criterion of the receipt of a command or signal as his basis for choice.[15]

Simon constantly reiterates the principle that organizational authority requires the "abdication of choice." In terms of the model I suggested earlier, this principle is part of the language-game; it is a logical requirement of the game, regardless of whether or not it actually corresponds to empirical reality. Furthermore, we may extend the notion of abdication of choice even further, to the hierarchy as a whole, for the authority of the superior official is itself based on the official's "abdication of choice" in favor of the social decisions of the organization. These social decisions are, strictly speaking, not "owned" by the official. The subordinates, as Weber says, "do not owe this obedience to the (person in authority) as an individual, but to the impersonal order."[16]

In summary, then, the organizational order requires that its social decisions be attributed to the organization rather than to the individual decision-maker, the "decision is to be made nonpersonally from the point of view of its organization effect and its relation to the organizational purpose,"[17] and the officials, as its agents, are required to abdicate their choice in obedience to the impersonal organizational order.

We now turn to another essential facet of the organizational language-game, namely, that every formal organization must have a goal, or a set of goals. In fact, organizations are differentiated and defined by reference to their aims or goals, e.g. the aim of the Internal Revenue Service is to collect taxes. The goal of most business ventures is to maximize profits, etc. We may find it useful to distinguish between the real and stated goals of an organization. Thus, as Galbraith has pointed out, although the stated goal of large industrial organizations is the maximization of profits, that is a pure myth; their actual, operative goals are the securing of their own survival, autonomy and economic growth.[18] There may, indeed, be a struggle over the goals of an organization, e.g. a power play between officials.[19]

For our present purposes, we may consider the real goal of an organization to be that objective (or set of objectives) that is used as a basis for decision-making, i.e. for prescribing and justifying the actions and decisions of the organization itself, as distinct from the actions and decisions of individual persons within the organization. As such, then, the goal is an essential element in the language-game of a formal organization's activities in somewhat the same way as the goal of checkmating the king is an essential element in the game of chess. Indeed, formal organizations are often differentiated from other kinds of social organizations in that they are "deliberately constructed and reconstructed to seek specific goals."[20]

The logical function of the goal in the organizational language-game is to supply the value premises to be used in making decisions, justifying and evaluating them. "Decisions in private management, like decisions in public management, must take as their ethical premises the objectives that have been set for the organization."[21]

It follows that any considerations that are not related to the aims or goals of the organization are automatically excluded as irrelevant to the organizational decision-making process. This principle of the exclusion of the irrelevant is part of the language-game. It is a logical requirement of the process of prescribing, justifying and evaluating social decisions. Consequently, apart from purely legal considerations, decisions and actions of individual officers that are unrelated to the organization's aims or goals are construed, instead, as actions of those individuals rather than of the organization. If an individual official makes a mistake or does something that fails to satisfy this criterion of social decision, he will be said to have "exceeded his authority," and will probably be sacked or made a vice-president! Again, the point is a logical one, namely, that only those actions that are related to the goal of the organization are to be attributed to the organization; those actions that are inconsistent with it are attributed to the individual officers as individuals. The individual, rather than the organization, is then forced to take the blame for whatever evil results.

Thus, for example, a naval officer who runs his ship aground is court-martialed because what he did was inconsistent with the aims of the naval organization; the action is attributed to him rather than to the Navy. On the other hand, an officer who successfully bombards a village, killing all of its inhabitants, in accordance with the objectives of his organization, is performing a social action, an action that is attributable to the organization and not to him as an individual. Whether or not the organization should take responsibility in a particular case for the mistakes of its officials is a policy decision to be made in the light of the objectives of the organization.

In other words, the concept of a social decision or action is bound up logically with the notion of an organizational aim. The consequence of this co-implication of action and aim is that the notion of an action or decision taken by an organization that is not related to one of its aims makes no sense. It is an unintelligible notion within the language-game of formal organizations. Within that language-game such an action would be as difficult to understand as it would be to understand how a man's knocking over the pieces in a chess game can be part of playing chess.

We finally come to the concept of "rationality," the so-called "ideal of pure rationality."[22] From the preceding observations concerning the organizational language-game, it should be clear that the sole standard for the evaluation of an organization, its activities and its decisions, is its effectiveness in achieving its objectives within the framework of existing conditions and available means. This kind of effectiveness is called "rationality." Thus, rationality is defined in terms of the category of means and ends. "Behavior . . . is rational insofar as it selects alternatives which are conducive to the achievement of previously selected goals."[23] And "the rationality of decisions . . . is their appropriateness for the accomplishment of specified goals."[24]

"Rationality," so construed, is relative, that is, to be rational means to be efficient in pursuing a desired goal, whatever that might be. In the case of organizations, "a decision is 'organizationally' rational if it is oriented to the organization's goals."[25] Rationality is consequently neutral as to "what goals are to be attained."[26] Or to be more accurate, "rationality" is an incomplete term that requires reference to a goal before it is completely intelligible.

To a philosopher it is clear that the technical use of "rationality" as it is found in social theory, e.g. in the writing of Weber and Simon, amounts to a persuasive definition. Like the other terms used in these analyses that carry ethical-emotive meanings, e.g. "good" and "should," it attests to a covert endorsement of a certain kind of formal organization, i.e. one structured according to the principle of efficiency they set forth.[27] Despite asseverations to the contrary, these analyses are not ethically neutral, much less "value-free."

Let us return to the organizational language-game. It was observed that within that game the sole standard of evaluation of, e.g. a decision, is the "rational" one, namely, that it be effective in achieving the organization's goal. Hence, any considerations that are taken into account in deliberation about these social decisions and in the evaluation of them are relevant only if they are related to the attainment of the organization's objectives. Let us suppose that there are certain factual conditions that must be considered in arriving at a decision, e.g. the available means, costs, and conditions of feasibility. The determination of such conditions is presumably a matter of empirical knowledge and a subject for empirical investigation. Among these empirical conditions there is a special class that I shall call limiting operating conditions. These are conditions that set the upper limits to an organization's operations, e.g. the scarcity of resources, of equipment, of trained personnel, legal restrictions, factors involving employee morale. Such conditions must be taken into account as data, so to speak, in organizational decision-making and planning. In this respect information about them is on a par logically with other information utilized in decision-making, e.g. cost-benefit computations.

Now the only way that moral considerations could be relevant to the operations of a formal organization in the language-game that I have been describing is by becoming limiting operating conditions. Strictly speaking, they could not even be introduced as such, because morality is itself not a matter of empirical knowledge. Insofar as morality in the strict sense enters into practical reasoning it must do so as an "ethical" premise, not as an empirical one. Hence morality as such must be excluded as irrelevant in organizational decision-making by the rules of the language-game. The situation is somewhat parallel to the language-game used in playing chess: moral considerations are not relevant to the decisions about what move to make there either.

Morality enters in only indirectly, namely, as moral opinion, what John Austin calls "positive morality."[28] Obviously the positive morality, laws and customs of the society in which the organization operates must be taken into account in decision-making and planning. The same thing goes for the religious beliefs and practices of the community. Decision-makers cannot ignore them, and it makes no difference whether they share them or accept them personally. But the determination of whether or not there are such limiting conditions set by positive morality, customs, law, and religion is an empirical matter. Whether there are such limitations is simply a matter of fact and their relevance to the decision-making is entirely dependent upon how they affect the efficiency of the organization's operations.

Social decisions, then, are not and cannot be governed by the principles of morality, or, if one wishes, they are governed by a different set of moral principles from those governing the conduct of individuals as individuals. For, as Simon says: "Decisions in private management, like decisions in public management, must take as their ethical premises the objectives that have been set for the organization."[29] By implication, they cannot take their ethical premises from the principles of morality.

Thus, for logical reasons it is improper to expect organizational conduct to conform to the ordinary principles of morality. We cannot and must not expect formal organizations, or their representatives acting in their official capacities, to be honest, courageous, considerate, sympathetic, or to have any kind of moral integrity. Such concepts are not in the vocabulary, so to speak, of the organizational language-game. (We do not find them in the vocabulary of chess either!) Actions that are wrong by ordinary moral standards are not so for organizations; indeed, they may often be required. Secrecy, espionage and deception do not make organizational action wrong; rather they are right, proper and, indeed, <u>rational</u>, if they serve the objectives of the organization. They are no more or no less wrong then, say, bluffing is in poker. From the point of view of organizational decision-making they are "ethically neutral."

Of course, I do not want to deny that it may be in the best interests of a formal organization to pay lip service to popular morality (and religion). That is a matter of public relations. But public relations operations themselves are evaluated and justified on the same basis as the other operations of the organization. The official function of the public relations officer is to facilitate the operations of the organization, not to promote morality.

Therefore, if one expects social decisions to conform to the principles of morality, he is simply committing a logical mistake, perhaps even what Ryle calls a category mistake. In a sense, as we shall see, organizations are like machines, and it would be a category mistake to expect a machine to comply with the principles of morality. By the same token, officials or agents of a formal organization are simply violating the basic rules of organizational activity if they allow their moral scruples rather than the objectives of the organization to determine their decisions. In particular, they are violating the rule of administrative impartiality, that is, the rule that administrative officials "faithfully execute policies of which they personally disapprove."[30]

Once again, it should be observed that the conclusions reached here relate only to the ideal-type, the theory of "how an organization should be constructed and operated in order to accomplish its work efficiently," that is, to what is essentially a normative order consisting of a set of nonmoral rules of conduct. It is unnecessary to point out that in actual fact many organizations fail to approximate the ideal outlined here. Nevertheless, it is important to recognize that this ideal makes demands and claims on our conduct if we are involved in the operations of formal organizations. And it is used to justify them.

The upshot of our discussion so far is that actions are subject to two entirely different and, at times, incompatible standards: social decisions are subject to the standard of rational efficiency (utility) whereas the actions of individuals as such are subject to the ordinary standards of morality. An action that is right from the point of view of one of these standards may be wrong from the point of view of the other. Indeed, it is safe to say that our own experience attests to the fact that our actual expectations and social approvals are to a large extent based on a tacit acceptance of a double-standard--one for the individual who is in the office working for the company and another for the individual at home among friends and neighbors. Take as an example the matter of lying: nobody would think of condemning Joe X, a movie star, for lying on a TV commercial about what brand of cigarettes he smokes, for it is part of his job. On the other hand, if he were to do the same thing in private among friends, we should consider his action to be improper and immoral. Or again, an individual who, acting in an official capacity, refuses help to a needy suppliant, would be roundly condemned if the individual adopted the same course of action in private life.

The pervasiveness of organizational activity throughout modern society makes the impact of this double-standard on the individual particularly unsettling. It produces a kind of moral schizophrenia which has affected us all. Furthermore, the dilemma in which we find ourselves cannot so easily be conjured away; for it has its logical ground as well as basis in the dynamics of social structure.

Before entering into the question of the nature and source of the dilemma created by these two standards, we must examine some of the further logical implications of this double-standard for the individual in relationship to a formal organization and for the organization's relationship to individuals.

## The Moral Relationship of Individuals to Organizations

It follows from what has already been said that the standard governing an individual's relationship to an organization is likely to be different from the one governing the converse relationship, i.e. of an organization to individuals. The individual, is supposed to conduct oneself in the relationship to an organization according to the same standards that one would employ in personal relationships, i.e. the standards of ordinary morality. Thus, one is expected to be honest, open, respectful, conscientious, and loyal towards the organization of which one is a member or with which one has dealings. The organization, represented by its officials, can however, be none of these in return. "Officials are expected to assume an impersonal orientation. . . . Clients are to be treated as cases . . . and subordinates are to be treated in a similar fashion."[31]

The question I now want to explore is whether or not the individual is justified in applying the standard of individual morality to relations with formal organizations. It will, of course, generally be in the interest of the formal organizations themselves to encourage one to do so, e.g. to be honest, although the organization as such cannot "reciprocate." But we must ask this question from the point of view of the individual or, if you wish, from the moral point of view: what good moral reasons can be given for an individual to assume a moral stance in one's conduct and relations with formal organizations, in contradistinc- tion, say, to conduct and relations with individuals who happen to be employees of such an organization?

The problem, which may be regarded as a question of loyalty and fidelity, puts the age-old problem of authority and obedience in a new light. Authority has become diffused, as I have already pointed out, and the problem of obedience can no longer be treated in terms of the personal relationship of an individual to a sovereign lord. The problem today is not so easily focused on one relationship; for the demands of authority, as represented in modern organizations, are at once more extensive, more pervasive and less personal. The question we face today is, for example,

why should I, as an individual, comply with the mass of
regulations laid down by an impersonal order, a bureaucratic
organization? Why, for example, should I comply with draft-
registration procedures? with passport regulations? with income-
tax requirements? with mortgage, credit, licensing, fair-trade
regulations or with anti-trust laws? Or, indeed, has the
individual any moral obligation at all to comply with them?[32]
It might be thought that, before trying to answer such
questions, we must be careful to distinguish between individuals
within an organization, e.g. officials and employees, and those
outside it who have dealings with it, e.g. clients and the general
public: what each of these classes ought to do is different.
Granting that the specific demands placed on individuals in these
various categories may be quite different, they all involve the
question of authority in one way or another. Hence, for our
purposes, the distinction is unimportant. For example, the
authority, or the claims to it, of governmental bureaucracies
extends far beyond those who are actually in their employ, e.g.
the Internal Revenue Service. For convenience, I shall call those
who come under the authority of an organization in some capacity
or other, directly or indirectly, the <u>subjects</u> of the
organization. Thus, we are all subjects of the IRS.
Can any moral reasons be given why individual subjects should
comply with the decisions of organizations? Or, what amounts to
the same thing, what is the basis of the authority of the
organizations by virtue of which we have an obligation to accept
and obey their directives? And why, if at all, do we owe them
loyalty and fidelity?
The most obvious answer, although perhaps not the most
satisfactory one ethically, is that it is generally expedient for
the individual to go along with what is required by formal
organizations. If I want a new automobile, I have to comply with
the financing requirements. If I want to avoid being harassed by
an internal revenue agent, I make out my income tax form properly.
If I want to be legally married, I comply with the regulations of
the Department of Public Health. In other words, I comply from
practical necessity, that is, I act under a hypothetical
imperative.
Still, this sort of answer is just as unsatisfactory from the
point of view of moral philosophy as the same kind of answer
always has been with regard to political obligation, namely, it
fails to meet the challenge of the conscientious objector.
Furthermore, there are many occasions and even whole areas
where self-interest is not immediately or obviously involved in
which, nevertheless, it makes good sense to ask: why comply? The
traditional Lockian argument that our acceptance of the benefits
of part of the social and political order commits us morally to
the acceptance and conformity with the rest of it rests on the
dubious assumption that the social and political order is all of
one piece, a seamless web. But when we apply the argument to
formal organizations it becomes especially implausible, because
there are so many competing claims and conflicting regulations,
not to mention loyalties. Not only logically, but as a matter of
practicality, it seems obvious that accepting the benefits of one

bureaucratic procedure, e.g. mailing letters, does not, from the moral point of view, _eo ipso_ bind us to accept and comply with all the other regulations and procedures laid down by the formal organization and, much less, those laid down by formal organizations in general.

Some of the traditional answers to the problem of political obligation might possibly be relevant to our questions about how we should relate to formal organizations. For example, we could try a contractarian, a utilitarian or a 'general will' kind of argument. Although all three of these have some initial plausibility, on closer inspection we will find, I think, that none of them will do; either they have no application whatsoever to organizations or else they are not specific enough for particular organizations.

Let us begin with the suggestion that our relations with formal organizations are based upon compacts of one sort or another. (I use the term "compact" to indicate that we are talking about a morally binding agreement as distinct from one that is merely legally binding, i.e. a contract.) It seems natural to suppose that we bind ourselves to organizations through agreements, tacit or explicit, of one sort or another. But if we distinguish between a moral agreement, which establishes mutual moral obligations, and a legal agreement, which establishes only legal obligations, it will be evident from what I have said earlier that it is impossible to make a compact with an organization. (Could we make a compact with a machine?) A compact is a bilateral promise and hence a compact can be made only between beings that are capable of making promises. But a formal organization cannot make promises, for it cannot bind itself to a performance that might conflict with the pursuit of its goal. The principle of rationality, as applied to formal organizations, makes no provision for the principle that promises ought to be kept; indeed, if the keeping of promises, or of a particular promise, is inconsistent with the goals of the organization, that principle requires that they be broken.

In sum, we cannot make compacts with organizations because the standard of conduct which requires that promises be honored is that of individual conduct.[33] It does not and cannot apply to formal organizations. This follows from the fact of a double standard.

The utilitarian answer to our question, like its ancestor the utilitarian theory of political obligation, maintains that somehow or other an individual act of compliance with the established order inevitably contributes to the stability of the whole system, whereas an individual act of defiance inevitably contributes to its instability. Thus Hume compares the social order of inflexible rules to a vault, where the "whole fabric is supported but by the mutual assistance and combination of its corresponding parts."[34] There is, it appears, no empirical evidence to support the contention that an individual act will strengthen or weaken the system. Nor is there any reason to suppose that the preserving of the status quo is either necessary or sufficient for promoting the public interest. In view of the complexity of the impact of modern social and political organizations on society, it is difficult, if not impossible, to accept a utilitarian argument as the basis of an individual's obligation towards formal organizations.

Finally, we come to those arguments that appeal to some sort of common interest or identity of goals as the basis of the authority of organizations over the individual. On this view, the goals of formal organizations are identified with the goals of its individual members, taken collectively perhaps. Galbraith, in The New Industrial State, refers to this as the "principle of consistency": "There must be a consistency in the goals of society, the organization and the individual."[35] He assumes that, in many cases at least, the objectives of all three are basically the same, their goal is the same, e.g. a rising standard of living. To serve the organization is to serve one's own goals and the goals of society.

So construed, the principle of consistency, like Rousseau's General Will, with which it has obvious affinities, represents a value-judgment. It places a premium on the sharing of goals, no matter what these goals might be. But, as I have already argued at some length, the standards of individual moral conduct and of rational organizational activity are so completely different that a collision between them is inevitable. The only way that the predicated consistency could be secured is for the individual to give up one's moral principles and adopt the goals of the organization as one's own. (This is the kind of consistency that exists in totalitarian political parties and that was so ably portrayed in Koestler's Darkness at Noon.)

In the final analysis perhaps the most plausible basis of the authority of formal organizations, or at least within formal organizations, is the Platonic one, namely, that the commands of officials should be complied with because they have superior knowledge. The superiors, like the guardians in Plato's Republic are experts; they have the expertise that the subordinates do not possess but need in order to act effectively. That much of the authority relationship within military and industrial organizations is founded on expert-know-how or alleged know-how is unquestionable. Many organizations, however, e.g. the public bureaucracies, make decisions that are not based upon superior knowledge, but involve the same kind of information and knowledge that is available to the general public, and in particular, to many individuals outside the organization. This is, of course, particularly true where issues of public (and foreign) policy are concerned.[36]

The breakdown of the argument from superior expertise is due, no doubt, to advances in technology, mass education and mass communication. More information of a higher quality is available to large numbers of people who are simply subjects and do not have command positions within the bureaucracies to which they are subject. It is too easy to see through the claims to superior knowledge when we also have some knowledge of our own about what is going on.

I have been able to touch only on some very limited aspects of the relationship of individuals or organizations. I hope, however, that it is now abundantly clear that some sort of crisis is taking place in our moral relationships, and in particular in our conceptions of authority, and that this crisis is due not only to complex historical, psychological and sociological factors, but also to an inherent <u>logical</u> paradox in the foundations of our social relations.

## The Moral Relationship of Organizations to Individuals

For logical reasons that have already been mentioned, formal organizations cannot assume a genuine moral posture towards individuals. Although the language-game of social decision permits actions to be attributed to organizations as such, rather than to the officials that actually make them, it does not contain concepts like "moral obligation," "moral responsibility," or "moral integrity." For the only relevant principles in rational decision-making are those relating to the objectives of the organization. Hence individual officers who make the decisions for and in the name of the organization, as its representatives, must decide solely by reference to the objectives of the organization.

According to the theory, then, the individuals who are officers of an organization, i.e. those who run it, operate simply as vehicles or instruments of the organization. The organization language-game requires that they be treated as such. That is why, in principle at least, any individual is dispensable and replaceable by another. An individual is selected for a position, retained in it, or fired from it solely on the grounds of efficiency, i.e. of what will best serve the interests of the organization. The interests and needs of the individuals concerned, as individuals, must be considered only insofar as they establish limiting operating conditions. Organizational rationality dictates that these interests and needs must not be considered in their own right or on their own merits. If we think of an organization as a machine, it is easy to see why we cannot reasonably expect it to have any moral obligations to people or for them to have any to it.

For precisely the same reason, the rights and interests of persons outside the organization and of the general public are <u>eo ipso</u> ruled out as logically irrelevant to rational organizational decision, except insofar as these rights and interests set limiting conditions to the effectiveness of the organization's operations or insofar as the promoting of such rights and interests constitutes part of the goal of the organization. Hence it is fatuous to expect an industrial organization to go out of its way to avoid polluting the atmosphere or to refrain from making napalm bombs or to desist from wire-tapping on purely moral grounds. Such actions would be irrational.

It follows that the only way to make the rights and interests of individuals or of the people logically relevant to organizational decision-making is to convert them into pressures of one sort or another, e.g. to bring the pressure of the law or of public opinion to bear on the organizations. Such pressures would then be introduced into the rational decision-making as limiting operating conditions.

Since formal organizations cannot have moral obligations,

they cannot have moral responsibilities in the sense of having
obligations towards those affected by their actions or subject to
their actions because of the power they possess. Organizations
have tremendous power, but no responsibilities. (The same goes
for a nuclear bomb!)

Paradoxically, perhaps, it follows from this analysis that
the more rational an organization is, the less likely it is to be
subject to moral or rational persuasion from the outside. Hence,
as I have pointed out, the only way to influence such a rational
organization is through coercion, legislative or otherwise. And
the more rational it is, the more necessary it is that such
external pressures be maintained.

Since, as I have argued in some detail, formal organizations
are not moral persons, and have no moral responsibilities, they
have no moral rights. In particular, they have no moral right to
freedom or autonomy. There can be nothing morally wrong in
exercising coercion against a formal organization as there would
be in exercising it against an individual. Hence, the other side
of the coin is that it would be irrational for us, as moral
persons, to feel any moral scruples about what we do to
organizations. (We should constantly bear in mind that the
officials themselves, as individuals, must still be treated as
moral persons with rights and responsibilities attached to them as
individuals.)

It is sometimes held that the ethical neutrality of
organizations, e.g. of a public bureaucracy, is a good thing, both
for the individual and for society. Thus Max Weber thought that
this kind of neutrality is commendable not only because it makes
for efficiency and "rationality," but also because it transfers
the responsibility for the ethical side of decision-making to
persons outside the organization. If and insofar as the
objectives of the organization, e.g. the governmental bureaucracy,
are set by others, e.g. the elected leaders, accountability to the
people, as required by the theory of democracy, is assured. There
has been much argument since his day as to whether a bureaucracy
of ethically neutral civil servants is conducive to or, on the
other hand, disruptive of democratic processes.

I do not wish to go into the empirical questions involved in
assessing the relationship between the ethical neutrality of
bureaucracies and democracy or totalitarianism. It suffices here
to observe that the concept of ethical neutrality is based on the
presupposition that once the objectives of an organization have
been decided on, then all the subsequent questions involved in
decision-making are merely empirical (factual) questions about
ways and means. The separation of ends and means in this analysis
is highly questionable from the philosophical point of view, as
any reader of Dewey's writings is well aware. Even the decision-
making of subordinate officials is bound to involve some sort of
evaluative assessment of alternatives going beyond the mere technological determination of means. Hence, the requirement of
"ethical neutrality" from bureaucratic officials is one that it is
impossible to fulfill, and to assume that it is possible or even
desirable is a pure myth, adopted, perhaps, for the purpose of
clearing officials of personal responsibility for their

decisions.[37]

## Utilitarianism and Alienation

It is abundantly evident that the use of a double standard for the evaluation of actions is not confined to the operations of formal organizations, as I have described them. The double standard for social morality is pervasive in our society. For almost all our social decisions, administrative, political and economic, are made and justified by reference to the "rational" standard, which amounts to the principle that the end justifies the means; and yet as individuals, in our personal relations with one another, we are bound by the ordinary principles of morality, i.e. the principles of obligation, responsibility and integrity.

The philosophical foundation of the theory of "rationality" in social decision is to be found in the whole family of theories generally known as utilitarianism. Utilitarianism in all its different forms is basically a theory of social decision rather than a theory of individual action. That is, it is a theory for legislators and social planners. Even rule-utilitarianism, which purports to have something to say about individual conduct, is in its utilitarian aspect a theory of moral legislation, a theory concerning what sorts of rules and practices ought to be adopted for society.[38] Sidgwick openly concedes this view of utilitarianism when he writes:

> Hence the stress which Utilitarians are apt to lay on social and political theory of all kinds, and the tendency which Utilitarian ethics have always shown to pass over into politics. For one who values conduct in proportion to its felicific consequences will naturally set a higher estimate on effective benevolence in public affairs than on the purest manifestation of virtue in the details of private life. . . .[39]

For reasons which should be obvious from the foregoing discussion, utilitarianism has always had great difficulty in bridging the gap between social morality, the morality of social decisions, and personal morality, the morality of individuals in their relations with each other. In most, if not all its versions, we end up with a double standard: the principle of utility, to be applied to social decisions; and rules, secondary principles, conventions, etc., to be applied to individual conduct. The double standard aspect of utilitarianism is openly acknowledged by Sidgwick, when he writes that "it seems expedient that the doctrine that esoteric morality is expedient should itself be kept esoteric. Or if this concealment be difficult to maintain, it may be desirable that Common Sense should repudiate the doctrines which it is expedient to confine to an enlightened few, etc."[40] In other words, the administrator of the principle of utility, the enlightened utilitarian, uses one standard, and the rest of us, the vulgar, use another one, the standard of Common Sense, i.e. the standard of ordinary morality.

This is not the place to discuss the merits of utilitarianism as a moral theory, although I think it should be pointed out that one of the consequences of the separation of the ideal theory (utility) of social action from the rules actually to be followed by the individual in one's personal conduct is an endorsement of the status quo as far as individual morality is concerned.

A great deal more needs to be said about the effects of working from a double standard of morality. In our highly organized (and utilitarian) society, most of us, as individuals, are forced to live double lives, and in order to accommodate ourselves to two different and incompatible standards, we tend to compartmentalize our lives, as I have already pointed out. For the most part, however, the organizational (or utilitarian) standard tends to take over.

Accordingly, our actions as individuals are increasingly submerged into social actions, that is, we tend more and more to use the social standard as a basis for our decisions and to evaluate our actions. As a result, the individual's own decisions and actions become separated from oneself as a person and become the decisions and actions of another, e.g. of an organization. They become social decisions, not decisions of the individual. And in becoming social decisions, they are, in Hobbes' terms, no longer "hers/his," they are "owned" by another, e.g. an organization or society.

This is one way of rendering the Marxian concept of alienation. As one's actions are turned into social decisions, the individual is alienated from them and is _eo ipso_ alienated from other people and from morality. In adopting the administrator's point of view (or that of a utilitarian) and so losing one's actions, the individual becomes dehumanized and demoralized. For morality is essentially a relation between people, as individuals, and in losing this relation, one loses morality itself.

## Closing Remarks on the Source of the Paradox

It is unnecessary to dwell on the intolerable character of the moral schizophrenia in which we find ourselves as the result of the double standard of conduct that has been pointed out. The question is: what can be done about it? The simplest and most obvious solution is to jettison one of the conflicting standards. But which one? The choice is difficult, if not impossible. If we give up the standard of "rationality," e.g. of organizational operations, then we surrender one of the chief conditions of civilized life and progress as well as the hope of ever solving mankind's perennial practical problems, e.g. the problems of hunger, disease, ignorance and overpopulation. On the other hand, if we give up the standard of ordinary moral conduct, then in effect we destroy ourselves as moral beings and reduce our relationships to each other to purely mechanical and materialistic ones. To find a third way out of the dilemma is not only a practical, political and sociological necessity, but a moral one as well.

Without in the least intending to dismiss the psychological and sociological aspects of the problem as unimportant and insubstantial, I should like to stress that it also has a logicoethical side that we cannot afford to ignore. For the dilemma arising out of the existence of two different standards is essentially a logical dilemma. We must therefore try to find out what logical assumptions or presuppositions underlie it. Hopefully if we can pinpoint the source of the difficulty logically, we may be able to escape between the horns of the dilemma and thus be on our way to a solution of the paradox - at least in its theoretical aspect.

Logically, the origin of the dilemma lies, I believe, in a certain theory of action which is taken for granted unquestioningly by many moral philosophers, namely, what I have elsewhere called the "causal theory of action."[41] (This theory is sometimes called the "consequentialist theory.") According to it, an action is a "making things to happen," the "production of a change," or the "causing of a state of affairs." It is the general theory of action on which utilitarianism and other theories of "rational behavior" are built.[42]

There are three propositions regarding action and responsibility that lie behind the double standard created by the organizational language-game and that are presupposed more generally by the utilitarian theory of social choice. All of them depend in one way or another on a causal theory of action.

The first of these propositions concerns the notion of a social decision, as I have called it. It is the effect that a logically and ethically tenable distinction can be made between the performance of an action by a representative (an actor) and the action itself, which is attributed to someone or something else (the author). Accordingly, a social decision is an action that is attributed to an organization although it is made (performed) by individual officers. The net effect of conceiving of social decisions as a distinctive kind of action of this type is that moral obligations, rights and responsibilities relative to them belong to the organizations as such, that is, are predicated of the organizations rather than of the individual officers who perform the actions as its representatives (actors). Furthermore, even questions about what kind of actions are right or wrong are construed as questions about what it is right or wrong for the organizations, rather than for its officers, to do; for it is really the organization that is doing the action and not its officers. In other words, the standards of conduct are applied directly to organizations, bypassing, as it were, the individual decision-makers. The next step in the development of the argument is, of course, to lay down a different standard for determining the rightness and wrongness of social decisions from that determining the rightness and wrongness of the actions of individuals.

The paradox arises, of course, from the notion of an action that is performed by an individual or group of individuals but is not attributed to them. It enables them to avoid responsibility for what they do by attributing the actions to the organization. The link with the causal theory of action is through the idea that an action consists in causing a change; social decisions are, on this view, causes of changes, sometimes changes of overwhelming importance. The relationship is obviously a complicated one and one that cannot be explored further at this point. The main question we have to face is whether or not we will allow social decisions, e.g. of formal organizations, to count as actions in the full, moral sense in which they are subjects of moral prescription, justification and evaluation.

The second proposition behind our paradox relates to the responsibility of individual decision-makers for the consequences of the decisions they make. The social decisions we have been discussing might, if we wish, be considered as collective actions, i.e. as actions to which a large number of individuals contribute. Then they would be like the kind of action in which a number of persons remove a table from the room by their joint efforts.[43] In that case, the part played by the individual is that of a partial, contributing cause to the effect that defines the action. Most of the decisions, i.e. actions, of formal organizations can be conceived as collective actions in this sense; for the part played by any single official is neither necessary nor sufficient to bring about the change. The efforts of the individuals in an organization are like strands in a rope; together they make up the rope, although any particular strand is dispensable. That is why the activities of the individual are simply lost in the complex social process.

We can see, then, how the individual might lose all responsibility for the decisions of the organization, if, as the causal theory supposes, moral responsibility is assimilated to causal responsibility, i.e. effectiveness. As the causal responsibility decreases, so does the moral responsibility. Hence, the less significant role a person plays in the social process, the less moral responsibility one has for it. Since most of the decisions made in formal organizations are in actual fact collective actions in which an indefinitely large number of individuals are involved, the responsibility of any single individual for the decision becomes minimal.

Here again we see how the causal theory of action gives aid and comfort to officials who want to avoid responsibility for the social decisions in which they participate. For in the operations of formal organizations there is a question not only of finding out who should be held responsible but also of determining what it means to be responsible. Only if we repudiate the theory, and the assimilation of moral to causal responsibility that it implies, will we be able to assess the actions of any particular official on their own merits without regard to the other causal factors contributing to the final result.

Finally, we come to the third proposition lying behind the theory of social decisions, namely, the proposition that an action is rational if and only if it is the best means to attaining one's objectives.[44] Whatever particular form this principle of rationality takes, subjective or objective, it is still based on the assumption that the essence of an action is its producing an end-state of affairs, an objective. Inasmuch as every action is, or ideally should be, purposive in this sense - by definition - then it naturally follows that a rational action could only be one that is defined in terms of a "bringing about a change" or a "production of a state of affairs." Given a causal theory of action, rational behavior, or action, has to be defined in causal terms, i.e. ends and means.

Quite apart from the question-begging nature of this conception of "rationality," it has certain obviously objectionable moral consequences; for it reduces the relationship between individual human beings to the category of means to an end, a category in which they do not belong. It makes the only point of a rational action the function that it plays in "means-ends" chains. The only point of keeping a promise, for instance, is the effect that doing so will have on my own ends or the ends of others. This way of looking at rationality reflects what seems to me to be essentially an amoral position, for it reduces morality, which is a matter of the relations between human beings, to what is useful or expedient for some purpose or other.

It is impossible to defend here in any detail the objections that I have presented against the concept of social decision, the concept of "rationality," and the causal theory of action, which in many ways is involved in the first two of these. It may suffice to point out that the kind of paradox which we are forced into by the basic concepts of organizational thinking and, of course, by utilitarian theory, calls for a radical re-examination of the theory of action that underlies them.

## FOOTNOTES

[1]Amitai Etzioni, _Modern Organizations_ (Englewood Cliffs, N.J.: Prentice-Hall, 1964), p. 4.

[2]Max Weber in Etzioni, quoted in Etzioni, _Modern Operations_ p. 53.

[3]Herbert A. Simon, _Administrative Behavior_, 2d ed. (New York: Free Press, 1965), p. 9. For a useful survey of the subject of formal organizations, see Peter M. Blau and W. Richard Scott, _Formal Organizations_ (San Francisco: Chandler Publishing Company, 1962).

[4]See Peter M. Blau and W. Richard Scott, _Formal Organizations_ for a survey of these questions.

[5]Ibid., p. 35.

[6]Hans Kelsen provides us with a good example of a nonethical normative system in his _General Theory of Law and State_ (Cambridge, Mass.: Harvard University Press, 1949). His pure theory of law bears certain analogies to the accounts of the ideal type of bureaucracy with which we are concerned here.

[7]Simon, _Administrative Behavior_, pp. 62, 249, 253.

[8]Ludwig Wittgenstein, _Philosophical Investigations_ (New York: Macmillan Company, 1953), p. 7.

[9]These rules are called "constitutive rules" by John Searle. See his _Speech Acts_ (Cambridge: The University Press, 1969), Ch. 2, Sec. 5.

[10]For further discussion of the game-model and this aspect of rules, see my, "Moral and Legal Obligation," in _Political and Legal Obligation_, ed. J. Roland Pennock and John W. Chapman.

[11]See Simon, _Administrative Behavior_, passim. Also, Blau and Scott, _Formal Operations_, p. 36.

[12]See Kenneth Arrow, _Social Choice and Individual Values_ (New York: John Wiley, 1951), passim.

[13]Quoted from A. Bergson by Kenneth Arrow in "Public and Private Values," in _Human Values and Economic Policy_, ed. S. Hook (New York: New York, University Press, 1967), p. 14.

[14]Thomas Hobbes, _Leviathan_, Chapter 16.

[15]Simon, _Administrative Behavior_, p. 11 and 126.

[16]Quoted from Max Weber in Robert Merton, Alisa Gray, Barbara Hockey, and Hanan C. Selvin, <u>Reader in Bureaucracy</u> (New York: Free Press, 1952), p. 19.

[17]Quoted from Chester I. Barnard in Simon, <u>Administrative Behavior</u>, p. 203.

[18]See John Kenneth Galbraith, <u>The New Industrial State</u> (Boston: Houghton Mifflin, 1967), pp. 171-78.

[19]See Etzioni, <u>Modern Operations</u>, pp. 7-9.

[20]Etzioni, <u>Modern Operations</u> p. 3. See Blau and Scott, <u>Formal Organizations</u>, p. 5. In a forthcoming article on "Community," I try to show that communities, as distinct from formal organizations, do not have specific goals. Indeed, the having of a specific goal may be what differentiates a Gesellschaft from a Gemeinschaft in Tonnies' sense. See Ferdinand Tonnies' <u>Community in Society</u>, trans. Charles P. Loomis (New York: Harper and Row, 1957), passim.

[21]Simon, <u>Administrative Behavior</u>, p. 52.

[22]"The ideal of pure rationality is basic to operations research and the modern management sciences." Yehezkel Dror, <u>Public Policymaking Reexamined</u> (San Francisco: Chandler Publishing Company, 1968), p. 336. Dror gives a useful bibliography of this subject on pp. 336-40.

[23]Simon, <u>Administrative Behavior</u>, p. 5.

[24]Ibid., p. 240.

[25]Ibid., p. 77.

[26]Simon, <u>Administrative Behavior</u>, p. 14.

[27]". . . 'good' administration is behavior that is realistically adapted to its ends. . . ." Simon, p. 62.

[28]"The name morality, when standing unqualified or alone, may signify the human laws which I style positive morality, without regard to their goodness or badness. For example, such laws of the class as are peculiar to a given age, or such laws of the class as are peculiar to a given nation, we style the morality of that given age or nation, whether we think them good or bad Hart. New York, Noonday Press, 1954, p. 125. The study of positive moralities belongs to what I call "descriptive ethics." See John Ladd's <u>Structure of a Moral Code</u> (Cambridge, Mass.: Harvard University Press, 1957).

[29]Simon, <u>Administrative Behavior</u>, p. 52.

[30]Reinhard Bendix, "Bureaucracy and the Problem of Power," in

Merton et al., <u>Reader in Bureaucracy</u>, p. 132.

[31]Blau and Scott, <u>Formal Organizations</u>, p. 34.

[32]See my "Moral and Legal Obligation," referred to in note 10.

[33]The fact that promising involves an extremely personal relation between individuals is almost universally overlooked by philosophers who discuss promises.

[34]David Hume, <u>An Enquiry Concerning the Principles of Morals</u>. ed. L.A. Selby-Bigge (Oxford: Clarendon Press, 1902), p. 305.

[35]Galbraith, <u>The New Industrial State</u>, p. 159.

[36]It is easy to understand why officials often go to such extremes to monopolize information; for monopolizing information is one of the few remaining ways for them to protect an authority that is already wobbling.

[37]It is obviously easier for an official to avoid responsibility for his decisions if he can maintain that his only role in the decision-making is that of ascertaining the facts.

[38]The rule-maker takes a "God's eye point of view," i.e. an impersonal approach of the kind that is required for social decisions in general. For expositions of this sort of moral legislation, see J. Rawls, "Justice as Fairness," <u>Philosophical Review</u> 67 (1958): 164-194. Also Kurt Baier, <u>The Moral Point of View</u> (New York: Random House, 1965), p. 107.

[39]Henry Sidgwick, <u>The Methods of Ethics</u>, 7th ed. (London: Macmillan, 1930), p. 495.

[40]Ibid., p. 490.

[41]See John Ladd, "The Ethical Dimensions of the Concept of Action," <u>Journal of Philosophy</u> 62 (1965): 633-45.

[42]See Eric D'Arcy, <u>Human Acts</u> (Oxford: Clarendon Press, 1963). Perhaps the most detailed exposition of the causal theory from the logical point of view is given in Georg Henrik von Wright, <u>Norm and Action</u> (London: Routledge and Kegan Paul, 1963).

[43]See Georg H. von Wright, <u>Norm and Action</u>, p. 38. Also Ernest Sosa, "Actions and Their Results," <u>Logique et Analyse</u> (Juin 1965) pp. 111-25.

[44]Various senses of "rationality" are distinguished in Simon, <u>Administrative Behavior</u>, pp. 76-77. An extremely sophisticated version of this concept of rationality is to be found in Carl G. Hempel, "Rational Action," Proceedings and Addresses of the American Philosophical Association 1961-62, p. 5. Hempel writes, "Broadly speaking, an action will qualify as rational if, on the

basis of the given information, it offers optimal prospects of achieving its objectives." The position he presents in this article is open to all the criticisms that I have presented here of the concept of rationality in social decision-making.

# ADMINISTRATION AND THE CRISIS IN LEGITIMACY:

## A REVIEW OF HABERMASIAN THOUGHT*

### William P. Foster

Traditionally, the applied field of educational administration has relied on theory and research generated in the study of corporate management. It has been concerned less with philosophies of administration than with the derivation of scientific principles designed to increase organizational efficiency and effectiveness. This paper is concerned with an analysis of some of those principles and with the relationship that may exist between the application of administrative science and public support of and confidence in the formal educational system.

The nature of administration has come increasingly under attack: "Public administration today faces a crisis of legitimacy so significant that the basic paradigm guiding thought and action in the field must now be called into question."[1] Organizational analysis has been held to be in a state of crisis by Benson.[2] The science of politics has been seriously questioned by Storing.[3] The field of educational administration has been indicted for its preoccupation with variables unrelated to the teaching-learning process by Erickson.[4] The succinct phrase of the moment is that these areas of administration are faced with a legitimation crisis. Even when overstated, there is undoubtedly a serious malaise among students of the administrative sciences, including that branch which deals with the governance of schools. In a period of critical reflection, a number of administrative scientists have begun not only to doubt the efficacy of their work but even to question the discipline's status as a science. Part of this self-questioning stems from a developing crisis of confidence in the abilities of administrators to govern public institutions. Public schools, highly visible and historically revered, are at the center of this crisis.

It would seem odd that, in a period when tremendous energy and money is being expended on attempting to develop more objectively scientific descriptions of administration, management, leadership, motivation and job satisfaction, that such questioning would occur. Indeed, it would seem that modern administrative theory represents a transition from the art of politics and administration, where value judgments predominate, to a science of politics and administration, where value-free statements dominate.

Max Weber, whose treatment of wertfrei social science sparked a number of continuing methodological debates, can be considered

*This is a revised and expanded version of "Administration and the Crisis in Legitimacy: A Review of Habermasian Thought," Harvard Educational Review 50 (November, 1980): 496-505. This version was prepared specifically for this volume.

to be the inspiration, despite later misappropriation, of an objectivistic social science. For Weber, "reality, whether natural or social, is extensively and intensively infinite; therefore any approach to the analysis of a given event or phenomenon in reality must be selective, and guided by values, as stated in the principle of value-relevance--Wertbeziehung."[5] Weber did consider that social, like natural, science, could investigate practical questions with methodological rigor, and that such investigations must be experential in nature; that is, a social science must look for "causes" in experience, not in metaphysics. The Weberian implications lie more in showing the impossibility of a <u>science of values</u> than in suggesting a value-free science. Science, was, essentially, concerned with facts, but this concern operates within a context of values which must be either accepted or rejected, not proven or disproven. Yet Weber did assert the neutrality of science in respect to value positions: a scientific approach can, and must, remain rationally objective. This position was, in the diet of later social scientists, converted into a methodologically hard positivism.

This, of course, is the crux of the problem. Can one develop an empirical basis for the proper governance of society in general and for such institutions as schools in particular? In his review of the state of contemporary social science, Bernstein points to the difficulties:

> When we examine those empirical theories that have been advanced, we discover again and again that they are not value-neutral, but reflect deep ideological biases and secret controversial value positions. It is a fiction to think that we can neatly distinguish the descriptive from the evaluative comments of these theories, for tacit evaluations are built into their very framework.[6]

Modern studies of administration and governance assumed that objective, empirically validated theories can and should be developed. The work of Herbert Simon, A Nobel Prize recipient in economics, is a case in point. His works, particularly <u>Administrative Behavior</u>, have been influential in both structuring inquiry in the field and providing justification for it. In reading the contemporary literature in public and school administration, one senses the spirit of Simon floating between the lines. The three particular postulates Simon advanced have become dogmas in the field of administrative science. He advocated the necessity of distinguishing between facts and values; he embraced a conception of human rationality that is peculiarly modern in its emphases; and he considered certain assumptions about the nature of science.[7]

First, Simon argued that administrators are not concerned solely with making decisions, but that the decisions they make be correct. But "correctness" can only be ascertained from "facts," since values are neither correct nor incorrect and therefore of no concern to administrators. Statements are only meaningful if they are true by definition or verifiable by the "facts of experience."[8]

This positivistic assumption is the basis for Simon's vision of rationality -- the utilization of correct means in the achievement of ends. These ends, being values, are, of course, beyond the realm of administrative action. In his earlier work, Simon adopted the "maximization" view of rationality, wherein the fully rational person is one who, given a particular end in sight, considers all possible means to achieve that end and then selects those means most consistent with the facts. Sensitive to the charge that this model of rationality leaves us without any truly rational people, Simon later revised his model to allow rationality to reflect the selection of means "good-enough" to achieve the end: our administrative decision makers, in the terms of a horrid neologism, "satisfice."[9]

As Storing has pointed out, neither the original maximization tenet nor the later "satisficing" argument allows Simon to escape from the problematic separation of facts and values. Facts are embedded in a context of values, and if one looks at administration as the direction of resources to solve problems then it should be clear that at the most basic level, problems are defined as such only because they conflict with certain values. It is of no use to claim, as Simon might, that the problem is defined by those outside administration and that therefore the fiat to stick to the facts still applies; even in the process of generation of solutions, the administrative decision maker receives facts that are interpreted within a system of values.[10]

But Simon held a rather positivist vision of science and hoped that by bracketing the rationality problem his administrators could proceed to become scientists.[11] He warned the uninitiated that "science is concerned with the factual aspects of meaning, but not with the ethical",[12] and he cautioned students to be concerned with only those propositions that are potentially verifiable. Yet, in the end, Simon could not escape the ethical basis of his science. Storing has effectively identified the problem:

> Wherever Simon's science is probed, it is found to depend upon some pre-scientific divination of the nature of man and the world. Simon does in practice assume that there are real problems which would exist even if they were not regarded as problems. He assumes that there are important problems and unimportant problems, and therefore important decisions. He believes that men ought to act rationally, ... (H)is description and analysis of administration depend absolutely on these beliefs, but on his own premises they are beliefs for which there cannot be any reasonable basis. They are the unarticulated value judgments on which the allegedly value-free science rests, to which it resorts for

guidance, and from which it draws whatever relevance it has to (the) real world of administrative behavior.[13]

One finds that much of what passes for administrative theory is strangely inappropriate for the "real world of administrative behavior," a consequence, in part, of the stress put on this new rationality and science. When Vroom, a management scientist, can write that management is charged with "determining how the problem is to be solved, not the solution to be adopted",[14] then clearly this science of management is unable to distinguish between such value-laden issues as democracy and dictatorship, and that each of these "solutions" to the problem of governance is scientifically irrelevant.

If, as I will claim, a science of administration must recognize the context of values and ethics, then one must develop a reconceptualization of the meaning of a science of administration and a critical awareness of the validity claims of its current practitioners. The work of Jurgen Habermas, a German social philosopher, provides a compelling framework for analyzing the nature of an administrative science, the fact-value distinction, and the role of the administrative apparatus in maintaining its legitimacy.

Habermas' seminal works, particularly Legitimation Crisis fostered an attack on the established dogma of institutional governance. While his endeavors are so broad as almost to defy classification - he has addressed such subjects as philosophy of history, sociology, psychoanalysis, and political science - he has nonetheless what Thomas McCarthy, Habermas' frequent translator and our guide through the sometimes dense prose, calls a "unity of perspective," based on a globable analysis of history and society and aimed at identifying the underlying causes of domination. One thrust of this analysis has been Habermas' critique of modern political and administrative strategies as they affect individual dignity. His critique of administration comes as necessary preface to his more far reaching analysis of advanced capitalism. Historically this was the major project of the Marxist-oriented Frankfurt School, whose members have included Horkheimer, Adorno, Marcuse, and Habermas. While Habermas has addressed many features of advanced capitalism, we will consider only that portion of his work concerned with education, administration, and the confidence crisis.[15]

Legitimation Crisis analyses both modern society and its administration; Communication and the Evolution of Society incorporates this analysis in a broader theory involving linguistic structures and developmental concepts. To decode Habermas' argument in terms of its relevance to modern political systems and to use it as a tool for recognizing the deficiencies of administrative thought requires an understanding of the premises that underlie the development of modern administrative science.[16]

A true democrat, Habermas argues that the fact-value distinction denies the possibility of a rational discussion of social norms in which generalizable political interests can be recognized and democratic consensus attained. While he acknowledges the distinction between empirically derived facts and socially derived norms, he questions the appropriateness of a positivistic separation of facts and values. He suggests that all theories, even those about the nature of scientific knowledge, rest on standards requiring critical justification. Thus, scientific description is "not independent of standards which are used, and standards rest upon attitudes which are in need of justification through supporting arguments."[17] The methodology of science, in this view, does not stand apart from the norms and attitudes of the scientific community. And the set of agreements about how science is conducted, which grows out of these norms and attitudes, is open to discussion. The implication is that rational processes are embedded in human action and do not stand objectively outside the world of human intercourse. Habermas' arguments strengthen the claim that it is possible to have a social science which is neither purely empirical nor purely interpretative.

Habermas provides an alternative view to positivistic developments in administrative theory which contrast starkly with the three areas Simon addressed. Habermas' thought is particularly significant in two respects. He outlines an argument which links modern administrative theory to a developing crisis in public confidence, and he embarks on a quest to construct a theory of empirically verifiable norms. this latter task may eliminate the fundamental basis for the assumptions of Simon and other modern theorists about a fact-value dichotomy by showing the veracity of certain normative standards.

In the first part of his argument, Habermas claims that advanced societies have developed tendencies toward crisis states which originate in capitalistic socioeconomic relations. But he espouses no vulgar critique of capitalism, rather, he reformulates the Marxian hypotheses by looking at the historical progression of human thought and analyzes developments from a perspective based on the philosophy and sociology of knowledge. His assertion, which he continually qualifies by underscoring the need for empirical validation, is that there are tendencies in modern governmental systems toward crisis in the areas of rationality, legitimation, and motivation.

The crisis in rationality arises in relation to the modern development of organizational rationality. This is what Weber identified as formal rationality, Horkheimer as subjective rationality, Habermas as purposive or instrumental rationality, and Simon as the objective rationality of means. This view of reason, as it appears in administration, is that ends are not subject to discussion, that only means can be considered to be more or less susceptible to rational analysis. By adopting an instrumental rationality, public governance provides no framework for belief in the system other than that it in fact provides the type of scientific, rational decisions that it says it will provide. But such rational decisions have not been typical, in part because of the complexity of the system and in part because of the productive relationships in a liberal capitalistic economy. One of the contradictions that arises in such a system is that two spheres of social interaction, the political and the economic, have different aims.[18] The political sphere is based on the premise of equality despite individual variations in talent and class origins, while the economic sphere is based on the premise of superiority on account of talent and class origins. Thus an individual can seek political equality, demanding representation and equal opportunity, but no individual can demand economic equality.

Modern states, for Habermas, are responsible for promoting economic growth, structuring production to meet collective needs, and correcting social inequalities.[19] When public administration promises full employment, economic growth, and limitation of inflation but does not deliver on these promises, then a rationality deficit emerges. The same effect might be described in education: if public schools are touted as the "means" to certain ends -- learned, disciplined students, a productive knowledgable society-but experience shows financial crises, problems of order and lack of achievement, then a public concern with "the quality of education" develops, symptomatic of a rationality deficit.

This in turn creates a legitimation deficit, that is, an erosion of belief in the system. This is the inchoate feeling that "things" are not what they should be and that certain "forces" have put the operation of the system beyond our control. Habermas explains his thesis this way:

> A rationality deficit in public administration means that the state apparatus cannot, under given boundary conditions, adequately steer the economic system. A legitimation deficit means that it is not possible by administrative means to maintain or establish effective normative structures to the extent required. . . . (W)hile organizational rationality spreads, cultural traditions are undermined and weakened. The residue of tradition must, however, escape the administrative grasp, for traditions important for legitimation cannot be regenerated administratively.[20]

By "organizational rationality," Habermas here means the formal means-ends rationality found in bureaucratic structures; there is a contractual demand for delivery of services. The question that is raised is whether such a rationality is in and of itself a basis for granting legitimacy to the institution. Norms and belief-structures are eroded by organizational rationality in the sense that such norms become required to justify themselves or be dismissed as irrelevant. Yet if this is the case, and organizational rationality is indeed not a sufficient basis for legitimizing an institutional universe, then what replaces the belief-structure which previously has asserted the moral "rightness" of the institution to do what it does? Thus, the legitimacy granted to the political structure depends on a set of beliefs external to that structure, e.g., "divine right," "self-evident truths," which allow the structure to claim the uncoerced allegiance of the populace. Modern theories of legitimacy, however, have become "secularized," divorced from their philosophical and ethical underpinnings.[21] Mueller claims:

> Today, efficiency is an important, if not the most important source of legitimacy in modern society. The disconnection of politics from a normative basis and the decline of traditional legitimating ideologies and collectively held political interpretations, on one hand, and the growing intervention of the state into the social and economic order, on the other, have created a symbolic void which has to be filled by legitimating symbols of a new nature.[22]

But the state cannot administratively create such new culture symbols, and, combined with the recognition of inefficiency (i.e., a rationality deficit), a legitimation crisis results. The state's dilemma is that in order to administer economic growth effectively and remove social inequality, it must use its legitimate power as a state: yet to use this power is to destroy one of the norms supporting its legitimacy, that "private autonomy may not be violated."[23] This norm, in a capitalistic democracy, secures the rights of individuals to succeed or fail in the (largely economic) affairs of men. The state's solution to this dilemma is to adopt increasingly technological strategies of administration oriented toward systems maintenance and adjustment. The increasingly scientific orientation of administration in itself creates problems of legitimation. A scientific administration is a depoliticized administration. Much of the newly established management science maintains that increasingly complex systems require highly technical control strategies beyond the grasp of the layperson. A fully efficient system is a fully rational system, but neither is compatible with a democratic political philosophy. Majority rule may not always be particularly rational nor particularly efficient. For systems theorists, democracy tends to be an outmoded concept inappropriate to quick, reactive control and steering capability within shifting environments. This technocratic consciousness is the logical conclusion of Simon's earlier work. But, as Habermas has pointed out, such technically refined systems cannot sustain the normative traditions needed for belief in the system.

The idea of a motivation deficit is related to the previous discussion of legitimation crisis. Habermas finds that the traditional sources of motivation lay in a normative structure that sanctions two types of privatism: civil, in which the citizen participated in the political fabric only to the degree permitted by institutions; and family-vocational, where family motivations tended toward the purchase of consumable goods and leisure time, and vocational motivations were oriented toward status achievement.

Habermas claims that the cultural traditions supporting these motivations, such as the Protestant Ethic, are being eroded and cannot be supplanted by new cultural traditions, since administration itself cannot create meaningful norms. Science, for example, can expose popular beliefs as ideological and mythical, but cannot recreate itself except as a paraideology.[24] A motivational deficit is reflected in a sense of powerlessness in the system as it is presently constituted.

This is evident in the schools. According to Tyack, "substantial segments of this society no longer believe in centralism as an effective response to human needs, no longer accept the inevitability or justice of the distribution of power and wealth along existing class and racial lines."[25] The severe fiscal problems in urban schools, the great public concern with discipline, the increasing distance between teachers and administrators, and the failure of schools to develop universal literacy and mathematics skills, suggest that public confidence in the system, indeed the educators' own confidence, has eroded to the point where the legitimacy of the institution itself is in question.[26] When the administration cannot deliver on the promise of equal and effective education, then the present organization of schools is not a rational means to the ends in question. The response by administration, however, has been not to reassess the adequacy of the system itself, but to attempt to adapt other institutions to the needs of the school system. Thus, preschool programs are established, and reputable psychologists encourage educators to go into homes of families with infants to correct inadequate child-rearing practices. Popular psychologists can suggest that parents establish formal contracts with children in order to secure appropriate behavior, apparently along the model of contracts between employers and employees.

The response to a crisis in confidence is to attempt to do what cannot be done: to objectify even further the ends of administration in the hope that these can be made susceptible to technical - that is rational-control. Thus, one author suggests that "it would seem useful to conceive of the educator - an administrator, a counselor, a teacher, a planner, or a curriculum specialist - as a manager of the learning process."[27] This refers, however, to systematic management concerned with systemic control. Applied to the school, the traditional legitimacy of the teacher becomes secondary to the means of administration. Teacher evaluations, for example, become mechanisms for administrative control, "objective" measurements of rational performance. Wolcott noted in his study that, "the evaluation ceremony reaffirmed organizational rules and policies imposed within the hierarchy, with the effect of keeping the locus of power in the central office and meeting out detailed elements of responsibility rather than delegating authority and responsibility on a broad scale."[28]

Planned curricula development which reduces the teacher's autonomy in developing educational aims similarly reflects an instrumental rationality whose failure to provide a meaningful education may threaten the legitimacy not of the academics who develop them but of the teachers who are forced to use them. Habermas offers these observations:

"Whereas school administrations formerly merely had to codify a canon that had taken shape in an unplanned, nature like manner, present curriculum planning is based on the premise that traditional patterns could as well be otherwise. Administrative planning produces a universal pressure for legitimation in a sphere that was once distinguished precisely for its power of self-legitimation."[29]

The rationale for a curriculum "That this knowledge is worth teaching," succumbs to an instrumental logic where all knowledge becomes a standardized means to achieving objectives set by the system itself. A Black Studies course is added not because it is a good thing to study but because it re-establishes a lost legitimacy in the eyes of a given constituency. The pressure to legitimate what is taught obfuscates discussion of what should be taught and results in a technical attempt to control the system. As one respected curriculum theorist writes:

A curriculum system is a system for decision making and action with respect to curriculum functions. A curriculum system has three primary functions: (1) to produce a curriculum, (2) to implement a curriculum, and (3) to appraise the effectiveness of a curriculum and a curriculum system. Curriculum engineering consists of all the processes and activities necessary to maintain and improve a curriculum system including leadership by such chief engineers as the superintendent, the principal, and the curriculum director.[30]

The "chief engineer" and his like-minded colleagues apparently see the curriculum not as a dynamic and evolving process but as a set of procedures to be implemented.

Yet, government administration continues to enter areas once the domain of tradition, such as educational curriculum planning, exposing them as new "problems" requiring administrative solutions. The identification of a problem, however, raises the entire question for public discussion. But in order to function effectively, Habermas claims, administrative solutions must be implemented quickly and accepted simply by the public. The identification of new "problems" can pose a threat to administrative authority and legitimacy by allowing public debate about a variety of solutions.

Compulsory education has succeeded in teaching a general acceptance of instrumental or purposive rationality and a faith in science and technology. The consequence is that reasons and evidence are required in support of the decisions the state makes, a requirement which challenges the natural legitimacy of the government. In addition, science can expose as ideological and

mythical the popular, traditional beliefs, but it cannot
substitute for those beliefs because it sets standards by which it
also can be exposed and critiqued. Thus, "theories of technocracy
and of elites, which assert the necessity of institutionalized
civil privatism, are not immune to objections, because they too
must claim to be theories."[31] A science of management which
requires the abstention of the public from decision making
(because of its advanced scientific status) can also be exposed
when it does not meet the purposive standards it has set for
itself. In this way, the traditional motivations which supported
preliberal capitalism are said to be eroded, creating the
repolitization of the public realm, as illustrated by the
frequency and variety of public protests on many issues.

Habermas has thus addressed the development of positivistic
social science and its corresponding fact-value distinction and
has related it to the development of crises in rationality,
legitimation, and motivation. Contemporary administrative science
is itself in something of a crisis state intellectually because of
its inability to completely rationalize the means of
administration. On a broad historical scale, there is a
relationship between this failure and legitimation crises in
welfare capitalism. A crisis in schools is not an isolated and
distinct problem, but is related to the general institutional
legitimation crisis, because both stem from the inadequacy of
scientific administration.

Habermas argues that a solution to the legitimation crisis is
possible. He suggests that a legitimation crisis can be avoided
in the long run only if the latent class structures of advanced
capitalist societies are transformed or if the pressure for
legitimation to which the administrative system is subject can be
removed. The latter, in turn, could be achieved by transposing
the integration of inner nature in toto to another mode of
socialization, that is, by uncoupling it from norms that need
justification.[32]

And this indeed is the second part of Habermas' argument: to
find a theory of verifiable norms whose existence can be
rationally discussed. He would, perhaps, agree with Dewey that
values do not come from the blue but are constructions based in
the human project. Its foundation, however, will rest not on the
legitimacy of the state but on a universal morality whose basis
lies in communicative ethics, a morality based on undistorted
discussion and consensus. The basis for this communicative ethics
lies in Habermas' analysis of a universal pragmatics, and the
underlying dimensions of speech acts. It is here that he makes
his stand on the possibility of rational discussion of norms and
implicitly dismisses the fact-value distinction.

On the assumption that speech itself is the common feature
that links the human species, Habermas, particularly in
Communication and the Evolution of Society, explores the
dimensions of the "ideal" speech situation, a presupposition
reflected in actual speech. What, he asks, underlies such a
situation? His answer asserts that basic to the process of
utterance is the requirement for intersubjective understanding,
which involves a speaker's claim that one is "saying something in

an understandable fashion, giving something to understand; has thereby made oneself understandable, and has thereby come to an understanding with another person."[33] Each of these factors can be described in terms of four dimensions basic to speech: comprehensibility, truth, truthfulness, and rightness. Comprehensibility is the claim that we have encased our sounds in a shared grammar; truth is the claim that there is a factual basis for the discussion; truthfulness is the claim that the speaker's intention in speaking is not deceptive; and rightness is the claim that the utterance is appropriate in the context in which it is uttered. These norms are offered as universal values embedded in human speech. If these dimensions are universal components of communication between people, there may be universalistic characteristics of norms such as "truth" and "rightness." The idea of norms themselves being generic to the human situation suggests, then, the possibility of a generic ethics based on communication norms. This argument is particularly significant because it could expose the false fact-value dichotomy and thus allow for new forms of justification for social institutions. Habermas writes: "Justifiable norms are like true sentences; they are neither facts nor values."[34]

The argument itself, however, depends on the assumption of an ideal of "pure" speech situation, an assumption which some sociolinguists would find to be unsupported at this point because of the complexity of patterns of language-in-use. Habermas, however, develops a logical rather than an empirical argument and, in so doing, at least provides the grounds for reconsidering the possibility of political praxis. The strength of his linguistically based argument lies in its theoretical liberation of the concept of rationality, which allow for the possibility of reconceptualizing the purpose and design of modern administrative theory. If it can be logically demonstrated that some norms or values have a real and meaningful base, then the dialogue on the administrative control of institutions can proceed rationally, in the expanded sense of rationality. Administrative scholars themselves have become dissatisfied with the heavy emphasis on rationality-as-efficiency, and a spirit of change seems to be affecting the discipline. The spirit, if not the form, of this critique is apparent in the words of Ramos: "The time is ripe for the practice of an unprecedented kind of administrative science sensitive to the diverse issues of human life and able to deal with them in a variety of settings where they appropriately belong, and of which the formal economizing organization is a case limit."[35]

This raises again the issue of values, norms and ethics in the development of an administrative science. On the one hand, there stands the position, as exemplified by Simon's work, that ethics and normative theory have no place in the structure of an administrative science (except, perhaps, as compulsory components of the persona of the individual scientist); on the other hand, we have seen the possibilities of including a normative element within the very structure of such a science.

One possibility, for example, would be to look at leader-member relationships within the organization and to ask what the

nature of such memberships might be were they to be based on the
generic norms that have been discussed. Such norms suggest,
perhaps, that individual freedom and mutual candor must influence
leader-member relations; they, in essence, provide a valid base
for suggesting that participative administration strategies, as
opposed to authoritarian strategies, are most appropriate for
organizations. As Gibb claims, a model of participative
leadership implies a theory of ethics: "That behavior is more
ethical which is most trusting, most open, most self-determining,
and most interdependent."[36] It can also be claimed that a theory
of ethics implies a theory of participative leadership. Thus a
science of administration becomes concerned not simply with the
correctness of a decision, but also with the implications of that
decision for human life, that is, with its rightness. Both which
solution and how it will be implemented become the proper concern
of those in administration.

Such norms, or such a theory of ethics, implies, however,
much more than the establishment of trustful relationships between
the administrative and membership apparatus. It is undoubtedly
important that mutual trust, candor and self-recognition be part
of the interaction structure in a school system; yet such ideals,
however, are by themselves not enough, and may even mask systemic
oppressiveness, when, for example, the internal dynamics of the
organization reveals satisfying relations but the organization-as-
a-whole taints its environment.

A three-part model might be used to explain how the function
of administration could be structured to incorporate both science
and ethics. Again, we turn to Habermasian concepts for our major
direction.[37] Posit for the moment three fundamental conditions
common to human life: action, interaction and development.* By
action we mean work and labor related activities which provide a
purposive framework to individuals, activities which involve
shaping, manipulating, controlling and producing. A product is
the end which is sought. By interaction, we mean the development
of meaning through shared communication and symbols; the
establishment of culture and norms; the beginning of inter-
subjective understanding. By development, we mean the progressive
emancipation of the individual, physically, cognitively and
culturally. Physically, of course, the individual grows and
begins to be able to control more adequately one's own functions;
one becomes less dependent. Cognitively, the child, according to
Piagetian theory, proceeds through several stages, each of which
allowing the mind more freedom to perform its tasks. Cultural
emancipation, however, requires the critical exposure of forms of
ideology which restrict developmental possibilities.

Corresponding to these three areas of human life are three
forms of knowing. One form would represent scientific knowledge

---

*These three categories are derived from Habermas' identification
of three primary human "interests": Technical, practical and
emancipatory. Each interest coincides with a form of science
The technical interest coincides with empirical science, the
practical interest with cultural science and the emancipatory
interest with critical science.

whose major purpose lies in developing law-like statements which are predictive in character. Another form represents knowledge aimed at discovering meaning between subjects, in much the fashion that an anthropologist enters a strange land to search for understanding. That these two forms of knowing must, particularly in the social sciences, be intertwined is a conclusion that often escapes proponents of either a completely objective or primarily subjective approach to science (natural science versus cultural science). Complete empiricists, however, in their practice embody the necessity of interpretation and understanding, while those who practice the art of hermeneutics also require data and "facts."

We would also suggest, however, that a third form of knowing is both necessary and appropriate; this is the development of a critical science. By this we mean the development of theory which addresses the degree to which human development is advanced or retarded by scientific and cultural forces, or, more specifically, the development of theory which exposes ideological biases which affect the human condition. The time has come, notes Richard Bernstein at the end of his remarkable exegesis of social and political theory that: "An adequate social and political theory must be empirical, interpretative, and critical."[38]

Thus, we see critical theory as being normatively based, an attempt -- through critique -- to come to terms with dimensions of truth and rightfulness. The inter-relationships can be demonstrated by the following model, where "objective" theory reflects the consensual but empirical testing of lawlike statements, "subjective" theory represents the interpretative, inter-subjective search for meaning, and "critical" theory reflects the dialectical consideration of the true and the good:

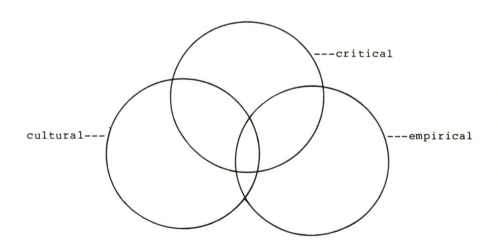

The implications of the model might be investigated by examining some dimensions of educational research, specifically an attempt to operationalize for educators the Maslowian based needs hierarchy. Sergiovanni and Carver report on such an attempt.[39] Their research can be examined in three dimensions.

First, they report the collection of empirical data. For example, they show that in 1969, 1,593 secondary school teachers scored (apparently on a scale of 0 - 2) in the following fashion: the level of need for <u>security</u> was .67; for <u>social belonging</u> .89; for <u>self-esteem</u>, 1.45; for <u>autonomy</u>, 1.25; for <u>self-actualization</u> 1.34. The higher the score, the greater the need. This information is then displayed on a bar graph, and then further scores, collected from 585 teachers in 1978, are added to the graph. The 1978 teachers far surpass the 1969 teachers in their "need deficiencies;" they rate a 1.21 for <u>security</u>, a .97 for <u>social belonging</u>, a 1.69 for <u>self-esteem</u>, a 1.71 for <u>autonomy</u>, and a 1.76 for <u>self-actualization</u>. Thus, Sergiovanni, Carver and their colleagues have amassed empirical data gathered through legitimate survey techniques and subject to statistical analysis. The methodology is described this way:

> . . . respondents completed a 13-item need deficiency questionnaire modeled after each of five categories of a modified version of Abraham Maslow's need heirarchy (sic). The instrument assessed on a seven-point scale the amount of need fulfillment available for each of the five categories as well as the amount each respondent felt he or she needed. The difference between actual and desired need fulfillment was computed and labeled a 'perceived need deficiency.' Mean differences between actual and desired need fulfillment were used to construct (the graphs).[40]

In this instance, subjects are asked to put a numerical value to their feelings concerning how much security, self-actualization, etc. they thought they had and should have. But the data of course do not provide us with any information without involving another form of knowledge, interpretation of meaning. This, surely, must take place on several levels.

One level, of course, lies in the selection of these categories as meaningful ones for research: that "esteem," "security," "actualization" and so on are legitimate constructs which are inter-subjectively shared. In this case, this is given more or less <u>a priori</u>, insofar as the methodology itself codes responses to certain questions as indicative of, e.g., "need deficiency." But the "fact" of such constructions can itself be problematic. In his review of research in the human relations domain, Perrow asks the following question: "But what if much of our world exhibits low coherence, accidental interactions and consequences, highly situational (rather than enduring or basic) determinants of behavior, and very specific rather than broad cultural reinforcements and demotivators?"[41] What if, indeed, the general conceptions of security, affiliation and so on are "recipes" or "scripts" which represent social expectations for behavior and that these expectations differ for different groups and change over periods of time?  Is the shared understanding of what these needs <u>are</u> truly shared?; can we also claim that one group's understanding of the meaning of "security" in 1969 is the equivalent of another group's understanding of that term in 1978? The interpretation of meaning and the understanding of what objective reality is pose a fundamental challenge to theorists concerned with the decoding of empirical research;  recognizing that there are these subcutaneous layers is one step forward in meeting the challenge.

Another area of concern when addressing theory and research lies with that notion we have labeled critical theory.  Efforts in this regard would involve, I believe, two principle strands:  the strand of negative dialogue, based on the critical examination and critique of educational theory and practice from the viewpoint of its social, economic and political implications, and the strand of positive dialogue, based on examination of educational theory and practice from the viewpoint of a search for generic norms (as discussed in an earlier section).

Turning to the research project in question, a perspective arising from critical theory would have asked some of these questions:  in what ways can this research be used to enhance teachers' effectiveness and in what ways can it be used to simply label certain teachers who don't fit into an administrator's idea of "motivated";  in what ways does this research ignore motivational structures which are social and political rather than psychological?;  in what ways does it ignore motivational structures of administrators as a group?;  in what ways does it create an ideology concerning why teachers wish to teach and thus perpetuates a vision of the profession which may be unfair?;  and, finally, in what ways does the research establish these motivational categories as organizational requirements which may be necessary for entry into the field but which may or may not have a great deal to do with effective job performance?

We are not, of course, implying that this particular piece of research does any or all of the above, but that these are legitimate, critical questions which can be addressed to any piece of competent educational research.  These questions, derived from critique, are both normative and ethical, and show how critical theory can add an ethical basis to science.

Critical theory also provides a perspective for investigating the essential foundations of research and framing them within ethical dimensions.  The process itself of gathering "data" and analyzing these same may itself contribute to the development of ideology.  Smith describes several "tricks" used in this regard:

> Trick 1.  Separate what people say they think from the actual circumstances in which it is said, from the actual empirical conditions of their lives and from the actual individuals who said it.

Trick 2.  Having detached the ideas, they must
now  be  arranged.  Prove then an order  among
them which accounts for what is observed.

Trick 3.  The ideas are then changed 'into  a
person',  that  is  they  are  constituted  as
distinct entities to which agency (or possible
causal efficacy) may be attributed.  And they
may  be  re-attributed  to  'reality'  by
attributing  them to actors who now  represent
the ideas.[42]

In  this  fashion,  ideas located in concrete  and  practical
circumstances are taken in abstract, sorted and arranged, and then
possibly given  as  causes for the behavior in which  they  were
originally located:  "Their beliefs, their values, their norms are
now  attributed  to this 'personage' as 'social  beliefs',  'social
values', and 'social norms'.[43]  A function of critical theory then
becomes  the  identification and critique of those instances  when
ideas become reified and then are taken as guides for policy.
This  is a major problem:  that research investigations  are
taken  at face value and then become guides to policy  and  action
without regard for the ethical,  normative and critical dimensions
involved.  A  model  which applies to educational  administration
three "moments" may be seen to re-institute these dimensions.  Two
moments are positive,  one is negative; empirical data formulation
and  hermeneutic  understanding reflect positive  moments  in
predicting  and understanding the educational environment and  its
administration;  critical reflection and theory tends to represent
a  negative  moment  in such understanding.  But  all  three  are
necessary  in  order  to  provide an  expanded  meaningfulness  to
education  and  to  base administrative  programs  in  firm
methodological as well as ethical foundations.
Legitimacy  of  institutions can be granted  in  the  popular
imagination  if  the institution serves accepted  beliefs  arising
outside  of itself.  Should a reconciliation between a theory  of
administrative science and a theory of norms be possible, then the
science of administration would be oriented not towards increasing
technical  control  but  towards a systematic search  for  social
justice and freedom.  By allowing both our theory and research the
freedom to have an orientation to the three fundamental conditions
of  action,  interaction,  and  development, can  an  ethical  and
normative dimension be introduced into administrative science.
In summary, we have attempted to show that if a set of values
common to a diverse and pluralistic society can be found,  it will
have to be located at a level deeper than we normally think about.
One probability is to examine carefully that feature of human life
that  is common to diverse groups:  the ability to engage in reasoned discourse.  If certain standards underlie that, then perhaps
we can impute certain universal values.  As indicated before, some
thinking  in  this  area  has  suggested  that  the structure of
discourse relies on standards of truth,  truthfulness,  rightness,
and  comprehensibility.  These in turn indicate a universal  need
for  such values as truth,  justice,  and freedom (truth,  in  the

sense that we make the automatic assumption that what we hear is not a lie - lies themselves are such only because they violate the norm; justice in the sense that we expect our discourse to be treated as comprehensible and right, and freedom, in the sense that we demand the opportunity to correct distortions.)

It was Socrates that pointed out that even among thieves was there honor, and it is this concept that is problematic for administrators. Despite our claimed existence of ideal norms, administrators are still confronted with the theory-practice problem: given a diverse constituency, how does one accomodate different versions of truth, justice or freedom? Must administrators deal with a type of ethical relativism?

Perhaps not, if we take care to distinguish between ethics and values. Values reflect the selection of preferences; ethics is concerned with qualities.[44] Ethics can identify a "good" without necessarily asserting that that "good" must be valued. We might, as administrators, suggest that education is good without also suggesting that education is valued by children, parents or the community. Ethically, it can claim that, in abstract, this good supports other basic qualities such as truth and justice (through, for example, reducing ignorance levels and providing routes of mobility for underclass youngsters) without claiming that the practice of education should be valued. The practice of education may in fact perpetuate class and racial divisions but this does not necessarily imply that education as a concept is not a good.

What follows then is the question of whether there can be a generic ethics for administration which can accomodate the values of a diverse constituency. If this can be answered positively, then I feel it must be based in two standards. One is an articulated philosophy of education which is linked to practical consequences; this is where a critical theory of administration must be used in order to evaluate positivist research programs in the context of understanding human relationships which can both liberate or enslave. The second standard is the principle of administrator-as-origin, not as agent. As an agent, an administrator simply carries out the orders of others and has no say into the process of problem identification, valuation and decision-making. The administrator-as-agent is concerned only with the _how_ of administrative solutions, not with the _what_. A generic ethics must refuse this: if the administrator is only an agent, then he or she has lost administrative freedom, necessary to achieve progress to the good. As Mackie states: ". . . the administrator is a decision-maker within the areas specified by the body which employs him. He ceases to be an administrator if he loses the right to make decisions."[45]

An articulated philosophy and the principle of administrator-as-origin allow for the beginning of a professional ethic which allows for the consideration of a constituency's conflicting value preferences. Consider the example of an administrator faced with the implementation of a voluntary desegregation program in a rather conservative district. Given, firstly, the ethical definition of education as a "good," the next question becomes how does integration promote that good? This must be approached from several angles. In a positivistic turn, the administrator may wish to know about the educational effects of integration as reported in research literature. In a phenomenological turn, the administrator may wish to explore the benefits of integration in developing understandings of the human condition and of means of constructing and maintaining cultural realities. In a critical turn, the administrator may wish to consider the relationship of integration to the creation of a more just and equitable society.

Further than this, the administrator must begin originating decisions which are based in the spirit of rational argumentation and discourse and which run counter to uninformed political action. The implementation of decisions in this view will then be ethically and professionally based, despite their political implications. This, however, is necessary. The administrator can no longer be seen as only a technician applying the techniques of system control. The crisis in legitimacy depends for its resolution on administrators whose concepts of action are based in a professional ethics which assumes the possibility of a substantive rationality. If administrative theory can break the cycle of dependence it has shown on a positivistic social science and business-oriented managerial practices, and begin reconsidering the ends of education, then perhaps it can also reestablish a lost legitimacy.

## FOOTNOTES

[1]Robert Denhardt and Kathryn G. Denhardt, "Public Administration and the Critique of Domination," Administration and Society 11 (May 1979): 107-120.

[2]Kenneth J. Benson, "Innovation and Crisis in Organizational Analysis," in Organizational Analysis, Critique and Innovation ed. J. Kenneth Benson, (Beverly Hills: Sage Publications, 1977), pp. 5-18.

[3]Herbert Storing, ed., "The Science of Administration: Herbert A. Simon," in Essays on the Scientific Study of Politics (New York: Holt, Rinehart and Winston, 1962), pp. 63-150.

[4]Donald Erickson, "Research on Educational Administration: The State-of-the-Art," Educational Researcher 8 (March 1979): pp. 9-14.

[5]Anthony Giddens ed., "Introduction," Positivism and Sociology, (London: Heinemann, 1978), p. 7.

[6]Richard J. Bernstein, The Restructuring of Social and Political Theory, (New York: Harcourt, Brace & Jovanovich, 1976), p. 228.

[7]Herbert A. Simon, Administrative Behavior, 2d ed. (New York: The Free Press, 1965), Chapter 3.

[8]Ibid., Ch. 3.

[9]James G. March and Herbert Simon, Organizations, (New York: John Wiley, 1958), Chaps. 6 & 7.

[10]Herbert J. Storing, ed. "The Science of Administration: Herbert A. Simon," in Essays on the Scientific Study of Politics pp. 63-150.

[11]See Simon, Administrative Behavior, n.p.

[12]Simon, Administrative Behavior, p. 249.

[13]Storing, Essays on the Scientific Study of Politics, p. 150.

[14]Victor Vroom, "A New Look at Managerial Decision Making," in Emerging Concepts (New York: Macmillan, 1975), p. 121.

[15]Jurgen Habermas, Legitimation Crisis, trans. Thomas McCarthy (Boston: Beacon Press, 1975).

[16]Jurgen Habermas, <u>Communication and the Evolution of Society</u> trans. Thomas McCarthy (Boston: Beacon Press, 1979).

[17]Jurgen Habermas, "Rationalism Divided in Two," in <u>Positivism and Sociology</u>, ed. A. Giddens, (London: Heinemann Educational Books, 1974), p. 216.

[18]Anthony Giddens, <u>Positivism and Sociology</u>, (New York: Harper and Row, 1975), pp. 1-22.

[19]Habermas, <u>Communication and the Evolution of Society</u>, p. 194.

[20]Habermas, <u>Legitimation Crisis</u>, p. 57.

[21]Claus Mueller, <u>The Politics of Communication</u>, (New York: Oxford, 1973), p. 135.

[22]Ibid., p. 143.

[23]Habermas, <u>Communication and the Evolution of Society</u>, p. 195.

[24]See Habermas' discussion of science as ideology in Jurgen Habermas, <u>Toward a Rational Society</u>, trans. Jeremy J. Shapiro (Boston: Beacon Press, 1970).

[25]David B. Tyack, <u>The One Best System</u>, (Cambridge, Massachusetts: Harvard University Press, 1974), p. 29.

[26]George Gallup, The Eleventh Annual Poll of the Public's Attitudes Toward the Public Schools," <u>Phi Delta Kappan</u> 61 (September 1979): 33-45.

[27]Kaufman, I. <u>Educational System Planning</u>, (Englewood Cliffs, N.J.: Prentice-Hall, 1972), p. 10.

[28]Harry F. Wolcott, <u>The Man in the Principal's Office: An Ethnography</u>, (New York: Holt, Rinehart, & Winston, 1973), p. 268.

[29]Habermas, <u>Legitimation Crisis</u>, p. 71.

[30]George Beauchamp, <u>Curriculum Theory</u>, 4th ed. (Itasca, Illinois: F.E. Peacock, 1981), p. 181.

[31]Habermas, <u>Legitimation Crisis</u>, p. 84.

[32]Ibid., pp. 93-94.

[33]Habermas, <u>Communication and the Evolution of Society</u>, p. 2.

[34]Habermas, <u>Legitimation Crisis</u>, p. 141.

[35]Alberto Ramos, "Misplacements of Concepts and Administrative

Theory," Public Administration Review 6 (November/December 1978): 555.

[36]Jack R. Gibb, "Dynamics of Leadership and Communication," in Leadership and Social Change, 2d ed. Edited by William R. Lassey and Richard R. Fernandez (La Jolla, California: University Associates, 1976), p. 119.

[37]Jurgen Habermas, Knowledge and Human Interests, trans. Jeremy J. Shapiro (Boston: Beacon Press, 1971), Trent Schroyer, The Critique of Domination; The Origins and Development of Critical Theory (New York: G. Braziller, 1973); Bernstein, The Restructuring of Social and Political Theory; Thomas McCarthy, The Critical Theory of Jurgen Habermas (Cambridge, Massachusetts, 1978).

[38]Bernstein, The Restructuring of Social and Political Theory p. 235.

[39]Thomas Sergiovanni and Fred D. Carver, The New School Executive, 2d ed. (New York: Harper & Row, 1980), p. 89.

[40]Ibid., p. 99, note 8.

[41]Charles Perrow, Complex Organizations: A Critical Essay 2d ed. (Glenview, Illinois: Scott, Foresman, 1979), p. 137.

[42]Dorothy Smith, "Theorizing as Ideology," in Ethnomethodology, ed. Roy Turner (Middlesex, England: Penguin), p. 41.

[43]Ibid., p. 42.

[44]Margaret Mackie, Philosophy and School Administration, (St. Lucia, Australia: University of Queensland Press, 1977), p. 20.

[45]Ibid., p. 41.

# CHAPTER V

## SECOND EDITION/ETHICS AND THE POLITICIAN

### Stephen K. Bailey

Any attempt to construct what John Buchan once called "an essay in recollection" is fraught with ethical puzzles. When it is addressed to the moral dilemmas of a political experience of some years ago, ethical issues are piled crazily one on top of the other. They are nudged into further disarray by the tricks that rationalization and memory play upon all autobiographers. In view of the number of friends whose good names must be protected against my possibly accurate reporting of their (and my) occasional moral lapses; in view of the impossibility, after the event, of my recapturing the precise pattern of considerations that shaped the matrix within which decisions were made; and in view of the inscrutability of many of the ethical issues with which I, as mayor of a city of 30,000, had to deal, it is clear that this article must be content with the probable rather than the precise.

In so far as I refer specifically to experiences in Middletown, Connecticut, during the years when I was mayor of that city, I hope that friends there will show me the same charity that Huckleberry Finn showed Mark Twain. Referring to The Adventures of Tom Sawyer, Huck commented, "That book was made by Mr. Mark Twain, and he told the truth, mainly. There was things which he stretched, but mainly he told the truth. That is nothing. I never seen anybody but lied one time or another, without it was Aunt Polly. . . ." Huck Finn was perceptive in spotting the moral flaw in Aunt Polly and in her old maid sister, Miss Watson: a flaw of self-righteousness so hideous that when Huck learned that Miss Watson was living "so as to go to the good place," Huck could "see no advantage in going where she was going," so he made up his mind he wouldn't try for it.

I have worried far more about the ethical consequences of my decisions as mayor since leaving office than I ever did as an incumbent. Perhaps this is the first point to be made. Most elected executives find that there is an ethics of action which is normally far more compelling than the urge to balance with precision the ethical niceties of pressing public issues. There are times when the good of the community demands firmness and decision at the expense of marginal injustice. Those who would make justice the sole criterion of the good society are, in my judgment, not only myopic in their ethical vision but establish an impossible norm for administrators.

Justice, in the sense of "just deserts," presumes omnipotence and omniscience. An elected mayor in a "weak-mayor" form of government, alas, has neither. One may desire to be just, but occasions arise when justice is not the highest ethical priority. If, for example, a local hospital that has run a county-wide ambulance service for years suddenly decides for budgetary reasons to disown this responsibility, it may be unjust to make the taxpayers of a single city in the county pick up the check for keeping the county-wide service going on an emergency basis. But, here, what is necessary overrides what is just.

Emergency actions by an authorized executive have meaning and value quite apart from the justice or injustice of any decision one may take under emergency authority. The justification for the emergency powers of the public executive are, I believe, not only in the necessities of organization under stress; there is a very significant social therapy in the public's sense that "somebody is in charge." The sight of Winston Churchill making his way through the rubble of blitzed London and barking orders to subordinates had the effect of strengthening resolve and dissolving fear among the affected public. Even lowly political executives at times perform this valuable role.

Even when an emergency does not exist, there are frequently statutory deadlines or political deadlines - budgets, elections, schedules of compliance established by a higher level of government - that precipitate decisions largely uncomplicated by ethical considerations. Deadlines are great strengtheners of the resolve to choose. Those who would build theories of decision-making removed from the context of the clock and the calendar know nothing of the inner life of a political executive. In brief, although almost every issue with which one must deal is charged with ethical dilemmas, it is rare that one has the time, the context, or the liver for constructing balanced ethical judgments. One does what one must. Ethically, elected executives tend, like successful fighter pilots, to "fly by the seat of their pants." Speed is the enemy of deliberation, and, in administration, speed - in the sense of dispatch - is often the condition of maintaining a tolerable if ineffable balance among those interests, obligations, and necessities which crowd the world of the elected executive.

All this is not meant to suggest that ethical considerations are somehow peripheral to the executive's life. It is only to say that ethical issues are rarely trotted out for leisurely inspection and deliberate choice. This may be unfortunate, but my guess is that if ethical considerations were always carefully and honestly articulated in decision-making, the ensuing chaos - moral and administrative - would be impressive. If we are talking about the real world, then, we are talking in large measure about the inarticulate moral premises of the office-holder, the ethical signposts that a harried political executive catches out of the corner of one's eye.

With this statement, of course, the essay could well end. Any attempt to list all the precepts, proverbs, fables (and their rationalized versions) that conscience picks to guide or justify actions would lead to an endless recitation of the obvious and inscrutable; ultimately, such a recitation would tell us nothing about conscience itself - that ego-tempered temperer of egos, that culture-bound transcender of culture, that ultimate sorter of ethical ambiguities. It gets us nowhere to suggest that all of the Philosophy 1-2 classroom stumpers are present in political life, as they are in all life. Should a cancer specialist be honest or kind? Ultimately, is it more honest to be kind or more kind to be honest? Is a half-truth a worse enemy of the truth than a falsehood? Should promises be kept if the situation changes (and when doesn't it change)? Should friends be reported if you know them to be mostly good and you know that they probably will not do it again? Should you subject someone to the consequences of wrongdoing if you are reasonably sure that the penalty is sufficiently harsh and inelastic as to be inequitable?

To pretend that there are clear religious, moral, or legal answers to such questions is to fly in the face of all sensitive moral inquiry. How difficult the means-ends questions really are is known by every parent who ponders such matters. Someone once commented that the Lord had left the two most difficult and important jobs in the world to amateurs: citizenship and parenthood. Elected political executives, at least most of them, are also amateurs, and their jobs may be no less difficult or important than the others mentioned. What is common to the life of all of these amateurs is that the value questions are extraordinarily complex, and the chances of adequate time for deliberation are slim.

But are there not some peculiar ethical risks run by elected political executives? Surely, most people are not faced frequently with questions of bribery, spoils, corruption, favoritism. The difficulty is, neither are elected political executives; and even when venality raises its head it rarely looks to the responsible political executive as ugly as it appears in newspaper cartoons or Sunday sermons. Venality, like virtue, is rarely unambiguous. G.K. Chesterton suggested that the error of Diogenes "lay in the fact that he omitted to notice that every man is both an honest and a dishonest man. Diogenes looked for his honest man inside every crypt and cavern. But he never thought of looking inside the thief. And that is where the Founder of Christianity found the honest man. He found him on a gibbet and promised him paradise."

When the nicest people have rationalized their selfishness with a tactical deference to the public interest, elected political executives are often grateful that they are too preoccupied to be ethically astute. Even where venality seems clearest, as in the rare case of an attempt at straight bribery – "Mayor, here's a thousand dollars in five-dollar bills if you get that easement through the council" – the ethical issues may not be self-evident. Let us make some assumptions: suppose that the mayor knows that the easement will go through "on its merits" (begging what the slippery phrase means). Suppose further that the mayor knows that the party needs money not only to run the forthcoming election but to pay debts on the past election. Suppose the mayor knows further that the voting public has not responded favorably to appeals for everyone to give to the party of his choice. Suppose, finally, that the mayor believes that a working two-party system is the community's greatest safeguard of democracy and freedom. If it could be proved to the mayor's satisfaction that the lack of a thousand dollars at the moment could do irreparable damage of the two-party system in the area, would it be higher principle in a naughty world for the mayor to accept the money on behalf of the party, or to refuse the money?

Stated this way, the issue is still not very complex for most people. They've known right from wrong since they've been ten. You do not accept bribes, period; and you most certainly do not compound evil by cheating the briber. This is all very clear. But is it, really?

There are ways of playing slight variations on this theme which would remove from the sternest Presbyterian moralist any burden of guilt. The briber has made a number of contributions to the party over the years. The latest thousand is simply another indication of his belief in the great principles of the party. On the easement question, every party member on the council, including the mayor, attempts to examine the issue on its merits. But a "will to believe" has set in - a subtle coloration of the problem. Good old Joe is a friend who provided all the favors for the party picnic. Isn't it fortunate that the merits of the easement case are on his side?

And bribery can take so many forms: money, favors, flattery, help in time of trouble, influence in building status. To pretend that bribery is a simple and easily spotted phenomenon is naive. To pretend it takes place only in politics is silly. I have seen the egos of older university professors successfully bribed by astute and ambitious instructors; I have seen great institutions bribe men into conformity with promises of promotions or demotions. I have seen them kill, spiritually, those who resisted. I have received threats that unless such-and-such happened, I would be voted out of office at the next election. Is this not attempted bribery? Is money any more a thing of value than power or status or re-election? If there are clear moral distinctions here, they escape me, even though our cultural inheritance sanctions certain kinds of bribery and frowns on others.

I once asked a municipal judge in Middletown to tell me what pressures were most constant in trying to influence his impartial administration of justice. He thought a minute and then said, with laughter, "The university deans and the town clergy." But why should he have laughed? Certainly few would question the motives of deans and clergy in attempting to save the reputations of individuals known to them, and under their keep, who have been accused of wrong-doing. But what of the wrongdoer who has no "friend in court"? Anyone who has ever watched a municipal court in action over a period of time knows that "political influence" is frequently a corrective for the partial justice that results from the rich litigant's capacity to purchase superior legal talent. Middle-class justice is not always equitable to the poor. This is not to condone political influence in courts of law; it is to suggest that without political influence certain inequities might be greater than they are and that those inequities need as much attention as overt or covert political influence.

I was never asked to fix a traffic or parking ticket in Middletown; but I cannot swear that tickets were not occasionally fixed while I was mayor. I am not sure that under certain circumstances - such as the situation of a harried woman who has been delayed in buying her six children school clothes - I would not have paid the dollar fine myself rather than penalize her for something beyond here effective control. Nothing is more unjust than unexceptional law except law that is all exceptions. Surely, one of the most difficult ethical problems in all governance is the drawing of lines between rules and exceptions. That the lines, to be moral, must be drawn near the rules end of the spectrum I do not question, but that exceptions are never warranted seems to me the most callous of all moral judgments.

To the moralist, words like bribery, favoritism, spoils, patronage, graft, are as clear and as evil as though bottled and marked with skull and crossbones. To those with political responsibility, on the other hand, it occasionally seems clear that poison can be therapeutic. The fact that poison is labeled with a skull and crossbones and placed back on a high shelf of the medicine closet may not mean that it is never to be used - only that it is to be used with care and in small doses. It is possible that if an elected executive had infinite time he might be able to discern ways to achieve his goals without using morally uncomfortable means, although the question of where rationalizations begin and end with this sort of game plays hob with moral certainty. However, if giving an unskilled job to a not-incompetent nationality group representative might make the difference between winning or losing on an urban renewal referendum of vast benefit to the entire city for years to come, I know few elected executives who would boggle over making such an appointment even if the executive was convinced that someone else might do the unskilled job better.

George Bernard Shaw once wrote what many politicians must at times have felt. Shaw learned that a Labor candidate named Joseph Burgess had refused to compromise on some issue and had thereby lost his seat in Parliament. Shaw commented bitterly: "When I think of my own unfortunate character, smirched with compromise, rotted with opportunism, mildewed by expediency - dragged through the mud of borough council and Battersea elections, stretched out of shape with wire-pulling, putrefied by permeation, worn out by twenty-five years pushing to gain an inch here, or straining to stem a backrush, I do not think Joe might have put up with just a speck or two on those white robes of his for the sake of millions of poor devils who cannot afford any character at all because they have no friend in parliament. Oh, these moral dandies, these spiritual toffs, these superior persons. Who is Joe, anyhow, that he should not risk his soul occasionally like the rest of us?"

I was once confronted with a possible kickback on a fire-truck purchase. The party representative reminded me that it cost money to run elections; that generosity from fire-truck manufacturers to those who had insight to see the need for public safety in their communities was rather standard; and that no one would really suffer. The gift would come as a preordained slice of the salesman's commission, who would give of his own income because "he believed in the principles of the Democratic Party." I drew myself up, stared at my good friend, and said, in what I am sure must have been the most patronizing of tones: "If the party needs four or five hundred dollars, I shall be happy to try to raise the money personally; but I shall not do it that way." I then went a step further. I called the poor fire-truck salesman into the office and made him add about four hundred dollars' worth of extra equipment to the fire truck at the bid price he had quoted. in a swift double blow I had proved my moral worth and defended the taxpayers' interests. I had proved that at least in one American community "public office is a public trust."

I had also proved that it is easy to be moral when the pressure is not really on. Suppose the party coffers had been empty? Suppose my confident bluff to raise "four or five hundred dollars" for the party had been called? Suppose the alternative to a Democratic re-election was the election of of a rather disreputable Republican gang who would have practiced "boodle" with more frequency and with infinitely less flair than the Democrats? And why should we refuse to accept money for the imperative cause of political party machinery, almost regardless of source, when the so-called "good" people of the community would not be caught dead giving to their political party - to the system of options that does far more than the Constitution to guarantee freedom and democracy?

I could not be a partner to a kickback, not because I had carefully weighed the moral issues but because my moral viscera told me it was wrong. Unfortunately, my moral viscera are not always right. If they were right in this particular case, they were right for reasons removed from the issue at hand. They were right because, without sufficient time and eloquence, I could not have explained any contrary action, if forced to by the local newspaper or in an official inquiry, that would satisfy the adult public whose moral viscera are quite as dogmatic as mine. I thereby would have undercut the public's faith in my honesty and would have damaged that most priceless of all public executive resources: the public's confidence. There would then have been an unhappy and unproductive feedback into everything else I did or tried to do as an elected official.

The moral dilemma remains, however: for I am confident that if I had had the insight to have taken the kickback and the time and eloquence to have explained to the public why I had done it - describing to them the impossible position they put politicians in by their not assuming disinterested responsibility for financing party campaigns - they would have seen the point and respected me for my action. They might even have taken the lesson to heart and decided to give to their party as frequently and as richly as they give to other causes they value, such as community chests and churches.

The only serious ethical struggle I had with party leaders in Middletown dealt with a request for a zoning exception. Here I was firm, morally aroused, and dogmatic, and would be to this day. A contractor, who had contributed liberally to both political parties locally, hired a leading Democratic lawyer to plead for a commercial spot zone in a strictly residential area. The people of the area were almost solidly opposed to the change. Even if they had not been, nothing can ruin the orderly and aesthetic development of a growing city like politically inspired spot zoning in contravention of a general plan. The members of the zoning committee, to their credit, said to me, "Mayor, there's a lot we'll do for the party, but we won't do this."

The final showdown on this case took place in the lawyer's office with all major party leaders present. I walked in swinging. I made it quite clear that if the plumbing broke down in city hall, I would hire a licensed Democratic plumber over a licensed Republican plumber any day of the week; that if the law did not force us to go to bid, I would buy insurance from a Democratic rather than a Republican insurance agent; but that when it came to what Edmund Burke once called "the permanent forces" in the community, I was ready to do battle. I suggested that although there was much in politics that one rendered to Caesar, almost without qualms, city planning was rendered only to God. A few party leaders were upset, but most of them were understanding; and the lawyer in question, who over the years has been one of the most brilliant as well as constructive influences in the community and state, had the grace to accept my position without rancor.

I have dwelt too long on such matters, for the fact is that in my two years as mayor party issues of this kind did not represent more than one-fiftieth of my working time. Contrary to what many people seem to believe, the hard ethical issues of public life rarely concern party politics. Party decisions tend to roll according to pre-set patterns. Every elected executive works out a few obvious benchmarks for relationships with political leaders (for example, "Consult party leaders on all appointments, but solicit their help in trading little appointments to the party for big appointments to you"). In any case, to suggest that most party officials are frequently ethical "problems" is to distort their normal role beyond recognition. For every occasion when a party leader asked me for a favor that disturbed my conscience, I can think of a dozen times when the same party leader helped me defend the public interest against the importunities of non-party pressure groups.

Upon reflection, it is my firm belief that in so far as party politics interferes with the pursuit of the public interest, it is largely a result of the necessities of campaign finance. Most venality in public life could be abolished or reduced to insignificance if the public would assume responsibility for broadly-based campaign financing and would insist upon the public auditing and disclosure of all campaign gifts and expenditures. This would not eliminate corruption entirely, for wherever power and money converge some venality will be found. But our method of financing political campaigns is, in my estimation, the single corrupting factor in our political life - local, national, and, especially, state.

If what has been discussed so far does not make up the major ethical issues of the elected executive, what does? To the man who is ethically sensitive, the hair-turning issues are those involving impossible choices among contending interpretations of the public interest. Again, the necessity of dispatch is psychologically therapeutic; but the drain on energy and conscience is substantial nonetheless. Take a dozen problems that faced me as mayor, and that are typical of perhaps a hundred I faced in two years.

(1) A peacock farm on the edge of town kept neighbors awake for a month or so a year during the peacock mating seasons. The city

government was asked by the neighbors to see to it that the birds were quieted. Ethical question: Is a temporary irritation - including loss of sleep - for ten families worth the destruction of a hobby and a partial livelihood for one person?

(2) A leading department store on Main Street said it had to have a rear-access service garage on Broad Street or it would be forced to leave town. But the street was zoned residential. Ethical question: Would the loss of the department store be a greater loss than a break in the city's zoning pattern?

(3) The best detective on the chronically underpaid police force is suspected of taking protection money from some local two-bit gamblers. The evidence is too vague and unsubstantial to stand in court. Ethical question: Is the possibility of the evidence being correct important enough to warrant a substantial investigation, with a consequent probable loss of efficiency and morale in the police department during, and long after, the investigation, a certain loss of public confidence in the whole force, and the ever-present possibility that the rumor was planted by a crank? In addition, out of the many pressing issues coming across the mayor's desk, how much time and effort does such an investigation warrant from the mayor himself?

(4) The whole scheme of volunteer fire departments is looked upon by the chief of the city's only paid department as wasteful, inefficient, and dangerous to the public safety. The volunteers claim that their firefighting record is topnotch, that they save the taxpayers money. Ethical question: If neither side can be proved incorrect, how does one weigh the values of volunteer community endeavors against marginal inefficiencies in operation of a vital service?

(5) Many years earlier, one department store was farsighted enough to have bought up some land for off-street parking, which gave the store quite a competitive advantage. The city, in a new municipal parking program, needed a portion of this private parking lot. When established, the municipal lot might destroy the store's competitive advantage. Ethical question: At what point does the public interest demand that private farsightedness be penalized?

(6) Two mayors in four years happened to have lived on Wyllys Avenue. Wyllys Avenue desperately needed repaving. But so did some other streets in the city. Ethical question: Should Wyllys Avenue be repaved, granted a heavy presumption that many citizens would claim that the mayor had "taken care of himself"?

(7) A federal grant-in-aid cut in half the city's welfare load, making a sinecure out of one of the two city welfare positions. The holder of the sinecure was a Black appointed by the opposition party. Ethical question: Should work somehow be "made" for the Black, or should she/he be dropped? (in view of the problems of status, morale, and upward mobility among Blacks in a largely white community, the political questions posed by this case are easy compared to the long-range ethical questions.)

(8) The virulent opposition of a local printer-publicist might be tamed on a few key issues with the proper placing of a few city printing contracts. Ethical question: Obvious.

(9) Buying of tires in wholesale lots would save the taxpayers

$300 a year - about one cent per citizen per annum. A score of little Middletown tire merchants would lose ten dollars or more in income. Ethical question: How does one balance one cent each for thirty thousand people versus ten dollars each for twenty merchants?

(10)    Parents concerned with the safety of their children on the way to and from school are constantly demanding increased police protection and more sidewalks. A more legitimate demand would be hard to imagine. But there are limits. Ethical question: granted that total safety never can be assured, what grounds beyond obvious necessity and "the squeaky wheel gets the grease" can be found for awarding or denying protection.

(11)    A health officer is technically qualified and conscientious, but egregiously officious. Ethical question: is the damage done to the city government's relations with its citizens by the meticulous and unfeeling enforcement of ordinances likely to be sufficiently serious to warrant the health officer's dismissal?

(12)    There is a likelihood that one of the major industries in town will have to close down a sizable slice of its operations. This may mean 2,000 unemployed. A steel company is looking for a New England site for a steel mill. It finds an "ideal" location in Middletown. That "ideal" location is a stretch of the Connecticut River which is unspoiled and is deeply treasured by small boat owners and by nature lovers. Ethical question: is the provision of employment for 2,000 people worth the destruction forever of natural beauty?

These are samples of the tough ones. And in most cases, the ethical values are sufficiently balanced so that no matter which side the mayor takes, half the concerned citizens in the community will charge the mayor - and with considerable justification in their own minds - with having sold out. This is one of the reasons for the low image of politicians in our society: the fact that the losing cause in public policy generally has substantial merit on its side, with the consequence that the loser can see nothing but venality or partiality in the elected official's decision. People get sore at politicians for the same reason they throw pop bottles at umpires: the disagreements always come on the close ones. If only citizens could pause on occasion to realize that the issues really are complex; that most elected officials do the best they can to be fair; that the peaceful resolution of conflict is a vast service to humankind, and is a most difficult art; that Solomon himself was perplexed by some of the issues posed by communities of people.

If I should be asked today how I resolved, in my own mind, the ethical dilemmas posed on the preceding pages, I should not know how to answer. Most of the dilemmas were not mine to resolve alone. Other people shared official power with me, and many citizens without official power assumed substantial unofficial responsibility for community decisions. There is not the loneliness and, perhaps, terror in executive decision-making at the local level which I assume there must often be at higher executive levels in American government. Consequences of errors in judgment are far less apocalyptic.

But insofar as I had to make up my mind by myself, or felt

that my judgment might be determining in the minds of others, I did repair to two or three very general propositions for ethical guidance. In practice, the propositions were never articulated, but in retrospect, I know that they were there. All of them had been woven into my life by parental, religious, and academic influences - in most cases by all three. My father, although never a minister, was a Professor of Religion and a firm believer in the Social Gospel. My studies at Oxford had brought me close to Immanuel Kant and Jean Jacques Rousseau. Ideas like "the categorical imperative" and "the general will" were connected in my mind with such biblical injunctions as "Let justice roll down as waters; and righteousness as a mighty stream." I had nothing in my system that told me what was right; but I did have something in my system that told me to search for what was right. The most helpful single question I could ask myself seemed to be, "What do you want Middletown to be like ten years from now?" Against this, many things fell into place. I wanted more beauty, fewer slums, less bigotry, more recreation, more community spirit, a more sustained sense of public responsibility, a more dynamic and prosperous economy, better education, a stronger and more truly competitive two-party system, and a heightened sense of personal dignity for all. These were some of the benchmarks against which specific ethical issues were measured or rationalized. They were not my marks. They were the marks of the civilization of which I was a miniscule and clouded reflection. As Carl Becker once wrote: "To have faith in the dignity and worth of the individual man as an end in himself; to believe that it is better to be governed by persuasion than by coercion; to believe that fraternal goodwill is more worthy than a selfish and contentious spirit; to believe that in the long run all values are inseparable from the love of truth and the disinterested search for it; to believe that knowledge and the power it confers should be used to promote the welfare and happiness of all men rather than to serve the interests of those individuals and classes whom fortune and intelligence endow with temporary advantage - these are the values which are affirmed by the traditional democratic ideology . . . . They are the values which since the time of Buddha and Confucius, Solomon and Zoroaster, Plato and Aristotle, Socrates and Jesus, men have commonly employed to measure the advance or decline of civilization, the values they have celebrated in the saints and sages whom they have agreed to canonize. They are the values which readily lend themselves to rational justification, yet need no justification."

There are, perhaps, two other matters that ought to be touched upon in an article of this nature. The first has to do with the effect of power upon personality. Acton is quite explicit: "All power tends to corrupt and absolute power corrupts absolutely." This I cannot gainsay. I remember one evening when I was returning with political friends from a television performance. For a half hour they told me what a brilliant performance mine had been. By the end of the half hour I was aware only that a new political star had been born on the horizon, namely myself, and that I could not long deny the people of the state of Connecticut the chance to vote for me for Governor or

United States Senator.    It was not until I got home that my  wife
reminded me that my performance had, in fact, been a little on the
mediocre side - but that she was sure I had just had an off-night.
The  most  devastating traps of public office are the ones set  to
catch the ego.   It is so easy to forget that the tribute is to the
office,   not  to the person.   Even a mayor stands out a little   -
fathers bring up their daughters to "shake the mayor's hand";   the
mayor sits at head tables;   the mayor officiates; and is often the
central  figure  in ceremonies.   All this inflates the  sense  of
personal  worth  and  waters the thirsty garden  of  vanity.   The
consequences are often pathetic, often silly, sometimes dangerous.
But  Acton was wrong in suggesting that the only  flowers  in
the  garden  of  vanity are the weeds of  corruption.   Power  may
corrupt,  but it also can ennoble.   The sense that you,  and  the
office  you  hold,  are widely valued often creates  a  heightened
sense  of  responsibility,  a desire to live close to  the  public
expectation,  a  wish to become a kind of community example.   Too
few  people appreciate the ennobling effect of public  office.   I
have seen people utterly transformed by a judgeship.   A politician
- an old pro in western Connecticut - once confided to me that  he
hated  all  judges.   "What  are they but some  hack  lawyers  who
happened  to  know a politician?"  And he went on,  "After  you've
made 'em,  what do they do?   They turn around and kick you in the
teeth!   They  draw  their robes around them as though  they  were
Solon or something!   You can't touch them!   Who the hell do they
think they are?"  The fact is that they think they are Solon; they
suddenly  realize  that instead of petty politicians they  are  an
essential  part of the fabric of civilization,  a fabric that  can
last  only  as long as there is a widespread  public  belief  that
judges in courts of law will try to be just.
What is true of judges is equally true of elected executives.
The  ennobling  effect of public office is one  of  its  greatest
psychic  dividends.   Those who believe that people seek to  hold
public  office only because it gives them power and status do  not
appreciate  the importance to many people of simply  feeling  that
the  job  they hold makes them better members of the  human  race.
The  heightened capacity for doing good in the world is one of the
key  attractions of political power and,  from my limited  observations,  is  a  far  more  fundamental factor  in  determining  the
direction  of a person's ambitions than the baubles and tinsel  of
temporary status and deference.
This  brings  me to my final point.   All  ethical  questions
ultimately revert to propositions about the nature of people.   The
underlying  complexity  of ethical questions stems from  the  fact
that  people  are  morally ambiguous and  ultimately  inscrutable.
Perched precariously on a whirling planet,  blind to our  origins,
blind to reasons for being,  beset by the terrors of nature and of
our  own  creation,  people wobble drunkenly between a  certainty
that  they are nothing and an occasional blinding revelation  that
one has a transcendent dignity and perhaps destiny.   When people
feel  alienated from their universe,  they may huddle in fear with
their fellow beings;  but one cannot reach them with that fullness
of feeling,  that intenseness of identity,  which is suggested  by
the  Christian  concept  of love,  or by  the  civil  concept  of

community.   I am not a mystical person, but I sense strongly that
my  best moments as mayor came when I felt in an almost  religious
way   that what we were attempting to do in Middletown had  meaning
beyond   itself.   I  remember the editor of the local  paper  once
writing  me  an intimate note when I was particularly  discouraged
about the public response to some issue.  "Never," he wrote, "lose
faith  in your neighbors."  He went on to explain,  not that  they
were perfect, but that he had known them for a long time, and that
they  would ultimately respond to the good if they could be  shown
the good.

     Surely this is the ultimate ethical postulate in a democracy:
Not that people are good,  but that they are capable of good;  not
that they are free from corruption,  but that they are desperately
sick  of it;  not that they have fashioned the good  society,  but
that they have caught an unforgettable glimpse of it.   Ultimately
the  ethical problems of the elected executive are what  they  are
for  all  human beings:   the struggle to discover ends and  means
that  will heighten people's sense of individual worth in an  ever
more extensive and inclusive community.

# MORAL DILEMMAS OF SCHOOLING*

### H. Millard Clements
### James B. Macdonald

For many years professional educators, under attack from critics and colleagues outside of education, have partially withdrawn from the challenge and responsibility of critically examining what goes on in our schools. This may well be due in some measure to the often irrelevant and sometimes irrational nature of the criticism, which encourages defense of present schooling practices. This is unfortunate, however, for no profession will be able to confront adequately its responsibilities unless it provides for the opportunity to engage in thoughtful criticism of its practices.

Are our schools a desirable place for the education of human beings? Do schools embody in practice the revered humanistic values of our culture? Are the schools essentially moral enterprises?

Educators often debate proposals, clarify aspirations and make plans related to schools. Yet, what sort of life do students and teachers lead in school? Unfortunately, we are apt to assume that noble aspirations, rational plans, and labored efforts on behalf of our school children result in desired accomplishment. We assume, in other words, that our good intentions and efforts are directly related to our achievements. The Conference on Moral Dilemmas was held in the spirit of challenge to this assumption.

It was not the intention of the speakers to challenge our aspirations, but instead to focus on the unintended consequences of schooling in the lives of teachers and students in the schools - in short, the moral dilemmas of schooling.

Consider, for example, the following living realities of most schooling:

1. Attendance is compulsory.
2. Children (and teachers even more) are compelled by assignment to live with each other for long periods of time regardless of personal wishes.
3. Children are compelled to take tests and examinations regardless of pupil or parent desire or approval.
4. Children experience a common compulsory curriculum regardless of individual desires or abilities.
5. Children must read a common established textbook literature.

---

*This article is an interpretation of the content of presented papers and their research implications of a Conference on Moral Dilemmas of Schooling, held at the University of Wisconsin, May 12, 13, 14, 1965. The full proceedings may be published at a later date.

6. Children experience school regulation of dress, time, social activity, and basic physiological functions.
7. Children are compelled to follow school routines, such as:

    a. Remaining inactive for long periods.
    b. Listening to someone talk two-thirds of the time.

To interfere to this extent in the lives of others is clearly a moral endeavor. Perhaps all these are good things for children to do, yet one must agree that these imperatives and others like them pose moral questions in the schools.

If we are to be satisfied with the moral character of our system of schooling, then we must be assured not only by our good intentions but by the consequences of what we do. The justice or morality of our willingness to dare to influence the lives of children must lie in our willingness to face both the intended and the unintended, both the manifest and the latent, both the hope and the accomplishment of schooling.

It is not enough to hope or intend. The manifest hope of Prohibition was the reduction of alcoholism and its unfortunate effects on our society. The unintended accomplishment of this legislation was the development of a criminal elite that flourished on the profits of illegal liquor. The manifest intention of anti-gambling legislation is to suppress gambling; the unintended consequence has been the creation of a nation-wide illegal gambling syndicate. The recent experience with thalidomide is a paradigmatic example of good intentions and unforseen and unsuspected consequences.

## A Moral Endeavor

Huebner suggests that there is no single satisfactory way to talk about schooling.[1] We may think and talk about schools with technical or manufacturing language, with political talk, or as instances of moral relationships of men. Each way of talking is neither true nor false, but more or less useful in gaining insight into the ways in which we work and influence each other.

He further suggested that if we are to talk about schools in moral terms we must utilize such concepts as justice, service and vitality. Schooling, if it is to be moral, must: (a) be just in the treatment of ideas and just in the treatment of children in school; (b) serve students rather than compel them to fit into ordained programs; (c) be vital, everchanging, rather than static, bureaucratic, routinized. Huebner argued that our schools are not just, vital or of service to students. The other speakers explored and illuminated specific aspects of this lack of justice, vitality and service. Each speaker illuminated a dilemma and identified a possibility for significant educational research.

Fielder explored the justice with which peoples and ideas were treated in social studies texts, and the service this performs for the learner.[2] He noted an appalling lack of justice in the treatment of Oriental Americans in California history, and proposed that books that distort what has been and is happening in the world are a fundamental disservice to students.

Macdonald discussed the justice and service to students of

tests and evaluation procedures in the classroom.[3] He asserted that much of present day evaluation is immoral when used to label, grade and promote students for the purposes of the school system. He pointed out the disservice and injustice tests and evaluation perform in the emotional life of the student, the development of healthy self-images, the restrictiveness of measurement, and in the distorted attitudes they foster about the nature and worth of scholarly or academic study.

Goslin continued in the discussion of testing, focusing upon the moral consequences of predictive testing in the schools.[4] He raised serious questions about the invasion of privacy and the rights of individual pupils and parents. He asserted that there is little evidence to suggest that predictive tests are essential to the conduct of schooling and may well perform injustices and be a disservice to students.

The question of the morality of psychological services for schools was raised by Szasz.[5] His contention was essentially this: A responsible psychologist or psychiatrist cannot serve both the interests of the individual and the school system. He was fearful that if psychologists or psychiatrists are in the employment of the schools they will serve the bureaucratic interests of the school (e.g., adjusting students to the norms of institutions) rather than serve individuals. In general, he contended that a state institution should not be in the business of arbitrating normality.

The morality of the bureaucratic agents of schools was challenged by Friedenberg.[6] He reported a study he had conducted in which he found that high school students believed that: (a) they had no right to privacy from school staff; (b) they were not disposed to defend the right of privacy of other students; (c) perceived students as problems to be "helped" and not as persons or individuals; and (d) believed that whatever was done in the name of being helpful by school personnel was morally acceptable. He further supported Szasz's contention that a person cannot serve justly as a "helper" to the student and as an agent of the school. He implied that schools are frustrating and often degrading to individuals and that the mythology of staff "helpfulness" proved to make school life more palatable for the students, as well as to legitimate the coercive behavior of school staff.

The final speaker of the conference, Coleman, proposed alternatives to the present lack of justice, service and vitality in the schools.[7] He suggested, briefly, that: (a) each school district establish fundamentally different kinds of schools that children may choose into or out of as they wish; (b) that to facilitate teaching and to reduce the need for marginally competent teachers, we make use of machines whenever they can be intelligently and appropriately used. Coleman discussed essentially the desirability of pluralized, optional, and task coercive (rather than teacher coercive) opportunities in schooling.

In would appear that the speakers above are in complete agreement about the moral dilemma of the individual versus the system. It is further implied that many of our present practices are in violation of the humanistic tradition and morality of our society, and are in conflict with the preservation of the dignity, worth and integrity of individual students.

If educators are concerned about human values, then it is imperative that we know what moral condition our schools are in. The Conference on Moral Dilemma of Schooling could well have generated the following kinds of questions for our study and research.

1. What better and/or different ways of talking about schools can be developed to account for moral as well as technical or political concerns?

2. Are textbooks and other commercial materials prepared primarily for markets or for service to students?

3. What attitudes, emotions, and self-images are created in individuals by our evaluation procedures?

4. What are the social consequences of testing?

5. Are bureaucratic practices and procedures (including psychological services) serving the individual?

6. How can we pluralize our school programs and activities to promote service, justice and vitality in the schools?

This is a time when we are looking again at the morality of our relationships. We are witnessing this phenomenon, for example, in the growth of existential literature, the civil rights movement, and the plea for control of nuclear weapons. It seems only too apparent that the moral pain people are experiencing grows out of the total context of our societies and cultures, of which our institutions of schooling are an integral part.

## FOOTNOTES

[1]Dwayne Huebner, "Moral Values and the Curriculum," paper presented at the Conference on Moral Dilemmas of Schooling, University of Wisconsin, 12-14 May 1965.

[2]William R. Fielder, "Education with Averted Eyes," paper presented at the Conference on Moral Dilemmas of Schooling, University of Wisconsin, 12-14 May 1965.

[3]James Macdonald, "Moral Problems in Classroom Evaluation and Testing," paper presented at the Conference on Moral Dilemmas of Schooling, University of Wisconsin, 12-14 May 1965.

[4]David Goslin, "The Social Consequences of Testing," paper presented at the Conference on Moral Dilemmas of Schooling, University of Wisconsin, 12-14 May 1965.

[5]Thomas Szasz, "Mental Health Services in School," paper presented at the Conference on Moral Dilemmas of Schooling, University of Wisconsin, 12-14 May 1965.

[6]Edgar Friedenberg, "Unintended Consequences of Bureaucratic Schooling," paper presented at the Conference on Moral Dilemmas of Schooling, University of Wisconsin, 12-14 May 1965.

[7]James Coleman, "Alternatives in Schooling," paper presented at the Conference on Moral Dilemmas of Schooling, University of Wisconsin, 12-14 May 1965.

# VALUES CLARIFICATION AND CIVIL LIBERTIES

## Howard Kirschenbaum

Among educational methods for dealing with controversial issues, the "values clarification approach" is one of the most consistent with democratic thought and practice. Much has been written about the educational, philosophical and psychological aspects of values clarification, but very little has been said of its political implications. I would like to take a fresh look at values clarification from this perspective.

Stated simply:

(1) Values clarification encourages individuals and groups to spend time thinking about and discussing important, value-laden topics--both of personal relevance and social concern.

(2) Values clarification encourages an atmosphere and a setting in which alternative viewpoints can be shared and where people are given the safety and respect that is so important for personal learning and social interaction.

(3) Values clarification has developed numerous educational methods and materials to help all this happen in an effective and interesting manner.[1]

This may not be a complete program for education in a democracy, but it is an important part of it.

## Important Topics

Sometimes the topics focused upon in value-clarifying activities are of personal importance to students or participants--leisure time activities, health priorities and practices, sexuality, material values, religious beliefs, etc. On other occasions, the topics may be of critical social importance--environmental issues, war and peace, economics, racism, sexism and other forms of oppression. As in all educational endeavors, teachers and students must make judgments about what topics are appropriate for attention and discussion in different situations. Certainly there are occasions when prudence and good judgment would suggest that specific topics not be discussed--with certain age groups, at certain times, with certain students, in certain communities.

Acknowledging this, the proponents of values clarification, explicitly and implicitly have taken a stand on the content of formal education. They have said, in effect;

> Too often we focus on bland and irrelevant issues in educational and group settings. Individuals are confused and conflicted about important value issues and choices in their lives. The society is being torn apart, its survival threatened by unresolved value conflicts among various interest groups. We can and we must focus on these issues in our

educational system. We underestimate students
too often. They are capable of discussing
these issues intelligently and responsibly.
If they lack knowledge or skills, then it is
our job to help them develop these, not to
shield them or keep them from facing some of
the very issues which could make education
exciting, indeed, the very issues (love, war,
money, aesthetics, religions, death, nature,
etc.) which have been central to the 'basic'
curriculum for centuries--history, literature,
science, philosophy and art.*

Thus, the literature of values clarification has been filled
with activities, questions, materials and units focusing on these
types of value issues. "Such a broadening of educational
objectives," writes Milton Rokeach, "now has a universal face
validity, largely because of the pioneering work of proponents of
values clarification."[2]

Unfortunately, Rokeach was exaggerating. The inclusion of
value-laden topics in the school has not met with universal
acclaim. There are groups in society who would rather that young
people not be exposed to various and divergent viewpoints about
politics and economics, material values, social behavior,
religious beliefs, attitudes toward drugs, sex, male-female roles,
and so on. For some, this opposition comes from the fear that,
while values clarification may be fine theoretically, in practice
it will be carried out poorly. Peer pressure will be too strong,
the teacher will impose his or her values, students will divulge
too much and be embarrassed, or even psychologically damaged.
Such fears are reasonable; but experience has shown that the large
majority of teachers employ the method quite safely, and the small
minority who misuse it soon stop using it, because their students
stop participating. Teacher training programs address all these
pitfalls and teach group leaders how to avoid them.

Other critics, however, have said that even when values
clarification is used most responsibly, at best, they are still
against it. They simply do not want their children and youth
exposed to viewpoints which they perceive as inimical to their
own. In some cases, they have held that the mere fact that
viewpoints different from theirs are treated with respect
undermines their religious teaching which views their own
spiritual and moral values as the only correct values. Therefore,
they argue, such a practice imposes a "secular humanism" (a non-
religious, liberal tolerance) and thereby violates the separation
of Church and State embodied in the Bill of Rights. (Not all
religious groups or individuals view values clarification in this
light. There are thousands of priests, nuns, ministers, and
rabbis who actively use values clarification and point out that
making a "free choice" from alternatives is the very essence of
religious faith.)

This is clearly a civil liberties issue. It takes two forms,

---

*Quotation not referenced.

depending on whether we are dealing with secular value issues or
religious value issues. On the secular side, in my opinion, the
question boils down to this: do teachers and students have a
right, in the context of the school curriculum, to focus on
controversial issues in the classroom? Do the First Amendment
rights of free thought, speech, assembly and press (e.g., a class
or school newspaper) extend to teachers and students? Proponents
of values clarification have clearly answered "yes" and have
encouraged teachers and students to use those rights.

On the religious side of the question, the situation is more
complicated, with an apparent conflict between two important
constitutional guarantees. To deny students the right to focus on
and discuss issues related to religion and morality would be a
denial of free speech and, ironically, freedom of religious
though. But to do so interferes with the religious training some
groups wish to provide for their youth. These are complicated
constitutional problems which, undoubtedly, the Supreme Court will
be called upon to clarify further. If it gets to that point,
however, I believe the First Amendment right of free speech will
again be upheld. As in the past, when the courts have decided
that certain civil laws take precedence over the doctrine of
separation of Church and State (e.g., polygamy was outlawed, even
though it was central to the Mormon religion), so it will be
decided that so long as nothing is done to hamper religious groups
from practicing their religion and conducting their own schools,
then in the public schools, the right of free speech will extend
to religious and moral issues.

While this matter is being clarified, however, schools may
find it expedient and wise to allow parents who object to their
children's participation in values clarification or other
activities that occasionally focus on religious or moral issues to
have their children excused from such activities and given
alternative learning experiences. This begs the constitutional
question, but respects the wishes of all concerned and may be the
most sensible course. In actuality, religious topics do not come
up that often, and only rarely does a parent, given the chance,
ask for such an exclusion for his or her child; so the alternative
learning option does not tend to become the logistical headache
that administrators or teachers might fear.

Values clarification is not the only educational methodology
that has had to face these questions. But as an educational
method, it finds good support in the Bill of Rights and, in turn,
it strengthens the First Amendment by giving students practice in
exercising those very rights.

## Safety and Respect

From time to time, I hear values clarification described as
being another form of brainwashing or a way of pressuring the
individual to conform to the group opinion. Nothing could be
further from the truth. Every major publication and training
event on values clarification emphasizes just the opposite--how to
encourage freedom of thought, how to reduce peer pressure, how to
eliminate ridicule or praise from the classroom as tools for
gaining conformity, how to avoid imposing one's own viewpoint on

the group, how to phrase questions so all opinions are legitimized, and so on. Granted the values clarification leader is human and sometimes fails to live up to this ideal; but if a leader wants students to think for themselves, they will get the message, in spite of an occasional imposition or instances of peer pressure. Conversely, if a teacher is highly authoritarian by nature, no amount of values clarification strategies is going to make it a safe place for them to voice their opinions.

The fact is that peer pressure and authority-imposed values existed long before values clarification came along. It was the worst example in history of authority and peer group pressure-- facism and the Holocaust--which in part motivated Raths, Harmin and Simon to develop the values clarification approach.[3] Its explicit goals and specific techniques support free thought and free speech, with the valuing processes of "choosing freely" and "publicly affirming" one's beliefs as central to the values clarification approach. They are also central to the democratic process.

Other critics have suggested that even when freedom of thought and individuality are encouraged, if students are "required" or "forced" to divulge their thoughts or feelings, this constitutes an insidious pressure toward group conformity, not to mention an invasion of privacy. If students were forced to reveal their inner thoughts, that certainly would be insidious. But it would not be values clarification. Again and again, the literature and training approaches of values clarification emphasize giving students (and adults) "the right to pass;" not only that, but the right to pass (to not participate or answer) with full respect, no further questions and no odd looks, as well as lots of support in case any class members question or make a comment about a student who passes. In other words, the values clarification facilitator is teaching his or her class that, at least in this classroom, it is safe to speak one's mind and safe to be silent--both behaviors are worthy of respect. If anything is imposed, it's that.

Methods and Materials

Long before values clarification appeared as an "educational approach," teachers, group leaders and others often created occasions for their students or members to share their views on important and controversial issues. What values clarification has added is a series of very practical activities for accomplishing its goal of stimulating thought and discussion.[4]

In small Focus Groups participants take turns, each getting an equal amount of time, to share their views on a particular subject. Rank Orders have participants respond to a question by arranging various alternative answers in order of their preference. Students place themselves on a Values Continuum to show where they stand between two end points on a given values issue. Various Inventories ask participants to make a list related to some aspect of their life (e.g., all the items in one's medicine cabinet, ten examples of prejudice one has experienced, etc.) and then examine that part of their life more closely (e.g., Which items in the medicine chest did you buy, in part, because of advertising? In which instances of prejudice did you respond in a way you were proud of? etc.) And on and on. Over thirty books and scores of articles contain hundreds of examples of strategies that might be appropriate in different situations, as well as ways of building such value--clarifying experiences into the subject matter curriculum.[5]

## Summary

Like any technique, values clarification can be abused. When this happens, students begin to "pass" and teachers stop using the method. But most of the time the results are just the opposite. Student and adult participants welcome the opportunity to share their thoughts, listen to other viewpoints, and clarify their values. Valuable citizenship skills are learned, such as affirming one's viewpoint in a group, evaluating alternative positions, learning to weigh the consequences of different positions, developing the ability to make one's own choice free from authority domination or peer pressure, and learning to take action in support of one's beliefs and values. This is a most important training ground for democracy. Not only is values clarification consistent with the principles of civil liberties, it helps teach and reinforce them.

**FOOTNOTES**

[1]For a complete listing of materials available on the values clarification approach, write National Humanistic Education Center, 110 Spring Street, Saratoga Springs, New York, 12866.

[2]Milton Rokeach, "Toward a Philosophy of Value Education," Values Education: Theory, Practice, Problems, and Prospects, ed. J. Meyer, B. Burnham, and J. Cholvat (Waterloo, Ontario: Wilfred Laurier University Press, 1975).

[3]Louis Raths, Merrill Harmin, and Sidney Simon, Values and Teaching (Columbus, Ohio: Charles Merrill, 1966).

[4]Sidney Simon, Leland Howe, and Howard Kirschenbaum, Values Clarification: A Handbook of Practical Strategies For Teachers and Students (New York: Hart Publishing, 1972).

[5]Merrill Harmin, Howard Kirschenbaum, and Sidney Simon, Clarifying Values Through Subject Matter (Minneapolis, Mn.: Winston Press, 1973).

# CAN SCHOOLS TEACH KIDS MORAL VALUES?*

## Amitai Etzioni

After meeting with a group of superintendents of schools in a neighboring state, I asked if I could talk to them about what I am working on currently, which is what the schools do and don't do in the area of civic ethics. They were somewhat reluctant to talk about that, saying that is was not an issue. So I asked them if they would recall any school problem which could be classified as belonging in the civic ethics arena and if we could discuss it. They told me two stories that I believe illustrate both the issues and our difficulties in handling them.

In one case, small amounts of money regularly disappeared from the principal's office. The principal felt that it showed a very serious defect in the disciplinary system. He decided to take matters into his own hand and put flourescent powder, obtained from the local police chief, on the cash in his office. After the next theft he put all the children's hands under a flourescent lamp and caught the culprit. It turned out, however, that the sister of the culprit's mother was married to someone on the school board, and so the principal quietly arranged for the situation to be handled without causing undue debate - "not to rock the boat," he said.

The other incident involved a Black child who was threatening to beat up some children unless they gave him a quarter each day. The principal felt the situation was particularly awkward because obviously the Black child was poor and came from a disadvantaged background. He felt, therefore, that he could not confront the issue the way he would with a white child from a privileged background. He thought that raising the issue would bring the Black community down on him. So he handled it by transferring the student to a different school.

In discussing these and other examples, it rapidly became clear that although the superintendents often faced serious problems in ethical misconduct in their schools, they lacked a sense of how, as official representatives of the larger community, they ought to deal with issues of students' ethical behavior and attitudes. Indeed, all thirty superintendents seemed unanimously agreed that even if they were of a mind to add ethics to the long agenda of their duties and to the problems they face, one could not define ethics. That is, what was ethical to one person (or segment of the community) was unethical to another. Accordingly, how could schools proceed with such a controversial program?

*This article is a transcript of the Abraham Weckstein Memorial Lecture presented by Dr. Etzioni at New York University's School of Education, Health, Nursing, and Arts Professions Alumni Day on March 12, 1977. Research used in preparation of this presentation benefited from a grant by the Humanities Division of the Rockefeller Foundation.

The anecdotes and the superintendents' response to the ethical issues they raise illustrate the uncertainty and ambivalence that currently beset efforts to come to terms with the role of schools in teaching civic ethics. We refer to "civic ethics" to distinguish a set of ethical principles which, whatever religious grounds they may also have, are fundamentally secular in that without them a civil society can be sustained only with great difficulty. The central tenet of civic ethics is the acceptance by members of society, as an ethical imperative (as opposed to a mere pragmatic expedient), that pursuing private and public goals ought to be done by legitimate means - i.e., according to rules demarcating right from wrong.

Clearly, if such concepts of right and wrong behavior in pursuit of personal and collective aims are to be maintained, each new generation must be taught the rules and the importance of following them. While the teaching of morality in general is a major mission of the family and religious institutions, instilling civic ethics is also, it can be argued, a task for the schools. Thus, it is a significant indicator of our society's lack of consensus on core values that teachers and school officials appear to be so ambivalent about the legitimacy of such a role and so confused as to how to go about fulfilling it.

## Views of Ethics Education

Indeed, there are at least three conceptions of what is meant by ethics education which are current in the literature on the subject, in discussions, and which come up again and again as the Center for Policy Research conducts interviews in the schools.

One is what may be called the conservative conception. It derives from those particular traditional values and thoughts which provide a kind of translation of the idea of law and order to the educational level. Basically it suggests that in a civilized society there are rules; you are not to argue about them unduly; they are transmitted from generation to generation as a kind of code; and it is the job of the elders - the parents, the teachers, and ultimately the policemen and the courts - to see to it that civilized society will survive by making the code transmitted, internalized, and, where it is not successfully internalized, enforced. While up to a point you can explain it, ultimately the code is its own virtue, because if you do not have a code you have anarchy; you have the Hobbesian state of society; and the only way to preserve a society in which we can exist is by having some set of rules. Even if the rules are not perfect and even it (sic) they ought to be changed, they must be enforced in the meantime. Therefore, the ultimate justification for a set of rules is the need for acceptance of authority, i.e., what a parent or teacher relies on when giving as a reason "because I say so," "I say so" is not an arbitrary term; "I say so" represents a society and a collectivity which needs to protect itself against social anarchy. In the school this means that the principal or the superintendent has a duty to get across, enforce, and uphold the set of rules.

Almost untouched by that is the left-liberal view that being moral, being ethical, is first of all being sensitive to others

and being just. As it is sometimes put, the greatest injustices
and therefore the greatest immorality is imposed by the code of
ethics that the "haves" insist upon imposing upon the "have-nots."
The code is never neutral; the code always reflects values society
has evolved historically, including its discriminatory practices,
its sexism, its racism, and its institutionalism. The need for
the ethical being, then, is to transform the system to make it
more responsive to the needs of the individual. According to this
view, the first order of duty is to dismantle the prevailing rules
in order to replace them with rules more reflective of egalitarian
individualistic values. Since new rules would signify transition
to a new social order, they would necessarily remain somewhat
formless until the outlines of that more socially just society
became more clear.

Some who espouse this view are also inclined to see children
as "noble savages" having an inborn or naturally developing sense
of ethics which is distorted or stunted by society. Some
educators interpret the developmental theories of Piaget and
Kholberg in this vein, though it does not seem to be the position
of either of these theorists themselves. However, this
perspective suggests to those who hold it that the way for the
school to influence children's ethical development is by giving
them maximum freedom, e.g., open classrooms to foster the growth
of their natural sense of right and wrong.

Then there is a third view. Lacking a better name, it might
be referred to as the rudimentary view of the Ten Commandments.
It seems that above and beyond whether a person holds a liberal or
conservative view of ethics, most seem to agree that we must
observe and heed some basic things, whatever our views. Most
elementary is "thou shalt not kill," and perhaps also "thou shalt
not steal," though some people are ambivalent about that.

The question of lying poses some interesting problems. On
the one hand, we still teach children that Washington never lied,
and we ask them to use their identification with the Founding
Father to internalize that value. We have various exercises in
specific ethics and books on morality about that value. At the
same time, a study done at the University of Michigan asked a
random sample of schoolchildren of various ages, ranging from
second-graders all the way up to age seventeen, if they would ever
tell a lie. When asked in that particular way, 87 percent said
never. But when they were asked, "Would you tell a lie to help a
friend if he were in a tight spot?" many said they would. What
they are really telling us in terms of the hierarchy of values is
that being particularistic is more important than being universal.
Not telling a lie is a general rule which is supposed to apply to
all circumstances. You occasionally transgress, but then you
should feel uncomfortable, or guilty about it (depending upon what
tradition you come from), and then you should try to go back to
the rule whenever you can. But you should not make a principle
out of transgression. When you say one ought to lie for friends,
then you are saying there is a higher value than telling the
truth, which separates all the people I know into two groups - my
buddies, who get extra treatment, and strangers. And that
particular value, my tribe against all others, then takes priority

over the more general rule.

These then are the three concepts of ethics education that are out there in the community; they all run into each other in the back of our minds and make it difficult for well-intentioned parents, educators, school officials, and board program formulators to frame a systematic attempt to deal with this matter. The result is avoidance of conflict, which is part of our national character. People are presently trying to come up with formulae that are neutral among the three conceptions. The most popular two deserve attention.

## Classroom Techniques

The best selling formula for ethics education says that we are not to tell you what you should believe in; our efforts are to help you to find out what your values are in order that you can clarify them in your own mind. If you are clear about your values, education has succeeded. It is not the duty or even the right of the educator to teach values, to step in and communicate values, certainly not to preach; he or she is not to affect your choices whatsoever. We are all equals - the youngest child is a human being just like the rest of us - and therefore what we should do for children is to refrain from imparting values and certainly from imposing values. But we should help the children discover what their own values are.

In that tradition there is a great interest in list-making. The teacher provides the paper and pencil, the children provide the list. In one of these exercises - and I am not interested in latching on to this or that example, I am interested in teasing out the educational philosophy and sociological feeling behind it - the pupils are asked to list the things they would like to do, e.g., go fishing, watch a movie, play basketball. Then it is explained to them that what they just listed is not simply a concrete list of activities, but one that captures their values, putting leisure and sport above learning, let us say. Then the students are asked to rank those activities. If they could not do them all, or if they had to divide their time or money among them, to which one would they give priority? It is this priority-ranking, then, that is read back to them to say, "You see, the fact that you put that one highest shows that while you value all of these things, you value one thing more than these others." And they get a feel for trade-offs, value hierarchy, and value structures. It helps people, whatever their age, to clarify what their preferences are.

To the extent that you stop here, you do not affect the value preferences of the people involved. However, if you do not allow a group discussion of why Jimmy chose that while Judy chose this, because that may raise a consensus that some preferences are not as acceptable as others, then in effect what you do, perhaps unwittingly, is cement people into their raw preferences, which may be reflective of their more anarchistic, more egoistic preferences. This also tends to foster the belief that all values are relative to point of view and that as expressions of individuals personally all are equally valid.

The other school again takes the position that you should not impose or transmit values, but, rather than helping people clarify their own values, you should help them understand how to reason about values. Here, the class is divided into two camps. One half is asked to argue, let us say, for the right of people to have an abortion if they wish, and the other half is asked to argue against that right. Disregarding what their preferences are, it is hoped that the student will learn to reason well for a value position. The next day the class is divided differently, and half are asked to argue for civil rights and the other half to argue against civil rights (of course with some preparation including substantive teaching materials). Again this helps people think through their premises, reach normative conclusions, and be able to talk with each other about their preferences. It is largely a cognitive exercise, dealing with reasoning and not with root preferences. Above all, it does not seek to affect preferences.

Against these two approaches stands the more old-fashioned idea that the teacher, and more generally other educators in the community and at home, represent the values of the society. While many of them are challenged in this time of redefinition and transition, there can be no normative vacuum. All persons should speak to the values they hold dear, and they should articulate and defend those. Yet it is argued that our capacity to sway other people, including children, is limited to begin with, and, therefore, the fear that we will brainwash them into our preferences is vastly exaggerated. In our pluralistic society children are subject to a large variety of inputs anyhow. They will get from their parents one set of values - or perhaps two or more sets of values if parents have conflicts on certain issues or if parents are divorced and remarried. They get some others from the neighborhood, or maybe some from churches and synagogues, and still others from their various teachers. Out of this plurality of normative inputs, each trying to sway the child to buy its set of values, the child will first of all gain the ability to deal with the fact that he/she lives in a society with a plurality of conflicting values. Second, she/he will learn to sort out what his/her true preferences are, not by reference to some rudimentary "human nature" that antedates society, but from the multiplicity of the values and culture in the society in which he/she lives.

Thus, to stick with an earlier example, there is a range of disagreement that a child cannot help but be exposed to, concerning how far one should carry personal loyalty. I.e., at what point is misconduct serious enough that for either the sake of the community, or another person's welfare, or the individual's own good, one is justified or even morally obliged to "tell on" a friend?

It is also implied that the school is not exempt from that process. In part because society is ridden with conflict and in part because teachers inevitably hold certain values as members of society, it is held that it is better for those values to be brought out into the open. The teacher should not say, "Well OK, everybody should have input, and I'll be just a neutral referee," or perhaps avoid the topic completely. Rather the teacher should see one's duty as adding one more voice to this constant array of normative inputs.

## Schools' Moral Climate

In addition to, and sometimes in opposition to, what the schools formally teach about ethics is the so-called "hidden curriculum" of what is learned via experience. It may well be that what affects children most in school in the area of civic ethics and ethicality and morality is not so much what they are taught in the classroom, but what they learn through the experiences the school as a climate and structure in society fashions for them. I am almost willing to disregard that in a civics class students are taught that the government has three branches, or how many members the Supreme Court has, or if they are taught value clarification or value reasoning or no values at all, if the school could be helped to become self-aware of the values it communicates so effectively in its total arrangements. In that case informal school experiences would be certain to convey values school officials would choose to submit were they more aware of the educational content of those experiences.

Let me illustrate with an example: grades. Grades, in most schools, are more or less the equivalent of money in adult society. They are one of the currencies with which people are rewarded for their efforts. They are a status symbol. They are psychological crutches onto which children latch. Grades help students assess how they are making out, how successful they are, and where they stand vis-a-vis each other. They stratify, they record, they help pupils feel their work is paying off even before they graduate and are able to make practical use of their learning and diploma.

Theoretically, of course, we should all learn for learning's sake and not heed the grades, but among the various psychological tools of the school, grades have some significance. It is as though you would come to a creative artist and say that he should enjoy the art and not worry about the cash value. Well, meanwhile artists have to live, not just in the sense of buying the bread, but in getting a sense of where they stand. Very few people can live on only vague psychological assurances that they are doing all right; most of them want an occasional precise reading, like an A- or an 83, which they need, in part at least, in the kind of society in which we live.

Students are also very concerned with the question of whether grades are allotted on a fair and just basis or on some other basis. In some of the schools, maybe as many as half of them, the children feel, perhaps with cause, that the main basis for allocation of these particular rewards and all others is not their achievements. The reasons may be many. One school we studied divided the children into two groups - an honor program and those who were considered just run-of-the-mill students. But once a student is put into the honor program, the honor program has to honor its honor, and therefore no one can flunk. Whatever students do, they get high grades. (That is very much like a medical school: once students are in, they have such an investment in them they are afraid to flunk them out.) That is known by both camps: the honor kids know it, the non-honor kids know it, and it creates a curious disaffection in both of them.

Some schools have trustees very much as we have them in the prisons. There are some inmates in the prison who work for the prison management and get extra "cookies." In one particular school there are seniors and juniors who work in the principal's office. They keep attendance sheets, they give passes, they stamp cards, and for the right to do so they have a power vis-a-vis all the other students and the trading of privileges. You get someone to do your French for you if you give him a pass. And so there is an unsavory trade going on. There are schools that make it quite clear to all concerned that coming from a disadvantaged background is worth at least one grade-point. I could make a very strong normative case for discrimination in reverse. But it does not take away from the fact that both groups of children are all too keenly aware that grades are awarded on some criteria other than their efforts or achievements.

When all these things come together - teacher's pet, the trustee system, "don't rock the boat," the social-justice issues, and all kinds of other political and ideological considerations such as teachers who believe that you should never fail anybody anyhow - when all this comes together you get, possible objectively, then magnified subjectively, the sense that there is a system of allotments, there is a system of ranking, but it is not based largely on the supposed effort-achievement criteria. Therefore, what one should do to graduate is to pay lip service to the presumed values, but to know that is not the way to make it. The way to make it is by taking one or all of these possible routes to get to what one wants with less effort than studying hard.

Let me just give you one more example: sports. We have been telling each other for many years, and telling each other correctly, that sports are experience-creating; they are character-forming; they affect people's ability to behave; they affect the inner traits, the inner qualities. How do we use sports though? There was a line that Nixon loved to quote from Vince Lombardi: "Winning is not the most important thing, it is the only thing." Such an attitude toward sports - or politics or any other human activity - is frankly unconcerned with ethics, because it implies that it does not matter what means you employ to attain your goal as long as you get there. Indeed it has the further connotation that "might makes right" - the world is unlikely to question the scruples of a winner, or to admire the ethics of a loser.

The ethical attitude toward winning, which the Lombardi quotation by implication mocks, is summed up in this old adage: It's not whether you win or lose that counts, but how you play the game. The point here is that the defining characteristic of the ethical viewpoint is a willingness to curb one's impulses and, if necessary, to sacrifice one's self-interest or personal desires in order to do what is right - and, especially, to avoid achieving desired aims via means which are unfair, dishonest, or otherwise improper.

Increasingly, however, sports are played in our schools via the Lombardi motto. Players are told to go by the rules only as

long as the referee is looking. They are either told so
explicitly when the coach says that you didn't do your best when
you did not pull the shirt or use the elbow in basketball, or do
worse in football. Even tennis, once the game of gentlemen, where
if there was a doubt in the point you would call it for your
opponent, is increasingly played as a competitive sport. It is
not competitive in the traditional American sense of playing by
some rules and making it, but competitive in the "no-holds-barred"
sense. I am not saying that all schools, or even most schools, do
it that way. I am saying that a fair number of them do.

I could go on to cite other examples of what students learn
about the inauthenticity of ethical rhetoric on the basis of
school reactions to vandalism, or alcoholism, or drug abuse. The
typical reaction to such violations might be characterized as an
odd mixture of toughness (a refusal to be shocked) and softness
(an avoidance of punishment). Suffice it to say that increasingly
ethical misconduct is explained or "plea-bargained" away in
private and seldom used for educational opportunities. In its
handling of such incidents the school is rarely working for civic
education but against it.

## The American-Dream Dilemma

Finally, I want to tie the notion of civic ethics to a
concept that is dear to me. Ultimately, what the school can or
cannot do, or more widely what education can or cannot do,
obviously reflects where the larger society is going. As I see
it, American society is facing on this very issue a decision that
is not directly in the realm of ethics, but has far-reaching
implications for it.

We started, roughly in the second half of the 1800s, to
rebuild the society around a particular "project." We moved from
a society and people who lived in agrarian and rural villages and
small communities into an urban, industrial society whose number-
one identity and purpose is the production of material objects and
instruments during the day and their destruction at night. When
we talk about the consumer project, the good life, what we mean by
it is really an industrial machinery capable of producing for
masses, not merely for a small aristocracy, an ever-larger flood
of goods and services. And it is deemed essential for the well-
being of the machinery that these products be eaten up. If not,
the whole system comes to a screeching halt the way the Detroit
assembly lines did during the energy crisis. So it is essential
for the system that at the other end there be people who consume a
lot and work to make more goods for a still higher level of
consumption. That is the way the cycle is closed. That is what
we value most. Captains of industry are paid the highest salaries
and often have more power than our elected leaders. Our schools
are engineered to make people able to function and behave and work
in that system.

Over the last ten to fifteen years this idea that the good
life was measured by working hard, playing hard, and consuming a
lot has been challenged in many ways and from many quarters. It
has been challenged by people who found out that you can play hard
and not work hard, that if you focus your having fun on activities

that are not rich in resources - from sex, to cheap wine, to marijuana, contemplating the sunset, or even reading a book - then you do not have to work eight hours a day, and you can still achieve the means you need for that lower level of consumption.

While the hippie counterculture quickly burned out, the counterculture idea stuck - as often happens in the history of ideas - among millions of Americans in a much more moderate fashion. So, for instance, we used to say that if you retire at sixty-five - and many people still feel this way - that terrible evil is done to you because you are going to die sooner. Not that people necessarily enjoyed work so much, but they felt that once a person no longer worked he was no longer useful and therefore did not really deserve to live. We have studies to prove that people who stayed at work after sixty-five lived longer than those who retired because work gave life purpose. Well there are many people who still feel this way, but there is a growing number of Americans who feel the opposite way. There has been a 20 percent increase over the last five years of Americans who retired at fifty-five and who say, "I'd rather earn less and have a lower pension, but what I really want to do is not work." There are 3 million Americans who are younger than this age who chose second careers; practically all of them traded higher-income jobs for somewhat lower-income jobs which are closer to what they enjoy. There are some 8 million Americans who make education, or culture, or learning, rather than work, their central life activity. They hang around the campuses or on their margins, scraping a living together. But their main activity is not "making it" in the old sense of building a better mousetrap, or amassing a million dollars before they are thirty, or climbing the corporate ladder. They want to write the great American novel or make the best piece of ceramic, or write poetry, or compose music, or print with their own hands.

On top of this comes the environmental challenge of pollution and the energy crisis, questioning the industrial project from that end, along with the increasing recognition that economic progress may not be the most important goal for our society. It has led about 30 to 40 percent of Americans to challenge in varying degrees what used to be called the American Dream, the American Way of Life.

The majority still hold to the traditional view of our industrial era, that the right way to live is to train yourself vocationally or at the university, to find a trade, become a doctor, an x-ray technician, or commercial artist, or whatever, which will lead you to ever-higher levels of income and to ever-higher levels of consumption, and that your measure is the size of your bankbook. Promise her/him anything, but buy her/him an object. This is the view that the majority still holds and that our educational system, for the most part, is geared to.

An increasing minority, in varying degrees, is endorsing an alternative definition of the good life, sometimes flagged by the term "quality-of-life society." The quality-of-life society here does not mean that everybody would have caviar and fine wine; quality-of-life would mean more relaxation, less "Type A," more "Type B," less heart attacks, more bicycle riding, less consumption, more free time, more educational activities, more public affairs, more of what is still known as alternate culture because the main culture is of the other kind.

The reason all this is relevant to our topic is because what kind of society we are going to have and, as educators, what kind of society we are gearing our efforts to, of course has a great impact on what set of values we are trying to sensitize people to. Is it more important for the next generation to learn the ethics of competition - how to beat the other guy fairly to success and a higher standard of living? Or do we want to place greater emphasis on the ethics of cooperation - not trying to get ahead vis-a-vis other people, but of working cooperatively with them to further collective, non-material life goals.

I do not dare to think that I could answer that question. My purpose, in these closing remarks, has been to flag the connection between the question of where society is headed and what we can do as educators, in and out of school, in the rearing of the next generation of Americans.

# WHO SAYS IT'S UNETHICAL

## Estelle Faulconer

"John Jones, a social studies teacher at Eastern High School, was guilty of highly unethical conduct for agreeing to serve as his political party's chairman in Eastern precinct in conjunction with an upcoming board election," said Tom Smith to his fellow members of the Board of Education.

"It was unethical for Jane Rogers to fail that student when he was so busy with his other duties as captain of the football team and president of the senior class," said Bob Clark, principal of Park View School.

The president of the Riverview Teachers Association announced, "Any teacher who does not support the association-sponsored boycott will be guilty of an ethics violation and will be automatically expelled from membership."

"It's unethical for a teacher to draw a salary and do no more work than Ann Brown does," Sue White told a small group gathered in the teachers' lounge.

These statements and others like them immediately raise questions in the minds of perceptive members of the profession:

1. By what standard is action measured to determine if it is ethical? Who sets the standard?
2. Who has the right to apply that standard and to make judgments about an educator's conduct?
3. What are the rights of educators who stand accused? Can educators defend themselves?
4. If one's actions are properly found to be unethical, what happens?

On first consideration, the teacher might feel that one would prefer to be subjected to no restraints whatsoever, to be completely free to practice one's profession in the manner one individually deems appropriate. However, a quick review of the people and agencies who have an interest in what teachers do and the potential of these groups to pressure or hurt them if a serious conflict should arise will disabuse teachers of the idea that they can practice their profession free from attempts to control their behavior.

Parental concern about the well-being of children leads to demands that other-than-individual controls be in effect. The standards advanced by parents would reflect the desire to protect their children as well as to promote their own viewpoints about the educational process. As a result, they might frequently ignore or intrude upon values that the profession would wish to protect. In the absence of controls, the parental community can make life miserable for the nonconforming teacher. Teachers who have been subjected to social ostracism, harassing phone calls, or even cross burnings can attest to the wisdom of avoiding or counteracting these forms of control.

Prime concerns of the board of education are to protect what it conceives to be the best interests of the school system and to ensure the loyalty of the employees against all odds. The board has the ultimate power to achieve these ends as long as it has the authority to control employment.

The main concerns of the school administration are to keep the school program running smoothly and to control dissension. Its ability to do so stems from its authority to make assignments and to determine some conditions of employment. Assignments to "Siberia" or to permanent bus duty can soon discourage those whom it identifies as troublemakers.

While the values of colleagues may be fairly consistent and include such matters as protection of freedoms and control of competition, the force used to influence behavior in an uncontrolled situation may be decidedly unpleasant. Gossip and innuendo or "star chamber" proceedings can destroy an unpopular colleague. Even action by peers must be structured to protect the individual's rights.

The overwhelming motive for joining an employee organization is protection and furtherance of one's professional self-interest. Some teachers might feel nervous over their organization's involvement in disciplining members, but most would prefer this to the damage inflicted by other behavior-controlling forces. When the organization sets the standards and establishes the procedures for their enforcement, the members may be assured of greater likelihood that their values will be expressed, that their rights to a fair enforcement procedure will be protected, and that ultimately their ability to practice their profession free of undue behavioral restraint will be increased.

During the last four decades, educators throughout the nation have published various statements of ethical principles. The most recent statement in general use is the Code of Ethics of the Education Profession, as revised by the NEA Representative Assembly in 1968 and adopted by most affiliated state associations. Unfortunately, the designation "unethical" has not always referred to violation of a Code standard, but frequently to conduct that the particular speaker doesn't like.

The educators who have developed statements of ethical standards can furnish the means of reviewing actions in light of those standards and the means of applying discipline where necessary. The immediate difficulty in implementing the process of self-discipline is the lack of a suitable base of power from which to operate. Membership organizations have the power to censure or to suspend or expel members. The greater power-control of employment - is held by the administration, or board. The opinion of the administration board is therefore more likely to prevail.

Self-discipline by the profession beyond organizational review of members' actions will depend on either delegation of power from boards of education or on special legislation authorizing a professional body to review acts alleged to be unethical and to impose discipline where necessary.

Several influences may cause boards of education to delegate power to professional agencies to prescribe discipline for Code violations. Boards may become conscious of the enhanced climate for the professional practice of education when the educator is freed from external constraint on professional conduct. Also, if a board has faced a show-cause hearing for the application of discipline or has confronted adverse community or teacher reaction to a judgment about professional conduct, it may be willing to share this source of controversy with a responsible body of practitioners. An active and alert association must be on the scene ready to assume the task of self-discipline and to provide the safeguards of due process that are necessary for an effective, responsible program.

Where boards of education are not inclined to relinquish any of the power they now hold to control the behavior of employees, some change may be effected through professional practices legislation. Such acts empower a commission of the profession to exercise control over certification or licensing or to take appeals from dismissal actions. Control over entry into the profession could give a professional commission sufficient power to balance the board's ability to terminate employment. The commission might thus establish itself as an authority in the field and eventually assume control of ethics enforcement.

In the absence of the delegation of power to professional bodies, the available alternative is for the professional organization to use its rights to oversee the actions of its members, to control membership privileges, and to speak out on questions of ethics. Use of this now-available power can increase confidence in the profession's ability to discipline itself, so that it may more easily attain additional authority. Without a doubt, responsible action by the appropriate agency of the association is far more desirable than discipline by fiat, by innuendo, or by political action as now practiced in some instances by boards, by individuals, and sometimes by organizations intent on advancing their particular interests.

Educators have much to gain in promoting professional self-discipline. The present failure of the educational structure to meet all the expectations of the public, coupled with the necessary welfare orientation of many association programs, has somewhat diminished the public's confidence in educators.

Actions guaranteeing to the public that the profession will discipline unscrupulous practitioners should enhance the public's trust. Another gain is the individual member's guarantee that one has an available remedy for the unscrupulous acts of fellow educators, subject to one's own initiative and not necessarily dependent on the goodwill of the governing board or administration. Further, opportunity to participate with one's peers in developing standards and procedures for enforcement guarantees one's rights of due process either as complainant or as defendant. The profession protects the collective reputation of the larger group and advances its cause by disassociating itself from the improper acts of the unscrupulous individual.

In advocating the cause of professional autonomy, spokesmen for the education profession have held that judgments about the practice of teaching should be made by those who are best informed

about the subject in order to lessen the likelihood of error.
Problems about professional conduct arise on the scene where
education is taking place:  in schools and local districts.  The
local association is faced with the obligation to provide an
organization for self-discipline based on the profession's
competence to make judgments free from political pressure and
other outside forces.

It is obvious that controls on behavior are going to be
applied.  The question is not whether there will be controls but
who will determine what they are and apply them.

# CHAPTER VI

## THE ROLE OF ETHICS IN

## DECISION MAKING BY EDUCATIONAL ADMINISTRATORS

### Joe R. Burnett

The title of the topic is capable of an indefinite number of interpretations. For instance, are we talking about the role of ethical theories or ethical behavior, or both, in decision making; are we talking about some special thing in either or both of those regards which sets off educational administrators from other administrators; what would be ethical decision making; etc.?

Let me briefly address a few of these questions. First, what would be ethical decision making? I think this simply would be an ethical act, fairly easily described as being one in which there are at least four things operating conjointly:

1. The act is one deliberately chosen from a set of genuine ("real," "non trivial") options;
2. The agent is capable of acting "sanely" and "maturely";
3. The agent can be expected to have knowledge of the situation and the likely outcome of acting on the various options;
4. The choice significantly affects the future welfare of others.

Of these four, I would single out the third and fourth as deserving of special attention in educational administration. The third one is special because, in many cases, the acts which the administrator performs are in areas in which he or she is not specially knowledgeable. I refer to acts bearing upon specialized areas of knowledge, research, teaching, learning, and services outside his or her domain.

Almost all educational administration ends by being administration by a small group of people, none of whom is competent in key regards about all the subject areas, method areas, research and service areas encompassed by the organization. Among other things this means that ethical decision making must forever reach out to ask others to help provide the expert knowledge available in the faculty; and, it must be cautious to make those others responsive to still others who might be involved.

Part of what is represented here is designated "academic freedom". There is something else as well, and that pertains to ideals of the educational institution as a community of scholars which has as its aim the internal enrichment of academic knowledge and initiating others--junior staff and students--wholly or partially into that community.

What is being rejected here is the corporate model of educational administration as ideal, however often it is imposed by legislative groups and however often administrators, faculty, and students desire it--perhaps only because they are habituated to it in other social institutions.

There is a special province in which the educational administrator has--or should have--special knowledge. That pertains to the organizational statutes, the organizational by-laws, and the likely behavior of those who externally hold special authority vis-a-vis the organization. These are governing boards, legislators, administration at other levels in the organization, student groups, parent and alumni groups. However, it should not be necessary to point out that most higher education administrators are not either educated about, or experienced with, the details of these matters. Even if they are graduates of programs or departments in educational administration, their mobility in professorial rank often has stressed scholarship rather than the items mentioned in this special province. So, here too, an ethical commitment requires that the administrator constantly seek out knowledgeable others, this time of others who are established and senior members of the academic faculty, the non-academic staff, alumni and friends.

The first criterion of the ethical act--that it be one which is chosen from a set of genuine options--is closely related to the one under discussion. An educational institution is governed like most institutions by laws, by-laws, mores and folkways. One does not know firmly when choices are options and when not except with great patience and experience--on the part of oneself and others.

There is a particular anomaly in all of this which is raised by what I think is inevitably true in a large organization. No one person makes decisions even if one person must "sign off" on them. The ordinary cannons of morality or ethicality thus are hard to apply, their violation or neglect hard to specify, a culprit hard to unambiguously identify.

However, let me turn to the fourth criterion: the choice significantly affects the future welfare of others. Obviously, any choice can do this in theory; but, in practice, few do so in a manner which can be argued to be significant. Education seldom is a high-risk enterprise in its immediately-traceable consequences.

Still, even for all of the non-educational variables involved, we are sure that it is in some important senses significantly high risk over a student's, a faculty member's, the institution's, and the society's respective long-range futures.

Here it is, I think, that ethical theories play a role, however covertly and tacitly, in many an administrator's decision making. Whatever else they are, they are models concerning what is significant, the nature of such, its contrasts, the supposed routes to it, etc. Not enough can be said about the worth of these, especially the classical ones, I think. But I think only a certain number are worthwhile in the standard repertoire of the educational administrator, and this is because he or she is typically chosen to "embody" a certain ethical theory or set of theories. Probably it would be better, for it is more truthful, to say he or she is chosen to embody a certain ethical or moral concept or certain such concepts. For instance, is one hired to administer in a private educational setting, a public one, a land grant one; a vocational high school, a liberal arts junior college; etc. All of these presuppose and demand certain conceptual commitments as a rule. When these conceptual commitments are called into question, then one often is favored (at least in argumentation) if he or she can find a rationale in behavior by appeal to supportive general theory.

I say little here about such theory because it would be rather like carrying coals to Newcastle. (I trust Newcastle still has plenty of coal!)

Let me say a brief word about the second criterion: the person is capable of acting "sanely" and "maturely". This criterion carries with it the same caveat as the third one (concerning use of knowledge of the situation). It is a group which deliberates, no matter who "signs off". The decision-making group must possess a good composite for sane and mature decision making. However good and fulsome the information acted upon, however clear and ethically circumspect the goals of the organization, the whole situation can go awry if there are not reflective, mature people to adjudicate the demands of the one to the other.

There are some things very different between administration in ameliorative institutions, one of which is education, and those institutions which are primarily self-service. These things should and do make the ethical task easier. One of these is that there is a much more pervasive awareness of unity or commonality of purpose between the participants, administrative and non-administrative. Several others especially relevant to (and inculcated by) educational institutions are the respect for facts, the respect for theory, and the respect for the consistency in thought and action which lead to reflectiveness and judiciousness on the part of all concerned. The degree to which these are not present in your and my educational settings probably is in direct proportion to the degree to which our institutions are less than genuinely educational.

# PROFESSIONAL DEVELOPMENT IN HIGHER EDUCATION:

## THE ETHICAL DIMENSION*

### Susan Sayer

## 1. SUMMARY

I am indebted to Jules Henry for his brilliant essay on "vulnerability"[1], its specific presence in education, and its pernicious effects throughout society. He explains why society requires and ensures vulnerability in all its members, allowing some people to achieve and defend their power by manipulating the vulnerability of others. He shows how this means deliberately educating our children to be stupid and passive, so that they will grow up to be vulnerable like their parents before them, and thus be able to be kept in their place to accept the unsatisfactory, the absurd, and the debilitating aspects of society that are thrust upon them.

On reflection, I believe that the "vulnerability" of colleagues and students in the highly competitive atmosphere of the university, and the direct or potential manipulation of that vulnerability, are what this paper too is about. It may in fact be that these are the realities that professional development personnel have to take into account, and perhaps should find ways to 'reveal' to others who are operating in that same system. But the fundamental question that I see arising repeatedly throughout this paper is: are these the means which professional development organizers too can or should adopt? What would be the implications of their doing so?

## 2. CONCLUSIONS

Sections 3 and 4 of this paper identify a series of ethical questions which should confront any professional development organizer in higher education. I have been both personally tempted and encouraged by colleagues to indicate my own answers (where I have them) to the questions presented, but this would require excessive background explanation concerning my own philosophy of professional development. I do not, for example, myself entertain the concept of an instructional role vis-a-vis my colleagues (although I am occasionally forced into such a posture), so certain questions arise for me with less force than others. Likewise, I see 'improvement' as a potential result, not an identified goal. The reason for this is that an intention to 'improve' implies both imposing one's own judgments about right and wrong/good and bad/etc., and an in-built pre-judgment that the relevant people and practices would, if tried, be found wanting (guilty until proven innocent). In the very complicated and

---

*The following is a revised version of a paper presented to the American Educational Studies Association convention in Boston, November 1981.

intractable context of the university, I see the 'improver-role' as naive, unjustifiable and infeasible--not least because academics reliably reject self-elevated individuals who come to judge them. This too influences my approach to answering the forthcoming questions.

I can only say here that, in my view, 'good aims' are not enough (aims are in any case evolutionary, not fixed). I judge 'methods' not so much by their abstract efficiency as by the 'example-of-how-life-may-be-lived' that they teach to people who experience them. I would have to say that, for me, it is 'outcomes' that matter most.

I hasten to add that emphasizing outcomes is not a sly way of conjuring up the old maxim that 'the end justifies the means'. On the contrary the counter-adage that 'means may become ends' is meant to be implied. Such a reversal is almost unavoidable in professional development where process and product are one concept, where tangible results may be far off and cause-and-effect is a speculative exercise, where outcomes are unmeasurable and unforseeable. What I really have in mind are the small, observable outcomes of any and all actions on a daily basis, from which one may (and must) extrapolate in seeking a larger view; they are, after all, the only source of ethical guidance in professional development that one currently has. In making such judgments for myself, I have found that the most reliable and useful (perhaps the only) guide that serves comfortably and well day after day is the embarrassingly-old-fashioned 'golden rule', "do unto others. . . ." This provides no answers in itself, but it helps one potentially to anticipate and understand the reactions of others or, at the very least, to feel that one is pointing one's enquiries in a morally defensible direction.

## 3.  THE ETHICAL RELATIONSHIP

What a professional development program for staff in higher education can/might/should consist of is a very personal as well as practical question for program organizers.[2] This decision is affected by job specification and resources, local possibilities for action, the organizer's particular inspiration and talents, and a wide variety of other relevent variables.[3] Despite the long list of possibilities, however, it is not necessarily defensible to conclude that, within a given set of opportunities and constraints, 'anything goes'.

> The occasion was a highly successful course for new staff at a British University. ('Success', in this instance, refers only to the observable, short-term result; the genuine appreciation of course participants and the earnestness with which they addressed the activities, ideas and views put by the organizer.) The last moments, however, were unexpectedly painful.
> On the final afternoon an interested Professor from the same university visited the course and was invited to comment at will. The

Professor inquired what it was that the new
staff thought that they had actually learned
from the course, and how they expected to put
that learning into practice. There were a
variety of replies about teaching methods,
objectives, strategies, etc.; there was the
intention of some personally to adopt methods
which they felt convinced were 'better' than
those in local use; there were a few who
wished actively to proselytize in their new
departments for revised approaches to teaching
and learning.
The Professor made what appeared to be his own
conscious contribution to the professional
development of the new staff. He advised them
that they would be ill-judged for
idiosyncratic behavior and attitudes, nor
could they, in his view, alter the opinions of
long-serving colleagues who felt keenly aware
of realities and constraints that the new
lecturers had yet to encounter.

The content of professional development programs will, in
practice, reflect many influences, the more obvious among them
being the aims of the organizer, the attitudes of hiring
institutions, the interests of participating colleagues, the
trends exhibited nationally or internationally within the field,
etc. What is less often considered, however, is whether
professional development organizers, who may be seen--especially
by new and inexperienced staff--to be acting on behalf of their
institutions, have a moral right to present, propound or encourage
ideas about professional development--especially in terms of
specific academic behavior--which the institution will not only
frequently not reward (while it so frequently rewards other
behaviors), but for which in some ways it may functionally
penalize members of its staff. This is not a dilemma for
professional development organizers alone in the sheltered privacy
of their own thought; its implications at least (if not the
underlying ambivalence about content) are widely recognized and
were clearly described some years ago during a staff workshop in
England at which recently-appointed staff commented about other
new colleagues who never attended:

They ought to come, but it's hard to blame
them. They're out there doing their research
and furthering their careers, while we sit
here being 'seen' to care about our teaching
and to be 'wasting' time on it--putting labels
on ourselves so that our heads of department
will know whom not to promote!

Little needs to be said to amplify those familiar remarks. Yet in
the author's experience, institutional leaders confronted head-on
with such disturbing attitudes tend strongly to deny their

reality. One must ask, therefore, are these staff suspicions
well-founded, or are they, as their deniers sometimes suggest,
academic fantasies born of rumor and ignorance combined with
personal and professional insecurity?

> She was attending a major international
> conference on university teaching 4,000 miles
> from home, but she had received bad news and
> her morale was very low. When she had become
> a new member of the faculty at an American
> university, she had taken seriously her insti-
> tution's public pronouncements about the then
> newly-emerging importance of good teaching and
> the high priority to be placed on it in future
> assessments for tenure and promotion. She had
> done her utmost, working closely with the
> local teaching improvement expert, attending
> relevant courses and conferences, preparing
> new material for departmental use, etc. After
> seven years it appeared that this was not
> appreciated. Indifferent teachers who had
> managed to publish a first book, or to secure
> a traditional research grant in the time, were
> awarded tenure and she was not.

A good deal of evidence suggests that there _are_ reasonable
grounds on which to conclude that the internationally-held staff
views in question are based as much on practice as paranoia. But
the origins of this problem are perhaps less obvious than its
outward effects. Institutional priorities do in fact fluctuate as
the fortunes and tribulations of universities change over time.
It is not necessary automatically to suspect 'corruption' or
'stupidity' in seeking reasons why institutions may not actively
implement desirable policy decisions even of recent vintage.
Academic institutions are complex structures composed of many
competing elements and contradictory forces over which the
leadership (fortunately or unfortunately, according to point of
view) has no reliable vision or direct control; institutions are
quick to react outwardly to pressures but slow to alter internal
attitudes and procedures. I do not comment on the above
colleague's situation because I know too little about it, but
theoretically her university's investment in teaching improvement
could have been a sincere and highly-regarded action on the day of
its inception, yet even with such background conditions it might
later have seemed of little moment, and the principles on which
support for it initially rested might have been barely remembered,
as other more pressing problems came to the fore. Hans Jalling,
national director of staff development in Sweden, put it much more
clearly and simply than that:

> Very few university presidents would state
> openly that they do not care about the
> teaching competence of their staff; this does
> not, on the other hand, mean that they find

this an important topic. As university
managers their duty is to concentrate on the
vital problems which, of course, vary from
time to time. When students started to
protest about bad teaching in the late 60s and
early 70s, university management was more than
willing to employ people who declared
themselves experts in teaching and who would
be willing--and competent--to influence their
colleagues. When these people now accuse
university management of no longer being
interested in change--meaning a change of
priorities from research to teaching--they are
themselves committing the same sin: they have
not realized that vital problems do change
over time, and that 'good' or 'bad' teaching
is not what is primarily bothering the
university system in the early 80s.[4]

I am certain that Jalling's observation has profound
implications for the activity called professional development--
especially that it is the responsibility not of the institution
but of the individual with responsibility for professional
development to be alert and cognizant about evolving institutional
interests and thus to worry about 'truth-in-professional-
development' according to the day and the hour. It is simply
unrealistic to expect that institutions will consistently honor
one's own, favorite, selected policy pronouncements as if they
were legal or sacred covenants. Accordingly, if there were any
concept of 'blame' to be attached in the above vignette, I would,
in principle, have to attach it to the hired 'expert' who, in his
efforts to assist the lady in question, failed to read the signals
and to bring institutional realities to her attention so that she
could make an informed choice about how to distribute her energies
and develop her professional life.

One sees emerging, therefore, a number of difficult and
interdependent questions which are of both practical and ethical
importance in assessing or devising the content of a professional
development program:

1. Should a professional development organizer
deliberately expose program participants to one's own
views and enthusiasms, or to any ideas or options
differing significantly from institutional norms of
practice, if the possibility of their adoption implies a
subsequent danger of professional difficulty or personal
disillusionment for participants?
2. Should an organizer encourage 'improvement' (change)
but give warning of professional dangers, thus
encouraging rejection of the work undertaken on behalf
of the institution, thus apparently accusing the
institution of bad faith or bad practice, and offering a
profile of disillusionment or disaffection for the
edification of colleagues?

3. Could the above conflicts reasonably and honorably be avoided by presenting merely 'what is' instead of 'what might be', hoping only to rely on the interest, critical faculties, and self motivation of colleagues to provide some sort of spontaneous, useful outcome?

Various ancillary questions also come to mind, in particular:

4. In formulating judgments about 'content', should the organizer's _first_ allegiance be to one's own aims and values, to the aims and values of the institution which provides the opportunity to undertake this work on its behalf, or to the aims and values of colleagues who place a measure of trust in the individual and the individual's work?

5. Can a professional development organizer responsibly encourage what one believes to be desirable behavior modification if one has not already tackled and begun to modify the most potent force constraining/penalizing such behaviors--i.e., counter-oriented value and reward mechanisms?

6. If a professional development organizer rejects or criticizes as negative the effect on individuals of an existing value and reward system, can one credibly and justifiably seek personal advancement within it?

7. In the act of seeking personal advancement, do any achievements by colleagues which (apparently) follow from the facilitative effects of a professional development organizer 'belong' to the organizer, or to the colleagues who produced them?

The questions above are central to the organizer's relationship with colleagues and represent conflicts not merely about legitimacy of content but also integrity of role. There are, moreover, occasions when these questions assume extra importance, e.g. when an experienced ('attitude-hardened') professional development organizer may move to a new post in a new environment or, as happens frequently at present, when a 'western' organizer operates on a limited consultancy basis in a so-called 'developing nation' where cultural needs, values and expectations may be at polar opposites from the ones which guide one at home.[5]
Some of the questions may, on the other hand, diminish in urgency from one country to another (or even one institution or sub-department to another), depending on the local leadership's tolerance for deviation from the norm, for critical assessment which may include itself, or to the extent that it exhibits reliable positive interest in innovative practice.[6] I would, nevertheless, argue that all the questions remain relevant in all cases so long as institutional tolerance has any limits, so long as times may change, and indeed so long as hiring and promotion procedures; the awarding of research grants, study leaves and other helpful privileges; the willingness of publishers to publish; the requirement for professional references; etc.; place power over professional lives in the hands of pre-designated

individuals and groups.

POSTSCRIPT TO SECTION 3
(a)  Responsibility
    I have argued above "that it is the responsibility not of the
institution   but   of   the   individual  with  responsibility   for
professional development" to identify realities, etc.   This   was
not   intended   to imply that institutions have no  responsibility;
merely   that   as   nebulous   as   they   are   (who,  exactly, is  the
institution?),   and   as constantly evolving,  this is a task  that
they   cannot   really   perform   on   their own  behalf.   I  do  not,
however,   believe   that   professional development  organizers   can
perform   this task on their own.   They must seek and learn those
realities from the individual and collective wisdom of  colleagues
who,   in   airing their perceptions and explaining to the organizer
and to each other, will themselves learn with greater clarity what
reality is and what options are genuinely before them.
    The   institution's major responsibilities of  course  include
the   nature   and   impact of its value and reward system   which   is
fundamental   to the priorities which staff will perceive,  and  to
which they are likely themselves to assign value in their   efforts
to   achieve a successful career.   But perhaps even more important
is   the   concept of congruence between  stipulated  institutional
policies   and   their   actual implementation.   It is not  so  much
'unpopular policies' and 'incongruous practices'--and the sense of
manipulation to which this gives rise--which produces cynicism and
disrespect, or sometimes confusion, anger and loss of morale.  Any
professional   development organizer who  can,  somehow,  help  his
institution   to appreciate this 'congruence-problem' and  re-think
and   take   steps   to   ameliorate it,  has  in  my  view  made  an
appropriate and major contribution.

(b)  Emphasis
    Section   3   may   also   appear   to   suggest   that   professional
development   personnel have little but a form  of  'institutional'
role,   and   a   function   only   to   'improve  teaching'  in  higher
education.[7]   This is not in fact a sufficient or viable concept of
professional   development[8].   It is merely a lingering remnant  of
'staff training'[9], often by another name.[10]  Nevertheless,  since
staff   training is logically subsumed under professional  development,   and   since a major portion of visible,  relevant activities
still   tend in that direction,   it is inevitable that this   aspect
gains   prominence   in inquiring about the ethics of  (observable)
professional development functions.[11]
    To   be fair most individuals now working in this field   would
reject the image implied above.[12]   They would consider  themselves
to   be operating within a much wider range of functions,  of which
instructional   activities--if countenanced at all--are merely  one
feature.[13]   Still very few practitioners yet use the broader  term
'professional   development' to refer to their work (this  may  be
either   an   evolutionary descriptor or a genuine rejection of  the
author's   point of view),   and in some cases the author would  not
spontaneously recommend it.  But since it would not entirely serve
to claim to represent a vast,  international field approaching nil

membership, all aspects and subsections of professional development are herein included--with or without their knowledge and
consent. Thus, while the remainder of this paper will also query
some 'non-instructional' aspects of the professional development
role, there will be no effort to do so comprehensively, and
further mention of instructional-sounding courses and workshops
will not be avoided.

(c) Aims
     Section 3, finally, will be seen by some to have omitted any
positive statement about the aims of professional development;
this is intentional. Aims and objectives, today, are akin to
educational 'motherhood', yet the noblest of aims remain
irrelevant if a corresponding curriculum (content) is precluded by
other factors. Moreover, it is not unknown or unthinkable to
'adjust' academic aims for reasons of 'pragmatism'--e.g. according
to what may prove actually to have been achieved, or achievable,
within a given situation (providing 'enhanced' retrospective
assessment/'improved' forward planning); according to what may
ring current socio-political bells among decision-makers and
finance committees (gaining initial or continued approval of
'desirable'/'inherently worthwhile' projects); etc.
     I would argue that certain aims have, in Section 3, been
conceptually called into question, and that helping to identify
unacceptable aims may, on some occasions, be equally productive as
the practice of positive recommendation. I am content therefore,
for the remainder of this paper, to leave aims unexamined except
by implication.

4. ETHICAL BEHAVIOR
     Seven brief, selected cases will be considered. Some of the
questions arising are mainly 'exploratory' in nature, serving
largely to support or illuminate others.

     I. An organizer outlined in full to new Professors the
        objectives of a workshop and its anticipated
        outcome. Participants were asked to follow a
        recommended planning procedure designed to make
        their lectures more effective. A common topic was
        assigned and lecture planning took place in small
        groups. One group produced a highly effective
        lecture which in no way followed the recommended
        procedure. The organizer was visibly disappointed
        and ignored the lecture that had not met the work-
        shop objectives.

     Questions:
        1. Was it defensible for the organizer to specify
     (one's own) objectives in such a way that the phenomenon of
     finding an 'effective' lecture negative to requirements could
     even have arisen?
        2. Further to (1), what was the potential effect of that
     occurrence on new Professors?
        3. Was the organizer facilitating the exercise, by

colleagues, of the responsibility, self-motivation and self-assessment that was espoused, or rather encouraging a form of dependence on the organizer?

4. For new Professors (on probation), who would be approved of by their superiors not for their willing reliance on the organizer but by how quickly they appeared to be equally self-confident and independent as their more experienced colleagues, was the organizer performing a beneficial, supporting service?

II. A course for new Professors identified two participants who appeared likely to experience difficulties in relating to their colleagues and students. The organizer contacted their heads of department and advised them, confidentially, of what in the organizer's opinion were the potential problems with their new staff.

Questions:
1. Was it a responsible act to assume that the behavior of these new Professors would, after time in their normal departments and daily routines, be equally problematic as that exhibited on a course for new staff where anxiety may be high, where they may have felt uniquely 'exposed' (felt that they were being judged by an 'expert' acting on behalf of the institution), where a sense of 'compulsion'--explicit or implicit--may have been their main or sole reason for attendance?

2. Does the organizer have a right to judge, and make predictions about, individuals to whom one is presumed to be offering an open-ended supporting and facilitative service on behalf of the institution?

3. Was it justifiable to contact the new Professors' heads of department without their knowledge (opportunity for self-defense) and approval (opportunity for self-determination)?

4. Was it fair to call their department heads' critical, worried attention to these new Professors with what could thereafter become a self-fulfilling prophecy?

III. A survey of department heads in one university revealed that what they would most appreciate from the professional development organizer was special attention to certain Professors that the chairmen claimed were deficient in their teaching. An offer was made to supply names to the organizer and, where necessary, to initiate contacts.

Questions:
1. If the organizer agreed to the proposal, and if the named individuals were reluctant to work with the organizer, would it be justifiable for the organizer and/or the department head to consider them 'resistant' and to apply any pressure, subtle or otherwise, to encourage the desired working relationship?[14]

2. In this context, would not the relevant 'contact' or 'invitation' itself constitute a form of pressure?

3. Is it fair to allow suspicion to develop about colleagues working with the organizer that they do so because they may in some way be 'deficient' or not well thought of by their heads of department?

4. Is it right or beneficial for the organizer to allow oneself to be used, no matter how indirectly, as an instrument of discipline, penalty or fear?

IV. A workshop on supervision of research convinced certain postgraduate students who participated in the workshop that the local professional development organizer was aware of and genuinely concerned about their needs. A group of them approached the organizer privately to ask for help. They were totally dissatisfied with the poor teaching, haphazard curriculum and lack of supervision on their highly specialized course, and were afraid that they might either fail the course or prove unsuitable thereafter to be hired in their small, chosen field. They had approached their supervisor to no avail and could not take the matter further within the department since their supervisor was also the department chairman. They were fearful of the consequences of complaining to unknown higher authorities about a powerful department head and asked the organizer to act on their behalf. The organizer told them there was nothing that he/she could do.

The organizer, in this instance, had reasoned that if the program became viewed as a vehicle for 'finger-pointing' and getting people into difficulties, it would lose its support overnight. It should also be pointed out that this was, in essence, not an isolated case. In practice, the professional development organizer is frequently in a position where, due to conditions of trust and frankness, a great deal of private information--often merely factual but sometimes highly critical or condemnatory of individuals and groups--comes to one's notice. (Sometimes even colleagues solicit the type of help the students were seeking.)

Questions:

1. Was the organizer justified in putting the welfare of the program before the welfare of the students?

2. Does the organizer have a right (perhaps a responsibility?) to identify problems to the institution when they become known in this manner, or is 'private' information which is revealed through trust in the organizer's program 'privileged'?

3. Would it be defensible to use private information for purposes of 'improvement' if doing so might affect reputations, individual careers, or the options available to groups?

V. An institution decided to elevate the importance of teaching and took steps to demonstrate its new policy. An invitation was issued to the professional development organizer to join the promotions board.

Questions:
    1. See again questions II 2; IV 2, and 3.
    2. Can the traditional function of <u>assessor</u> be justified when an 'exceptional' relationship (including unusual openness and self-exposure) is the main basis for one's knowledge of colleagues rather than a normal, academic working relationship?

VI. An organizer offered a course on study methods to undergraduates which included a session on 'intelligent notetaking'. A student complimented the organizer for the most enjoyable session of the term, but complained that it was irrelevant because on the course in computational statistics it was required that the students copy faithfully everything written on the board. The student concluded that the lecturer in statistics was a bad teacher.

Questions:
    1. Can the organizer justifiably claim (to students <u>or</u> staff) that one possesses useful 'expertise' in connection with student needs when one is not present to see, understand or control the learning environment in which those students must function?
    2. Is it helpful for the organizer to transmit ideas to students which may make them dissatisfied with the teaching they receive when one cannot guarantee any corresponding change in that teaching?
    3. Is the organizer performing a supporting service to staff if one contributes to making the relationship with students more difficult?
    4. Does the organizer perform a beneficial service to students if one assists them to blame 'poor teaching' for their difficulties rather than to focus on their own responsibility to work and to succeed?

VII. A professional development workshop judged very successful by its organizer was criticized as "unethical" by colleagues who heard about but had not observed it. A deceit had been practiced on two volunteers who unknowingly participated in a different experiment than the one described to them. All other participants knew in advance of the organizer-proposed deception which they collectively agreed to perpetrate in order to test the hypothesis that student behavior could profoundly influence the behavior, intentions and ability of a Professor. In the event, one volunteer was totally 'appreciated' by the audience, regardless of performance, while the other subsequently endured sustained disattention and disrespect. The effects were direct and dramatic, leading to an intensive group analysis of Professors' needs and of structured mechanisms for obtaining fuller and more useful information about student responses.

It should be added that on the above occasion there was no resentment from the volunteers who had known and trusted, in advance, both the organizer and the other colleagues present, and who themselves--like the other participants--applauded the workshop at its conclusion.

Questions:
1. Did the post-approval of the volunteers justify the initial deception?
2. Does ethical procedure in human research include an unalterable requirement for full (advance) disclosure?
3. Does the fact that there was no 'external' benefit for the organizer (i.e., no subsequent reports or publications, etc.) affect one's perceptions of the case?
4. When other people are involved, are 'non-risk-taking' procedures the only acceptable practice, or can the strong likelihood of 'beneficient results' be self-justifying?
5. Is 'full-disclosure' a genuine and reliable safeguard against abuse of individuals?

The above is but a small sampling of the type of questions which should interest anyone concerned with the ethical dimension in professional development and in the relationship between higher education 'teaching staff' and their chosen profession.

# FOOTNOTES

[1] J. Henry, "Vulnerability in Education," Essays on Education (New York: Penguin Books, Inc., 1971), Chap. 1.

[2] S. Sayer and Harding, A.G. "Intervention, Interference and Intimidation in Professional Development," Proceedings of the Third International Conference on Improving University Teaching, (Newcastle, 1971).

[3] S. Sayer, "The Nature and Purpose of Professional Development," Irish Educational Studies 1 (Educational Studies Association of Ireland, 1981).

[4] H. Jalling, "Exploring the Organizational and Political Boundaries of Staff Development: Internationalism in Staff Development," Proceedings of the Seventh International Conference on Improving University Teaching, (Tokyo, 1980).

[5] Well described in Harding, Kaewsonthi, Roe and Stevens, Professional Development in Higher Education: State of the Art and the Artists (England: Bradford University Educational Development Service, 1981).

[6] See, for example: Educational Development at Michigan State University, report 11, MSU Educational Development Program, 1979.
The report states: "The overall goal of the (educational development) program is to facilitate development and implementation of innovative educational policies. . . ."

[7] Most of the literature still stresses primary focus on the improvement of teaching. My own assigned title (Director of Teaching Development) illustrates this emphasis of viewpoint. A major international conference (annual), is entitled "Improving University Teaching."

[8] S. Sayer, "Directions in Professional Development, in Staff Development for the 1980's: International Perspectives," ed. D. Rhodes, and D. Hounsell, Illinois State University Foundation, and Institute for Research and Development in Post-Compulsary Education at the University of Lancaster, 1980. See also H. Jalling, "Exploring the Organizational and Political Boundaries of Staff Development: Internationalism in Staff Development."

[9] This atmospheric influence has been strong in the UK where there was, until 1981, the official presence of a national "Co-ordinating Committee for the Training of University Teachers." See for example: S. Trickey, "Staff Training: A Polytechnic Perspective," Impetus no. 6 (1977).
The centralized Swedish National Board for Universities and Colleges apparently also contributed, at least initially, to such

an atmosphere. See for example: H. Jalling, "University Teacher Training in Sweden," Impetus no. 7.

Other countries too are not immune, even in the 1980s. See for example: P. Lauvas, "Perspectives of Inservice Training in Education for Teachers in Norway," Staff Development for the 1980s: International Perspectives, 1980.

R.A. Scott, "The Development of Competence: Administrative Needs and Training Goals in American Higher Education," Staff Development for the 1980s: International Perspectives, 1980.

[10]Examples include, G. Brown, "Some Myths of Staff Training and Development," Impetus no. 6 (1977).

Boyle and Giorgiades, "The Teaching Development Programme at Birkbeck College," Impetus no. 7 (1977).

D. Harris, "Staff Development as an Agent of Change," Impetus no. 9 (1978).

Jalling, Behre, and Larsson, "Teaching Teachers to Teach? Ten Commandments for those who Plan and Lead Courses that Experiment with Pedagogical Ideas," Impetus no. 10 (1978).

R. Swain, "How to Recognize the Real Thing: Professionalism and Expertise in Teaching Development," Impetus no. 11 (1979).

G.R. Meyer, "The Development of Mini-Courses (with a Basis in Educational Technology) for the In-Service Education of Teachers and Trainers," Programmed Learning and Educational Technology 16 (1979).

T. Habeshaw, "Continuing Self-Development for Teachers," British Journal of Educational Technology 11 (1980).

[11]An international over-view may be found in Staff Development in Higher Education, ed. D. Teather and Kogan Page, (1980).

[12]This was confirmed by a substantial survey (1978 unpublished) of relevant personnel in Britain, carried out by the Working Party on Professional Development, (sub-committee of the Educational Methods Committee) at Salford University.

[13]The following gives a variety of individual, institutional or national indicators:

C.R. Coles, "Developing Professionalism: Staff Development as an Outcome of Curriculum Development," Programmed Learning and Educational Technology 14 (1977).

A. Shannon, "Staff Development in Course Development," Impetus no. 8 (1978).

A. Moore, "Adaptive Change for the Improvement of Teaching and Learning in the University," Impetus no. 10 (1978).

E. Hewton, "Towards a Definition of Staff Development," Impetus no. 11 (1979).

J.G. Hadberg, "Client Relationships in Instructional Design," Programmed Learning and Educational Technology 17 (1980).

H. Greenway and A.G. Harding, "The Growth of Policies for Staff Development," Society for Research into Higher Education Monograph no. 34 (1980).

D. Rhodes and D. Hounsell, ed., "Staff Development for the 1980's: International Perspectives," Illinois State University

Foundation, and Institute for Research and Development into Post-Compulsory Education at the University of Lancaster, 1980.

[14]The concept of 'resistance' is neither unknown nor an invention by the author. See for example:

C. Matheson, "Francis Gibb Talks to the New Man Responsible for Training University Teachers." <u>Times Higher Education Supplement</u> 1 (September 1976).

## CENSORSHIP:  CASES AND CATEGORIES*

### Ken Carlson

Introduction
   This paper is designed to lead you through some exercises
that should cause you to come to my conclusions. Putting it that
bluntly could result in your resistance; however, since you will
not know the conclusions to which you are being led unless you
read ahead, there will be no way of knowing what to resist.  Thus,
the conclusions will be truly your own, but I expect that we will
agree on most of them. The extent of our agreement or disagreement
is of sufficient interest to me to solicit your written reaction.

EXERCISE I
   Look at the Chinese Menu (on the next page) and decide which
items are the most censorable from your standpoint.  You may not
wish to see any of the items actually censored, but still some may
strike you as being more censorable (objectionable) than others.
   Once you've made your selections, look to see whether they
cluster in a single column.  If so, does that column have any
theme or pattern?  How does it differ from the other columns?  My
conclusions from this can be found on pages 257-258.

EXERCISE II
   This exercise consists of reading the statement on the
following page and formulating a response.  The author of the
statement, Reverend Harrah, was opposed to the reading material
that was being introduced into the Kanawha County, West Virginia
schools because of what he thought was the sinful sexual content
in that material.  How would you reply to Reverend Harrah?
   My conclusion is on page 258.

*Paper presented to the 1977 Annual Meeting of the American
Educational Research Association, as part of the symposium on "The
Political Ideology of Schooling," April 8, 1977, New York City.

## EXERCISE I

### A CHINESE MENU

Column A

Down These Mean Streets

Slaughterhouse Five

Catcher in the Rye

The Affluent Society

Soul on Ice

The Scarlet Letter

Brave New World

Lysistrata

Portnoy's Complaint

MACOS

Column B

The Merchant of Venice

Huckleberry Finn

Uncle Tom's Cabin

Birth of a Nation

A. Jensen's theories

W. Shockley's theories

Reifenstahl's films

Death Wish

TV violence

cigarette ads

Column C

St. Augustine

Shakespeare

Dryden

Ben Franklin

Chaucer

The Bible

Swift

Column D

Playboy

Hustler

Deep Throat

masturbation

Earl Butz's jokes

4-, 5-, and 12-letter words

## EXERCISE II

I am a minister of the Pentecostal Church. The standards and articles of faith of our church rest completely in our belief that the Bible is the absolute, infalliable Word of God. We do not intend to compromise our beliefs, nor do we intend to agree to go to Hell, even if the majority of the people vote to do so. This is not a situation where opposing views can be reconciled. As you well know, there are some things that are somewhat like night and day, or darkness and light - they are beyond the point of reconciliation. There is no dusk or dawn or in between or neutral zone. There is a line drawn and the people stand either on the right or the left of it.[1]

## EXERCISE III

Read the U.S. Supreme Court definition of obscenity below. Answer the following questions:

1. Who is the "average person" in your community?

2. What are the "standards" of your community?

3. What is your "community" for purposes of defining obscenity?

4. What is "prurient interest?"

5. What kinds of sexual conduct do you find to be "patently offensive?"

6. How much value amounts to "serious" value?

7. What are "ultimate sexual acts?"

8. Is there anything other than sex or excretion which you consider to be obscene?

For my conclusions from this exercise, see pages 258-260.

## EXERCISE III

DEFINITION OF OBSCENITY BY THE U.S. SUPREME COURT IN MILLER V. CALIFORNIA, JUNE 21, 1973:

1. The average person applying contemporary community standards finds that the material taken as a whole appeals to prurient interest.
2. The work depicts or describes, in a patently offensive way, sexual conduct specifically defined by the applicable state law.
3. The work, taken as a whole, lacks serious literary, artistic, political, or scientific value.

The Court went on to suggest two areas which the state law could specifically define:

a. Patently offensive representations or descriptions of ultimate sexual acts, normal or perverted, actual or simulated.
b. Patently offensive representations or descriptions of masturbation, excretory functions, and lewd exhibition of the genitals.

## EXERCISE IV

Read the New Jersey test of obscenity below and determine whether it is an improvement on the Supreme Court test. Should the New Jersey law be a model for the nation?
My conclusions are on page 260.

## EXERCISE IV

THE NEW JERSEY TEST OF OBSCENITY FOR MINORS AND NON-CONSENTING ADULTS CHAPTERS 446-448, LAWS OF 1971:

a. "Material obscene for persons under 18" means any description, narrative account or depiction of a specified anatomical area or specified sexual activity contained in, or consisting of, a picture or other representation, publication, sound recording or film, which, by means of posing, composition, format or animated sensual details, emits sensuality with sufficient impact to concentrate prurient interest on the area or activity.

b. "Specified anatomical area" means
   (1) less than completely and opaquely covered human genitals, pubic region, buttock or female breast below a point immediately above the top of the areola; or
   (2) human male genitals in a discernibly turgid state, even if covered.

c. "Specified sexual activity" means
   (1) human genitals in a state of sexual stimulation or arousal; or
   (2) any act of human masturbation, sexual intercourse or sodomy; or
   (3) fondling or other erotic touching of covered or uncovered human genitals, pubic region, buttock or female breast.

## EXERCISE V

Read Bill 919, below, and decide whether it should have been enacted into law and if it would be a desirable law in your state. My opinion is on pages 260-261.


NEW JERSEY SENATE BILL NO. 919, INTRODUCED MARCH 18, 1974 BY SENATORS MARTINDELL, BUEHLER, AND MENZA:

> Every teaching staff member employed in any public school or institution in this State and every person employed in an academic capacity in any public college in this State shall have the right to use and present any available subject matter, facts, materials and methods which are relevant to the course of study, discussion or lecture being presented, including the presentation of diverse sides of any controversial matter, provided, however, that the expression of personal opinions shall be so indicated. This act shall take effect immediately.

## EXERCISE VI


On the diagram on the next page write in the major levels in the bureaucracy of your school district. See whether the authority of these levels increases with increases in the expertise of the levels. That is, does each higher level in the hierarchy possess both more authority and more expertise in curricular matters than the level below it?

My conclusions are on page 261.

## EXERCISE VI

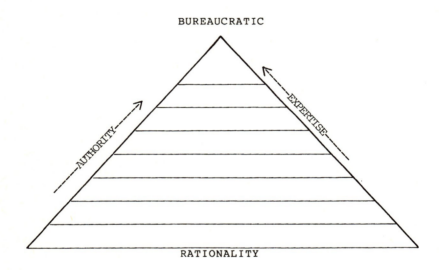

### EXERCISE I - CONCLUSION

1.  The likelihood is that your items do tend to cluster in a single column.
2.  The columns do have distinguishing themes. The themes for Column A are sex and iconoclasm. Homosexuality, promiscuity, adultery, rape and ribaldry are the sexual themes. Defiance of secular authority and lampooning of religion are the themes of iconoclasm.

    Something else that unites the themes in Column A is that they have all been the targets of censorship from the right. Kurt Vonnegut recently alleged that several of the items in Column A, including his own Slaughterhouse Five, are on a list being circulated nationwide by right-wing groups intent on having the materials suppressed.

    If your selections fell into Column A, you are probably a conservative. That such items are not likely to bring out the censoriousness of those on the left can be seen in the list of celebrities who signed the full-page New York Times ad of February 20, 1977 in defense of Larry Flynt, publisher of Hustler - an ad which likened Flynt to Andrei Sakharov.
3.  Column B contains the themes of prejudice and violence. The first seven items in this column have been alleged to be racist or anti-Semitic, with the last three items relating to some form of violence. These are themes which are especially offensive to those on the left, and which liberal groups have tried to censor, sometimes successfully. The most recent example of such objectionable material is Arthur Butz's The Fabrication of a Hoax, which asserts that "the Nazi extermination of European Jews was nothing more than a Zionist-inspired myth."[2] Whether Butz will retain his position as an associate professor of electrical engineering at Northwestern University remains to be seen. If the items you selected are in Column B, chances are that your ideology is somewhere from liberalism leftward.
4.  Column C is a listing of items which those nineteenth century expurgators, Thomas and Harriet Bowdler, tried to "bowdlerize," and often succeeded. What rattled the Bowdlers was not just sex but human anatomy.[3] It is interesting to note how persistent sex is as an object of censorship. Although greater license toward sex seems always to be the rule, sex itself is still the main target of censorship. If the items you selected are in Column C, you are an anachronism in the objects of your displeasure if not the theme.
5.  As for Column D, that might be called "the family special." Playboy, Hustler, and Deep Throat are certainly objectionable to those on the right, but these items have also incurred the censoriousness of women's groups which are otherwise on the left. Women resent the objectification and dehumanizing of women that occurs in these materials. It is worth noting in this regard that Shana Alexander, the liberal commentator on

60 Minutes, thinks that Hustler should be censored, whereas
Jack Kilpatrick, her conservative opponent, thinks it should
be tolerated.
Masturbation is a bugaboo to that good liberal medium, the
BBC. In a Monty Python episode, a character was supposed to
describe his hobbies as "golf, masturbation, and strangling
animals," The BBC struck the mention of masturbation.
Earl Butz's jokes were censored as news that's not fit to
print by The New York Times. It was not the racist character
of the jokes but their smutty content that invoked the Times'
censorship. To learn what Butz really said, and whether he
should have been sacked for it, one had to read sources that
were left of the Times, i.e., Rolling Stone or New Times
And, of course, The New York Times will not print four-letter
words, even in reviews of poetry which quote lines containing
these words. In the September 29, 1974 and September 7, 1975
issues of The New York Times Book Review, Helen Vandler had
long articles on several new collections of poetry in which
she quoted liberally from the poems themselves. The reader
repeatedly came upon Times' elisions such as c---, f---, and
s---. It is obvious then that the Times doesn't print shit.
If you selected items in Column D, it may be that you are
feminist or a staff member at one of the "respectable" liberal
media.
6. A general conclusion from the foregoing is that censorship is
a trans-ideological urge, even though the targets may be
ideologically specific. That the urge can be irresistible is
shown by the fact that the American Civil Liberties Union
denied Elizabeth Gurley Flynn a place on its board of
directors because of her politics at the same time that it was
defending the rights of other Communists.[4]

## Exercise II - Conclusion
There is no reply that can be given to the Reverend Harrah.
He has stated his position in metaphysical terms, by which I mean
terms that are not susceptible of empirical or logical persuasion
or dissuasion. When ideology is rooted in religion this way, one
is down to (or up against) absolute presuppositions for which
there is no court of appeal. Many censorship battles are of this
nature - a melancholy fact, but one which no amount of sweet
reasoning can change. Compromise, reconciliation are not
possible, as Reverend Harrah makes clear. The only thing left is
to fashion a system for deciding who the winners and losers will
be. Ideally, this system would have been worked out before the
censorship controversy arose.

## Exercise III - Conclusion
1. The U.S. Supreme Court definition of obscenity is hopelessly
vague. Worse, it is mischievously vague. It is an incitement
to profiteers on either side of the issue, both the peddlers
and the prosecutors. The Court has defined a crime in terms
that make it impossible to identify the criminal. What other
legal offense is left to so many subjective interpretations?
2. The "average" person only exists as a statistical abstraction.

It is illusory to think that twelve, or even six, "average" people can be found to serve as a jury in an obscenity case. It is just as foolish to believe that twelve atypical people can collectively constitute one "average" person. "Average" how? The most meaningful "average" might be average in attitude toward censorship. But how many people advertise these attitudes or can articulate them or have even developed them?

3. The purveyors of smut claim that the sales of their merchandise is the best index of the community's "standards." It's at least a quantitative index. It's also a behavioral index and not a rhetorical one. The question then arises as to whether people should be held to higher standards than those they display in their behavior. If so, how does one piece together a standard from a welter of conflicting and peripherally relevant opinion? Assuming that a standard can be assembled, how does it get applied to specific instances and by whom?

4. Then there is the question of the relevant community. Is it the nation, the state, the county, the municipality, the ward – or no geopolitical community at all? Perhaps it should be a community of interest, e.g., the gay community. For purposes of litigation, it might be well to make it a jurisdictional community, e.g., the territory covered by the Third Circuit Court of Appeals. If the "community" is defined in too restricted terms, it may reduce access by the larger community to the things it wants. On the other hand, a broad definition of "community" can mean the imposition of alien standards on smaller communities.

5. "Prurient interest" and "patently offensive" are other subjective terms. It could also be argued that these terms are mutually exclusive. Anything that titillates one's prurient interest is hardly going to <u>patently</u> offensive.

6. In the matter of "serious literary, artistic, political, or scientific value," the question of expert judgment occurs. That means that each side parades its "experts" before a jury in a charade in which all three parties operate from ideologically derived prejudgments.

7. As for "ultimate sexual acts," I, at age 40, would like to think that I have not yet experienced such acts and still have those to look forward to. What Chief Justice Burger, who wrote the Court's majority opinion, means by such acts I do not know. If ever you should chance upon him, you could ask.

8. Finally, it is noteworthy that the Court considers only two forms of human behavior to come under its obscenity criteria: sex and excretion. What Freud could have made of that ! On the issue of obscenity, the U.S. Supreme Court is clearly more compatible with those on the right than those on the left. In its Miller v. California ruling, the Court seemed to be intent upon extricating itself from the obscenity-adjudication business by passing the buck to localities along with some <u>procedural</u> guidelines. However, the Court did not stop there, but added the <u>substantive</u> areas of sex and excretion. In doing so, the Court may have, wittingly or unwittingly, spared

both the right and the left from being savaged for nonsexual ideology, however execrable.  Thus, the Court is to be faulted for the vagueness of its ruling and the ideological bent of its specific references to sex and excretion, but the Court can be commended for at least limiting the substantive specificity of the ruling.

## Exercise IV - Conclusion

The New Jersey law is good in that it omits adults from its "protection."  The reader should be informed, however, that New Jersey has a separate law for adults and does not eschew a role for government in regulating private morality. The law on page 253 is also good insofar as sections b and c are clear statements of the proscribable.  It would be difficult to plead incomprehension of these sections.  Such is not the case with section a.  There we are back to the Supreme Court criterion of "prurient interest." All a juror can do with this is see whether the material at issue arouses his or her own prurient interest, and run the risk of publicly pronouncing a kind of personal guilt.

Sections b and c, for all their preciseness, are ludicrously and anachronistically specific.  They have the clarity of calipers.  Some of the things they prohibit are already available to kids through R-rated movies to which they can be taken by their parents.  The law was quickly made obsolescent by the culture.

The Supreme Court was too vague and the New Jersey legislature was too specific.  The conclusion this suggests is that there is a large element of futility in trying to devise formulae that will preclude censorship problems or give clear guidance when the problems occur.

At any rate, the New Jersey legislature agrees with the Court that it is sex and not other forms of human activity that are legally obscene.  And since the New Jersey law was intended to protect minors, it, like the Supreme Court ruling, could be used to safeguard the rights of minors to be exposed to nonsexual ideologies.  An interesting illustration of this is the brochure that Larry Flynt mailed to his fellow Ohioans.  It contained grisly color photographs of bodies blown apart in Vietnam.  It was revolting but, legally, it was not obscene.

## Exercise V - Conclusion

Bill 919 would confer upon teachers an immunity to censorship and an impunity to censure.  Teachers, especially those with tenure, would be the final arbiters of their own actions.  They would have virtual carte blanche in curricular decisions.  Not only would they be exempt from supervision by the school board and administration, they would be beyond supervision by their peers.

The initial impact no doubt would be to inject greater ideological diversity and vigor into the schoolwide curriculum. In time, however, the classroom curriculum could well degenerate into ideological indoctrination.  On the college level, where students have the sophistication to resist the teacher's blandishments and where they are not likely to have one teacher all year, this is no great danger.  At lower levels, it could create impediments to critical analysis rather than being a stimulus thereto.

Thus, the effort to preclude problems of censorship by writing preventive legislation fails in this case as it does in the case of obscenity.

## Exercise VI - Conclusion

An argument can be made that the people who know the most about social studies teaching, say, are the social studies teachers. They know the subject and they know the kids. The social studies supervisor may be out of touch with the latter, never mind the administration or the board. Therefore, the people at the bottom of the bureaucratic hierarchy - those with the least authority - are the ones with the most expertise. The rationality of the Weberian bureaucratic medal, where authority and expertise ascend together, may be applicable to the Prussian army, but it does not reflect what goes on in the American school. There, the bureaucracy is irrational because authority is inversely related to expertise. Given their relative superiority in expertise, teachers should be free to deal with ideology as they see fit. Bill 919 makes sense after all.

But does it? Does the teacher's expertise extend to ideology - to values - or is it restricted to factual knowledge and pedagogical strategies? Why should teachers presume to be more expert in matters of ideology than the public whom they serve? Even if a case could be made for this superiority with certain teachers in some school systems, giving these teachers authority commensurate with their expertise might make the bureaucracy rational but it would not make the school system democratic. The ideology of democracy requires that schooling be popularly determined. The experts can attempt to influence this determination, but they cannot preempt it.

## Summary

The several conclusions which the author has drawn from the six exercises can be summarized in seven general conclusions.

1. Censorship runs the full ideological spectrum, both in the kinds of material that get censored and the kinds of people who do the censoring.
2. Censorship disputes frequently defy resolution through rational discourse.
3. A vague policy governing controversial materials does little good and may do harm.
4. A policy that is substantively detailed may prevent censorship problems but at the price of flexibility and reasonableness.
5. Ideological representativeness is too important in education to be left to individual teacher judgment.
6. In a democracy, matters of ideology and censorship are subject to popular control and not expert fiat.
7. What is needed is a procedure for democratically resolving the issues as they arise - a procedure which will include all the parties to the issue. In cases of school censorship, this means students, teachers, parents, administrators, board, and public. The

procedure may not be fun, but it's bound to be educational.

**FOOTNOTES**

[1]Statement to the NEA Panel by Lewis Harrah, Pastor of the Church of Jesus Christ, North Charleston, as quoted in A Textbook Study in Cultural Conflict (NEA Inquiry Report on the Textbook Controversy in Kanawha County, West Virginia) p. 13.

[2]Seth S. King, "Professor Causes Furor by Saying Nazi Slaying of Jews is a Myth," New York Times, 28 January 1977, p. A-10.

[3]See Noel Perrin, Dr. Bowdler's Legacy: A History of Expurgated Books in England and America, (New York: Athaneum, 1969), n.p. .

[4]For a discussion of this episode, see Peggy Lamson, Roger Baldwin, Founder of the American Civil Liberties Union, (Boston: Houghton-Mifflin), 1976, n.p. .

# THE AASA CODE OF ETHICS*

## Policy 1

The Professional School Administrator
Constantly Upholds the Honor and Dignity of
His Profession in All His Actions and Rela-
tions with Pupils, Colleagues, School Board
Members, and the Public.

The following examples illustrate but do not limit
applications of this policy.
The professional school administrator:

A. Is impartial in the execution of school policies and the
enforcement of rules and regulations. It is a breach of ethics to
give preferential consideration to any individual or group because
of their special status or position in the school system or
community.

B. Recognizes and respects fully the worth and dignity of
each individual in all administrative procedures and leadership
actions.

C. Demonstrates professional courtesy and ethical behavior
by informing a colleague in another system of his intention to
consider for employment personnel from that system.

D. Never submits official and confidential letters of
appraisal for teachers or others which knowingly contain erroneous
information or which knowingly fail to include pertinent data.

E. Never fails to recommend those worthy of recommendation.

F. Is alert to safeguard the public and his profession from
those who might degrade public education or school administration.

G. Seeks no self-aggrandizement.

H. Refrains from making unwarranted claims, from inappropriate advertising, and from misinterpreting facts about his
school system to further his own professional status.

I. Never makes derogatory statements about a colleague or a
school system unless he is compelled to state his opinion under
oath or in official relationships where his professional opinion
is required.

J. Exhibits ethical behavior by explaining and giving
reasons to individuals affected by demotions or terminations of
employment.

## Policy 2

The Professional School Administrator
Obeys Local, State, and National Laws; Holds
Himself to High Ethical and Moral Standards,
and Gives Loyalty to His Country and to the
Cause of Democracy and Liberty.

---

*The gender references appear as written in the original.

The following examples illustrate but do not limit applications for this policy:

A. A legal conviction for immorality, commission of a crime involving moral turpitude or other public offense of similar degree shall be sufficient grounds for expelling a school administrator from membership in the American Association of School Administrators.

B. Affiliation with organizations known to advocate the forcible overthrow of the government of the United States is evidence of unworthiness of public trust. A person who is so affiliated shall not be permitted to become or to continue as a member of the American Association of School Administrators.

C. A professional school administrator, in common with other citizens, has a right and in many instances an obligation to express his opinion about the wisdom or justice of a given law. An opinion questioning a law, however, does not justify failure to fulfill the requirements of that law.

D. The ideals of his profession require a school administrator to resist ideological pressures that would contravene the fundamental principles of public education, or would pervert or weaken public schools, their educational program, or their personnel.

E. It is unethical to ignore or divert attention from laws which are incompatible with the best interests and purposes of the schools, as a way of avoiding controversy. Rather the professional school administrator will take the initiative to bring about the reconsideration, revision, or repeal of the statute.

F. The professional school administrator will not withhold evidence or knowingly shield law breakers.

## Policy 3

The Professional School Administrator Accepts the Responsibility Throughout His Career to Master and to Contribute to the Growing Body of Specialized Knowledge, Concepts, and Skills Which Characterize School Administration as a Profession.

The following examples illustrate but do not limit applications of this policy:

A. In addition to meeting the minimum standards required for legal certification in his state, the professional school administrator has a responsibility to satisfy the preparation standards recommended by his professional association, and has an obligation to work toward the adoption of these professional standards by the appropriate certification authorities in his state.

B. The school administrator has a professional obligation to attend conferences, seminars, and other learning activities which hold promise of contributing to his professional growth and development.

C. It is in keeping with the highest ideals of the profession for the administrator to support local, state, and national committees studying educational problems and to participate in such activities whenever and wherever possible, consistent with his obligations to his district.

D. The school administrator has a leadership responsibility for the professional growth of his associates which requires encouragement of their attendance at appropriate professional meetings and their participation in the work of local, state, and national committees and associations.

E. Concern for improving his profession, and for education generally requires that the school administrator seek out promising educational practices and relevant research findings and that he share with others any significant practices and research from within his own institution.

F. The school administrator has a special obligation to contribute to the strengthening of his own state and national professional association.

## Policy 4

The Professional School Administrator
Strives to Provide the Finest Possible
Educational Experiences and Opportunities to
All Persons in the District.

The following examples illustrate but do not limit applications of this policy:

A. The school administrator will base differentiation of educational experiences on the differing needs and abilities of pupils, giving no preference to factors such as social status or other undemocratic or discriminating considerations.

B. A school administrator has an obligation to inform the board and the community of deficiencies in educational services or opportunities.

C. A school administrator resists all attempts by vested interests to infringe upon the school program as a means of promoting their selfish purposes.

D. A school administrator resists all attempts to exclude from consideration as teaching personnel members of any particular race or creed. He also resists pressures to employ teachers on the basis of the political, marital, or economic status of the applicant. The ability and fitness of the candidates for teaching positions are the sole criteria for selection.

E. A school administrator recognizes that the provisions of equal educational opportunities for all pupils may require greater or different resources for some than for others.

F. A school administrator is professionally obligated to assume clear, articulate, and forceful leadership in defining the role of the school in the community and pointing the way to achieve its functions.

## Policy 5

The Professional School Administrator Applying for a Position or Entering into Contractual Agreements Seeks to Preserve and Enhance the Prestige and Status of His Profession.

The following examples illustrate but do not limit applications of this policy:

A. A school administrator is morally committed to honor employment contracts. He shall refuse to enter into a new contractual agreement until termination of an existing contract is completed to the satisfaction of all concerned.

B. A school administrator does not apply for positions indiscriminantly nor for any position held by an administrator whose termination of employment is not a matter of record.

C. Misrepresentations, use of political influence, pressure tactics, or undermining the professional status of a colleague are unethical practices and are inimical to his professional commitment.

D. Advertising, either to solicit new school positions or to offer professional consultation services, is inconsistent with the ideals of the profession of school administration.

E. A school administrator refrains from making disparaging comments about candidates competing for a position.

F. A school administrator refuses to accept a position in which established principles of professional school administration must be seriously compromised or abandoned.

G. A school administrator does not apply for or accept a position where a competent special professional investigating committee endorsed by the Association has declared working conditions unsatisfactory until such time as appropriate corrections in the situation have been made.

## Policy 6

The Professional School Administrator Carries Out in Good Faith All Policies Duly Adopted by the Local Board and the Regulations of State Authorities and Renders Professional Service to the Best of His Ability.

The following examples illustrate but do not limit applications of this policy:

A. Adoption of policies not in conformity with the administrator's recommendations or beliefs is not just cause for refusal by the administrator to support and execute them.

B. It is improper for an administrator to refuse to work at his optimum level.

C. A school administrator has an obligation to support publicly the school board and the instructional staff if either is unjustly accused. He should not permit himself to become involved

publicly in personal criticism of board or staff members. He
should be at liberty, however, to discuss differences of opinion
on professional matters.

D. If a situation develops whereby an administrator feels
that to retain his position would necessitate that he violate what
he and other members of the profession consider to be ethical
conduct he should inform the board of the untenable position. In
the event of his imminent dismissal the superintendent should
request adequate reasons and if they are not forthcoming or if the
situation is not resolved to his professional satisfaction he
should report to the public.

## Policy 7

The Professional School Administrator
Honors the Public Trust of His Position Above
Any Economic or Social Rewards.

The following examples illustrate but do not limit
applications of this policy:

A. To resist, or to fail to support, clearly desirable
approaches to improving and strengthening the schools is
unbecoming to a professional person and unethical conduct on the
part of a school administrator.

B. The school administrator has a commitment to his position
of public trust to resist unethical demands by special interest or
pressure groups. He refuses to allow strong and unscrupulous
individuals to seize or exercise powers and responsibilities which
are properly his own.

C. The rank, popularity, position, or social standing of any
member of the school staff should never cause the professional
school administrator to conceal, disregard, or seemingly condone
unethical conduct. Any and all efforts to disregard, overlook, or
cover up unethical practices should be vigorously resisted by a
school administrator.

## Policy 8

The Professional School Administrator
Does Not Permit Considerations of Private Gain
nor Personal Economic Interest to Affect the
Discharge of His Professional Responsibilities.

The following examples illustrate but do not limit
applications of this policy:

A. A school administrator refuses to permit his relationship
with vendors primarily interested in selling goods and services to
influence his administration of the school system he serves.

B. It is improper for a school administrator to accept
employment by any concern which publishes, manufactures, sells, or
in any way deals in goods or services which are or may be expected

to be purchased by the school system he serves.

C. It is improper for a school administrator to be engaged in private ventures if such endeavors cause him to give less than full-time concern to his school system.

D. This policy in no way precludes private investment of personal funds of the school administrator in ventures not influenced by his position in a given school system provided his own professional obligations are not neglected.

E. During the time of his employment the school administrator shall have no personal interest in, nor receive any personal gain or profit from, school supplies, equipment, books, or other educational materials or facilities procured, dispensed, or sold to or in the school system he serves.

F. It is a breach of public trust for a school administrator to use confidential information concerning school affairs (such as the knowledge of the selection of specific school sites) for personal profit or to divulge such information to others who might so profit.

G. It is inappropriate for a school administrator to utilize unpublished materials developed in line of duty by staff members in a school system in order to produce a publication for personal profit, without the expressed permission of all contributors.

H. A school administrator must be wary of using free consultative services from a commercial concern which may in effect be a skillful technique for promoting the sale of instructional or other materials in which that concern has a pecuniary interest.

I. A school administrator does not publicly endorse goods or services provided for schools by commercial organizations.

J. The school administrator should not recommend the appointment of immediate relatives to positions under his jurisdiction.


### Policy 9

The Professional School Administrator Recognizes That the Public Schools Are the Public's Business and Seeks to Keep the Public Fully and Honestly Informed about Their Schools.

The following examples illustrate but do not limit applications of this policy:

A. A school administrator has an obligation to interpret to the community the work and activities of the school system, revealing its weaknesses as well as its strengths. It is unethical for a school administrator to present only the favorable facts to the patrons of the district.

B. A school administrator maintains confidences or qualified privileged communications entrusted to him in the course of executing the affairs of the public schools. These confidences shall be revealed only as the law or courts may require or when the welfare of the school system is at stake.

C. It is proper for a school administrator to discuss confidential information with the board of education meeting in executive session.

D. A school administrator considers that those with whom he deals are innocent of any disparaging accusations until valid evidence is presented to substantiate any charges made.

## Overview

High Standards of Ethical Behavior for the Professional School Administrator Are Essential and Are Compatible with His Faith in the Power of Public Education and His Commitment to Leadership in the Preservation and Strengthening of the Public Schools.

The true sense of high calling comes to the superintendent of schools as he faces squarely such widely held beliefs as the following:

A. The effectiveness of the schools and their programs is inescapably the responsibility of the superintendent.

B. Every act, or every failure to act, of the superintendent has consequences in the schools and in the lives of people.

C. In many situations and to many people in a community the superintendent is the living symbol of their schools.

D. The public entrusts both the day-by-day well-being and the long-range welfare of its children and of its school system to the superintendent and board of education.

E. The ultimate test for a superintendent is the effort which he makes to improve the quality of the learning opportunity for every child in the schools.

F. In the long run, what happens in and to the public schools of America happens to America.

# THE ETHICS OF CHIEF SCHOOL ADMINISTRATORS:

## A STUDY OF ACCOMMODATION*

### Roy Dexheimer

> So long as a businessman complies with the
> laws of the land and avoids telling malicious
> lies, he's ethical. If the law as written
> gives a man a wide-open chance to make a
> killing, he'd be a fool not to take advantage
> of it. If he doesn't, somebody else will.
> There's no obligation on him to stop and
> consider who is going to get hurt. If the law
> says he can do it, that's all the
> justification he needs. There's nothing
> unethical about that.

That statement was written by Albert Carr in a 1968 article
about the ethics of businessmen, published in the Harvard Business
Review. This definition is, we hope, foreign to the concept of
ethics in a profession, because a prominent tenet in any
definition of a profession is that it have an enforceable code of
ethics. Otherwise the public may not perceive the group as being
professional. One can only assume that the American Association
of School Administrators was so motivated when, after nearly a
hundred years of existence, it promulgated a Code of Ethics in
1962.[1]

Let me retreat from this opening line of thought just for a
minute. When I was a chief school administrator in a rural school
district, I confess to giving little or no attention to ethics as
a separate entity, although I certainly hope my administrative
behavior was ethical. Last year I returned to the University of
Rochester for a final year of graduate study. One day, almost
casually, I mentioned in a seminar how odd it was we talked so
often about the mechanics of administering people and things, but
how little we investigated the ethical implications of such
administration. The professor gave what can best be described as
a snort of derision. Other members of the seminar group felt
almost embarrassed by the open mention of ethical behavior, as if
a naughty word had been uttered. One peer even indicated that any
talk of ethics in administrative behavior was irrelevant!

As is often the case in graduate studies, I discovered that
the professor was putting me on, daring me to defend or to retreat
from my observation. He eventually led me to a book entitled
Lawyer's Ethics: A Survey of the New York City Bar, by the
distinguished lawyer-sociologist Jerome Carlin.[2]

---

*Paper presented at the American Association of School
Administrators annual meeting, Atlantic City, New Jersey, February
15-19, 1969.

In 1965-66 Professor Carlin conducted an exhaustive and ingenius study of the New York City Bar Association and its Code of Ethics. His goal was to discover the relationship between the outward acceptance of this code and the actual adherance to it. Carlin's methodology was to get at actual ethical behavior through a combination of depth interviews and a questionnaire. This approach was determined after ruling out direct observations (too time-consuming), informants (too unreliable), and the official records of misconduct (too few infractions ever saw print). His approach depended upon the candor of his respondents as they replied to his questions about thirteen borderline ethical situations which were likely to face any lawyer in the normal duties of their profession.

The conclusions were illuminating. Lawyers, at least in the New York City Bar Association, were barely honest in many instances, let alone ethical. There was a material discrepancy between the ethical standards that lawyers acknowledged were binding upon them and the standards of conduct that many of them observed in fact. Further, the deviations from ethical standards of conduct were not significantly inhibited by formal devices for fostering compliance; i.e., the official sanctions of the Bar Association itself. The Association really punished only those offenses which transgressed upon societal morality, and not the ethical breaches of professional standards as outlined in its own code of ethics.

Back from these digressions to the American Association of School Administrators and its Code of Ethics.

A report given to this Convention a year ago indicated that only thirty-two states had active Ethics Committees; only five states were investigating or in some way acting upon a case involving a violation of ethics; only two states had officially adopted the AASA Code of Ethics as a state guideline; and generally, most states had no significant activities to report in 1967.

In another AASA report, the 1960 Profile of the School Superintendent,[3] the superintendents surveyed never once listed ethical behavior as one of the qualifications for an effective school administrator, nor did the report ever list the study of ethics in its discussion of pre-service and in-service programs for chief school administrators.

In short, it is possible that the same situation Carlin discovered among New York City lawyers might be prevalent among chief school administrators; viz., that despite serious professional concern on the part of AASA for the ethical behavior of its members, there could be a relatively wide gap between the outward acceptance of the AASA Code of Ethics and the individual member's internal or even public adherence to that Code.

These conclusions became the basis of a study I conducted this past fall. A questionnaire was devised containing fifteen anecdotal situations which might face any typical school administrators sometime in the course of their career. Each of the anecdotes was based upon some statement in the AASA Code of Ethics; e.g., accepting gifts from vendors, hiring one's spouse in the district, and so forth.

With each anecdote went a range of answers, including the option of writing in a completely different answer if none of the choices was relevant. Also, the respondent was to indicate whether or not the response was based upon an actual experience in one's career, or if the answer selected was only what might be done in theory if ever faced with the situation. Finally, the range of answers offered contained one--sometimes two--replies which corresponded almost exactly with the course of action which is clearly a part of the AASA Code of Ethics.

With this questionnaire went a single sheet asking for some autobiographical information. The respondents were asked about their age; the major field of study as an undergraduate; the number of years as chief school administrator in the present district; and the number of years totally as a chief school administrator; what position did they hold immediately prior to becoming a chief school administrator, and was that position in the current district or elsewhere; the size of the school district in numbers of students; a general statement on the strength of religious convictions; a question about frequency of attendance at AASA Conventions such as this one; the salary for 1968-69; and finally, whether or not the graduate training had contained any special attention directed toward the ethical implications of administrative decisions.

The sampling technique was very simple: I took the 1967 Roster of Members, and selected the first superintendent on each page. Since the Roster is divided by states, this guaranteed geographical distribution. In an attempt to elicit candor, complete anonymity was guaranteed. No code numbers were used, no signatures were asked. An extremely supportive covering letter was attached, signed by Forrest Connor and Steve Knesevich. I also had a letter of explanation, and I enclosed a self-addressed and stamped envelope for returning the responses.

Two hundred and forty-two replies were received, out of a grand total of four hundred and forty-four mailed questionnaires. Although personal anonymity was assured, I did keep a rough tabulation of postmarks; thus I can assert positively that all fifty states were represented in the final tabulation.

One final bit of background information, and then to some findings. The first and most obvious fault to find in this research design is that respondents might not be candid. The supposition here is that only the most ethical answer will be selected, and not the one which reflects actual behavior. Partly to answer this argument, and partly to sharpen the questionnaire itself, I conducted a pilot study among fifteen chief school administrators known to me personally. Their replies were completely candid, believe me! No man picked more than twelve ethical answers. When the same questionnaire was given to a group of graduate students, who were instructed to select the answers they thought to be most ethical and not what they actually would do, no respondent got less than seventeen ethical replies (there were twenty items on the pilot questionnaire). The pilot study and the results I am about to describe from the national study seem to indicate candor, if nothing else.

The results of the final questionnaire were interesting.

More non-ethical responses were made than ethical responses. The mean score of ethical responses for the entire group of respondents was 7.1, out of a possible score of 15.

Over 55% of the responses were based upon actual experiences. One nice result here: the replies based upon actual experience were almost 2 - 1, ethical to non-ethical responses. Among the replies based upon theoretical responses, the ethical -- non-ethical ratio was equal. The significance of this escapes, unless it is that we are more ethical in actual practice than we are when only guessing what we might do in any given situation.

You'll remember that each respondent was asked to give some autobiographical information. This information was matched against the replies on the questionnaire. Here are some quick overviews of the results of that analysis:

1) age of the respondent has no significant bearing upon the responses.

2) the humanities majors of undergraduate years had relatively low mean scores -- 6.2, vs. the 7.1 mean of the whole group. Hooray for philosophy!

3) longevity in the present job had no significance, but career longevity did. The longer one is a chief school administrator, apparently, the lower the number of ethical responses.

4) I asked what job was held prior to the superintendency, and whether or not this job had been in the current or another district. The only interesting sidelights here were these: coaches from other districts were not very good on sportsmanship, because their mean score was pretty low. The highest number of ethical responses was in the group I termed "outsiders" - people who moved into the superintendency from jobs that ranged from payroll clerk to college president.

5) membership in AASA, religious convictions, and graduate studies in ethical behavior did not produce any significant deviations from the group mean of 7.1.

6) finally, two bits of autobiographical information did yield very interesting and statistically significant results. In an almost straightline progression, the size of the district and the amount of salary did show marked differences. That is, the smaller the district and the lower the pay, the lower the mean number of ethical replies. And conversely, the people responding from the largest districts and/or the people with the best salaries clearly had the greatest number of ethical replies.

Let me offer some concluding remarks. First, remember that this is only a graduate student's study, subject to all the limi-

tations that term implies. There is no much that could be faulted
in  this or any other questionnaire study that the results must be
looked at with a skeptical eye.
   Still, it's <u>startling</u> to find more non-ethical replies than
ethical  replies.  It's <u>interesting</u> to note  the  variations  in
replies.  It's <u>significant</u> that  the foremost  leaders  in  our
profession -- i.e., those who are in the largest districts and who
are  recognized  by  the status of high salaries -- are  the  most
ethical among us.  It's <u>important</u> to note that ethical  responses
on  a  questionnaire  are  no measure at all  of  a  chief  school
administrator's  effectiveness.  The  least  ethical among us  may
accomplish the most good.
   There  is some question,  especially in terms of contemporary
thought  on  ethical behavior,  whether or not  codified  rules  of
conduct  have any real effect upon the behavior of  human  beings.
For example:

>   A committee set up by the late President Kennedy to deal
>   with  questions of business ethics,  of which the writer
>   of this book was a member, got nowhere at all because it
>   was code-minded, wrote a code to cover all business, and
>   found itself possessed of nothing but platitudes.[4]

Yet  the public seems to put faith in such codes,  and  wants
guidelines of some type:

>   . . .  in  almost  every chapter of a study  reporting
>   ethical  issues  in  a  number  of  occupations,  the
>   participants  voiced their longing for ethical  guidance
>   in  their  particular  vocational  problems.  The
>   incontrovertible  fact  is  that  many  must  ever  be
>   protected against the human propensity to seek one's own
>   advantage.  It  is  at this point that  the  forces  of
>   ethics and religion make their contribution to the well-
>   being of society.[5]

Ethical philosophies from Aristotle to Phenix,  Barnard,  and
Maslow have all indicated that the real source of ethical behavior
exists  within  the individual and not in any code of  ethics.  A
major  writer  in  the field  of  educational  administration  has
agreed:

>   Equally  as  important as the  possession  of  desirable
>   character  attributes for the educational  administrator
>   is  the possession of a value framework upon which these
>   attributes are based.  George S.  Counts once  proposed
>   that  the major sources of American values are found  in
>   the Hebraic-Christian ethic,  the humanistic spirit, the
>   scientific  method,  faith in the rule of the  law,  and
>   faith  in  democracy . . . .  In other  words,  as  a
>   prospective  administrator,  one  should  be  able  to
>   translate  this system into action as he faces the  many
>   moral and ethical decisions which will occur both on and
>   off the job.[6]

My study has tried to focus some attention on the possibilities of adherance to the professional AASA Code of Ethics being something less than their apparent acceptance, and also to highlight some of the variables which might affect that adherance.

The study has <u>not</u> attempted to make judgment on how adherance might be fostered. Greater emphasis upon ethics in preservice training, perhaps through simulation materials, is one possibility. Stronger sanction for the AASA Code of Ethics, plus a greater willingness to enforce this sanction might bring about more adherance. Some high-powered public relations techniques in pointing out the salient features of the Code of Ethics are methods which might be explored.

Whatever the road to be selected, this study seems to have reinforced what philosophers from Aristotle to Phenix have stressed: ethical standards are internalized personally, and are not determined by public codes, no matter how important such codes are to maintain the public image of any profession. Perhaps the only code of ethics possible was expressed by Philip Phenix - "if the consequences of the act are good, the act is right; if they are evil, the act is wrong. Good, not right, becomes primary."

## Ethical Situation Questionnaire for the Actual Study

### INSTRUCTIONS

In the next few pages you'll read over some anecdotal situations. These situations involve the making of decisions by chief school administrators, and they have been selected on the presumption that they - or something relatively similar - have occurred at one time or another during your own administrative career.

Your task is to select a solution from among the alternatives offered which most resembles what you did when faced with the necessity of making this decision. If none of the solutions matches your personal experience, there is an opportunity for you to write in a solution of your own choice.

If nothing even remotely resembling the situation as described has come up in your administrative career, please do not omit the question. Instead, choose a solution from the alternatives offered based upon what you would do if ever faced with a similar or identical situation (again, the write-in privilege exists).

> To repeat: please respond to each situation, either based upon your actual experience, or upon what you would do if that situation did arise.

The final page of this questionnaire is an Answer Key.

### ANSWER SHEET

The column headed SITUATION NUMBER refers to the anecdote on the questionnaire.

The column headed LETTER OF ANSWER refers to your choice among the alternatives.

The column headed ACTUAL should be checked if your choice was based upon actual experience.

The column header HYPOTHETICAL should be checked if your choice was based upon what you would do, since you have never faced the situation described, or even anything similar.

The column headed WRITE-IN RESPONSE should be completed only if none of the alternatives offered with the anecdotal situation were suitable to your own past experience and/or hypothetical solution.

280

| SITUATION NUMBER | LETTER OF ANSWER | ACTUAL | HYPOTHETICAL | WRITE-IN RESPONSE (if any) |
|---|---|---|---|---|
| 1. | _____ | _____ | _____ | _____ |
| 2. | _____ | _____ | _____ | _____ |
| 3. | _____ | _____ | _____ | _____ |
| 4. | _____ | _____ | _____ | _____ |
| 5. | _____ | _____ | _____ | _____ |
| 6. | _____ | _____ | _____ | _____ |
| 7. | _____ | _____ | _____ | _____ |
| 8. | _____ | _____ | _____ | _____ |
| 9. | _____ | _____ | _____ | _____ |
| 10. | _____ | _____ | _____ | _____ |
| 11. | _____ | _____ | _____ | _____ |
| 12. | _____ | _____ | _____ | _____ |
| 13. | _____ | _____ | _____ | _____ |
| 14. | _____ | _____ | _____ | _____ |
| 15. | _____ | _____ | _____ | _____ |

Below is a sample illustration from the Answer Sheet.

| SITUATION NUMBER | LETTER OF ANSWER | ACTUAL | HYPOTHETICAL | WRITE-IN RESPONSE (if any) |
|---|---|---|---|---|
| 1. | C | X | _____ | _____ |
| 2. | A | _____ | X | _____ |
| 3. | other | X | _____ | My solution is... |

In other words, you saw alternative "C" as the response best suited for the first anecdotal situation based upon an actual incident in your career.

For the second situation, you picked "A" as the best response. Since you've never actually encountered this situation in your career, this answer is based upon what you do hypothetically in similar circumstances.

And, finally, for number three you wrote in an answer because none of the alternatives offered in the questionnaire described exactly what you did when once faced with the same situation.

1. Because of the requirement for evaluation in the new federally financed programs, your state has instituted a yearly program of standardized testing in certain grades. The results have just arrived for the current year. They show your district trailing other districts in your immediate geographic area, especially in the skill area of reading. This is especially distressing because there have been many Board-sponsored workshops, and subsidies for teachers to attend appropriate seminars and conferences on the teaching of reading. What should you do with this report?

   A. File it, re-adjust some of your planning, but do both privately and without any formal presentation of data either to the Board or the total staff.

   B. Make the contents of the report known to the Board, the staff, and the community at large.

   C. Review the report with the total staff and ask for guide-lines.

   D. Make a presentation - in executive session - to the Board, pointing out that the district ranks well ahead of other areas in the state, if not in the immediate area.

   E. Talk privately with key staff members about the report, and especially with those in charge of the reading program, and begin planning new approaches.

   F. None of the above, but rather: _____

   _____

2. The Board sends you, at district expense, to a major convention for administrators (for example, the Atlantic City Convention of AASA). While you are there, you meet a group of friends in the lobby. As you're talking about the convention, the group is approached by the sales representative of a product used by all of your schools. The person mingles with the group, and before long, insists that all of you go to dinner at one of the better restaurants in the city . . . at the company's expense. How do you handle the invitation.

   A. You accept with thanks.

   B. You try to get the salesman aside, indicating that you'd love to have a meal, privately, sometime.

C. You refuse the invitation, pleading a prior appointment, even though this is not exactly the case.

D. You accept the invitation, but only if you are allowed to pay for your own meal.

E. None of the above, but rather: _____

_____

3. The parents of a good student and generally responsible youngster have come to you with complaints about the teaching style of a social studies teacher. They claim the teacher is using biased materials and slanted opinions in the classes. Further, they claim that when their son tried to question these approaches, he was greeted with sarcasm and thinly veiled threats to have his grades lowered. The matter is not relieved by the father's active role in town matters, and he demands evidence of action immediately. What action do you take.

A. Agree with the parents that the teacher is in the wrong, and indicate that censure will be applied in some form.

B. Have the boy transferred into another classroom with a teacher whose techniques and methods are well known to you, and which you know will placate these irate parents.

C. Call the most immediate supervisor of the teacher and ask for some corroboration of the incidents; then proceed with action.

D. Indicate to the parents that you will take the matter up with the teacher and the teacher's supervisors, but that no direct action will be taken until both sides of the controversy have been aired.

E. None of the above, but rather: _____

_____

4. You are leaving the district at the end of this school year. The Board, not wishing to involve itself with outside consultants, has decided to handle the recruitment of your successor itself, using you as the main resource of advice and help. After going through the normal procedures, a final group of five candidates remains. These candidates have visited the district, have met with the Board, and have chatted with you and other staff members. Now the final selection process has begun, and the Board is asking for some firm opinions from you on these candidates. What advice do you offer?

A. You excuse yourself and leave the Board entirely to its

283

own devices in these final stages.

B. Since some of the candidates have exhibited personal characteristics which you believe would not fit in well for this particular district, you enter these opinions freely.

C. Any advice you give is restricted to commentaries upon the professional qualifications of the candidates, as revealed in the placement folders and letters of recommendation.

D. Knowing that the Board would probably want this advice, you have done additional follow-up work with each candidate (for example, telephone calls), have arrived at what you believe would be the best choice for this district at this time, and now offer that opinion to the Board.

E. None of the above, but rather: _____

_____

5. Your Board, taking its cues from the original exhortations of the National School Boards Association, has maintained a policy of refusing any federal funds for school programs. Now you have been approached by the state department of education and urged to conduct a federally financed program in your district. They ask this because they know that your district is particularly well suited for such a program. You are sympathetic and flattered, especially since the experimental program fits in very well with what you consider to be educationally desirable and sound. Now what?

A. You stand on the Board's policy, however regretfully, and decline the offer.

B. You approach the Board, asking that they reconsider their previous stand.

C. You devise a plan where the special aid can be masked as a type of state aid, a plan which has the support of the state education department. Then you implement the program in your district.

D. You not only ask for Board support in the program and a reversing of their previous policy statements, but indicate that such a reversal is a deciding factor regarding whether or not you'll remain on as superintendent.

E. None of the above, but rather: _____

_____

6. Your district is a rural one, and homogeneous in its

population. The teaching staff reflects this homogeneity; that is, they're mostly white, middle-class, and Protestant. In your search for new staff members, an excellent candidate with extremely promising credentials appears. The interview turns up an additional fact: the candidate is Jewish (or Black, or Italian, or of any other group not generally found in your area). The Board has made it clear in the past that all hiring is entirely in your hands; they'll ratify any recommendation you make to them. What is your recommendation?

A. You turn to other candidates, not because of prejudice, but as a form of protection for the candidate, who would be clearly in a lonely and vulnerable position.

B. The Board is given a list of the candidates, with all credentials, and asked to make its own decision.

C. Exercising your usual prerogative of a nearly final decision in hiring, you sign the teacher on.

D. Although other candidates are clearly inferior as prospects, you hire one of them as the best course of action for this particular community at this particular time.

E. You do not hire the candidate, but you do make efforts to seek placement for the person in the form of contacts you have in other districts.

F. None of the above, but rather: _____

_____

7. It's late July and your best math teacher has suddenly taken a position as supervisor of student teaching in a nearby university. A young teacher, a graduate of your school several years back, is teaching math in a neighboring district. The occasional contacts you've had with the person have indicated a desire to move back home one day. Is now the time?

A. A news article announcing the vacancy is quickly placed in the local newspaper - and you hope for the best!

B. You send the teacher a note stating that the person would be welcome.

C. By planting a few seeds in the informal system of communications you know that personal word will get to the teacher.

D. If the teacher applies with no special effort on your part, you hire the person immediately, not needing the recommendations.

E. You call the chief school administrator of the nearby district, explain your problem, and ask if you can approach the teacher.

F. You call the placement agency of the young teacher's college, with specific instructions that the teacher get a personal notice.

G. None of the above, but rather: _____

_____

8. That time of year to begin writing recommendations for teachers has arrived. Your general policy is to give a basically honest recommendation, including weaknesses as well as strengths. One of this year's requests comes from a teacher who has always wanted to move to "X" district, mainly because the teacher's future husband/wife lives there. The teacher is not a particularly strong candidate, but you know how important it is for the teacher to make this move. What kind of letter will you write?

A. Realizing that the teacher will probably get married and stop teaching soon anyway, you write a glowing recommendation - knowing the teacher will be accepted on the basis of this letter.

B. No deviation from your usual policy is taken, and you make no attempt to gloss over weaknesses.

C. You decline to write any letter, and instead ask the most immediate supervisor to handle this particular case, so that no compromise with your usual standards is made.

D. You write the glowing letter of recommendation, and you call the administrator in "X" district - an old friend - to increase the chances of the teacher being hired.

E. None of the above, but rather: _____

_____

9. Spring has arrived, and it's time for that new tennis racket and perhaps even the new set of golf clubs you have been promising yourself for some time. The athletic director in the district has just purchased a lovely personal set of irons, and you suspect he did so through the district's contractor for athletic supplies at a cost price. How will you get your set?

A. You call the supplier, strictly as an unidentified buyer, and price the clubs.

B. You stay away entirely from the school supplier,

preferring to make your own deal elsewhere.

C. The athletic director offers to negotiate the new clubs at a good price, especially since he does all the ordering for the district.

D. You call the supplier, identifying yourself and your position, and asking him what he can do.

E. None of the above, but rather: _____

_____

10. Your district has an unusually high turnover of elementary teachers this year, with many of the vacancies coming very late in the spring and early summer. Despite a feeling that it would not be the wisest thing to do, you have to give consideration to the teaching capabilities of your spouse. Although your spouse has been out of teaching for eight years, all the youngsters are safely in school now and your spouse wants to return to active teaching. Your spouse's reputation from teaching in other districts is excellent, and no written policy prevents you from hiring your spouse.

A. You approach the Board, explain the problem, and seek their approval for the appointment.

B. The search continues for other candidates, with the understanding that you'll hire your spouse if no better candidate turns up by Labor Day - even if your spouse has to turn down good jobs in the neighboring districts in the meantime.

C. You offer to exchange spouses, regarding a teaching position, with a neighboring school administrator.

D. You avoid hiring your spouse, even if lesser candidates must be considered.

E. None of the above, but rather: _____

_____

11. The education statutes of your state contain a number of laws which you believe to be of questionable value. Two in particular have an effect upon your daily program: that no regular program of prayers may be offered in the classrooms, and that a flag salute is required each day as classes begin. You know full well that some prayers are still continued in certain classrooms (generally with tacit parental support); and you know also that many teachers are relatively lax on the flag salute. What actions ought you to take?

A. Issue a bulletin which points out the statutes, and that

you expect them to be followed to the letter in this district.

B. Simply look the other way until some official complaints are forthcoming from staff or parents, and then act.

C. In cooperative planning with the teachers, find some way to fall within the statutes while helping them to meet what are apparently individual beliefs and needs.

D. Campaign actively and politically to have the offending statutes revised, and support in addition any teacher who apparently feels the same.

E. Have the Board take some action in the form of a supportive policy for these awkward situations.

F. Speak to individual teachers, asking that their practices be brought into line with the statutes.

G. None of the above, but rather: _____

_____

12. A local service organization, of which you are a member, puts on an impressive talent show annually to raise funds. This year they have designated the proceeds to help the AFS Exchange Student program in your school. All rehearsals and the final show will be in the high school auditorium. The chairperson of the talent show has come to you to ask for a reduction in the normal rates charged by the school for use of the facilities, so that a maximum profit may be realized. As a loyal member of the organization, you respond by:

A. Recommending to the Board that the request be granted.

B. Refusing the request, point out the policy as it stands, and noting that other equally deserving groups use the auditorium during the year.

C. Since the request will mean more benefits to the district's AFS program, you grant it as an administrative action.

D. You give no definite answer, but urge the chairperson to state the case before the Board - with your support guaranteed.

E. None of the above, but rather: _____

_____

13. The Board has lately taken to adopting a number of "protective" policies for the district. Examples include: a

policy requiring male teachers to wear ties and jackets. No teacher may have beards and/or mustaches, and the hair must be neatly trimmed. The mailboxes are off-limits for Teacher Association literature. A statement is adopted discouraging the active role of teachers in local politics . . . and so forth. You are not exactly ecstatic about some of these policies, and now it has come to your attention that a young history teacher is going to campaign as a candidate for the town council. What is your action?

A. Call in the teacher, try to discourage the candidacy, and warn the teacher of the policy in effect.

B. Say nothing to anyone, hoping that the Board will not feel that the policy is enforceable in this case.

C. Go immediately to the Board, inform them of the actions, and point out that the teacher is probationary and therefore relatively easy to release.

D. While ostensibly taking a neutral stance, you openly support the candidacy in a staff meeting, feeling that this might be an excellent way to get at what is, in truth, a dubious Board policy.

E. None of the above, but rather: _____

_____

14. Each year the American Legion, in cooperation with the Coca-Cola distributors, offers - free of charge - bookcovers for the children in your district. Aside from one Coke symbol and a few patriotic quotations, they are unmarked and in school colors. How do you handle these bookcovers?

A. By offering them on a first-come, first-serve basis.

B. By passing them out, on a rationed basis, to all the children in the district.

C. By sending them back, with a note of thanks, to the donors.

D. By keeping the covers, but also by accidentally "filing" them in a place where they don't get distributed.

E. None of the above, but rather: _____

_____

15. The competition for teachers, especially in the critical subject matter areas of reading, math and science, is always keen. Because of the economic limitations in your district-- as in neighboring districts--salary schedules are generally

below state averages. This in turn means you sometimes have to bargain with individual candidates in these critical subject areas, and the resulting salary offers often exceed what is called for by the local salary schedule. This puts the new teacher some dollars ahead of the already employed teachers of similar training and/or experience. The situation has come up again: your science teacher in chemistry has left, and the best candidate you have unearthed will come, but not at the salary the schedule calls for. How can you fill this critical teaching position?

A.  Try to find some other way of making the job attractive, such as rearranged class load, unique fringe benefits, emphasizing the local scenery.

B.  Offer whatever salary is necessary, on the assumption that superior teaching will overcome possible staff grumbling at the extra pay differential.

C.  Continue the search, hoping that an adequate teacher will be attracted by the salary your schedule calls for.

D.  Look at your current staff to see if someone can be retained for the critical science job, and thus making it possible for you to recruit in a less critical and therefore less competitive market.

E.  Continue to offer the job at the proper step, but indicate that rather substantial "merit" increases will be forthcoming after some time on the job.

F.  None of the above, but rather: _____

_____

## AN ANSWER KEY FOR THE QUESTIONNAIRE

The following Table is a "key" to the questionnaire.  In the first
column   are   listed   the   numbers   of   the   anecdotes   on   the
questionnaire.   Column 2 has the most ethical response among   the
choices   offered.    And the third column contains the section from
the AASA Code of Ethics upon which the anecdote is based.

| ANECDOTE | MOST ETHICAL RESPONSE | "CODE" REFERENCE |
|---|---|---|
| 1 | B | 4-B |
| 2 | D | 8A, 8E |
| 3 | D | 9-D |
| 4 | A | 5-E |
| 5 | D | 7-A |
| 6 | B or C | 4-D |
| 7 | A or E | 1-C |
| 8 | B | 1-A |
| 9 | B | 8-E |
| 10 | D | 8-J |
| 11 | A | 2-C |
| 12 | B | 1-A |
| 13 | A | 6-A |
| 14 | C | 4-C |
| 15 | A | 1-A |

## FOOTNOTES

[1]American Association of School Administrators, Code of Ethics, 1962.

[2]Jerome Carlin, Lawyer's Ethics: A Survey of the New York City Bar (New York: Russell-Sage, 1966).

[3]American Association of School Administrators, Profile of the School Superintendent, 1960.

[4]Joseph Fletcher, Situation Ethics: The Morality (Philadelphia: Westminister Press, 1966).

[5]Victor Obenhaus, Ethics for an Industrial Age: A Christian Inquiry (New York: Harper and Row, 1965): p. 2.

[6]Roald Campbell, John Corbally, and John Ramseyer, Introduction to Educational Administration (Boston: Allyn and Bacon, 1958).

# A CASE STUDY ON SEXISM

## Carol Sarvello

In a rural area of Wildcat County athletics, especially at the high school level, play a vital role in the community. The building of community spirit, and the fostering of competition are two aspects of the role of organized sports. In Wildcat County, during the past five years both the football and basketball teams have won the state championships.

Like many other counties during the past few years a declining enrollment plus poor economic conditions forced the school board of Wildcat County to begin the process of budget cutting. Over the years the teachers had negotiated a contract that included an agreed upon provision and procedure for terminating teachers. During the past year the school board began the difficult process of cutting academic programs. This led to implementing the procedure to begin terminating teachers. This procedure was based on a seniority list of names plus school program demands. The procedure also had a recall provision.

For eleven years Ms. Jeans and Mr. Blue team-taught the elementary school physical education courses. Three weeks prior to the beginning of the fall term, Ms. Jeans was notified by phone that her position had been terminated. Two days later official written notification was provided. Mr. Blue had three years seniority over Ms. Jeans. He would teach the physical education courses with the help of a woman locker room assistant.

During this three week period the position of high school boys' physical education teacher/boys' varsity basketball coach was posted. Since Ms. Jeans was certified to teach K-12 and since she had just lost her position, according to the contract procedure for recalling terminated teachers, she should have been automatically appointed to this teaching/coaching position. This was not done. However, Ms. Jeans applied for the position and initiated a grievance procedure against the school board for not following the process outlined in the contract.

When the members of the school board were informed of Ms. Jeans' actions, the board president called a closed session (which was not legal) to discuss the turn of events. The day after the board met, Ms. Jeans was offered her original position and a Mr. Green was hired for the high school physical education/varsity coach position.

## Questions To Help Discussion

1. Does community sentiment play a greater role in this case than legal contracts? Why?

2. Where was the Superintendent of Schools during this battle?

3.   Should Ms. Jeans fight to win the teaching/coach position or settle for her old job?

4.   The   issue of sexism is obvious,   however,   look   at   this issue from the perspective of:
  A.   School Board;
  B.   Community;
  C.   Teachers – Male and Female;
  D.   Legal aspects of contract;

# A CASE STUDY:  RACE RELATIONS

## Michael Katz

## Introduction
In this situation a principal must decide how to deal with a desegregation task force leader whose attitude and conduct undermine the purposes of the task force.

## Description of the Situation
In September 1983, Mr. James Harris, the principal, formed a task force to develop and implement a plan for promoting interracial understanding among teachers and students in Johnson Elementary School. This school was desegregated in the previous year and transformed from an all-white school to one whose student population consisted of 60% Whites, 40% Blacks, and 10% Hispanics. Mr. Harris has been appointed principal two years ago and has received strong backing for this promotion from the Associate Superintendent, Robert Carson, a former colleague of Mr. Harris' at Blair Elementary School. When the task force was being formed, Mr. Carson persuaded Mr. Harris to ask John Waters to chair the work of the task force. Mr. Waters was a teacher at Johnson Elementary School and was married to Mr. Carson's sister, June.

Mr. Waters' selection to the task force angered several Black leaders of the community and a few of the liberal teachers as well, for Mr. Waters had been personally opposed to desegregation and busing for many years (although he had not been outspoken in his opposition).

Several Black community leaders wrote letters to the editor of the newspaper expressing their concern. Others contacted members of the Superintendent's staff and Mr. Harris to note their disapproval of Mr. Waters.

Mr. Waters' conduct as task force leader gave substance to the concerns of the Black leaders. At the first and second meeting of the task force, he made several racial and ethnic slurs about "uppity Blacks." Moreover, he cancelled two meetings at the last minute for personal reasons and appeared forty minutes late at still another. He expressed little enthusiasm for the goal of the task force and at one point questioned its legitimacy. Finally, Mr. Waters spoke disparagingly of several task force members who wished to develop an ambitious program of teacher-led workshops to raise racial and ethnic consciousness about the cultural backgrounds of the school's Blacks and Hispanics.

By December, no plan for developing and implementing interracial understanding among teachers and students had been constructed. Moreover, several members of the task force had begun to complain to the principal about Mr. Waters' conduct as a leader. One of them claimed that his racial insensitivity made it difficult, if not impossible, to accomplish one of the central goals of the task force--to promote respect for persons of different cultural backgrounds. The failure of the task force to develop a plan contributed both to widespread rumors about the intentions of the principal and to increased anxiety among the teachers and parents about desegregation.

## Analysis:  Topics for Consideration
### 1.  The Moral vs. Self-interested Point of View

Moral philosophers, especially those whose perspective is categorized as "deontological," often distinguish between doing what is right (i.e. acting in accord with some fundamental moral rule or principle) and acting purely out of self-interest (i.e. acting to enhance one's own personal interest). Individuals who act out of self-interest, for example, seldom are willing to take risks which may harm their position. On the other hand, to assume a moral point of view is to ask "What is the morally right thing to do?" This point of view suggests that one's choice should be, in some sense, detached or rationally arrived at. To strive for the moral point of view is to strive for a choice one would want to generalize for others acting in a very similar situation.

Moral rules and principles may not dictate one's choice of an action but they can guide one's decision-making conduct. Among one's moral considerations, one may find some version of the following principles:

A)    Show Respect for Persons!

Treat people as ends in themselves, not as means. Do not use or exploit people for one's own purposes; do not treat them with contempt or indifference. Treat each person as an individual with dignity, i.e. as a creature endowed with moral worth.

B)    Benevolence

Do unto others as you would have them do unto you (Golden Rule); consider the well-being of others in one's decision.

C)    Do Not Intentionally Harm People*

(This is the correlative of the benevolence principle.)

In this case, it is important to consider whether or not Mr. Waters' conduct is morally suspect. Has he violated certain moral rules or principles? If so, how has he done so? What kind of moral interpretation do we want to place on his conduct. How reprehensible is it?

### 2.  Intentions and Consequences
Different approaches to moral theorizing place different weight on the respective roles of intentions and consequences in making and justifying moral judgments. Nonetheless, it is plausible to argue that the intention one has should play a role

---

*Other moral rules often appealed to are "telling the truth" and keeping one's promises.

in making moral judgments. For example, we do distinguish between murder in the first degree (with premeditative intent) from murder in the second degree (no premeditative intent), although the outcome is the same--a dead person. Similarly, we distinguish between first and second degree murder and manslaughter on the basis that manslaughter implies no intent to kill.

Thus, in our case study, we may ask whether Mr. Waters intends by his actions to undermine the task force and whether such a consideration is important. We might also ask whether punishing Mr. Waters for his irresponsible conduct (cancelling meetings, showing up late) would be a morally acceptable intention on the part of either the principle or other teachers? What conclusion do we draw about the teachers who complained to the principal? Did they act morally? Do we need to know more about their intentions before we can decide?

In considering the consequences of a decision, we are often faced with balancing different kinds of consequences. Many decisions have different types of consequences and not all of them may be commensurate with each other. For example, if a decision were to be made to dismiss Mr. Waters from the team (depending of course on how the dismissal is made and interpreted), this action will have different effects for the following: 1) Mr. Waters; 2) the individual members of the Task Force; 3) the Task Force as a Whole; 4) other teachers and students in the school; 5) the Principal himself; 6) the community members who opposed Mr. Waters' selection to head the Task Force; and 7) Mr. Waters' family members, his friends, and his supporters in the community.

Most decisions have both short-term and long-term consequences. Although the short-term consequences may sometimes be easier to predict than the long-range consequences, neither set of consequences are completely predictable or subject to control. In this regard, some uncertainty usually accompanies our predictions of what the results of our decisions will be -- both the immediate and long-range results. In the case of Mr. Waters, what are the immediate and long-range results of 1) letting him continue in his job; 2) replacing him as the Task Force leader? What other choices are available.

3.    The Way in Which Decisions are Made

Decisions are not only made, but they are made in certain ways. The way a decision is made will usually be extremely important -- perhaps as important as the content of the decision itself. In this case study, if the principal decides to discuss the Task Force and Mr. Waters' conduct with him before making a decision, how will such a discussion proceed? For example, will the principal listen in a caring and open-minded way? Or will the principal listen to Mr. Waters out of courtesy, having already made up his mind in advance? Or will the principal approach Mr. Waters with accusations and contempt.

If a decision to dismiss Mr. Waters is made, how will it be communicated to him? Will he be given a written notice of the decision? Will the decision and its rationale be explained to him before it is announced? Will the decision be discussed openly with others after it is made?

In raising such questions, we call attention to the ethical importance of the style and manner of decision making itself. In the law, the notion of "due process" is often invoked to underline the importance of the values of "fairness." Fairness involves the effort to hear both sides of the story before making a decision (which may be punitive); it involves not presuming someone guilty until he/she is proven to be in the wrong. It involves giving someone who is charged with misconduct the opportunity to a fair, impartial hearing with legal representation.

Individuals will and should react not only to the content of decisions but to the process leading up to and following them. Was the decision made in a way that showed consideration (or even compassion) for those involved? Or was the decision made insensitively? The way we arrive at our decisions and the way we communicate them have significant ethical implications that should not be ignored.

## 4. A Concluding Note on the Interpretive and Human-Relations Elements in Ethical Decision Making

It should be clear at this point that the questions raised in the previous sections illustrate the importance of interpreting a situation prior to making a decision. The "facts" of the case are seldom so objectively given that two rational people might not disagree about the significance or meaning that should be given to these facts. Interpreting why someone acted is often a very subjective affair, one not lending itself to experimental validation. Similarly, assessing the consequences of one's decisions is usually a matter of educated guessing, not scientific prediction.

Wise decisions demand good judgment, but such good judgment seems predicted upon an understanding of what makes individuals act as they do. Understanding what makes individuals act as they do is psychological matter, but not one that can be dismissed because of its subjective dimensions. Quite the contrary. We must remember that administrative decisions alter the nature of organizations and the nature of the human relationships that exist within them. However much we may want to construct organizations on some model of impersonality, we must remember that human beings exists in relationship to other human beings. The sustenance of human relationships based on fairness, concern for others, and decency lies at the heart of ethical decision-making.

The following questions may help you in analyzing the ethical issues involved:

1. Put yourself into the principal's shoes. What is the nature of your ethical concern about Mr. Water's "alleged conduct?"

2. What should you do? What options are available to you?

3. How would you explain and justify your choice on ethical grounds?

4. In making your decision, how would you balance your concern for the task force with your concern for Mr. Waters as a teacher and a person?

# MORGAN JUNIOR COLLEGE

## Scott Fisher

The maintenance crew arrived in President Adams' office as scheduled at exactly 2:00 P.M., December 10, 1974, to set up the furniture, display easels, overhead projector and screen for the College's annual meeting of the Board of Trustees. They followed the usual routine finishing quickly, glad to retire from the Boardroom atmosphere already made tense and oppressive by the deep scowl on the President's brow. It was just as well that they, the faculty, and the students were not privy to the agenda that day. It promised to be one of the most significant meetings since the college's founding in 1903.

Morgan Junior College was originally organized as a proprietary institution boasting 13 students in its first entering class. The college was established to teach business skills of shorthand, typing, bookkeeping, and penmanship to enhance the employment opportunities of its students. Virtually all of the original students were first-generation collegebound. For the most part, they were sons and daughters of the European immigrants who arrived in great numbers around the turn of the century..

Enrollment grew, branch operations were established, and except for the depression years a general trend of healthy growth prevailed. By 1974, the college had settled in the heart of a metropolitan city, became non-profit, was regionally accredited by the New England Association of College and Schools, and offered 17 Associate in Arts or Associate in Science degree programs. Its tradition in business education still prevailed. Over 60% of its students were enrolled in business and secretarial programs. The remainder pursued liberal arts or allied health majors.

The college's original mission had remained intact. A standard glossy college catalogue gave the familiar description of lofty goals and purpose, but it all boiled down to what the president liked to refer to as "a meat and potatoes education", that in two years prepared students for the job market and gave them the skills to seek employment successfully. College personnel were very proud of their results in this regard and boasted a 100% placement record for all graduates seeking employment. It was felt that this was a unique feature of the college, demonstrated its excellence, and made it stand almost alone among other colleges. Graduates transferred all credits without difficulty to almost every senior college in the nation.

Corporate policy was formed and revised by a formidable and diverse Board of Trustees, most of whom were chief executive officers in their institutions and companies. Presidential-Board rapport was excellent, but the independent attitude of trustees always kept President Adams on his toes.

In 1966, the college registered 507 students, the highest enrollment in its history. Unfortunately, the rate of incoming students did not keep pace with the successful placement of outgoing graduates. The following year, 1967, showed a decline in enrollment and so did almost every successive year thereafter, including the current September 1974 registration. National projections and the consistency of the enrollment decline, despite two changes of Admissions Directors, worried the President. Similar trends were being recorded nationally in most of the other 250 independent two-year colleges. Despite hip-shooting last-minute changes such as single sex to coed or two-year to four-year, a number of those colleges had closed their doors forever.

Morgan Junior College had for years, during its growth, relied on tuition and fees as its sole source of funds. Realistically two-year women's colleges had nowhere else to look for significant funding. Two-year graduates generally went into the job market at nominal salaries with limited long-range potential for executive-level compensation. Graduates continuing their education at a four-year college, tended to give to the baccalaureate institution, if they gave at all. Married alumnae giving usually flowed to the husband's alma mater. Nevertheless, Morgan maintained contact with it's alumni, and annually asked for contributions. Each year averaged $3-4,000. In 1968, a major alumni giving campaign was held and $30,000 was given or pledged. The following year contributions returned to their previous level. Successive alumni newsletters and mailings were considered worthwhile in the hope that alumni would remember the college and recommend that young women whom they knew might enroll.

Due to the singular source of funding, a "hand to mouth" financial condition prevailed. Some years brought a modest surplus, others a deficit. Commercial borrowing during the lean summer months in anticipation of September income was the order of the day. As enrollments were building in the early 60's, surplus income resulted. A peak $176,000 surplus was recorded in 1966. Then, following the pattern of enrollment, decline and deficits became more familiar. It had been possible during the period of prosperity to purchase 13 buildings grouped along two streets in a prestigeous neighborhood. The bulk of the property was in one consolidated parcel overlooking the Silver Bow River. By 1974, three of these buildings, used as dormintories, were being sold to meet operating capital needs. The fiscal year ending August 31, 1974, showed an additional deficit of $103,000. The current year budget projected another $111,000 deficit.

In 1968, the President had hosted 15 partners from large legal firms in the city. These firms looked each year to graduating classes of legal secretaries to fill vacancies. A tour of the premises was followed with luncheon, and a general discussion about the college. There was a clear suggestion of willingness on the part of the college to accept any donations that the firms might like to extend. None were subsequently forthcoming.

In 1974, development consultants were hired for a one-year contract to research and make contacts for the President with potential foundation or corporate donors. The President exercised a six-month escape provision when nothing had been achieved nor in his opinion such seemed likely in the second six-months. Tuition and fees were discussed each year, as a possible source of additional revenues. Despite periodic increases, the college tuition seemed only to be able to maintain a relative position of just under the median of charges by similiar institutions. The raises tracked, pretty well, the general inflation rate and did not provide the additional revenue desired.

From time to time it was rumored that an alumna had become wealthy by marriage, inheritance, or other means and perhaps would look kindly upon the college. Several of these rainbows were pursued, but no pot-of-gold discovered.

Consortium efforts with other colleges to lower overhead expenses always deteriorated to cooperative, bulk-buying of common commodities such as paper, computer service, or fuel oil. The savings projected were meager and compared unfavorably with the more serious loss of individual institutional flexibility. Several institutional mergers had been explored, these could be classified in two categories. The first were healthy institutions (generally large colleges or universities), willing to accept the college as a donation, probably for liquidation. The second were smaller colleges, desperately weak themselves, seeking strength through consolidation. Careful evaluation of the latter category had convinced the President and Trustees that two weaks probably do not make a strong.

Congress, alarmed by the number of college closings in the early 1970's, provided in the 1972 Educational Amendments, an emergency fund for distressed colleges, but had not provided the corresponding appropriations. No State aid of this type existed for independent-colleges, nor did existing legislation provide any means whereby a two-year private college could become part of the community college-system. These three government-related refuges had been explored by a similar institution in the same state, before it closed in the summer of 1972.

The information illustrated here had been reviewed in fragmented form at every trustee meeting since 1966, but received its most comprehensive attention at the meeting on October 1, 1974. The President concluded the presentations of his chief administrators with the statement, "It is not economically feasible for Morgan Junior College to continue its current type of operation." "By judicious management of assets and lean budgets" said the President, "we will cease educational operations in two, possibly, two and one-half years with virtually no assets after liquidation." "The timing depends on how well we manage the decline." Following some further discussion of the components, the trustees reached a consensus that the President's statement was essentially accurate. A motion was made, seconded and voted to have the President clarify and present the options for the college at the annual meeting two months hence.

With one hour left before the annual board meeting, the President reflected on all the data collected, opinions offered by staff, trustees, and peers. Much information was available nationally and locally and the President felt he knew the limits of his own institution. While the trustees were in the same dilemma, they expected the President to make a serious recommendation for guidance. No new information had been uncovered to alter the judgement expressed at the last meeting.

At a critical time in the college's life for whom should the decision be made? The Trustees?, The Alumni?, Current Students?, Current Faculty?, The General Public?, The Higher Education Industry? Three rational choices had emerged over the past two months.

1. Plan A - A managed termination of operations to cease this summer or next so that all constituencies affected could plan adjustment well in advance. The college could maintain its present form to the end, preserving its dignity, its image and tradition. One Trustee had referred to such a plan as "Dying in Genteel Poverty."

2. Plan B - Continue to run as long as possible (presumably this meant until payrolls could no longer be met), and then ceasing operations abruptly. The advantage of this would be to keep open any opportunity to exploit some unforseen relief, governmental or private. The major disadvantage was that the condition of the college must remain secret until the last moment to prevent a faculty and student exodus. Unfortunately, a sudden cessation would appear unplanned and irresponsible. Students and faculty would be left high and dry with partial credits and uncompleted contracts. Alarmed creditors would grasp at any available asset. The media would blow the affair out of proportion, and the fine traditions and reputation which had taken almost 75 years to build, would be torn asunder to become an ignominious memory. Not a pretty picture, but perhaps this plan would keep hope alive longer than plan A. . . "just in case."

3. Plan C - A recent development. Two "consultants" one recently an assistant basketball coach at Harvard, the other a free-lance advertising agent had submitted a proposal to President Adams. Their scheme was based on a recent raise in Veteran's educational benefits. The consultants proposed to act as exclusive managers of a new division of the college, market G.I. Bill benefits by advertising, phone calling, and direct mail. They said, the benefits plus the college reputation and degree authority would attract hundreds of students. They predicted that full-time enrollment would triple in the first year.

Tripling enrollment seemed too good to be true perhaps even miraculous. Adams pondered what alumni, students, faculty, trustees and general public would think of such a commercial approach. If the plan succeeded, the 15% of gross and five-year contract that the consultants requried seemed no barrier. If it didn't succeed, the seed money and disruption of all factions might hasten the closing date a year or so. This course of action was risky to say the least.

As Chairman Granville Custis Nickels raised his gavel to convene the Annual Meeting, President Adam's recommendation remained uncertain.

# IROQUOIS PUBLIC SCHOOLS

## A Case Study Concerning Ethics
## and Practical Politics

### Ira W. Krinsky

> Ben, if you support this, you'll really
> be in for it!

As Dr. Benjamin Peterson looked back over his four years as Superintendent of the Iroquois Public Schools, he most vividly remembered the events which led the School Board President to make the above statement to him. These events led to Peterson's ultimate firing and subsequent 18-month agonizing job search.

## The Community

Iroquois, New York, is a predominantly white, middle-class suburban community located approximately 35 miles north of New York City in Northview County. There are thirty thousand residents, most living in private homes and many are executives in corporations located in New York City or owners of small businesses throughout Northview and neighboring counties. Politically, Iroquois has been in sharp contrast to its neighbors within Northview County. While most of Northview and the better part of twelve adjacent counties have been solidly Democratic, Iroquois has been the scene of a very strong Republican come back. Some explain this phenomenon as being directly related to the prevailing strength of the Conservative Party, which dates back to the late 1940s. Others, explain it as a community backlash to the progressive fiscal policies of the Democratic Northview County Legislature, which has had an especially strong impact on the taxes of Iroquois home owners.

## The Schools

The Iroquois Public Schools are governed by a seven-member Board of Education which is elected at large for three year terms of office. Terms are staggered such that there are usually no more than two seats up for election in any year. School budget elections occur concurrently with the Board elections. Although the amount of State Aid to Education being received by Iroquois has remained fairly constant, expenses have increased and elementary school enrollment has begun to decline. The Board was most concerned about these conditions, and in choosing Benjamin Peterson as their new Superintendent in 1972, they had hoped that his background in PPBS (Planning Programming Budgeting System), labor relations, and school management, would help improve the efficiency and effectiveness of the schools.

When the Board unanimously voted not to renew Dr. Peterson's contract in 1976, six of the seven votes cast against him came from members of the same Board that hired him four years earlier. As Iroquois was solidly Republican, it came as no surprise to Peterson that the Iroquois Board of Education was also solidly Republican. For the first two years of his tenure as Superintendent, this did not seem to be of any significance to him. It eventually led to his downfall!

## The Problem

In 1974, Paul Rogan, a twenty-four year old resident of Iroquois defeated incumbent congressman Charles Hauser for one of the New York seats in the United States House of Representatives. Rogan was a Democrat, and a graduate of Iroquois High School. He narrowly defeated Hauser who had served his constituancy for five successive terms. Hauser's elections were usually won by safe margins and some felt that this had caused him to become complacent about campaigning during election years.

When asked why Rogan managed to defeat Hauser, Ben Peterson said the following:

> Rogan is a young Irish/Italian American -- and he played it for all it was worth. What followed was a bizarre series of events: the complacency of Hauser, who didn't even canvass that year; the fact that two newspapers, the influential Northview Press and the local Iroquois Lamplighter; strongly supported the Rogan candidacy; and the large crossover voting which a young Irish-Italian candidate attracted, were just enough to push him over the top.

Marshall Frank was the President of the Iroquois Board of Education. He was also a very close personal friend of Charles Hauser. The two had served together as naval officers during the 1950s. Frank was shocked and a bit annoyed by the defeat of his long-time friend. Also distressed by the election results was Board Vice President, Richard Hutchins. Hutchins had always been active in partisan politics and in 1972 was a member of the Republican National Committee.

Board members Stephen Gersten and Carl Polilli were also staunch Republicans. Both were early Rockefeller supporters and Gersten had worked in every Rockefeller gubernatorial campaign since 1960. Polilli was also a personal friend of Hauser and shared Marshall Frank's annoyance over the entire situation.

Board member Samuel Post was a long-time member of the Iroquois Board of Education. Post had grown up in Iroquois and had been an Honors Graduate in Veterinary Medicine at Ohio State. He returned to Iroquois after World War II to begin one of the first Veterinary Medical Clinics in Northview County. Approximately equalling his devotion to animals is his commitment to the Northview Conservative Party, having been its first and only president. For the last ten years, the Conservative Party had been among the staunchest supports of Republican Charles Hauser.

Another Conservative Republican was Board Member Alfred Gordon. He too supported Charles Hauser and was also a personal friend. Finally, Sylvia Barber, the newest Board member, was an independent voter whose family was friendly with the Hauser family through the local church.

One plank in the Rogan platform was a commitment to improving job opportunities for young people. Shortly after his first victory over Hauser, Rogan decided to sponsor a Job Fair targeted at the teenagers of Iroquois. Planned were information booths, guest speakers, local businessmen, and career and vocational counselors from the New York State Division for Employment Security. Rogan and his staff submitted a routine "Building Use Request" through the Business Office of the Iroquois Public Schools. The request was routinely approved and forwarded to the Superintendent for his review. All requests are then submitted to the Board for final review and approval.

Ben Peterson:

> I only vaguely recalled initialing Rogan's request. It was probably in a pile with 20 or 30 others. The Board's clerk picked it up and entered it on the agenda for Monday's regular Board meeting. The next thing I heard about it was at 11:15 p.m., Monday, when we reached the part of the meeting entitled 'Requests for Use of Facilities.' Then all hell broke loose!

As the Business Manager was making some random comments about several requests, Board Vice President Richard Hutchins asked Ben Peterson to explain why he (Peterson) had approved a request for the use of an Iroquois Public School Building for a political function? Board members Samuel Post and Alfred Gordon joined in and began to lambast Peterson who was taken completely by surprise by this interrogation. Peterson explained that he saw the event as a youth activity -- not a political activity, and he therefore saw no reason whatsoever to reverse his initial favorable recommendation. Each Board member, in turn, disagreed. The heated discussion on the issue ended with Board President Marshall Frank making the following motion, which was seconded and approved unanimously:

> That the request for the use of the Iroquois High School Gymnasium submitted by Mr. Paul Rogan be tabled pending further review by the Board of Education.

To Ben Peterson, the support of the Job Fair became an issue of principle -- and he therefore chose to resist the intense pressure (coming principally from the Board) to reverse his recommendation. Meanwhile, the Board's action was rapidly becoming a community issue as both papers carried front page articles condemning the Board for allowing partisan politics to

interfere with a program which seemed to be beneficial to the
Iroquois teenagers.

Anger and frustration were particularly noticeable at
Iroquois High School. In preparation for the event, the Rogan
staff had developed ample publicity. Posters, advertisements in
the school paper, a town-wide mailing, and 60 second radio
announcements had been successful in generating much interest in
the Job Fair. It was also significant that a large number of
Iroquois High School students were volunteers during the Rogan
campaign. The Board's action was particularly suspect from their
point of view.

Despite Peterson's advocacy of the Job Fair, despite the
support of the press, despite the groundswell of public opinion in
favor of it, and despite pleas, petitions, and (even) threats from
many High School students, the Board took no further action on
either the initial request or the motion. This resulted in the
Job Fair not taking place -- by default.

In the months following the confrontation, things did seem to
settle down in Iroquois. The Board and the staff became immersed
in the annual budget review and the high school students became
concerned with SAT's and college admissions. And although Ben
Peterson felt that he had won a moral victory and managed to
survive the experience, he never assumed that the Board would
forget what had happened.

In 1975, Paul Rogan was again narrowly re-elected to
Congress. While he never again attempted to request the use of
school facilities for youth activities, he did on one occasion
speak (in school) to the juniors and seniors on how a Bill becomes
a Law. He also continued to sponsor events and help Iroquois
teenagers in many ways on numerous occasions. His popularity
among the senior class ('76) of Iroquois High School was
overwhelming. It therefore did not come as any real surprise when
a delegation of students visited the High School Principal to
request that Paul Rogan be the keynote speaker at graduation that
June.

Charles McCarthy had been the Iroquois High School Principal
for twelve years. He reflected on prior student requests for
graduation speakers.

Charles McCarthy:

> In 1968, they came in and requested that Soupy
> Sales be the keynote speaker at graduation!
> They were quite serious, but somehow, reason,
> humor, and Sales' inaccessibility helped us
> get through that one. That summer, the Board
> adopted a policy limiting graduation speakers
> to either the Board President or the
> Superintendent. I think they really did this
> because in those days, we were graduation
> classes of 800 to 1,000 seniors, and we just
> didn't want to sit through hours of speeches.

It was late April. After listening to the students' request

for Rogan, McCarthy explained the Board's Policy on graduation speakers to them. Because of the policy and because he did not wish to establish a precedent for future requests of this nature, McCarthy felt that he could not support the request. When the students left his office, McCarthy telephoned Ben Peterson.

McCarthy:

> Ben, I've just had the senior class officers in my office. They want Rogan to speak at graduation. I explained Board Policy to them, but they didn't seem to accept it. I just thought that you should know.

Peterson:

> O.K., Charlie, but Board Policy not withstanding, what's your view of the issue.

McCarthy:

> Personally, I like Paul -- I had him in class. He's done a lot for the kids and would probably not use the rostrum to make a political speech. However, all fairness, to have Rogan, we'd have to extend an invitation to some Republican office-holder. This would be consistent with existing practice which has been to provide balance on all controversial issues. Frankly, with 900 diplomas to pass out and the probability of a heat wave, thundershower, shortage of chairs or other contingencies, I'd just as soon let it alone.

Peterson:

> Well, let's keep in touch on this one. You know, its not every high school that has access to a Paul Rogan -- what a great role-model he is! How do you think the Board will react?

McCarthy:

> Honestly, Ben, I think they'd even turn down a Republican -- I mean that!

In the days that followed the meeting between the senior class officers and the High School Principal, support for Rogan's appearance at graduation began to mount. The Board was innundated with letters and telephone calls. Charles McCarthy attempted to stay clear of the issue by continuing to support Board Policy. Ben Peterson told the delegation of students who came to see him (with a petition) that he was in the process of considering his position on the matter. The <u>Iroquois Lamplighter</u> featured an article supportive of the idea. The <u>Northview Press</u> did not cover the story. The issue was scheduled for discussion at the May first meeting of the Board of Education.

## The May First Board Meeting

That evening, three hundred parents and two hundred students packed the Iroquois High School auditorium. As the audience filed in, Board President Marshall Frank called Ben Peterson aside.

Frank:

> Ben, what kind of a recommendation are we getting from you tonight on Rogan?

Peterson:

> Marshall, I believe that Rogan would be a good speaker. He's a graduate and a great role model for the kids. He's done many things for the community and he deserves the honor. Besides, we've got that petition with 800 student signatures on it to demonstrate their support.

Frank:

> His presence is a political gesture no matter what he says. We have a policy on this and the entire Board opposes any change. Ben, if you support this, you'll really be in for it!

Agenda items coming before the issue were disposed of quickly. At 8:30 p.m., permission was granted for the president of the senior class to address the Board. After reading a fifteen minute prepared speech which praised Rogan's service to Iroquois and his concern for youth, each Board member was handed a photostatic copy of a petition with 800 signatures. The petition requested that Board policy be set aside in order that Paul Rogan be permitted to speak at graduation. A thunderous applause arose from the audience following the speech.

Marshall Frank then turned to Ben Peterson and asked for a recommendation. Peterson made the following brief remark.

Peterson:

> The only thing that I can add to the speech that we have heard is -- my support.

The audience rose and again applauded -- for five minutes. Marshall Frank then pounded the gavel for order. He then announced that the Board would go into executive session for no more than 20 minutes to discuss the issue. They then adjourned to an adjacent classroom. Ben Peterson was asked to remain outside.

After fifteen minutes, the Board returned to the auditorium and Marshall Frank reconvened the meeting:

Marshall Frank:

> The Chair recognizes Board Vice President Richard Hutchins.

Richard Hutchins:

> I'd like to make the following motion:

> That Board Policy GS-202-4 entitled, Speakers at Graduation, be waived for the purpose of extending an invitation to Mr. Paul Rogan to be the keynote speaker at commencement exercises for the Iroquois High School Class of 1976. Further, that he be asked to limit his remarks to non-political subjects.

Alfred Gordon:

> I second the motion.

Marshall Frank:

> All in favor say "Aye" (unanimous response).
> All opposed. . . (no response) -- the motion is carried.

The audience's roar of approval was thunderous! Exuberent students and satisfied parents dashed out into the parking lot. Cars, over-loaded with students sped off towards Main Street with horns blowing and trailing fire-crackers -- much like what occurs after a football game.

Ben Peterson had 15 months remaining on his contract. It somehow seemed anti-climatic, that evening, when Marshall Frank came over and said, ". . . Ben, I think we should talk. . ."

QUESTIONS

1. Did Ben Peterson have a firm philosophical basis to argue from regarding his requesting space for the Job Fair?

2. Was the Job Fair issue a politically motivated issue?

3. How was Ben Peterson pressured by special interest groups?

4. Discuss Superintendent Peterson's position regarding the Board of Education's policy pertaining to graduation speakers.

5. Should community sentiment play a role regarding altering School Board policy?

# NEGLECTED LANDMARK:  CALIFORNIA'S JACK OWENS CASE

## Charles Tyner

Legal action in the case of Board of Trustees v. Jack Owens came to a halt in October, 1962, three years after Owens, a Susanville, California, teacher, was charged with unprofessional conduct for writing letters critical of the school district to the local newspaper. Owens returned to his teaching. California Teachers Association publications carried brief reports of the final decision, as did a few of the state's and metropolitan papers, and then . . . silence. thus, one of the most important cases in years involving a teacher slipped past before its full story could be revealed or its deeper significance appreciated.

It is difficult to discover why the case did not receive more attention at the time. Some reasonable guesses are possible, of course. The position of the CTA, with over 120,000 members the giant of California educator groups (and the largest state teachers' organization in the country), had been sharply defeated in the courts. Having expended money, energy, and hope in a losing cause, its leaders were understandably reluctant to give further publicity to the case. Also, the supporters of Owens were a tiny minority, lacking the means to broadcast and interpret the victory.

More vital than the reasons why the affair was neglected, however, are the reasons for examining it now. The Jack Owens decision established an important new principle for the profession, but its implications reach, like tendrils of ivy, in many directions. The story of the case bears upon such matters as the nature and use of ethical codes, the function of educational journals, the status of California's nationally-heralded "professional witness" law, the role of the teacher in shaping policy, and the scope of the free-speech clause of the United States Constitution.

In 1955 a bill was passed in the California legislature allowing any teacher organization that had a personnel standards commission and written code of ethics to furnish "professional witnesses" in court cases. The bill was framed -- and shepherded through the legislature -- by the CTA.

The new law excited the CTA. For years teacher organizations throughout the country had had codes of ethics, but they were scarcely more than words on paper. In thirty years the National Education Association had found only one person guilty of violating its code, and his punishment was not exactly shattering: he lost his NEA membership.[1] The "professional witness" law, however, seemed to signal a breakthrough into the realm of responsible professionalism. By sharing with doctors, psychiatrists, and others the legal title of "expert," educators would gain much-needed prestige. Furthermore, when another teacher's conduct was under examination in a courtroom, the educator-expert would, naturally base his opinion on the provisions of the CTA code of ethics. The document would thus acquire tremendous power to control the behavior of teachers throughout the state.

It remained for the CTA to show how the new law would operate. The chance did not come until December, 1958. Then, the organization's Burlingame headquarters received news that two school superintendents, in mountainous, thinly-populated Lassen County had complained about a letter, written by a Susanville junior college teacher and decidedly "unprofessional" in content, which had appeared in the weekly Lassen Advocate. The Jack Owens affair was under way.

That Owens should have become the intended "victim" was ironic. The thirty-nine-year-old teacher was easily the most energetic CTA member in Lassen County. Whether a new teacher needed help moving in his furniture[2] or the teachers in the state's twenty-one northeastern counties clamored for a credit union, Owens was there to do the job. During the two years he taught in Herlong he was vice-president of the local association of elementary teachers. After moving forty miles to teach political science and history at Lassen Junior College in Susanville, he organized the teachers there into a CTA chapter. Twice he was made its president. He served one three-year term as a member of the Board of Directors, CTA Northern Section, and was elected to another just prior to his resignation.[3]

In many California school districts, those who are hired for a fourth consecutive year reach the shelter of tenure. Accordingly, in their third year at a school many teachers keep their mouths shut and stay out of sight. In 1956, however -- his third year at the junior college -- Owens was vigorously presenting to the Board of Trustees the results of a fourteen-month study made of the local high school by the teachers' association. The study pointed to a complex of weaknesses -- poor student discipline, sagging teacher morale, absence of a planned curriculum, and lack of written policies on various matters.[4]

## Board Fires, Then Re-hires Owens

Though it adopted a few of the suggestions accompanying the study, the board was evidently infuriated that so many educational shortcomings had been exposed to public gaze. Owens was informed that he would not be re-hired.[5] At this, the Susanville teachers rallied to his defense. They recommended to the board that Owens be retained; they demanded to know the reasons why he was not going to be given a contract. At first the board answered that it did "not feel it advisable to accept recommendations other than those of the administrators in this sort of personal matter."[6] Then, perhaps sensing the flimsiness of any reasons it might offer, the board backed down and re-hired Owens.[7]

During the first few years in Susanville, Owens had helped organize and became the first moderator of the Public Affairs Forum, a series of town-meeting-like discussions. On December 24, 1958, the Lassen Advocate published a letter from Owens, the same letter that piqued the superintendents. In it, Owens announced that the forum meetings beginning in January would center on the subject, "Education in Lassen County." He also mentioned the difficulties encountered by the public in finding out what the teachers thought of the educational system. "The public has been taught not to listen," he wrote. "It chooses a board (of trustees) who in turn choose an administrator -- who then speaks for everyone." Finding out how things are going becomes a near impossibility, Owens suggested: "Has anyone ever seen . . . an office manager tell his boss that he (the manager) has been doing a poor job?"[8]

Reaction came swiftly. The board contacted Erwin Howlett, the CTA field man in Chico. Shortly thereafter, the chairman of the Northern Section ethics commission invited Owens to attend the commission's January meeting, a two-day affair held in Auburn. The chairman explained that the members of his group were keenly interested in hearing how Owens and the Susanville teachers had solved a particularly touchy ethics problem two years before. Feeling complimented, Owens accepted. He went to Auburn, told the story to the members of the commission, and answered their questions. The next day, the hidden reason for his being invited there came out into the open. The commission asked if he would meet with them again. They wanted to discuss his recent activities, they said. They wanted to talk about the December 24 letter he had written to the Advocate.

Again, Owens accepted. Questioning by the members of the Commission made clear that they were disturbed by what they called the "implied criticism" in his letter. Didn't he realize that he was breaching the CTA code of ethics, specially the section stating that the professional teacher "conducts school affairs through the established channels of the school system"?

Owens replied that there were big problems to be eased in the Lassen County schools. He was convinced that public discussion and examination of the problems would help to effect solutions. As for the code: evidently his interpretation of it was different from theirs. He had the impression, he told them, that the CTA code was often used to smooth things over. Seldom did it cure problems; it only left them to simmer. He saw no reason, he concluded, to discontinue his letter-writing.[9]

The January 21 Advocate contained another letter from Owens, and over the next eight months he and some fellow teachers composed twelve other letters, all of which were printed, over his signature, in the newspaper. His February 4 letter stated his belief that educators, administrators, and the CTA combined to keep the classroom teacher powerless. "I offer for consideration the ethically and intellectually castrated American, first echelon -- the teacher in the classroom," he wrote.[10] A communique appearing on March 4 contained the statement, "The Lassen Union High School and Junior College administration and a part of the Board of Trustees have well illustrated a disease that is rapidly sinking American public education . . . autocracy."[11]

## CTA Sees Chance To Kill Two Birds

Seeing a remarkable chance to validate its code of ethics and its professional witness law at one stroke, the CTA began to work closely with the educational and legal authorities in Susanville. Signs of a combined operation appeared. The Board of Trustees authorized $1,000 for the services of a special legal consultant, who was added to the staff of District Attorney James Pardee, along with another stenographer;[12] District Superintendent L. Vernon Greenleaf persuaded the Susanville Secondary Teachers Association to carry out its own investigation of the letter-writing;[13] and Howlett took an opinion survey of district teachers, placing the results in the district attorney's office for safe-keeping.[14]

The activity against him was duly reported by Owens in a steady flow of letters-to-the-editor. On March 11 he let _Advocate_ readers know that Howlett and Greenleaf were working together to have him dismissed for unprofessional conduct. "Now do you understand why teachers complain bitterly in private but refuse to talk or take a stand in public in opposition to the educator?" he queried.[15]

As Owens left his classroom a little before 3:00 on the afternoon of May 14, he found a deputy sheriff waiting for him in the corridor. The man pushed a paper into his hand and walked away. It was a notice that the board intended to dismiss him at the end of thirty days unless he demanded a court hearing. The notice listed four charges against him -- unprofessional conduct, dishonesty, evident unfitness to teach, and persistent violation of the law. These charges were based on portions of five of the letters Owens had sent to the Lassen newspaper.[16] (Oddly enough, the letter which had first gotten the CTA on his trail, and which the ethics commission had declared was a breach of the ethical code, was not included.)

With a wife, four children, and a comparatively low salary, Owens had no savings. Some of his friends among the teachers and some of the citizens who had helped in starting the forums sprang to his aid. They began soliciting funds for the Owens defense. One of the forum boosters, attorney Harold Abbott, consented to take his case.

The hearing was set for October 7, 1959. During the summer and early fall each side worked furiously to strengthen its legal position and to capture public support. Harold Abbott managed, after a deluge of demurrers, to remove "persistent violation of the law" from the list of charges.[17] Petitions urging the board to reconsider and retain Owens, signed by nearly 700 people, poured in.[18] For the other side, James Williamson of the CTA came to town with a five-member Personnel Standards Commission panel. The panel interviewed forty-two teachers and residents, then released its predictable conclusion: Owens had violated several portions of the CTA code of ethics and was therefore guilty of "unprofessional conduct."[19]

Twice during the same period the board tried to get Owens to quit without a hearing. District Attorney Pardee told him in July that if he resigned the board would see that he had no trouble getting another job. The implied threat was unmistakable, but Owens refused.[20] Then the list of district employees -- and their assignments -- came out in the fall, and Owens could not find his name on it. He hurried down to Superintendent Greenleaf's office. Greenleaf shrugged off his questions. "You've been dismissed," he said. He added that someone else would be teaching Owens' classes, and that even if Owens won his case in court he would never teach his junior college classes again.

"Don't forget," Greenleaf reminded him, "the board can assign you to any position it wishes."[21]

Dazed, Owens phoned Abbott to tell him what has happened. The lawyer rushed out and obtained a court order restoring Owens to the payroll. But he was unable to get him back into the classroom. Each school day Owens had to report to a tiny office in the Lassen High School, sharing it with the attendance clerk. He was given trivial paper work to do, some of it euphemistically labeled "research."[22]

While Owens was marking time, the local residents found themselves gradually being drawn into the battle. Fiery exchanges appeared in the letter columns of the Lassen Advocate, and soon threats of libel suits were whizzing back and forth.[23]

## Owens Sympathizers Pressured

Eventually, subtle but powerful forces were brought to bear on those who were trying to help Owens. An assistant bank manager who openly favored him lost his job. So did an assistant to the county farm adviser whose wife was a fund-raiser. These may have been coincidences, but no one in the Owens camp could be sure. It was certainly no coincidence that the manager of one of the local banks, who resisted the efforts of a wealthy board member to get him to cease his support of Owens, received a telephone call from his main bank office directing him to withdraw from the cause.[24] As the opening date for the trial neared, the number of people working for Owens began to dwindle. Those who hung on had to face an unpleasant fact: Most of the townspeople who had promised to contribute to the defense fund had changed their minds.

Susanville was in such a state by the time the trial began in the Superior Court that the local judge prudently disqualified himself. Seventy-nine-year-old Judge A. Kester Wylie came down from Alturas, near the Oregon line, to try the case.[25]

During the three weeks of the hearing Abbott tried to show that conditions in the area justified Owens' criticisms. His strategy was largely undermined, however, by a shortage of witnesses. Owens, reasoning that one teacher jeopardizing his career at a time was enough, would not ask his colleagues to testify.[26]

It was impossible for the courtroom crowd not to be impressed with the case presented by Pardee, the prosecutor. He and his special consultant, Mrs. Paula Tennant, brought on a steady parade of educational witnesses. They began with the CTA state executive secretary, Dr. Arthur Corey, who informed the court that "any behavior which tends to tear down the profession is unprofessional conduct."[27] He made it clear that Owens' letter-writing was an example of such behavior. F. McElwain Howard, head of the CTA Northern Section, Miriam Spreng and Richard V. Matteson, two of the expert witnesses from the Personnel Standards Commission panel, field man Howlett, and two men from the California State Department of Education followed Corey to the stand. Of the Lassen educators called by the prosecution, one -- whose presence furnished eloquent testimony to the pressures exerted over the summer -- was a teacher who had helped Owens write some his earlier letters.[28]

A major contention of the prosecution was that Owens had violated the CTA code of ethics. With aid of Mrs. Tennant, Pardee also launched a two-pronged assault on the Owens defense. One drive, to prove that things weren't really so bad in the Lassen County district, was weakened somewhat by Abbott's nimble cross-examination, but the second thrust, to challenge the ultimate basis for Owens' beliefs, was relentless and devastating. At one point in the trial Owens admitted that his knowledge of a statement was based on something he had read. The prosecution pounced:

Q. A newspaper account?

A. That is correct.

Q. Therefore you based it on a newspaper account without personal knowledge of how or where or when or under what circumstances it was said?

A. Yes.[29]

Again, a bit later:

Q. And you based your criticism on this news article in the Sacramento Bee?

A. Yes.

Q. The authenticity of which you did not know?

A. Correct.[30]

In another courtroom dialogue, this persistent effort to fix the notion that only personal knowledge is trustworthy was coupled with an obvious attempt to bamboozle Owens. In one of his letters he had stated that in Lassen County "we have serious problems in education." A few lines later he had written, "If we don't see and cure our problems the Russians quite probably soon will; they also will cure us of the 'liberty' habit." Mrs. Tennant began her examination of these statements with a phrase that was becoming familiar:

Q. On what do you base your opinion, that they probably soon will?

A. . . . We have been engaged in a cold war with Russia; in recent times they have made some notable and outstanding achievements known to the public in the scientific area, Sputnik 1, 2, and so on; I have great faith in people, and I feel we will cure our problems, but if the time ever came when we no longer had the internal strength to look out for ourselves I would feel we would quite probably fall to some outside power. I don't personally feel then, nor now, that time will come.

**Mrs. Tennant.** Your honor, I ask that be stricken as not responsive to the question of "probably how soon." He has said "if the time ever comes." Previously he said "probably soon will."

**The Court.** Yes, this is the statement: "If we don't see and cure our problems the Russians quite probably soon will. They will also cure us of the liberty habit."

**The Witness.** If we don't cure our problems; if we don't.

**Mrs. Tennant.** But you did not say "if we don't."

**A.** It is right here.

**Q.** And you continue "quite probably."

**A.** If we don't cure our problems.

**Q.** What is your personal knowledge of the military strength of the United States?

**A.** About what the average citizen's is.

**Q.** What is your personal knowledge of the military strength of Russia?

**A.** Again, the same answer, about what the average citizen's is.

**Q.** What is your training in tactics and logistics of war?[31]

Thus, for 953 pages of recorded testimony, the hearing went on.

The trial over, Jack Owens went back to his tiny office and his piddling busywork. He waited until January 27, 1960, for Judge Wylie to file his findings and conclusions.

## Puzzling Prose But a Clear Verdict

The septuagenarian's decision issued in a Shenandoah of words, rolling on in great tumbling sentences full of curious redundancies ("it seems to me that . . . Mr. Owens was rather beside himself in working in a stratosphere above the ground"[32] and semantic gaffes (". . . the plaintiff in this case, Board of Trustees of the Lassen Union High School District, may dismiss said Jack Owens as a teacher thereof (sic)"[33]. Yet even puzzling and ungrammatical prose did not obscure the verdict: ". . . Jack Owens, by virtue of said five publications aforesaid, which he edited and published, constitute (sic) unprofessional conduct."[34] Judge Wylie did not rule on the charges of dishonesty and evident unfitness to teach.

Wylie indicated that, "ignoring all codes of professional

ethics,"[35] Owens had written letters critical of the district, even though there was "irrefutable evidence that the junior college and the high school are functioning in a proper manner."[36]

When he heard the decision, Owens recalls, he felt "completely humiliated and destroyed."[37] He had a deep sense that further action was futile. Only about $350 had been raised in the fund drive, and that barely covered court costs. Abbott, in Owens' words, "had donated three weeks' time."[38]

Both his supporters and his detractors assumed that Owens would appeal the decision. He did not seriously consider further legal action, however, until, unexpectedly, the money problem was solved. Before the hearing ended more than twenty Susanville citizens had written to the Northern California branch of the American Civil Liberties Union in San Francisco. They urged Ernest Besig, the organization's executive, to jump into the case on free speech grounds. At its monthly meeting in late February, the ACLU's Board of Directors, after hearing Chief Counsel Albert Bendich's opinion that Owens had been deprived of constitutional rights, voted to carry the Owens appeal."[39]

On some California teachers the report that Owens would appeal had a galvanic effect. The California State Federation of Teachers, an AFL-CIO affiliate which, though small, is the CTA's only rival, gave much of the space in an issue of its monthly paper to the case, started a fund-raising drive, and began drafting an amicus brief in his behalf.[40] Seventy-six professors of the University of California at Berkeley proclaimed their "agreement with Mr. Owens' position as presented in the five letters," and sent money to the ACLU.[41]

And now, for the first time, came a faint stirring in the ranks of the CTA. Forty-five members at Capuchino High School in San Bruno, practically in the shadow of CTA headquarters, let James Williamson know that they could see nothing wrong with what Owens had done. They asked for a clarification of the CTA's stand. Instructors at Fresno City College lodged a similar objection.

Williamson made a trip to Fresno first. He explained the CTA position. In answer to questions dealing with the free-speech issue, he shook out Holmes' famous example in the Schenck case: Writing those letters, Williamson insisted, was like falsely shouting fire in a theater and causing panic. Williamson moved on to Capuchino, gave much the same presentation, and once again resurrected the ghost of Justice Holmes. The teachers at both schools listened politely, but they considered his arguments fantastic. The Fresno instructors wrote and distributed a thoroughgoing analysis of the CTA code of ethics, showing its inadequacies as a guide to rational behavior. Capuchino teachers wrote to Dr. Corey assailing the CTA stand; copies of the letters were sent to sixty CTA chapters all over California.[42]

## CTA Presents One Side

Without fuel, the flames of dissent did not spread far. Because they were hearing about the case through skimpy newspaper accounts and CTA releases, most California teachers had to assume that Owens was dead wrong. And the CTA apparently had no desire to let its members hear the arguments on Owens' side. The ACLU's Ernest Besig read the CTA Journal's April article on the Owens affair, thought it tumbled a row of straw men, and wrote the magazine offering to present, in a subsequent issue, the civil liberties argument. He received no answer.[43] Jack Owens wrote to Dr. Corey, protesting what he called "false statements, half-truths, distortions, and glaring omissions of fact" in two Journal articles and demanding space in the September issue to reply.[44] Owens, too, might have saved the postage.

What there was to say for Owens had to be said by the ACLU's Bendich, in legal briefs that few California educators ever saw. Bendich's argument in his opening brief was that dismissing Owens violated constitutional guarantees of freedom of speech, due process, and equal protection of the law. None of the kinds of speech usually restricted -- slander, libel, defamation of character, the use of "fighting words" -- was involved, he asserted. Furthermore, no "clear and present danger" would or did result from the letters.[45] "In other words," Bendich said, "the sole basis for the finding of 'unprofessionalism' would seem to reduce itself to the astonishing fact that a teacher said what anyone else would have an unquestionable and constitutionally protected right to say."[46]

According to James Pardee's brief for the respondent, all the arguements and citations given by Bendich were simply "not in point."[47] Free speech was not the issue. Pardee drew a parallel between Owens' case and two other California cases dealing with firings of public employees for "unbecoming" conduct. One, Board of Education v. Swan, concerned a principal who was ousted for consistently refusing to obey district rules and regulations, and who had referred to the administrators as "henchmen" and to the Board of Education's office as "the little Kremlin."[48] The other, Pranger v. Break, dealt with a civil service employee who lost his job for advocating an illegal strike.[49] Since the CTA code of ethics clearly states what conduct is becoming to a public employee who is a teacher, Pardee argued, and the CTA panel had shown that Owens violated the code, he must be judged "unprofessional."[50]

## Constitution Protects 'Political' Speech

In his closing brief, Bendich was careful to distinguish the Owens case from Swan and Pranger. Relying on Alexander Meiklejohn's now-famous analysis of free speech, Bendich showed that Owens had engaged in "political" speech -- that is, he had presented ideas to the public so that it could consider whether, and if so, how, to change policy in the field of education.[51] Of course, all speech is not protected by the Constitution, Bendich admitted, which is why Pranger lost, but political speech is protected -- another way of saying that it is "free."[52]

While he was at it, Bendich could not refrain from expressing his "shock" at the treatment accorded Owens during the trial -- the persistent inquiry into opinion; the assumption, underlying the prosecution's questioning, that only personal knowledge was worth considering; and the unfair attempts to mislead the witness.[53]

Months passed while the briefs were written and the oral
arguments heard. Waiting for the decision was but one of many
problems Owens faced. He had to sell his 15-acre farm at
Janesville in order to live. After a brief stint as chain man on
a survey crew, he ran unsuccessfully as a Republican candidate for
state assemblyman, then moved to Redding, where he was employed as
a real estate salesman. Someone asked the State Department of
Education to take away his credential on the strength of the Wylie
decision, but the department's Commission of Credentials refused,
holding that "Mr. Owens may be a successful teacher in another
school district."[54] Then Owens' oldest daughter was mysteriously
crippled for several weeks. The doctor who treated her said he
believes her troubles were "a psychological result of this
mess."[55]

## Court of Appeals Files Verdict

It was not until July 26, 1962, that the Third District Court
of Appeals filed its verdict. Justice (now California Supreme
Court Justice) Paul Peek wrote the prevailing opinion, with
Justice Pierce concurring. The opinion paraphrased Bendich's
chief argument: "that one of those limits applicable to his
(Owens') case is his constitutional right to publicly criticize
the educational process, including his superiors, without fear of
losing his teaching position.[56]

"This," the appellate majority declared in a headshaking
phrase, "is too broad a proposition."[57] An employee in public
service, the court explained, does not have a constitutional right
to such employment.

Having shied away from Bendich's position on this point, the
Court of Appeals then proceeded to accept the bulk of his
arguments. They agreed that neither Swan nor Pranger was
controlling.[58] Although conceding that few teachers had appeared
to give evidence in support of Owens' views, the justices added,
"Considering the quasi-inquisitional nature of Plaintiff's trial
tactics and the fact that charges had been filed against
defendant, it is not surprising. . . ."[59]

The court implied that much of the trial had been a waste of
time. The question to which the lower court should have directed
itself was "whether there had been any disruption or impairment of
discipline or the teaching process as a result of defendant's
letters."[60] In other words, the court should have been concerned
not with whether Owens' comments were true but with whether
his making them had disrupted the teaching process.

In reaction to Judge Wylie's praise of the "proper manner" in
which the high school and junior college were being conducted, the
opinion produced its most telling sentence: "Within the
limitations previously discussed (disruption or impairment of
discipline or the teaching process), defendant had the
constitutional right to differ with the court and the
administrators over what is proper management, at least in a
responsible manner."[61]

## Judges Deliver Two Jolts to CTA

Before concluding, the justices took time to deliver the CTA two terrific jolts. The Court of Appeals said that the trail court had been wrong in saying that Owens had ignored "all codes of professional ethics," since Owens and some of the other teachers had stated that their personal codes differed in some respects from that of the CTA. CTA members take no oath to support the code, the appellate court said; nor do they agree to subscribe to it when they join.[62] The justices also said that they had been able to find only a "scintilla of evidence bearing on the decisive issue . . . whether defendant's conduct had resulted in impairment of the teaching process."[63] This "scintilla" was the CTA panel's claim that Owen's letter had created an antagonism which in turn had "caused a rift, which if continued, would undermine the educational program. . . ."[64] But the basis for this claim, the court noted, was never established: no evidence for it was ever submitted in court.[65]

The Court of Appeals concluded by reversing the judgment allowing dismissal.

Jack Owens prepared to resume teaching at the junior college in the fall of 1962. When school opened, however, he was still not in his classroom. In early September Pardee had filed a petition in the California Supreme Court for a hearing on the decision, thereby suspending everything. The CTA, perhaps thinking that its code of ethics and its expert witness law were swirling down the drain, filed a long and agonized brief in support of the petition.

The Supreme Court scheduled October 24, 1962, as the date on which it would give its answer to the petition, but in the first week of October it announced suddenly that it had decided not to grant the hearing.[66]

## Final and Complete Victory for Owens

Finally and completely, Owens had won.

Once the ebb tide turned, the flood was quick and heavy. Owens was promptly reinstated, and the school board gave him $15,545 in back pay.[67] There was a touch of poetry in the fact that Miss Lucille Gansberg was given the chore of announcing his restitution. She was one of the two administrators who had originally reported him to the CTA.[68]

The importance of the Owens affair is not limited to a single aspect. Nearly all of its implications, however, are either legal or professional. At least four legal implications are discernible. One is that the CTA code of ethics (and, presumably, any other code) has no legal standing in cases involving questions of "unprofessional conduct." What else can one assume from the court's view that the personal ethical code of a single teacher carries as much weight as the CTA's standard?

A second legal implication is that the "expert witness" law is not as strong as it was originally hoped. It is quite true, as the CTA has put it, that "nothing in the ruling . . . invalidates the 'expert testimony' procedure of the Personnel Standards Commission."[69] (This was a curious point to seize upon, though. It was not the procedure which the CTA desired to establish in the

Owens case, but the link between the procedure and the code of ethics.) Witnesses, in keeping with the California Education Code, may still be called on "any matter of . . . skill, fitness, competency, performance, or other such professional matter,"[70] but no teacher or administrator can set oneself up as an authority on "personnel standards" – and neither can a professional organization.

## 'Unprofessional Conduct' Better Defined

Of much wider legal import is a third aspect of the case. In Board of Trustees v. Owens the term "unprofessional conduct" was rendered more precise. The appellate court made plain that, barring disruption or impairment of discipline or of the teaching process, the term may not be applied to public criticism, by teachers, of the educational system of which they are a part.

The fourth, and most crucial, legal meaning of the case is this: Teachers have been granted the protection of the First Amendment in circumstances where they had previously been completely vulnerable. As the winning lawyer Albert Bendich said when asked if he thought the final reversal was a victory for free speech: "I think it was. This is the main point -- we now have, for the first time, a decision that says teachers have got free speech rights. Before, the idea was that the teacher was a 'hired hand' who could be fired without looking at the Constitution."[71]

The professional implications may turn out to be even more important than the legal ones. For instance, the history of the entire affair shows the danger in the widespread use of professional publications for persuasive purposes. The inadequate coverage of the issues by CTA publications -- no matter what the reasons -- was a professional disaster. CTA members simply did not have enough information to judge their organization's role in the matter. After Owens and Besig failed to place the opposition's viewpoints in the Journal, teachers and administrators were left with only one frame of reference -- the CTA's -- for interpreting the few facts they had. Worse, after the final decision the CTA seemed to be using its publications to shield its members from the hard facts. Taking the Court of Appeal's comment that the only scintilla of evidence bearing on the central issue was the CTA panel's completely unsubstantiated claim, Action, a CTA newspaper, turned it into an assertion that the District Court "acknowledged that the only valid evidence was contained in the CTA panel's report."[72]

One concept in the teaching profession may undergo a change because of the Owens opinion. A basic assumption in contemporary education is that policy should be formed by boards of education and then enforced by superintendents and principals. Until the Owens case, it has also often been assumed that public discussion of policy, at least on the secondary and primary school levels, is properly initiated and controlled by those in authority, i.e., boards, superintendents, and principals.

Owens effectively challenges the second assumption, and, by earning for teachers everywhere the right to public comment on the policies in effect in their own districts, may also have opened the way to a challenge of the first.

A final lesson which the Jack Owens story provides for the profession lies in the three-year torment which Owens experienced. Though it has not been the purpose of this paper to focus on his mental anguish, sensitive readers will already have guessed what it must have been like for Owens during the long battle to establish what he thought was his right. Those same readers may perceive that, if the status and strength of the profession are ever to be enhanced, teachers must do a great deal more than pay dues, pass resolutions, and huddle together in wishful groups. Like Jack Owens, they must join the company of the brave.

## FOOTNOTES

[1]Myron Lieberman, <u>The Future of Public Education</u>, (Chicago: The University of Chicago Press, 1960), pp. 185-86.

[2]This detail was reported to me by Mr. Byron McCaughey, former Lassen High School teacher who also taught at Capuchino High School, San Bruno, California.

[3]Jack Owens, "The CTA and Me." March 15, 1960, p. 1 (Mimeographed).

[4]Brief of Amici Curiae in Support of Respondent's Petition for a Hearing by the Supreme Court, <u>Board of Trustees of the Lassen Union High School District v. Jack Owens</u>, pp. xii-xiii. (All subsections relate to <u>Board of Trustees v. Owens</u>.).

[5]Appellant's Opening Brief, p. 10.

[6]Ibid., p. 11.

[7]Ibid., p. 10.

[8]Ibid., Appendix A, p. i.

[9]For this account of the trip to Auburn, I have relied upon Owens, pp. 2-4.

[10]Appellant's Opening Brief, Appendix A, p. xi.

[11]Ibid., p. xiv.

[12]Owens, p. 15.

[13]Ibid., p. 9.

[14]Ibid., pp. 11-13.

[15]Appellant's Opening Brief, Appendix A, p. xvii.

[16]Owens, p. 15.

[17]Appellant's Opening Brief, pp. 4-5.

[18]Owens, p. 17.

[19]Ibid., p. 22.

[20]Ibid., p. 18.

[21]Ibid., p. 19.

[22]Ibid., p. 20.

[23]San Francisco Examiner, 28 February 1960.

[24]Jack Owens to Charles Tyner, undated, received in November, 1962.

[25]San Francisco Examiner, 28 February 1960.

[26]Owens "CTA and Me," p. 28.

[27]Appellant's Closing Brief, p. 32.

[28]Owens to Tyner.

[29]Appellant's Closing Brief, pp. 26-7.

[30]Ibid., p. 27.

[31]Ibid., Appendix, pp. iv-v.

[32]San Francisco Examiner, 28 February 1960.

[33]Appellant's Opening Brief, p. 6.

[34]Ibid.

[35]Respondent's Brief, p. 21.

[36]Appellant's Answer to Respondent's Petition for a Hearing by the Supreme Court, p. 4.

[37]Owens to Tyner.

[38]Ibid.

[39]California Teacher, March-April, 1960.

[40]Ibid.

[41]American Civil Liberties Union News, June 1960.

[42]Ibid.

[43]Ibid.

[44]Jack Owens to Dr. Arthur F. Corey, dated May 15, 1960. (Dittoed).

[45]Appellant's Opening Brief, p. 20.

[46]Ibid., p. 23.

[47]Respondent's Brief, p. 31.

[48]Ibid., pp. 25-26.

[49]Ibid., p. 28.

[50]Ibid., p. 32.

[51]Appellant's Closing Brief, pp. 17-18.

[52]Ibid., p. 18.

[53]Ibid., p. 26.

[54]According to a Thermo-Fax copy of p. 4514 of the Minutes of the Commission of Credentials covering the case. Action was taken on March 22, 1960.

[55]Owens to Tyner.

[56]Respondent's Petition for Hearing by the Supreme Court. Appendix A, p. 8.

[57]Ibid., pp. 11-12.

[58]Ibid., pp. 11-12.

[59]Respondent's Petition for Hearing by the Supreme Court. Appendix A, p. 8.

[60]Ibid., p. 8.

[61]Ibid., p. 9.

[62]Ibid., p. 12.

[63]Respondent's Petition for Hearing by the Supreme Court. Appendix A, p. 8.

[64]Ibid.

[65]Ibid., p. 16.

[66]See the ACLU News, October, 1962, and CTA Action, 12 October, 1962.

[67]San Francisco Chronicle, 11 October 1962.

[68]Owens to Tyner.

[69]CTA Action, 12 October 1962.

[70]California, Education Code (1961), Vol.1, Sec.13417, p.584.

[71]Albert Bendich to Charles Tyner, 24 October 1962.

[72]October 12, 1962.

## BIBLIOGRAPHY

### BOOKS

Abbott, Jacob. A Primer of Ethics. Edited by Benjamin B. Camegys. Boston: Ginn and Company, 1891.

Adler, Felix. An Ethical Philosophy of Life Presented In Its Main Out-Lines. New York: D. Appleton and Co., 1918.

Adler, Mortimer and Cain, Seymour. Ethics, The Study of Moral Values. Chicago: Encyclopedia Britannica, 1962.

Anderson, Thomas C. The Foundation and Structure of Sartean Ethics. Lawrence: Regents Press of Kansas, 1979.

Anshen, Ruth N. ed. Moral Principles of Action, Man's Ethical Imperative. New York: Harper, 1952.

Apel, Karl Otto. Analytic Philosophy of Language and the Geisteswissenschaften. Translated by H. Holstelilie. Dordrect, Holland: D. Reidel & Co., 1967.

Aries, Philippe. Centuries of Childhood. Translated by R. Baldick. New York: Vintage Books, 1962.

Aristotle. The Nicomachean Ethics of Aristotle. Translated by F.H. Peters. 9th ed. London: Kegan Paul, Trench, Truber and Co., 1904.

Arrow, Kenneth. Social Choice and Individual Values. New York: John Wiley, 1951.

Arygis, C. Intervention Theory and Method: A Behavioral Science View. Reading, Mass: Addison-Wesley, 1970.

Ashby, Eric. Adapting Universities to a Technological Society. San Francisco: Jossey-Bass, 1974.

Ashworth, Kenneth H. American Higher Education in Decline. College Station: Texas A&M University Press, 1979.

Ayer, Alfred Jules. Language, Truth and Logic. New York: Dover Publications, n.d.

Baier, Kurt. The Moral Point of View: A Rational Basis of Ethics. New York: Cornell University Press, 1958.

Baier, Kurt. The Moral Point of View. New York: Random House, 1965.

Banner, William A. Ethics: An Introduction to Moral Philosophy. New York: Scribner, 1968.

Barbour, Ian G. Science and Secularity: The Ethics of Technology. New York: Harper and Row, 1970.

Barnes, Hazel E. An Existentialist Ethics. New York: Knopf, 1967.

Barrett, Clifford. Ethics: An Introduction to the Philosophy of Moral Values. New York: Harper and Brothers, 1933.

Baumgardt, David. Bentham and the Ethics of Today. Princeton: Princeton University Press, 1952.

Bax, Ernest. The Ethics of Socialism. 3d. ed. New York: C. Scribner's Sons, 1893.

Beauchamp, George A. Curriculum Theory. 4th ed. Itasca, Illinois: F.E. Peacock, 1981.

Bendix, Reinhard. "Bureaucracy and the Problem of Power." In Merton, Robert, et. al. Reader in Bureaucracy. New York: Free Press, 1952.

Benson, J. Kenneth. "Innovation and Crisis in Organizational Analysis." In Organizational Analysis, Critique and Innovation. Edited by J. Kenneth Benson. Beverly Hills: Sage Publications, 1977.

Bentham, Jeremy. An Introduction to the Principles of Morals and Legislation. Foreward by Laurence J. LaFleur, New York: Hafner Publishing Co., 1948.

Bentham, Jeremy. Anarchical Fallacies. In the Collected Papers of Jeremy Bentham. Edited by John Bowring. Vol. 2. Edinburgh, 1843. Reprinted in Human Rights. Edited by A.I. Melden. Belmont, California: Wadsworth Press, 1970.

Berdiaeu, Nikolai A. The Destiny of Man. New York: C. Scribner's Sons, 1937.

Bergson, Henri L. The Two Sources of Mortality and Religion. Translated by R. Ashley Audra and Cloudesley Brercton with the assistance of W. Horsfall Carter. New York: H. Holt and Co., 1935.

Bernstein, Richard J. The Restructuring of Social and Political Theory. New York: Harcourt, Brace & Jovanovich, 1976.

Blau, Peter M. and Scott, W. Richard. Formal Operations. San Francisco: Chandler Publishing Company, 1962.

Blumenthal, Albert. Moral Responsibility Mankind's Greatest Need:

_Principles and Practical Applications of Scientific Utilitarian Ethics_. Santa Ana, Cal: Rayline Press, 1975.

Bok, Sissela. _Lying:  Moral Choice  in  Public  and Private Life_. New York:  Pantheon Books, 1978.

Bourke, Vernon.  _Ethics in Crisis_.  Milwaukee:  Bruce Publishing Co., 1966.

Brandt, Richard B.  _Ethical Theory_.  Englewood Cliffs, New Jersey: Prentice-Hall, 1959.

Brandt,  Richard B.  "Toward a Credible Form of  Utilitarianism." In _Contemporary Utilitarianism_, pp.  143-86.  Edited by M. Bayles.  Garden City:  Doubleday Anchor Books, 1968.

Brandt,  Richard.  _A Theory of the Good and the Right_.  New York: Clarendon Press, 1979.

Breed,  Frederick  S.  "Education  and  the  Realistic  Outlook." Philosophies  of Education.  In the _Forty-first Yearbook  of the  National Society for the Study of Education_.  Edited by Nelson  Bollinger  Henry.  Chicago:  University  of  Chicago Press, 1942.

Brennan,  J.M.  _The Open-Texture of Moral Concepts_.  New  York: Barnes and Noble Books, 1977.

Brett, George.  _The Government of Man:  An Introduction to Ethics and Politics_.  London:  G. Bell and Sons, Ltd., 1920.

Broad,  Charlie. _Five Types of Ethical Theory_.  London:  K. Paul, Trench, Truber and Co., 1930.

Brubacher,  John  S.  _Modern Philosophies of Education_.  New York: McGraw-Hill Book Company, 1962.

Cabot,  Richard.  _The Meaning of Right and Wrong_.  New York:  The MacMillan Co., 1933.

Campbell, Roald,  Corbally, John and Ramseyer, John.  _Introduction to Educational Administration_.  Boston:  Allyn  and  Bacon, 1958.

Carlin,  Jerome.  _Lawyer's Ethics:  A Survey of the New York City Bar_.  New York:  Russell-Sage, 1966.

Carritt, Edgar.  _The Theory of Morals:  An Introduction to Ethical Philosophy_.  London:  Oxford University Press, 1928.

Carter,  Curtis.  _Skepticism and Moral Principles:  Modern Ethics in Review_.  Edited by C.L. Carter.  Evanston, Illinois:  New York University Press, 1973.

Chazan, Barry, comp. <u>Moral Education</u>. Edited by Barry Chazan and Jonas Soltis. New York Teacher's College Press, 1973.

Cicero, Marcus. <u>On Moral Obligation</u>. Berkeley: University of California Press, 1967.

Clark, Gordon and Smith, T., ed. <u>Readings in Ethics</u>. 2d ed. New York: F.S. Crofts and Co., 1935.

Cohen, M.D. and March, J.G. <u>Leadership and Ambiguity: The American College Presidency</u>. New York: McGraw Hill, 1972.

Conover, Charles. <u>Personal Ethics in An Impersonal World</u>. Philadelphia: Westminister Press, 1967.

Crittenden, Brian. <u>Form and Content in Moral Education</u>. Toronto: Ontario Institute for Studies in Education, 1972.

Crittenden, Brian. <u>Education and Social Ideals</u>. Toronto: Academic Press, Canada, 1973.

Crittenden, Brian. <u>Education for Rational Understanding</u>. Melbourne: Australia Council for Educational Research, 1981.

Culbertson, Jack A., Jacobson, Paul B. and Reller, Theodore L. <u>Administrative Relationships</u>. Englewood Cliffs: Prentice-Hall, 1960.

D'Arcy, Eric. <u>Human Acts</u>. Oxford: Clarendon Press, 1963.

Dewey, John. "Aims in Education." In <u>Democracy and Education</u>, pp. 100-110. New York: Macmillan Co., 1916.

Dewey, John and Tufts, James. <u>Ethics</u>. Rev. ed. New York: H. Holt and Co., 1932.

Donagen, Alan. <u>The Theory of Morality</u>. Chicago: University of Chicago Press, 1977.

Dougherty, Kenneth. <u>General Ethics: An Introduction to the Basic Principles of the Moral Life According to St. Thomas Aquinas</u>. Peekskill, N.Y.: Graymoor Press, 1959.

Dror, Yehezkel. <u>Public Policymaking Reexamined</u>. San Francisco: Chandler Publishing Company, 1968.

Duncan, Alistair. <u>Practical Reason and Morality: A Study of Immanuel Kant's Foundations for the Metaphysics of Morals</u>. New York: Nelson, 1957.

Dworkin, Gerald. "Paternalism." In <u>Morality and the Law</u>. Edited by Richard A. Wasserstrom. Belmont, California: Wadsworth, 1971.

Dworkin, Ronald. *Taking Rights Seriously*. Cambridge, Massachusetts: Harvard University Press, 1977.

Dye, Thomas R. *Understanding Public Policy*. 2d ed. Englewood Cliffs, New Jersey: Prentice-Hall, 1975.

Eble, Kenneth E. *The Art of Administration*. San Francisco: Jossey-Bass, 1978.

Edel, Abraham. *Ethical Judgement: The Use of Science in Ethics*. Glencoe, Ill.: Free Press, 1955.

Edwards, Paul. *The Logic of Moral Discourse*. Foreward by Sidney Hook. Glencoe, Ill.: Free Press, 1955.

Eisler, Lee. *Morals Without Mystery*. New York: Philosophical Library, 1971.

Erickson, Millard. *Relativism in Contemporary Christian Ethics*. Grand Rapids: Baker Book House, 1974.

Etzioni, Amitai. *Modern Organizations*. Englewood Cliffs, New Jersey: Prentice-Hall, Inc., 1964.

Ewing, Alfred. *Ethics*. London: English University Press, 1953.

Everett, Millard. *Ideals of Life: An Introduction to Ethics and the Humanities*, with Readings. New York: Wiley, 1954.

Feibleman, James. *Moral Strategy*. The Hague: Martinus Nijhoff, 1967.

Feinberg, Joel. *Social Philosophy*. Englewood Cliffs, New Jersey: Prentice-Hall, 1973.

Feinberg, Joel. "The Rights of Animals and Unborn Generations." In *Philosophy and Environmental Crisis*. Edited by W.T. Blackstone. Atlanta, Georgia: University of Georgia Press, 1974.

Flathman, Richard. *The Practice of Rights*. Cambridge: Cambridge University Press, 1976.

Fleischer, Martin, ed. "A Passion for Politics: The Vital Core of the World of Machiavelli." *Machiavelli and the Nature of Political Thought*. New York: Atheneum, 1972.

Fletcher, Joseph. *Situation Ethics: The New Morality*. Philadelphia: Westminister Press, 1966.

Flew, Anthony. "Ends and Means." The *Encyclopedia of Philosophy*. Edited by Paul Edwards. New York: Macmillan and the Free Press, 1967.

Foot, Philippa. "Goodness and Choice." In The Is/Ought Question. Edited by W.D. Hudson. London: Macmillan, 1969.

Foot, Philippa. Virtues and Vices and Other Essays in Moral Philosophy. Berkeley: University of Cal. Press, 1978.

Forrest, John K. Reality or Preachment, the Moral Crisis of Our Time. Boston: Beacon Press, 1967.

Frankena, William. Ethics. 2d ed. Englewood Cliffs, New Jersey: Prentice-Hall, 1973.

Fried, Charles. An Anatomy of Values, Problems of Personal and Social Choice. Cambridge: Harvard University Press, 1970.

Friedrich, C.J. "Public Policy and the Nature of Administrative Responsibility." In Public Policy, pp. 6-7. Edited by C.J. Friedrich and E.S. Mason. Cambridge: Harvard University Press, 1940.

Fromm, Erich. Man for Himself, An Inquiry into the Psychology of Ethics. New York: Rinehart, 1947.

Fromm, Erich. The Heart of Man, Its Genius for Good and Evil. New York: Harper and Row, 1964.

Fuller, Lon L. The Morality of Law, rev. ed. New Haven: Yale University Press, 1969.

Galbraith, John Kenneth. The New Industrial State. Boston: Houghton Mifflin, 1967.

Garner, Richard and Rosen, Bernard. Moral Philosophy, a Systematic Introduction to Normative Ethics and Meta-Ethics. New York: McMillan, 1967.

Garnett, Arthur. Ethics: A Critical Introduction. New York: Ronald Press Co., 1960.

Gastil, Raymond D. Social Humanities. San Francisco: Jossey-Bass Publishers, 1977.

Gewirth, Alan. Reason and Morality. Chicago: University of Chicago Press, 1978.

Gibb, Jack R. "Dynamics of Leadership and Communication." In Leadership and Social Change. 2d ed. Edited by William R. Lassey and Richard R. Fernandez. La Jolla, California: University Associates, 1976.

Giddens, Anthony. The Class Structure of the Advanced Societies. New York: Harper & Row, 1975.

Giddens, Anthony. "Introduction." Positivism and Sociology.

Edited by Anthony Giddens. London: Heinemann, 1978; Reprint edition.

Gilson, Etienne Henry. _Moral Values and the Moral Life, the Ethical Theory of St. Thomas Aquinas._ Translated by Leo Richard Ward. Hamden, Conn.: Shoe String Press, 1961.

Ginsberg, M. _On the Diversity of Morals._ London: Mercury Books, 1956.

Gladwin, Thomas. _East Is a Big Bird._ Cambridge, Mass.: Harvard University Press, 1970.

Goode, William. _The Family._ Englewood Cliffs, New Jersey: Prentice-Hall, 1964.

Goodrow, F.J. _Politics and Administration._ New York: Macmillan Company, 1900.

Graff, Orin B. and Street, Calvin M. "Developing a Value Framework for Educational Administration." _Administrative Behavior in Education._ Edited by Rose F. Campbell and Russell T. Gregg. New York: Harper and Brothers, 1957.

Habermas, Jurgen. _Toward a Rational Society._ Translated by Jeremy J. Shapiro. Boston: Beacon Press, 1971. (Paperback edition)

Habermas, Jurgen. _Toward a Rational Society._ Translated by Jeremy J. Shapiro. Boston: Beacon Press, 1970.

Habermas, Jurgen. _Knowledge and Human Interests._ Translated by Jeremy J. Shapiro. Boston: Beacon Press, 1971.

Habermas, Jurgen. _Legitimation Crisis._ Translated by Thomas McCarthy. Boston: Beacon Press, 1975.

Habermas, Jurgen. "Rationalism Divided in Two." In _Positivism and Sociology._ Edited by Anthony Giddens. London: Heinemann, 1978, Reprint edition.

Habermas, Jurgen. _Communication and the Evolution of Society._ Translated by Thomas McCarthy. Boston: Beacon Press, 1979.

Hampshire, Stuart. "Public and Private Morality." In _Public and Private Morality._ Edited by Stuart Hampshire. New York: Cambridge University Press, 1978.

Harding, Kaewsonthi, Roe and Stevens. _Professional Development in Higher Education: State of the Art and the Artists._ England: Bradford University Educational Development Service, 1981.

Hare, Richard. _Freedom and Reason._ Oxford: Clarendon Press, 1963.

Hare, Richard M. The Language of Morals. London: Oxford University Press, 1964.

Hare, Richard M. The Language of Morals. Oxford: Clarendon Press, 1972.

Harmin, Merrill, Kirchenbaum, Howard, and Simon, Sidney. Clarifying Values Through Subject Matter. Minneapolis, Mn: Winston Press, 1973.

Hart, Herbert Lionel Adolphus. The Concept of Law. Oxford: Clarendon Press, 1961.

Hartman, Heinz. Psychoanalysis and Moral Values. New York: International University Press, 1960.

Hartmann, Nicolai. Ethics. Translated by Stanton Coit. New York: The Macmillan Company, 1932.

Henry, Jules. Essays on Education. New York: Penguin Books, Inc., 1971.

Hollingworth, Harry. Psychology and Ethics, A Study of the Sense of Obligation. New York: Ronald Press Co., 1949.

Holt, Edwin. The Freudian Wish and Its Place in Ethics. New York: H. Holt and Co., 1915.

Hook, Sidney, ed. Human Values and Economic Policy. New York: University Press, 1967.

Horkheimer, Max. Eclipse of Reason. New York: The Seabury Press, 1974.

Hospers, John. Human Conduct, Problems of Ethics. New York: Harcourt Brace Jovanovich, 1972.

House, E.R. The Logic of Evaluative Argument. Center for the Study of Evaluation, University of California at Los Angeles, 1977.

Hume, David. A Treatise of Human Nature. Edited by L.A. Selby-Bigge. Oxford: Oxford University Press, 1888.

Hume, David. An Enquiry Concerning the Principles of Morals. Edited by L.A. Selby-Bigge. Oxford: Clarendon Press. 1902.

Hume, David. Moral and Political Philosophy. Edited by Henry D. Aiken. New York: Hafner Publishing Co., 1948.

Huxley, Thomas. Evolution and Ethics and Other Essays. New York: D. Appleton, 1897; St. Clair Shores Michigan: Scholarly Press, 196?

Hyde, William. The Five Great Philosophers of Life. 2d ed. New York: The Macmillan Co., 1956.

Illich, Ivan. Toward a History of Needs. New York: Pantheon Books, 1977

International Encyclopedia of Unified Science. 1939 ed. S.v. "The Technique of Theory Construction" by J.H. Woodger.

Jalling, Hans. "Exploring the Organizational and Political Boundaries of Staff Development: Internationalism in Staff Development." Proceedings of the Seventh International Conference on Improving University Teaching. Tokyo, 1980.

James, William. Essays on Faith and Morals. Selected by Ralph B. Perry. Cleveland: World Publishing Co., 1962.

Kaestle, Carl F. The Evolution of an Urban School System, New York City, 1750-1850. Cambridge, Mass.: Harvard University Press, 1970.

Kandel, Isaac Leon. The Cult of Uncertainty. New York: Macmillan Co., 1943.

Kant, Immanuel. Fundamental Principles of the Metaphysics of Ethics. 10th ed. Translated by Thomas Kingsmill Abbott. New York: Longmans, Green and Co., 1934.

Kant, Immanuel. Critique of Practical Reason and Writings in Moral Philosophy. Translated and edited by Lewis W. Beck. Chicago: University of Chicago Press, 1949.

Kant, Immanuel. Groundwork of the Metaphysics of Morals. Translated by H.J. Paton. New York: Harper and Row, Harper Torchbooks, 1964.

Kant, Immanuel. The Metaphysics of Morals. Translated by John Ladd. Indianapolis: Bobs-Merrill, 1965.

Kant, Immanuel. On the Old Saw: That May Be Right in Theory But it Won't Work in Practice. Translated by E.B. Ashton. Foreword by George Miller. Philadelphia: University of Pennsylvania Press, 1974.

Kattsoff, Louis. Making Moral Decisions: An Existential Analysis. The Hague: Martinus Nijhoff, 1965.

Kelsen, Hans. General Theory of Law and State. Cambridge, Mass.: Harvard University Press, 1949.

Keyes, Charles. Four Types of Value Destruction: A Search for the Good Through an Ethical Analysis of Everyday Experience. Washington: University Press of America, 1979.

Kirk, Kenneth. _The Threshold of Ethics_. London: Skeffington and Sons, Ltd., 1952.

Komisar, Paul. "Need and the Needs-Curriculum." _Language and Concepts in Education_. Edited by B. Othanel Smith and Robert H. Ennis. Chicago: Rand McNally & Company, 1961.

Kovesi, Julius. _Moral Nations_. New York: The Humanities Press, 1967.

Kropotkin, Petr. _Ethics, Origin and Development_. Translated by Louis S. Friedland and Joseph Piroshnikoff. New York: B. Blom, 1968.

Labov, William. _Language in the Inner City_. Philadelphia: University of Pennsylvania Press, 1972.

Ladd, John. _The Structure of a Moral Code_. Cambridge: Harvard University Press, 1957.

Ladd, John. "Moral and Legal Obligation." In _Political and Legal Obligation_, Nomos, 12. Edited by J. Roland Pennock and John W. Chapman. New York: Atherton Press, 1970.

Lamson, Peggy. _Roger Baldwin, Founder of the American Civil Liberties Union_. Boston: Houghton-Mifflin, 1976.

Langer, Susanne. _Philosophy in a New Key_. 3d ed. Cambridge, Mass.: Harvard University Press, 1972.

Larrabee, Harold A. _Reliable Knowledge_. Boston: Houghton Mifflin, 1945.

Lasch, Christopher. _The Culture of Narcissism: American Life In an Age of Diminishing Expectations_. New York: W.W. Norton & Co., Inc., 1978.

Lauvas, P. "Perspectives of Inservice Training in Education for Teachers in Norway." _Staff Development for the 1980s: International Perspective_. Edited by D. Rhodes and D. Hounsell. Illinois State University Foundation and the Institute for Research and Development into Post-Compulsory Education at the University of Lancaster.

Leys, Wayne. _Ethics for Policy Decisions, the Art of Asking Deliberative Questions_. New York: Greenwood Press, 1968.

Liberman, Myron. _The Future of Public Education_. Chicago: The University of Chicago Press, 1960; pp. 185-186.

Lockwood, A.L. "Moral Reasoning and Public Policy Debate." In _Moral Development and Behavior_. Edited by Thomas Lickona. New York: Holt, Rinehart and Winston, 1976.

Louch, A.R. "Sins and Crimes." In Morality and the Law. Edited by Richard A. Wasserstrom. Belmont, California: Wadsworth, 1971.

Lyons, David. The Forms and Limits of Utilitarianism. Oxford: Clarendon Press, 1969.

Macdonald, James. "An Image of Man: The Learner Himself." In Individualizing Instruction.Edited by R. C. Doll. Washington, D.C.: Association for Supervision and Curriculum Development, 1962.

Mackie, John. Ethics: Inventing Right and Wrong. Harmondsworth, England: Penguin Books, 1977.

Mackinnon, Donald. A Study in Ethical Theory. London: A and C Black, 1957.

March, James and Simon, Herbert, A. Organizations. New York: John Wiley and Sons, 1958.

Maritain, Jacques. An Essay on Christian Philosophy. Translated by Edward H. Flannery. New York: Philosophical Library, 1955.

Maritain, Jacques. The Person and the Common Good. Notre Dame. Indiana: University of Notre Dame Press, 1966.

Maslow, Abraham H. "Some Basic Propositions of a Growth and Self-Actualization Psychology." In Perceiving, Behaving, Becoming. Edited by A.W. Combs. Washington, D.C.: Association for Supervision and Curriculum Development, 1964.

McCarthy, Thomas. The Critical Theory of Jurgen Habermas. Cambridge, Massachusetts: MIT Press, 1978.

McCloskey, Henry. Meta-Ethics and Normative Ethics. The Hague: Martinus Nijhoff, 1969.

McCloskey, H.J. "The Rights of Parents." In Rights and Inequality in Australian Education, pp. 359-378. Edited by P.J. Fensham. Melbourne: Cheshire, 1970.

Melden, Abraham. Ethical Theories: A Book of Readings. 2d ed. Edited by A.I. Meldon. Englewood Cliffs, New Jersey: Prentice-Hall, 1967.

Merton,Robert, Gray, Alisa, Hockey, Barbara and Selvin, Hanan. Reader in Bureaucracy. New York: Free Press, 1952.

Meyer, G.R. "The Development of Mini-Courses (with a Basis in Educational Technology) for the In-Service Education of Teachers and Trainers." Programmed Learning and Educational Technology 16, 1979.

Midgley, Mary. Beast and Man: The Roots of Human Nature. Ithaca: Cornell University Press, 1978.

Mill, John S., ed. Utilitarianism, On Liberty, and Essay on Bentham. Introduction by Mary Warnock. Cleveland: World Publishing Co., 1962.

Miner, John B. Management Theory. New York: Macmillan Co., 1971.

Mintzberg, Henry. The Nature of Managerial Work. New York: Harper and Row, 1973.

Missions of the College Curriculum: A Commentary of the Carnegie Foundation for the Advancement of Teaching. San Francisco: Jossey-Bass, 1977.

Monro, David. Empiricism and Ethics. Cambridge: Cambridge University Press, 1967.

Moore, George E. Ethics. London: Oxford University Press, 1912.

Moore, George E. Principia Ethica. Cambridge: Cambridge University Press, 1903.

Moore, George E. "The Indefinability of Good." A Modern Introduction to Philosophy. Edited by Paul Edwards and Arthur Pap. New York: Free Press of Glencoe, 1957.

Morris, Charles S. "Axiology as the Science of Preferential Behavior." Value A Cooperative Inquiry. Edited by Ray Lepley. New York: Columbia University Press, 1949.

Mueller, Claus. The Politics of Communication. New York: Oxford, 1973.

Murdoch, Iris. The Sovereignty of Good. London: Routledge and Kegan Paul, 1970.

Nagel, Thomas. "Ruthlessness in Public Life." In Public and Private Morality. Edited by Stuart Hampshire. Cambridge: Cambridge University Press, 1978.

National Education Association. A Textbook Study in Cultural Conflict. NEA Inquiry Report on the Textbook Controversy in Kanawha County, West Virginia, p. 13, n.d.

Newmann, Fred, Clarifying Controversial Issues: An Approach to Teaching Social Studies. Boston: Little, Brown & Co., 1970.

Northrop, F.S.C. The Logic of the Sciences and the Humanities. New York: The Macmillan Company, 1948.

Northrop, F.S.C.  The Logic of the Sciences and the  Humanities. New York:  Meridian Books, 1959.

Obenhaus, Victor.  Ethics for an Industrial Age:  A Christian Inquiry.  New York:  Harper and Row, 1965.

Office of the Dean, Faculty of Arts  and  Sciences.  Report to the Faculty and Students on the Core Curriculum.  Harvard University, May 1979.

Perrin, Noel.  Dr. Bowdler's Legacy:  A  History  of  Expurgated Books in England and America.  New York:  Athaneum, 1969.

Perrow,  Charles.  Complex Organizations:  A Critical Essay.  2d ed.  Glenview, Illinois:  Scott, Foresman & Co., 1979.

Perry,  Ralph.  The Moral Economy.  New York:  C. Scribner's Sons, 1909.

Perry,  Thomas  D.  Moral Reasoning and Truth.  Oxford:  Clarendon Press, 1976.

Peters, R.S.  "Ambiguities in Liberal Education and the Problem of Its Content."  In  Ethics and Educational Policy, pp.  3-21. Edited  by  Kenneth  A.  Strike  and  Kieran  Egan.  Boston: Routledge & Kegan Paul, 1978.

Peters, R.S.  Ethics and Education.  London:  Allen & Unwin, 1966.

Peters, R. S.  Ethics and Education.  Atlanta:  Scott,  Foresman, 1967.

Pound, Roscoe.  Law and Morals.  2d ed.  Chapel Hill,  North Carolina:  The University of N.C. Press, 1926.

Rashdall, Hastings.  The Theory of Good and Evil.  2d ed.  London: Oxford University Press, H. Milford, 1929.

Raths, Louis,  Harmin, Merrill,  and  Simon, Sidney.  Values  and Teaching.  Columbus, Ohio:  Charles Merrill, 1966.

Raup, R.B.,  Axtelle,  G., Benne, K. and Smith, B.  "Why We Need a Method  of  Practical Judgement," and "Putting the Method  to Work."  In  The Improvement of Practical Intelligence.  New York:  Harper and Brothers, 1950.

Rawls,  John.  A Theory of Justice.  Cambridge,  Massachusetts: Harvard University Press, 1971.

Rhodes,  D.  and Hounsell, D., ed.  Staff  Development for  the 1980s:  International  Perspectives.  Illinois State University  Foundation,  and Institute for Research and Development into  Post-Compulsory Education at the University of  Lancaster, 1980.

344

Roberts, William. The Problem of Choice: An Introduction to Ethics. New York: Ginn and Co., 1941.

Rokeach, Milton. "Toward a Philosophy of Value Education." In Values Education: Theory, Practice, Problems, and Prospects. Edited by J. Meyer, B. Burnham, and J. Cholvat. Waterloo, Ontario: Wilfred Laurier University Press, 1975.

Ross, W.D. The Foundations of Ethics. Oxford: Clarendon Press, 1939.

Ross, W.D. The Right and the Good. Oxford: Clarendon Press, 1939.

Royce, Josiah. Studies of Good and Evil: A Series of Essays Upon Problems of Philosophy and of Life. New York: D. Appleton and Company, 1898.

Royce, Josiah. The Philosophy of Loyalty. New York: The Macmillan Co., 1919.

Russell, Bertrand. Human Society in Ethics and Politics. New York: New American Library, 1962.

Ryle, Gilbert. Dilemmas. Cambridge: Cambridge University Press, 1954.

Sahakian, William. Systems of Ethics and Value Theory. New York: Philosophical Library, 1963.

Sayer, Susan. "Directions in Professional Development." In Staff Development for the 1980's: International Perspectives. Edited by D. Rhodes and D. Hounsell. Illinois State University Foundation and the Institute for Research and Development in Post-Compulsory Education at the University of Lancaster, 1980.

Scheffler, Israel. "Definitions in Education." In the Language of Education. Springfield, Illinois: C.C. Thomas Publishers, 1960.

Schopenhauer, Arthur. On the Basis of Morality. Translated by E.F. Payne. Foreword by Richard Taylor. Indianapolis: Bobbs Merrill, 1965.

Schurr, George M. "Toward a Code of Ethics for Academics." Unpublished.

Schweitzer, Albert. Civilization and Ethics. 3d ed. Translated by C.T. Campion. London: A and C Black, 1946.

Scott, R.A. "The Development of Competence: Administrative Needs and Training Goals in American Higher Education." Staff Development for the 1980's: International Perspectives.

Edited by D. Rhodes and D. Hounsell. Illinois State University Foundation and the Institute for Research and Development in Post-Compulsory Education at the University of Lancaster, 1980.

Searle, John R. _Speech Acts_. Cambridge: The University Press, 1969.

Searle, J.R. "How to Derive 'Ought' from 'Is'." In _The Is/Ought Question_. Edited by W.D. Hudson, London: Macmillan, 1969.

Sellars, Wilfrid and Hospars, John. _Readings in Ethical Theory_. New York: Appleton-Century Crofts, 1952.

Sergiovanni, Thomas J. and Carver, Fred D. _The New School Executive: A Theory of Administration_. New York: Harper and Row, 1973.

Sergiovanni, Thomas J. and Carver, Fred D. _The New School Executive_. 2d ed. New York: Harper & Row, 1980.

Sergiovanni, Thomas J. and Starratt, R.J. _Supervision: Human Perspectives_. 2d ed. New York: McGraw Hill, 1979.

Sidgwick, Henry, _The Methods of Ethics_. 7th ed. London: Macmillan, 1930.

Simon, Herbert A. _Administrative Behavior: A Study of Decision-Making Processes in Administrative Organization_. New York: The Macmillan Company, 1950.

Simon, Herbert A. _Administrative Behavior_. New York: Macmillan Co., 1957.

Simon, Herbert A. _Administrative Behavior_. 2d ed. New York: Free Press, 1965.

Simon, Herbert A. "Technology and Environment." In _Emerging Concepts in Management_. 2d ed. Edited by Max S. Wortman and Fred Luthans. New York: Macmillan Co., 1975.

Simon, Sidney, Howe, Leland, and Kirschenbaum, Howard. _Values Clarification: A Handbook of Practical Strategies for Teachers and Students_. New York: Hart Publishing, 1972.

Singer, Peter. _Practical Ethics_. New York: Cambridge University Press, 1979.

Smart, J.J.C. _An Outline of a System of Utilitarian Ethics_. Melbourne: University Press, 1961.

Smart, J.J.C. "Extreme and Restricted Utilitarianism." _The Philosophical Quarterly_ 6 (1956). In _Contemporary Utilitarianism_. Edited by M. Bayles. Garden City: Doubleday

346

Anchor Books, 1968.

Smith, Dorothy. "Theorizing as Ideology." In Ethnomethodology. Edited by Roy Turner. Middlesex, England: Penguin, 1974.

Smith, P.G. "Philosophic-Mindedness," and "Philosophic Mindedness and the Preparation of School Administrators." In Philosophic-Mindedness in Educational Administration. Columbus, Ohio: Ohio State University, College of Education, 1956.

Stephen, Sir Leslie. The Science of Ethics. London: Smith Elder and Co., 1882.

Storing, Herbert, ed. "The Science of Administration: Herbert A. Simon." Essays on the Scientific Study of Politics. New York: Holt, Rinehart & Winston, 1962.

Strawson, P.F. "Social Morality and Individual Ideal." In Christian Ethics and Contemporary Philosophy. Edited by I.T. Ramsey. London: SCM Press, 1966.

Strike, Kenneth and Egan, Kieran. "Liberality, Neutrality and the Modern University." Ethics and Educational Policy. Boston: Routledge and K. Paul, 1978.

Szasz, Thomas. "Mental Health Services in School." Paper presented at the Conference on Moral Dilemmas of Schooling, University of Wisconsin, 12-14 May 1965.

Teather, D. and Page, Kogan, eds. Staff Development in Higher Education. New York: Nichols Publishing Co., 1979.

Toulmin, Stephen. The Uses of Argument. Cambridge: Cambridge University Press, 1958.

Toulmin, Stephen. Human Understanding. Vol. 1. Oxford: Clarendon Press, 1972.

Triandis, Harry C., ed. Variations in Black and White Perceptions of the Social Environment. Urbana, Ill.: University of Pennsylvania Press, 1972.

Tyack, David B. The One Best System. Cambridge, Massachusetts: Harvard University Press, 1974.

Urban, Wilbur. Fundamentals of Ethics, An Introduction to Moral Philosophy. New York: H. Holt and Company, 1930.

von Wright, Georg Henrik. Norm and Action. London: Routledge and Kegan Paul, 1963.

Vroom, Victor. "A New Look at Managerial Decision-Making." In Emerging Concepts in Management. 2d ed. Edited by Max S. Wortman and Fred Luthans. New York: Macmillan Co., 1975.

Warnock, Geoffrey J. The Object of Morality. London: Methuen, 1971.

Wasserstrom, Richard A., ed. Morality and the Law. Belmont, California: Wadsworth, 1971.

Weber, Max. As quoted in Etzioni, Amitai. Modern Organizations. Englewood Cliffs, New Jersey: Prentice-Hall, 1964.

Williams, Bernard. Morality: An Introduction to Ethics. Cambridge: Cambridge University Press, 1972.

Williams, Bernard. "A Critique of Utilitarianism." In J.J.C. Smart and Bernard Williams, Utilitarianism: For and Against. Cambridge: Cambridge University Press, 1973.

Winch, Peter. The Idea of a Social Science and Its Relation to Philosophy. London: Routledge and Kegan Paul, 1965.

Wittgenstein, Ludwig. Philosophical Investigations. New York: Macmillan Company, 1953.

Wolcott, Harry F. The Man in the Principal's Office: An Ethnography. New York: Holt, Rinehart & Winston, 1973.

Wundt, Wilhelm. Ethics: An Introduction of the Facts and Laws of Moral Life. Translated by Bradford Titchener, Julia Gulliver, and Margaret Washburn. London: S. Sonnenschein and Company, Ltd., 1897-1901.

Yut'ang, Lin. The Importance of Living. New York: The John Day Co., 1937.


**ARTICLES**

Abrell, Ronald and Archer, Douglass. "Education's Search for the Ethical." Educational Leadership 33 (February 1976): 377-80.

Adams, Henry B. "The Moral Test of Communicability." Ecounter 27 (Spring 1966): 158-66.

Alinsky, Saul D. "Of Means and Ends." Union Seminary Quarterly Review 22 (January 1967): 107-24.

Allison, Graham T. "Conceptual Models and the Cuban Missile Crisis." The American Political Science Review 63 (1969): 684-718.

American Association of School Administrators. Profile of the School Superintendent. 1960.

American Association of School Administrators. Code of Ethics.

1962.

American Civil Liberties Union News, June, 1960; October, 1962.

Armstrong, Hubert C. "The Place of Values in American Education." California Journal of Elementary Education 23 (February 1955). 141-54.

Bahm, Archie. "Is American Society Ethically Deficient." Journal of Social Philosophy 5-7 (1974-76): 8-9.

Ballinger, S. "The Nature and Function of Educational Policy." Center for Study of Educational Policy: Occasional Paper 65-101. Bloomington: Indiana University Press, 1965.

Bartky, John A. "The Depressive State of Educational Leadership." The Clearing House 38 (November 1963): 131-35.

Bartle, Roe. "Educational Administration in a Changing World." National Association of Secondary School Principals 34 (April 1950): 168-80.

Bayles, Ernest E. "Democratic Education and Philosophic Theory." Educational Administration and Supervision 36 (April 1950): 217-25.

Behre, Jalling and Larsson. "Teaching Teachers to Teach? Ten Commandments for Those Who Plan and Lead Courses that Experiment with Pedagogical Ideas." Impetus no. 10. Co-ordinating Committee for the Training of University Teachers, 1978.

Bernstein, Basil. Class, Codes and Control 1 London: Routledge and Kegan Paul, 1971.

Black, Max. "Philosophy: A Hope for Higher Education." The American Scholar 13 (Summer 1944): 300-8.

Blanchard, Everard. "Education Through Philosophy." Educational Leadership 12 (January 1955): 227-30.

Board of Trustees of the Lassen Union High School District v. Jack Owens.

Bobbe, Richard and Connolly, Phyllis. "Educational Decision-Making: Collaboration Among School Board, Administrators and the Community." Educational Technology 19 (November 1975): 21-25.

Bode, Boyde H. "Where Does One Go For Fundamental Assumptions in Education?" Educational Administration and Supervision 14 (September 1928): 361-70.

Boyle and Giorgiades, "The Teaching Development Programme at Birkbeck College." Impetus no. 9. Co-ordinating Committee for the Training of University Teachers, 1977.

Brackenbury, Robert L. "Philosophy and Values For the Future." Educational Leadership 14 (February 1957): 280-84.

Brameld, Theodore. "Ethics and the School Superintendent." School and Society (March 1969): 166-68.

Brameld, Theodore. "Philosophies of Education In An Age of Crisis." School and Society 65 (June 1947): 449-52.

Brameld, Theodore. "The Philosophy of Education As Philosophy of Politics." School and Society 68 (November 1948): 329-34.

Braybrooke, David. "The Firm but Untidy Correlativity of Rights and Obligations." Canadian Journal of Philosophy 1 (March 1972): 351-63.

Briner, Conrad and Campbell, Ronald F. "The Science of Administration." Review of Educational Research 34 (October 1964): 485-92.

Brown, G. "Some Myths of Staff Training and Development." Impetus no. 6. Co-ordinating Committee for the Training of University Teachers, 1977.

Brown, Ray F. "No Place for Perfectionists." The Nation's Schools 74 (November 1964): 53-56.

Browning, Robert. "Philosophy and Education." The Educational Forum 19 (January 1945): 203-11.

Bruner, Jerome S. "Education as Social Invention." Journal of Social Issues 20 (July 1964): 21-33.

Burnett, Charles T. "Philosophy and Education." Educational Administration and Supervision 3 (1917): 284-90.

"By Way of Comment." Educational Administration and Supervision 35 (November 1949): 434-37.

"By Way of Comment." Educational Administration and Supervision 35 (February 1949): 103-4.

California. Education Code (1961).

California Teacher, March-April, 1960.

Calkins, Robert D. "Decision-Making in Administration." California Journal of Secondary Education 33 (April 1958): 251-54.

Callahan, Daniel. "Should There Be an Academic Code of Ethics?" Paper presented at the National Conference on Higher Education, American Association of Higher Education.

Washington, D.C., April 1979.

Carr, William. "Recent Books That Deal With Superintendents' Problems." The Nation's Schools 8 (July 1931): 26-29.

Cassell, Eric J. "Making and Escaping Moral Decisions. The Hastings Center Studies 1 (1973): 52-62.

Champlin, Carroll. "Education and Philosophy-Fusion or Confusion." School and Society 56 (September 1942): 231-34.

Champlin, Carroll. "The Content of Our Philosophy of Education." Educational Administration and Supervision 35 (May 1949): 257-69.

Champlin, Carroll. "This Philosophy of Education Business." Educational Administration and Supervision 37 (October 1951): 291-98.

Champlin, Nathaniel L. "Value Inquiry and the Philosophy of Education." Educational Leadership 13 (May 1956): 467-73.

Charlesworth, M.J. "The Liberal State and the Control of Education." In Melbourne Studies in Education 1967. Edited by R.J.W. Selleck. Melbourne University Press, 1968.

Charters, W.W., Jr. "A Critical Review of Erickson's Readings in Educational Organization and Administration." Paper prepared for Annual Meeting of the American Educational Research Association, Toronto, Canada, March 30, 1978.

Chase, Alstan. "Skipping Through College." The Atlantic 24 (September 1978): 35.

Childress, James F. "The Identification of Ethical Principles." Journal of Religious Ethics 5 (Spring 1977): 39-68.

Cleary, Robert. "University Decision Making." Educational Forum (November 1978): 89-98.

Clements, Millard and Macdonald, James. "Moral Dilemmas of Schooling." Educational Leadership 23 (October 1965): 29-32.

Cochrane, Donald. "A Proposal for Certifying Administrators." Education Forum 39 (January 1975): 177-79.

Cohen, Carl. "Have I a Right To a Voice in Decisions That Affect My Life?" Nous 5 (1971): 63-79.

Cole, Robert. "A Basic Philosophy of Administration," American School Board 118 (June 1949): 27.

Coleman, James. "Alternatives in Schooling." Paper presented at the Conference on Moral Dilemmas of Schooling, University of Wisconsin, 12-14 May 1965.

Coleman, James S. "Rawls, Nozick, and Educational Equality." The Public Interest 43 (Spring 1976): 121-28.

Coles, C.R. "Developing Professionalism: Staff Development as an Outcome of Curriculum Development." Programmed Learning and Educational Technology 14 (1977). n.p.

Crawford, Berry A. and Brown, Warren R. "Missing: A Viable Aim for American Education." Educational Theory 21 (1971): 407-17.

Crittenden, Brian D. "Durkeim: Sociology of Knowledge and Educational Theory." Studies in Philosophy and Education 4 (Fall 1965): 207-53.

Crittenden, Brian D. "Moral Education: Some Aspects of its Relationship to General Values Education and the Study of Religion." n.d.

CTA Action. 12 October 1962.

de Charms, Richard, Carpenter, Virginia and Kuperman, Aharan. "The Origin-Pawn Variable in Person Perception." Sociometry 28 (1965): 241-58.

Denhardt, Robert B. and Denhardt, Kathryn G. "Public Administration and the Critique of Domination." Administration and Society 11 (May 1979): 107-20.

Dexheimer, Roy. "Ethics and the School Administrator." School Management 14 (March 1970): 36-44.

Diederich, Paul B. "An Ethical Basis for Educational Objectives." The School Review 59 (February 1951): 78-86. (An Abridgement and Revision of original article)

Diederich, Paul B. "An Ethical Basis for Educational Objectives." Ethics 58 (January 1948): 123-32.

Dilley, Norman E. "Personal Values Held By College Students Who Enter A Teacher Education Program." Journal of Teacher Education 8 (September 1957): 289-94.

Donohue, Francis J. "Education Needs a Philosophy." Educational Administration and Supervision (September 1940): 462-66.

Doughty, Julia M. "Philosophy of A High School Principal." California Journal of Secondary Education 19 (January 1944): 45-47.

Downie, R.S. "Personal and Impersonal Relationships." Proceedings of the Philosophy of Education Society of Great Britain 1 (July 1971): 129-30.

Educational Development at Michigan State University - Report 11 MSU Educational Development Program, 1979.

Edwards, C.S. "Humanism in Administration." Pennsylvania School Journal 115 (February 1967): 296-97.

England, Walter, ed. "Ethics for Teachers, Superintendents and for School Boards." Minnesota Journal of Education 27 (April 1948): 376-77.

Ennis, Robert H. "Equality of Educational Opportunity." Educational Theory 26 (Winter 1976): 3-18.

Erickson, Donald. "Moral Dilemmas of Administrative Powerlessness." Administrator's Notebook 20 (April 1972): 3-4.

Erickson, Donald. "Research on Educational Administration: The State-of-the-Art." Educational Researcher 8 (March 1979): 9-14.

Evans, Donald. "Paul Ramsey on Exceptionless Moral Rules." American Journal of Jurisprudence 16 (1971): 184-214.

Everhart, Robert B. "From Universalism to Usurpation: An Essay on the Antecedents to Compulsory School Attendance Legislation." Review of Educational Research 47 (Summer 1977): 502.

Faulconer, Estelle. "Who Says It's Unethical?" Today's Education 59 (January 1970): 62-63.

Fielder, William R. "Education with Averted Eyes." Paper presented at the Conference on Moral Dilemmas of Schooling, University of Wisconsin, 12-14 May 1965.

Fisk, Robert S. "The Activity of Administration Professors." The School Executive 75 (January 1956): 72-73.

Fowlkes, John Guy. "An Educator Gives His Concept of School Administration." The Nation's Schools 9 (April 1932): 66-67.

Fox, Michael. "The 'Relevance' of Philosophy and Its Relevance For Teaching." Metaphilosophy 4 (July 1973): 261-68.

Frank, Lawrence K. "Reorganizing Our Prejudices." Educational Leadership 1 (April 1944): 389-92.

Freeman, Frank H. "Psychology as the Source of Fundamental Assumptions in Education." Educational Administration and Supervision 14 (1928): 371-77.

Friedenberg, Edgar. "Unintended Consequences of Bureaucratic Schooling." Paper presented at the Conference on Moral Dilemmas of Schooling, University of Wisconsin, 12-14 May 1965.

Gallup, George. "The Eleventh Annual Poll of the Public's Attitudes Toward the Public Schools." Phi Delta Kappan 61 (September 1979): 33-45.

Goslin, David. "The Social Consequences of Testing." Paper presented at the Conference on Moral Dilemmas of Schooling, University of Wisconsin, 12-14 May 1965.

Greenway, H. and Harding, A.G. "The Growth of Policies for Staff Development." Society for Research into Higher Education Monograph, 1980.

Grimes, Robert. "Structuring Teachers Into the Decision Making Process." Journal of Secondary Education 44 (December 1969): 346-51.

Habeshaw, T. "Continuing Self-Development for Teachers." British Journal of Educational Technology 11, 1980.

Hadberg, J.G. "Client Relationships in Instructional Design." Programmed Learning and Educational Technology 17 (1980).

Hales, M. "Management Science and the 'Second Industrial Revolution'." Radical Science Journal 1 (January 1974): 5-28.

Harris, D. "Staff Development as an Agent of Change." Impetus, no. 9. Co-ordinating Committee for the Training of University Teachers, 1978.

Hempel, Carl G. "Rational Action." Proceedings and Addresses of the American Philosophical Association. 1961-62.

Hewton, E. "Towards a Definition of Staff Development." Impetus, no. 11. Co-ordinating Committee for the Training of University Teachers, 1977.

Hills, Jean. "Problems in the Production and Utilization of Knowledge in Educational Administration." Educational Administration Quarterly 14 (Winter 1978): 2.

Huebner, Dwayne. "Moral Values and the Curriculum." Paper presented at the Conference on Moral Dilemmas of Schooling, University of Wisconsin, 12-14 May 1965.

Hullfish, Henry G. "A Crucial Problem for Philosophy of Education." Educational Administration and Supervision 16 (April 1930): 241-48.

Iowa State Teacher's Association. "Ethics for Teachers." The

Journal of the National Education Association (January 1923): 40.

Jalling, Behre and Larsson. "Teaching Teachers to Teach? Ten Commandments for those Who Plan and Lead Courses that Experiment with Pedagogical Ideas." Impetus, no. 10 (1978).

Jalling, Hans. "University Teacher Training in Sweden." Impetus no. 7. Co-ordinating Committee for the Training of University Teachers, 1977.

Jenson, T.J. "A Code of Ethics for School Administrators." The American School Board Journal 122 (June 1951): 44-45.

Johnston, Charles H. Educational Administration and Supervision 1 (November 1915): 635-37.

Johnston, Charles H. "The School Administrator and His Philosophy of Education." Editorial. Educational Administration and Supervision 2 (November 1916): 591-95.

Johnston, Charles H. "Our Special Issues." Editorial. Educational Administration and Supervision 2 (December 1916): 649-51.

Johnston, Charles H. "Our Party Platforms." Editorial. Educational Administration and Supervision 2 (December 1916): 654-56.

Johnston, Charles H. "The Deeper Meaning of High School Administration." Editorial. Educational Administration and Supervision 3 (1917): 307-8.

Johnston, Charles H. "Party Platforms-Internal Government of Schools." Editorial. Educational Administration and Supervision 3 (1917): 435.

Kaltsounis, Theodore. "Decision Making and Values." The Instructor 80 (April 1971): 51-54.

Kattsoff, Louis O. "The Role of Consequences in Moral Decisions." Studi Internazionali difilosofia - A Yearbook of General Philosophical Inquiry (Fall 1973): 53-62.

Kaufman, J. F. "Education and Ethics." National Association of Women Deans and Counselors 30 (Fall 1966): 3-6.

King, Seth S. "Professor Causes Furor by Saying Nazi Slaying of Jews is a Myth." New York Times, 28 January 1977, p. A-10.

Kuenzli, Irvin. "Unethical Practices in School Administration." The American Teacher 33 (December 1948): 6.

Kuenzli, Irvin. "What Group Does the Administrator Represent?"

Progressive Education 30 (November 1952): 46-50.

Kyte, George C. "How Functional Philosophy Applies to Elementary Education." The Nation's Schools 12 (November 1933): 24-26.

Ladd, John. "The Ethical Dimensions of the Concept of Action." Journal of Philosophy 62 (1965): 633-45.

Ladd, John. "Morality and the Ideal of Rationality in Formal Organizations." Monist 54 (1970): 488-516.

Lean, Martin E. "Aren't Moral Judgements 'Factual'?" The Personalist 51 (Summer 1970): 259-85.

Lemmon, John. "Moral Dilemmas." Philosophical Review 71 (1962): 139-58.

Lilge, Frederic. "Reason and Ideology in Education." Harvard Educational Review 22 (Fall 1952): 247-56.

Lindblom, C.E. "The Science of Muddling Through." Public Administration Review 19 (Spring 1959): 79-88.

Love, Jean. "Professional Ethics in Education." Educational Administration and Supervision 40 (November 1954): 385-94.

Macdonald, Jam s. "Moral Problems in Classroom Evaluation and Testing." Paper presented at the Conference on Moral Dilemmas of Schooling, University of Wisconsin, 12-14 May 1965.

Martin, William. "Values, Too, Can Cause Discrimination." Educational Leadership 12 (November 1954): 90-93.

Matheson, C. "Francis Gibb Talks to the New Man Responsible for Training University Teachers." Times Higher Education Supplement 1 September 1976.

McDonald, Gerald E. "Cooperation In Education Between the Thomist and Experimentalist." Educational Administration and Supervision 45 (January 1959): 13-25.

McDonald, Gerald E. "Is the School Administrator Capable of Receiving Effective Guidance from Philosophy." Educational tional Administration and Supervision 42 (October 1956): 358-67.

McLaughlin, Andrew. "Science, Reason and Value." Theory and Decision 1 (December 1970): 121-37.

McNassar, Donald. "Decision Making Process In a Revolution." Journal of Secondary Education 44 (October 1969): 265-70.

McWilliams, Carey. "Ethics in an Affluent Society." The Christian Century 22 (June 1966): 797-802.

Midgley, Mary. "Trying Out One's New Sword." The Listener (December 1977): 787-88.

Mead, Margaret. "Are Any School Administrators Listening?" Nation's Schools 87 (June 1971): 41-45.

Michigan State University Educational Development Program. Educational Development at Michigan State University, report 11, 1979.

Moore, A. "Adaptive Change for the Improvement of Teaching and Learning in the University." Impetus, no. 10. Co-ordinating Committee for the Training of University Teachers, 1978.

Newton, Jesse H. "The Importance of a Point of View in Educational Administration." School and Society 45 (March 1937): 361-68.

Norton, John K. "Functional Philosophy of Education is the Administrator's Compass." The Nation's School 12 (October 1933): 11-13.

Nozick, Robert. "Moral Complications and Moral Structures." Natural Law Forum 13 (1968): 1-50.

Owens, Jack. "The CTA and Me." 15 March 1960. (Mimeographed).

Pincoffs, Edmund. "Quandry Ethics." Mind 80 (1971): 552-71.

Pittenger, Benjamin F. "A Philosophy for School Administrators." The School Executive 67 (December 1947): 25-26.

Popper, Samuel. "In Dispraise of Existential Humanism in Educational Administration." Educational Administration Quarterly 7 (1971): 26-50.

Price, Kingsley. "On Having an Education." Harvard Educational Review 28 (Fall 1958): 320-37.

Pugmire, O. Ross. "Challenge to Educational Administrators." Educational Forum 20 (March 1956): 329-39.

Ramos, Alberto Guerrero. "Misplacements of Concepts and Administrative Theory." Public Administration Review 6 (November/ December, 1978): 550-56.

Rawls, John. "Justice As Fairness." Philosophical Review 67 (1958): 164-94.

Reavis, William C. "Administration as a Profession." Phi Delta Kappan 28 (January 1947): 205-8.

Reeder, Ward. "Professional Ethics-A Code For Administrators." The Nation's School (January 1941): 50-51.

Robinson, Willard F. "Moral Aspects of Educational Leadership." The Clearing House 34 (March 1960): 387-89.

Russell, William F. "Philosophical Bases of Organization and Operation of American Schools." Teachers College Record 50 (January 1949): 221-31.

Russell, William F. "Philosophical Bases of Organization and Operation of American Schools," Teachers College Record 50 (March 1949): 386-95.

San Francisco Examiner, 28 February 1960.

Sayer, Susan. "The Nature and Purpose of Professional Development." Irish Educational Studies 1. Educational Studies Association of Ireland, 1981.

Sayer, Susan and Harding, A.G. "Intervention, Interference and Intimidation in Professional Development." Proceedings of the Third International Conference on Improving University Teaching. Newcastle, 1971.

Schroyer, Trent. "Toward a Critical Theory for Advanced Industrial Society." In Recent Sociology No. 2. Edited by Hans Peter Dreitzel. New York: Macmillan Co., 1970.

Sears, Jesse B. "Analysis of School Administrative Controls." Educational Administration and Supervision 20 (September 1934): 401-30.

Sears, Jesse B. "Administrative Discretion vs. (or with) Rules and Regulations." Educational Administration and Supervision 29 (May 1943): 257-83.

Sears, Jesse B. "Ethics in School Administration." Educational Forum 15 (November 1950): 29-37.

Sears, Jesse B. "Ethics an Element in Administrative Authority." Educational Administration and Supervision 37 (January 1951): 1-24.

Sears, Jesse B. "A Program of Instruction for School Administrators." Educational Administration and Supervision 35 (March 1949): 129-49.

Sellars, Roy W. "In What Sense Do Value Judgements and Moral Judgements Have Objective Importance?" Philosophy and Phenomenological Research 28 (September 1967): 1-16.

Shannon, A. "Staff Development in Course Development." Impetus, no. 10. Co-ordinating Committee for the Training of

358

University Teachers, 1978.

Shrag, Francis. "The Right to Educate." _School Review_ 79 (May 1971): 359-78.

Sosa, Ernest. "Actions and Their Results." _Logique et Analyse_. June 1965.

Strauch, R. E. "A Critical Look at Quantitative Methodology." _Policy Analysis_ 2 (1976): 121-44.

Swain, R. "How to Recognize the Real Thing: Professionalism and Expertise in Teaching Development." _Impetus_, no. 11. Co-ordinating Committee for the Training of University Teachers, 1979.

Trickey, S. "Staff Training: A Polytechnic Perspective." _Impetus_, no. 6. Co-ordinating Committee for the Training of University Teachers, 1977.

Wittrock, M.C. "The Cognitive MovementinInstruction." _Educational Researcher_ 8 (February 1979): 5-11.

Wood, Stephen and Kelly, John. "Toward a Critical Management Science." _Journal of Management Studies_ 15 (February 1978): 1-24.

101